Understanding and Sharing

Second Edition

Understanding and Sharing

An Introduction to Speech Communication

Judy Cornelia Pearson   Paul Edward Nelson

Ohio University   Ohio University

wcb

Wm. C. Brown Company Publishers
Dubuque, Iowa

Book Team
Louise Waller Editor
Julia A. Scannell Designer
Julie A. Kennedy Production Editor
Mary M. Heller Visual Research
Editor

Acknowledgments
The authors and publishers of this book
would like to thank all sources for the
use of reprinted material.
Acknowledgments to authors and
publishers for permission to reprint from
copyright material is made at the end of
the chapter in which the material
appears.

Credit lines for photographs and
cartoons appear on the extension of the
copyright page at the end of this book.

2-04196-03

**wcb
group**

Wm. C. Brown Chairman of the Board
Mark C. Falb Executive Vice President

wcb

**Wm. C. Brown Company
Publishers, College Division**

Lawrence E. Cremer President
Raymond C. Deveaux Vice President/
Product Development
David Wm. Smith Vice President/
Marketing
David A. Corona Assistant
Vice President/Production
Development and Design
Janis M. Machala Director of
Marketing Research
Marilyn A. Phelps Manager of Design
William A. Moss Production Editorial
Manager
Mavis M. Oeth Permissions Editor

Cover photo/Bob Coyle

Dedicated to our parents:
Sophia and J. D.
Ferne and H. B.

Preface   *xi*

Part 1

Elements of the Communication Process   3

1 The Nature of Communication   4

Definition of Communication   6

Communication Is the Process of Understanding and Sharing Meaning/Communication Begins with the Self/Communication Occurs in a Context/ Communication Involves Codes/ Communication Is Transactional

Functions of Communication   16

Social Functions/Task Functions

Problems in Communication   18

Lack of Interest/Lack of Understanding/Lack of Common Goals and Assumptions

Summary   22

2 Perception: The Process of Understanding   26

How Does Communication Involve Perception?   28

The Process by Which We Come to Understand Ourselves/The Process by Which We Come to Understand Others

What Is Perception?   30

Why Do Differences in Perception Occur?   32

Physiological Factors/Past Experience/Present Feelings and Circumstances

What Occurs in Perception?   36

Selection/Organization/ Interpretation

Summary   42

Contents

**3 Verbal Codes:
A Tool of Sharing** **46**

Words Can Be a Major
Obstacle to Communication 49

*We Intentionally Use Language
to Distort or Alter Our
Meaning/We Assume that
Words Have Universal Meaning
and Are Real*

Verbal Skills Can Be Improved 63

*Avoid Intentional Confusion/
Descriptiveness/Concreteness*

Summary 70

**4 Nonverbal Codes:
A Tool of Sharing** **74**

Importance of Nonverbal Codes
in Communication 76

Definition and Identification of
Nonverbal Codes 78

*Bodily Movement and Facial
Expression/Space/Touching/
Vocal Cues/Clothing and Other
Artifacts*

Interpretation of Nonverbal
Cues 88

*Problems of Interpretation/
Solutions to Problems of
Interpretation*

Summary 90

Part 2

**Intrapersonal and
Interpersonal
Communication** **95**

**5 Understanding
Yourself** **96**

Self-Awareness 98

Self-Concept 103

*Two Components of Self-
Concept/Self-Concept in
Process/Self-Concept Affects
Communication/Improving Self-
Concept*

Journal Writing 115

*Increasing Self-Awareness/
Improving Self-Concept*

Summary 118

6 Sharing Yourself **122**

Definition of Self-Disclosure 124

Importance of Self-Disclosure 125

*Self-Disclosure Allows Us to
Develop a Greater
Understanding of Ourselves/
Self-Disclosure Can Result in
Self-Improvement/Self-
Disclosure Allows Us to
Establish More Meaningful
Relationships with Others/Self-
Disclosure Allows Us to
Establish More Positive
Attitudes toward Ourselves and
Others*

Interference with Self-Disclosure 129

Guidelines for Self-Disclosure 131

*Self-Disclosure Should Be
Reciprocal or Shared/Self-
Disclosure Is Related to the
Duration of a Relationship/Self-
Disclosure Should Be
Appropriate for the Person to
Whom You Are Self-Disclosing/
Self-Disclosure Depends on the
Person Who Is Disclosing*

Summary 136

**7 Understanding
Another** **140**

A Basic Skill in Understanding
Another 142

Three Kinds of Listening 144

Interference with Our Ability to
Listen 148

*The Message and the Occasion/
Ourselves/Our Perception of the
Other Person*

Improving Our Ability to Listen 155

Behavioral Components of
Effective Listening 157

Summary 158

8 The Interview: An Application of the Principles of Interpersonal Communication 162

Questions and Questioning 165

Open or Closed/Primary or Secondary/Neutral or Leading

Answers and Answering 168

Purposes of Interviews 170

Informational Interviews/ Persuasive Interviews/ Employment Interviews

Summary 182

9 The Small Group Discussion: An Application of the Principles of Interpersonal Communication 186

Definition of Small Group Discussion 189

Unique Features of the Small Group Discussion 190

The Function of Small Group Discussion/The Process of Small Group Discussion: Preparation and Presentation

Interaction in the Small Group 198

Communication Networks/ Participating in a Small Group Discussion/Leadership

Summary 203

Part 3

Public Communication 207

10 Understanding through Topic Selection and Audience Analysis 208

Selecting and Limiting the Topic 210

Brainstorming/Personal Inventory/Involvement/ Knowledge/Narrowing the Topic

Understanding Your Audience 216

Level 1: Captive and Voluntary Audiences/Level 2: Demographic Analysis/Level 3: Audience Interest in and Knowledge of the Topic/Level 4: The Audience's Attitudes, Beliefs, and Values

Three Methods of Audience Analysis 225

Method 1: Observation/Method 2: Inference/Method 3: The Questionnaire

Adapting to the Audience 229

Adapting Yourself/Adapting Your Verbal and Nonverbal Codes/Adapting Your Topic/ Adapting Your Purpose/ Adapting Your Supporting Materials

Summary 233

11 Sharing Yourself: Source Credibility and Credible Sources 236

Four Aspects of Credibility 239

Competence/Trustworthiness/ Dynamism/Coorientation

Some Ways of Increasing Credibility 244

A Highly Credible Speaker Will Change an Audience's Opinion More than a Speaker of Low Credibility, but the Difference Diminishes in Time/A Speaker Can Gain Credibility by Establishing Common Ground with the Audience/Credibility Is Influenced by the Introduction of the Speaker, by the Status and Sincerity of the Speaker, and by the Organization of the Speech

Finding Credible Sources 250

Citing Your Sources/ Materials for Evidence, Proof, or Clarification

Summary 264

ix   Contents

12 Sharing Your Message through Organization   **268**

The Introduction: Gaining and Maintaining Attention   270

Principles of Outlining   274

Composing a Sentence Outline

The Sentence Outline   279

The Key Word Outline   281

Organizational Patterns   284

Time-Sequence Pattern/Topical-Sequence Pattern/Problem-and-Solution Pattern/Other Organization Patterns

Transitions   288

The Conclusion   289

Summary   293

13 Sharing Yourself through Delivery and Visual Aids   **296**

Four Modes of Delivery   299

Manuscripts and Papers/The Extemporaneous Speech/The Impromptu Speech/The Memorized Speech

Vocal and Bodily Aspects of Delivery   302

Vocal Aspects of Delivery/ Bodily Aspects of Delivery

Using Visual Aids   312

Some Helpful Hints for Delivery   318

Summary   320

14 The Informative Speech: An Application of the Principles of Public Communication   **324**

Preparing an Informative Speech   327

The Topics for Informative Speaking/Behavioral Purposes for Informative Speaking

Presenting Information to an Audience   332

Information Hunger/ Information Relevance/Extrinsic Motivation/Informative Content

Organizing Content   338

Special Skills for Informative Speaking   339

Definitions/Descriptions/ Explanations

An Example of an Informative Speech   342

Summary   345

15 The Persuasive Speech: An Application of the Principles of Public Communication   **350**

Preparing a Persuasive Speech   352

Persuasion Defined/The Goals of Persuasive Speaking/Topics for Persuasive Speeches/ Behavioral Purposes for Persuasive Speeches

Persuading an Audience   357

Motive Appeals/Source Credibility/Logical Appeals/ Emotional Appeals/ Organizational Plans/Ethical Considerations

Special Skills for Persuasive Speaking   364

Argumentation/Evidence/ Refutation

An Example of a Persuasive Speech   368

Summary   372

Topics for Activities   376

Glossary   378

Bibliography   394

Name Index   406

Subject Index   410

Preface

The second edition of *Understanding and Sharing* reflects not only our experiences as instructors of speech fundamentals but also the use that we and our colleagues and students have made of the text since it was first published. A textbook must fit the goals of the course, the background and experience of the teacher, and the abilities of the students. *Understanding and Sharing* is an appropriate text for a beginning course in speech fundamentals that emphasizes interpersonal communication and public speaking. In the area of interpersonal communication, this edition supplies new material on small group communication and problem solving. To meet the needs of students, an extensive section on interviewing has been added, with particular attention to the employment interview. In public speaking, the main emphasis is on the informative and the persuasive speech, but the material on public communication is adaptable to a wide variety of speech purposes. Listening, audience analysis and appeals, and ethical considerations have also been added to this text.

Understanding and Sharing takes a skills approach to help students learn effective communication behavior in interpersonal and public situations. The book attempts to combine speech heritage with the results of recent experimental studies, pedagogy, and classroom experience. *Understanding and Sharing* can help a student discover the kinds of questions to ask in an interivew; the characteristics of the leader in a small group; and the functions of an introduction, body, and conclusion in a public speech. However, it is the instructor who can help students apply on a practical level the skills that are described here. The book, the instructor, and the students become partners in a creative transaction that results in learning communication skills through practical application.

Audience

Understanding and Sharing is for both the experienced instructor, who can richly supplement any textbook with personal knowledge, and the graduate teaching assistant, who is in the classroom for the first time.

It is intended for students in their first speech course at a community college, technical school, four-year liberal arts college, or university; and it was designed to appeal to their interests and written on their own vocabulary level. We have tried to make speech communication concepts clear by defining them when they are introduced, by listing key terms at the beginning of each chapter, and by assembling concepts and terms alphabetically in the glossary.

Organization

Understanding and Sharing is divided into three major parts, each of which focuses on communication skills.

Part 1, "Elements of the Communication Process," begins with a chapter on the nature of communication, in which communication is defined and related to the self. Then perception is related to communication in chapter 2. Chapter 3 focuses on language and how it can both help and hinder communication. The last chapter in part 1, concentrates on the nonverbal aspects of human communication.

Part 2, "Intrapersonal and Interpersonal Communication," opens with a chapter on self-awareness, self-concept, and journal writing as an exercise in understanding intrapersonal communication. Chapter 6 emphasizes self-disclosure, how it operates in interpersonal communication, when it is appropriate, and when it is inappropriate. Chapter 7 focuses on active listening and empathy, and the last two chapters of part 2 consist of practical application of interpersonal communication skills in the interview and in the small group discussion.

Public communication is the subject of part 3. It begins with a chapter on topic selection and audience analysis and adaptation. Source credibility is examined in chapter 11, which focuses on the speaker. Speech organization and visual aids are covered in chapter 12; while chapter 13 discusses the vocal and bodily aspects of speaking in public. The last two chapters of the text are devoted to practical applications that examine in detail the two most common types of speeches in the basic course: the informative speech and the persuasive speech.

All of the chapters emphasize application of speech concepts; all of them concentrate on skills that can be immediately employed in interpersonal and public communication.

Special Features

Each chapter begins with objectives that state specifically what students should be able to do when they have completed the chapter. Educational research indicates that students learn better if they know specifically what is expected of them. The chapter is previewed in the introduction, and throughout the chapter application exercises are strategically placed so that students can test ideas for themselves immediately after learning about them. Contemporary cartoons, photos, and line drawings illustrate concepts effectively for those students who learn best through visual means. Chapter 8 on the interview, chapter 9 on small groups, chapter 14 on the informative speech, and chapter 15 on the persuasive speech are especially helpful to students in implementing their knowledge through practical applications. Subject matter is summarized, and annotated sources for further reading are listed at the end of each chapter.

Instructor's Resource Manual

Understanding and Sharing and the Instructor's Resource Manual that accompanies it are our answer to the text selection problems that we have encountered over the years. Because many textbooks were too theoretical for our pragmatic students, we wrote a skills-oriented book with ideas for everyday application. Because some books were good for public speaking and others were good in interpersonal communication but few were good in both areas, we tried to write an effective book in both areas of speech communication. Because we found the development of useful classroom activities to be lacking, we have pro-

vided a resource manual filled with them. Finally, because we found exam questions difficult to develop and resource materials time consuming to find, the Instructor's Resource Manual provides them for every chapter.

Each chapter of the Instructor's Resource Manual includes true-false, multiple-choice, and essay questions; an annotated list of films, records, and slides that reinforce concepts; and an annotated list of additional readings. Beginning instructors will find the manual's quarter and semester schedules for a course based on *Understanding and Sharing* especially helpful. All instructors will be helped by the manual's resource material and activities, from which instructors can select those items that best fit their own teaching style and the objectives of their course. These classroom-tested exercises include explanations of what usually occurs when students do the exercises, what the students are supposed to learn, and what implications of the exercise the instructor should emphasize.

The Authors

Because the textbook is an impersonal entity—the reader does not see the writer and, even worse, the writer cannot see the reader—we self-disclose to reduce the distance between us and the persons who read *Understanding and Sharing:*

Judy Cornelia Pearson is first and foremost a teacher. She earned her doctorate at Indiana University and served as basic course director at

Bradley University, Indiana University-Purdue University at Fort Wayne, Iowa State University, and at Ohio University.

Paul Edward Nelson earned his Ph.D. at the University of Minnesota and was the basic course director at the University of Missouri, chair of the Speech Department at Iowa State University, and is currently the Dean of the College of Communication at Ohio University.

We have taught speech fundamentals all of our professional lives. More importantly, fundamentals is what we like best. We both were honored to win the Central States Speech Association's Outstanding Young Teacher Award, and both of us attribute much of our abiding interest in fundamentals to the enthusiastic support of our colleagues in the Midwest Basic Speech Director's Conference.

Don Yoder is particularly well qualified as co-author of the instructor's manual because he is a sensitive teacher and knows first-hand the needs of a beginning teacher. He received his Master's degree at the University of Nebraska, has taught at Iowa State University and the Ohio State University, where he is a Ph.D. candidate, and currently teaches at Creighton University. Don assembled and developed many of the activities in the Instructor's Resource Manual, collected and developed examination questions, and wrote the objectives for each of its chapters.

Acknowledgments

Understanding and Sharing is a cumulative effort by publishers, editors, critic-evaluators, students, fellow teachers, and the authors. Encouraged by Iowa's harsh winters and hot summers to stay inside to write, we typed our own material, criticized each other's writing, and—because we are husband and wife—encouraged each other lovingly to the completion of the book.

Our graduate professors at Indiana University and the University of Minnesota, our colleagues at many colleges and universities who share our affection for speech fundamentals, and our six children, who can blame us in later years for ignoring them to write a book, deserve our special thanks. The people at Wm. C. Brown Company Publishers have earned our grateful appreciation. We are also grateful for the helpful suggestions from college and university faculty members who evaluated the manuscript at several stages of development: Martin H. Brodey, Montgomery College; Jerry D. Feezel, Kent State University; Judith Friedman, Bergan Community College; Marilyn Kelly, McLennon Community College; Edward J. Harris, Jr., Suffolk University; Harry Hazel, Gonzaga University; Larry D. Miller, Indiana University, Bloomington; Michael B. Minchew, Mississippi University for Women; David E. Mrizek, San Antonio College; William J. Seiler, University of Nebraska, Lincoln; and Curt Siemers, Winona State University. Finally, we were granted time occasionally by the Iowa State University Department of Speech to work on this book. For that too we are thankful.

Judy C. Pearson
Paul E. Nelson

Understanding and Sharing

PART 1

Elements of the Communication Process

Communication is the process of understanding and sharing meaning. In this first section of the text, the elements of the communication process are considered. Among the topics discussed are perception, verbal codes, and nonverbal codes. Chapter 1, "The Nature of Communication," includes a consideration of the definition of communication, the function of communication, and problems involved in communication. Chapter 2, "Perception: The Process of Understanding," contains an explanation of the role of perception in the communication process, why differences occur in perception, and the activities involved in perception. Chapter 3, "Verbal Codes: A Tool of Sharing," contains an examination of how words create a major obstacle to communication, but also describes methods by which verbal skills can be improved. Chapter 4, "Nonverbal Codes: A Tool of Sharing," includes descriptive material on various nonverbal codes such as bodily movement and facial expression, space, touching, vocal cues, and clothing and other artifacts.

1

The Nature of Communication

Objectives

1. Define communication and the relationship between understanding and sharing
2. Differentiate among intrapersonal, interpersonal, and public communication
3. Differentiate among action, interaction, and transaction views of communication and discuss the perspective each of these views gives to the study of communication
4. Discuss the ways in which communication is used for survival of the individual and society in today's world
5. Identify three factors that can create barriers to communication and relate these factors to specific personal experiences

Key Terms

communication
process
understanding
sharing
meaning
messages
thought
Barnlund's "six people"
intrapersonal communication
interpersonal communication
public communication

codes
verbal codes
nonverbal codes
encoding
decoding
action
interaction
transaction
feedback
noise
hidden agenda

Oh, talk to me
'Cause it's surely not just you
Needing to talk, you see
You can bet I feel it too
We need not try and blame
'Cause I know we feel the same
Won't you talk to me?
You know I want to understand[1]

The usual pedagogy in teaching a baby to talk is so poor that if people were taught to read by the same crude methods, we would be a nation of illiterates.[2]

Americans report that their greatest fear is the fear of speaking in front of a group.[3]

Communication pervades all aspects of our lives. A number of studies have shown that we spend more time in verbal communication than in any other single activity.[4] Nonetheless, as the last two passages above suggest, we spend very little time and effort studying communication, and public speaking remains as one of our greatest fears. In the same way that the ocean is necessary for the survival of sealife, communication is essential to the survival of humankind. Still, many of us do not feel confident about our ability to communicate with others.

This text will help you to improve your ability to communicate with other people. Each of us has experienced the feelings expressed in the lyrics by Jimmy Messina, reprinted above. We communicate to fulfill our social needs and to understand others. Similarly, we communicate in order to fulfill more task-related needs—to get a job, to solve a problem, or to persuade others. This text will help you to achieve your social and task-related needs by discussing intrapersonal communication, interpersonal communication, and public communication. You will learn how to improve your ability in communication activities such as the journal, the interview, the small group discussion, the informative speech, and the persuasive speech. As you read the text and as you participate in the suggested activities and exercises, you will increase in confidence as a communicator and become more successful in achieving your personal and job-related goals.

Definition of Communication

Communication Is the Process of Understanding and Sharing Meaning

The word **communication** is used in a variety of ways. Before the term is used further, a common understanding of the word should be established. *Communicate* comes from the Latin *communicare*, which means *to make common*. Originally, communication suggested that some thought, some meaning, or some message was held in common. Contemporary definitions suggest the manner in which these are shared: we "exchange thoughts," we "discuss meaning," and we "transmit messages."

We shall define communication as *the process of understanding and sharing meaning.* Communication is defined as a **process** because we recognize that it is an activity that is characterized by action, change, exchange, and movement. Alterations that occur in the individuals who are communicating, the context of communication, the message that is selected, and the nonverbal elements of the exchange affect the entire communication situation. Communication is marked by shifts and turns, variation and modification. We cannot stop the process of communication nor does it have a beginning and an end. The concept of process was presented as long as two thousand years ago by Heraclitus who wrote that "a man cannot step in the same river twice" and as recently as Bob Dylan's lyrics, "The times—they are a-changin.' " David Berlo, a well-known communication scholar, probably provides the clearest statement about communication as a process. Berlo writes,

If we accept the concept of process, we view events and relationships as dynamic, ongoing, ever-changing, continuous. When we label something as a process, we also mean that it does not have a beginning, an end, a fixed sequence of events. It is not static, at rest. It is moving. The ingredients within a process interact; each affects all of the others.[5]

The process nature of communication is especially relevant in our culture today. Our society has grown in scope and size, relationships have increased in complexity in our culture, and changes occur with even greater rapidity than in the past. The media affects our view of reality more today than it did ten or twenty years ago; family structures are being altered so that the traditional "nuclear" family is no longer the norm; there are more older people in the 1980s than in the 1960s or 1970s; individuals in our culture are increasingly mobile and frequently move across the country for job advancement; and the labor force evidences unemployment and misemployment—people with little training or interest in their current jobs. All of these changes affect the communication *process.*

Communication involves **understanding.** People involved in communication must understand what they are saying and hearing. All of us have been in situations where we could repeat another person's message but could not understand it. Communication does not occur unless understanding exists. The importance of understanding was emphasized by Carl Rogers in his book, *On Becoming a Person,* when he wrote, "I have found it of enormous value when I can *permit* myself to understand another person."[6]

Communication requires **sharing.** Consider the popular use of the word sharing. We share a meal, we share an event, we share a sunset. Sharing is a gift that people exchange. We can also share with ourselves—when we allow ourselves time to relax and daydream, time to consider who we really are and what our goals truly are. We share with ourselves in intrapersonal communication; we share with others in interpersonal and public communication. Regardless of the situation, communication requires sharing.

The sharing that occurs in communication is not necessarily the almost saccharin sharing of offering someone a gift. Our romantic inclination would encourage us to view sharing as a totally positive experience. We must remember that it can also be neutral and even negative; nonetheless, it does involve sharing. Let us consider three examples of sharing in communication to illustrate this point. When you softly touch someone you love, you share an understanding of the meaning of the caress, and the shared message is most likely positive. When you offer directions to a stranger, the two of you must share an understanding of the meaning of such words as "third stop sign," "large church," "left," and "right," but the shared message is neutral. Finally, when you are told that your job has been eliminated and that your services are no longer needed, you and your employer share a common understanding of the situation, and yet the sharing is probably a negative experience.

In the process of communication, the object of our understanding and sharing is **meaning.** Earlier definitions of communication have identified messages or thoughts as the objects of sharing. Neither of these terms is as accurate as meaning, however. The term **message** is not sufficient, because it does not imply any level of understanding. If I repeat an Iranian phrase to a student from Iran, this only shows that I have heard the phrase and can repeat it. No communication has occurred, even though we shared a particular message. **Thought** is also a troublesome term. It is very difficult to define thoughts, and even more difficult to determine when our thoughts are the same as another person's. The term meaning refers to that which is felt to be the significance of something and is a more accurate and useful descriptor of the object of communication.

These examples of sharing can also illustrate the difference between message, thoughts, and meaning. When we reach out to touch a loved one, we may be thinking about a past experience that was particularly touching or made us feel especially close to another person, and our message may be that we want to repeat that experience; however, the meaning of the nonverbal communication exchange arises from the definition that the two people attach to it. When someone asks for directions to a large classroom building, we might think about a class we had in the building last term and send a message about our negative experience, but the meaning is the shared understanding of how to proceed to the building from our current location. Thinking about our employer firing us may be complicated, even if the message on the "pink slip" is euphemistic and brief; but the meaning of the event will have long-range implications.

Communication Begins with the Self

Communication begins with oneself. As Carl Rogers wrote, "Every individual exists in a continually changing world of experience of which he is the center."[7] All of our communication is viewed from the perspective of self. Chapter 2 discusses the role of perception in communication and the difficulties that occur because each of us has separate perceptions of reality. Chapter 5 discusses the central role of self in communication and stresses the importance of self-awareness and self-concept in the communication process. Sharing ourselves with others in the interpersonal and public communication settings is discussed in chapters 6 and 10.

Dean Barnlund, a communication scholar, introduced the notion that communication is viewed from one's own perspective in his discussion of the "six persons" involved in every two-person communication situation (fig. 1.1). These six persons emerge first from the way in which you view yourself; second, the way in which you view the other person; third, how you believe the other person views you; fourth, how the other person views himself or herself; fifth, how the other person views you; and sixth, how the other person believes you view him or her. Barnlund believes that we "construct" ourselves, as well as other persons, through the relationships that we have, wish to have, or perceive ourselves as having. He encourages us to consider the various perspectives that are involved in communication and to recognize the centrality of the self in communication.

An example may clarify **Barnlund's "six people."** Suppose you see yourself as a slightly overweight, intelligent college junior (1). You perceive your roommate as a very attractive, slightly "spacey" college sophomore (2). She views you as an older and wiser friend (5), but sees herself as very bright, but in need of a good diet (4). Nonetheless, you treat her as though she has no weight problem, while you do; and you tend to discount her opinions because you think that she doesn't have much insight and, as a consequence, she seldom talks to you about her negative feelings about her body image and rarely shares her ideas (6). In addition, she does not view your body to be heavy, but she does think you are experienced and bright so you tend to "mother" her with your advice and guidance, and you talk a great deal about your "weight problem" to try to convince her of the seriousness of your feelings (3).

Figure 1.1 Barnlund's "six-people" involved in every two-person communication. (Adapted from Dean C. Barnlund, "A Transactional Model of Communication," in *Foundations of Communication Theory*.)

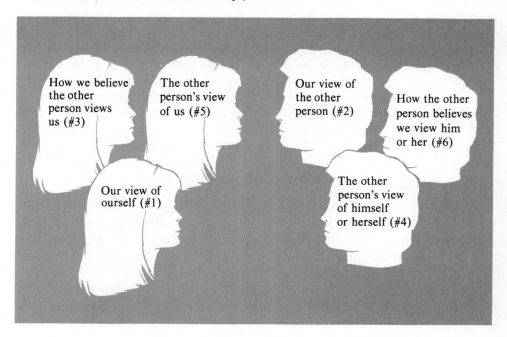

How we believe the other person views us (#3)

The other person's view of us (#5)

Our view of the other person (#2)

How the other person believes we view him or her (#6)

Our view of ourself (#1)

The other person's view of himself or herself (#4)

All of our perceptions of communication are tied to ourselves. In our descriptions, explanations, and evaluations of communication, we reflect a great deal of ourselves. As participants in communication, we are limited by our own view of the situation. For example, a woman might describe a heated conversation with her spouse as "Nothing at all. He made a mountain out of a molehill." The husband, on the other hand, might conclude that "She never really has understood me."

Communication Occurs in a Context

Communication does not occur in a vacuum. We communicate with ourselves, with another person, or with a number of other people. The differences between these contexts affect the communication that can and does occur. Communication scholars discuss the various contexts in which communication can occur and categorize them on the basis of the number of people involved or on the purpose of the communication. They also use such criteria as the degree of formality or intimacy, the opportunities for feedback, the need for prestructuring messages, and the degree of stability of the roles of speaker and listener.

For our purposes, we distinguish among the various contexts in which communication occurs on the basis of our definition of communication as the process of understanding and sharing meaning.

Intrapersonal communication is the process of sharing and understanding that occurs within a person. It is internal communication. Intrapersonal communication includes internal problem solving, resolution of internal conflict, planning for the future, emotional catharsis, and evaluations of oneself, others, and relationships between oneself and others. Intrapersonal communication involves only the self, and it must be clearly understood by the self because it constitutes the basis for all other communication.

We are engaged in intrapersonal communication almost continually. We might become more easily absorbed in "talking to ourselves" when we are alone—walking to class, driving to work, taking a shower—but most of us are involved in this form of communication in the most crowded circumstances as well—during a lecture, at a party, or visiting friends. Think about the last time you looked at yourself in a mirror. What were your thoughts? Intrapersonal communication is almost continuous, and yet we seldom focus on our communication with ourselves.

Interpersonal communication is the process of understanding and sharing meaning between oneself and at least one other person when relatively mutual opportunities for speaking and listening occur. Interpersonal, like intrapersonal, communication occurs for a variety of reasons: to solve problems, to resolve conflicts, to share information, to improve our perception of ourselves, or to fulfill such social needs as the need to belong or to be loved. Interpersonal communication includes interviews with an employer or teacher; talks with a parent, spouse, or child; and small group communication in clubs or in small civic, social, and church groups.

The addition of another person complicates communication greatly. Although each of us holds conflicting perceptions, beliefs, values, and attitudes (indeed a great deal of our intrapersonal communication concerns these conflicts), the differences between two people are generally far greater than those within an individual. In addition, we all have different ways of expressing what we feel. Consequently, the possibility of successful communication decreases.

Next to intrapersonal, interpersonal communication is generally considered the most influential form of communication, and the most satisfying to the individuals involved in it. Interpersonal communication typically occurs in an informal setting and includes face-to-face verbal and nonverbal exchanges, a sharing of the roles of speaker and listener, and minimal planning.

Public communication is the process of understanding and sharing meaning with a large number of other people when one person is generally identified as the speaker and others are recognized as listeners. It is recognized by its formality, structure, and planning. One person speaks, the others listen. We are frequently the listeners in public communication: as students in lecture classes, at convocations, and in church. Sometimes we are speakers: when we speak before a group, when we try to convince other voters of the merits of a particular candidate for office, or when we introduce a guest speaker to a large audience. Public communication most often has the purpose of informing or persuading, but it can also have the purpose of entertaining, introducing, announcing, welcoming, or paying tribute.

Communication Involves Codes

All communication is coded. We typically use the word *code* to describe the secret language that children use or to refer to specialized, stylized, or shortened languages, such as Morse Code. For our purposes, however, a **code** is any systematic arrangement or comprehensive collection of symbols, letters, or words that has an arbitrary meaning and is used for communication.

We can distinguish between two major kinds of codes that are used in communication: verbal codes and nonverbal codes. **Verbal codes** consist of words and their grammatical arrangement. It is easier to think of the German language as a code or to consider French as "some kind of code," than it is to realize that our own language is a code. All languages are codes. The English symbols, letters, and words we use are arbitrary. We have no more reason to call a heavy outer garment by the word *overcoat*, than a German does to call it *der mantel*. Nature does not provide a rationale for any particular language. Chapter 3 discusses the importance and role of verbal codes in communication.

Nonverbal codes consist of all symbols that are not words, including our bodily movements, our use of space and time, our clothing and other adornments, and sounds other than words. Nonverbal codes should not be confused with nonoral codes. All nonoral codes—such as bodily movement—are nonverbal codes, but nonverbal codes also include oral codes such as pitch, duration, and rate of speech, as well as sounds like *eh* and *ah*. Nonverbal codes refer to *all* codes that do not consist of words. Chapter 4 discusses the nature and role of nonverbal codes in communication.

Communication Consists of Encoding and Decoding

If communication involves the use of codes, the process of communicating can be viewed as one of encoding and decoding. **Encoding** is defined as the act of putting a message or thought into a code. **Decoding** is assigning meaning to that message. For example, suppose you are interested in owning a St. Bernard, and you are trying to describe this breed of dog to a relative who wants to help you find such an animal. In your own mind, you visualize a friend's St. Bernard who lived in your childhood neighborhood. You picture the dog's frisky gallop, his silky hair, the mischief he caused, and his big brown eyes. When you put your vision into words, you might say that a St. Bernard is a large brown and white dog with long hair. You encode your memories and perceptions of a particular dog into words that describe the breed. When your relative hears this definition, she decodes the words and creates a picture of her own. Her own experience with smaller dogs affects her encoding. The picture that she gains from your definition is of a German shepherd. As we can see, misunderstanding often occurs because of the limitation of our language and the inadequacy of our descriptions. Nonetheless, the process of holding a message or thought in our mind, encoding it for another person or persons, and decoding the verbal and nonverbal codes into another person's consciousness is the method by which we communicate.

The relationship between encoding and decoding is unclear. Three views have been popularized by researchers: (1) encoding and decoding are separate functions; (2) encoding and decoding are successive phases of a single ongoing process; and (3) encoding and decoding are the same operation viewed from opposite ends of the system.

Communication Is Transactional

These three views of the relationship between encoding and decoding influence the way we view communication. In the past, people believed that communication could be viewed as **action**, that is, one person sends a message (encoding) and another person receives it (decoding). This view is depicted in figure 1.2. This view can be compared to the situation in which one person holds a basketball and throws it to another. The second person does not return the ball, she only catches it or fumbles it.

A second view evolved. Communication is viewed as **interaction**: one person sends a message to a second person who receives it and, in turn, responds with another message. The communicators take turns encoding and decoding messages. This point of view is pictured in figure 1.3. To continue with our basketball analogy, this perspective would be similar to a game of catch. Each person catches (or drops) the ball and each person throws the ball. However, the ball cannot be thrown until it is caught.

**Figure 1.2
Communication as action.**

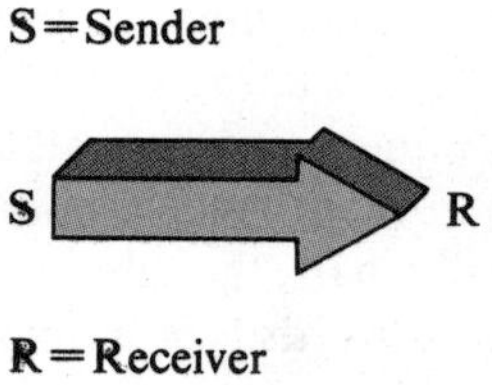

S=Sender

S   R

R=Receiver

**Figure 1.3
Communication as
interaction.**

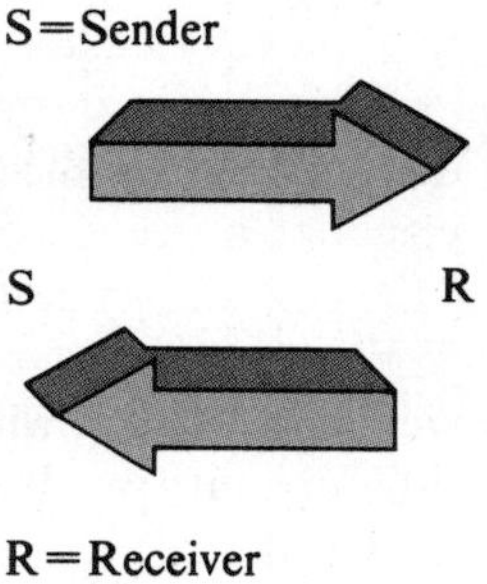

S=Sender

S   R

R=Receiver

**Figure 1.4
Communication
as transaction.**

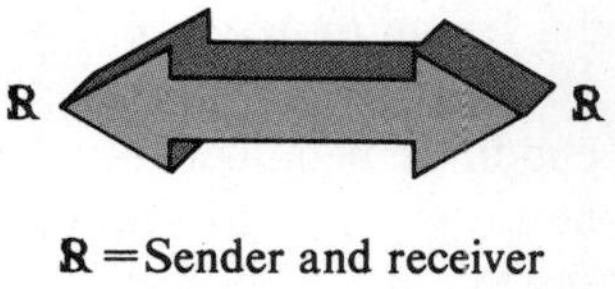

Я   Я

Я=Sender and receiver

     The **transactional** view of communication may have originated with Oliver Wendell Holmes who explained problems in communication by considering the role of differing perceptions, constructs, and ideas that two people might have regarding the people involved in communication.[9] Although this view of communication may have germinated with Holmes in the mid-nineteenth century, it has been only recently discussed by communication scholars. John Stewart suggests that transactional communication may be called relationship communication, because meanings are largely born out of the perceptions that we create or hold about others while we are actively engaged in interaction with them.[10]

     Viewing communication as a transaction means that we believe that communicators simultaneously encode and decode (fig. 1.4). Rather than identifying people as senders and receivers, we suggest that people simultaneously serve as senders and receivers of messages. Recently, two communication scholars coined the term "transceivers"[11] for communicators, which stresses the simultaneity of transmitting and receiving messages. Thus, encoding and decoding are not separate activities, nor do they occur one at a time. According to the transactional view, people are continually sending and receiving messages. They cannot avoid communication. This most recent view of communication is accepted in this text. We view communication as a confusing ballgame in which a person catches and throws an unlimited number of balls at any time, in any direction, to any other person. An individual's throwing a ball is not dependent upon his ability to catch one first. He or she does not always "take turns" in this game. The game has some rules and some predictability, but from time to time, balls fly through the air without preplanning or preparation.

     In some settings, one person may serve as the primary transmitter of messages while another person or persons serve primarily as receivers of messages. For example, in public speaking, we can identify a speaker and an audience of listeners. In interpersonal communication, such a distinction frequently cannot be made. In those situations in which one person is perceived as the initiator of messages, or as the speaker, we refer to the listeners' transmission of verbal and nonverbal messages as **feedback**. **Feedback** is the verbal and nonverbal responses to messages that are received and understood by the speaker. Feedback provides important information to the speaker concerning the need to alter, embellish, correct, or reinforce the messages that he or she is sending. The role of feedback will be discussed in more detail in chapter 7.

Any factor that intervenes between encoding amd decoding is known as **noise**. Noise is generally thought of as static—stimuli that are external to the person or persons engaged in communication. But it also includes interference that is internal to one or both of the communicators. External noise includes loud banging, confusing lights, a strong and unpleasant odor, and so forth. Internal noise may result from worries, daydreams, or a negative reaction to a particular word.

To recapitulate, we have defined communication as the process of understanding and sharing meaning that begins with oneself, occurs in a variety of situations, involves codes, and consists of encoding and decoding. Communication is one of our most basic activities. Let us examine its functions.

The Case of Sharon Black

Sharon Black, a freshman at an extension university, worked thirty hours a week at a local department store—a very busy schedule. Sharon wanted to spend more time with her co-workers, but her college work interfered. The other workers usually ate lunch together, but Sharon had a class that started at 12:30 four days a week. She usually couldn't attend parties because she had homework to do.

Sharon became increasingly quiet at work and felt more alienated as time passed. Her co-workers began to suspect that "the college girl" was avoiding them because she felt superior. They began to plan activities that would exclude Sharon.

Sharon's work was exemplary and she became eligible for promotion to supervisor. Her boss told her that a lot depended on whether the other workers would accept her leadership and cooperate with her. But Sharon's co-workers were resentful of the possible promotion of a person who had so little experience at the store. They also felt that she was being "pushed ahead" because she was a college student. At lunch that day, they decided that Sharon would not get the promotion if they had anything to say about it. One of the women offered to tell the boss how they felt.

Sharon was called into the office two days later. Her boss said "Sorry." Sharon didn't seem to be getting along well with the others, and it did not look like they would cooperate with her. Sharon broke into tears and ran from the office.

1. Does communication begin with self in this example? If so, how does it begin with self?
2. Identify the communication situations that are involved in this case.
3. Does this case illustrate communication as action, interaction, or transaction? How?
4. Discuss the "noise" in the communication between Sharon and her co-workers.
5. What conclusions can be drawn about this breakdown in communication?

Functions of Communication

At the beginning of this chapter we said that we communicate in order to fulfill social needs—the need to understand ourself and others—and to fulfill task-related needs—to gain employment, to maintain a job, to solve problems, and to inform and persuade others. The function of communication, according to this view, is to help the individual gain control of his or her life. While we reject the simple, quick, and easy answers of est, transcendental meditation, and weekend short courses, we do believe that communication skills can be learned and that people can function better as a result of their understanding of communication fundamentals.

Understanding and Sharing is designed to help you achieve your social and task-related goals. The skills approach that is offered in this book includes the identification of effective communication skills, understanding the theory that supports these skills, and being able to practice them when appropriate. The function of communication is to help you gain control of your environment. Let us consider some of the social and task-related functions in more detail.

Social Functions

The social functions that communication serves are:

1. Increasing our personal awareness
2. Presenting ourselves to others
3. Improving social relationships
4. Enhancing the continued existence of our society

We increase our personal awareness or discover who we are through communication. Other people tell us—verbally and nonverbally—important information about ourselves. They tell us that they respect us when they ask for, and listen to, our opinions. They tell us that they enjoy our company when they seek opportunities to spend time with us. They tell us that we have a well-developed sense of humor when they encourage us to relate humorous anecdotes.

It is also by communicating that we present ourselves to others. As other people communicate to us who they believe we are, we can communicate to them who we believe we are. Our behavior is influenced by the impressions that others have of us, but we also influence those impressions. We communicate who we are verbally—"I try to be patient with my husband and children," "I think I really did a good job!"—and nonverbally—by the clothing we wear, the expression on our faces, the posture we assume, and the way we touch other people.

We communicate to improve social relationships and to enhance the continued existence of a society. Few people would choose the hermitlike existence that Howard Hughes maintained during his last years. Most of us are socially oriented. We seek out and enjoy the company of others. We communicate to help establish, maintain, and improve the relationships that are the foundation of our society.

We also communicate to enhance the continued existence of our society. The theorist Kenneth Burke describes the American society in very bleak terms. He maintains that our society is on the brink of extinction and warns people that they should not forget that we build our cultures by "huddling together."[12] While Burke was speaking abstractly, he was emphasizing the point that a society can exist only to the extent that people are able and willing to communicate with each other.

Task Functions

Communication also helps us achieve certain task-related goals. Our current economic situation has caused people to focus on the importance of working. A few years ago, Studs Terkel, author of the best-seller *Working,* emphasized this same point.

As the automated pace of our daily jobs wipes out name and face—and, in many instances, feeling—there is a sacrilegious question being asked these days. To earn one's bread by the sweat of one's brow has always been the lot of mankind. At least, ever since Eden's slothful couple was served with an eviction notice. The scriptural precept was never doubted, not out loud. No matter how demeaning the task, no matter how it dulls the senses and breaks the spirit, one *must* work. Or else.[13]

We communicate in order to gain employment, to maintain jobs, to improve our marketable skills, and to change careers. The employment interview, the small group discussion, and the speeches to inform and persuade can all be useful in these endeavors.

Task functions do not only concern actual employment and job-related communication. We also use communication to help us solve problems and to achieve our ambitions. We communicate in committees and in discussions with instructors, parents, and larger groups. We attempt to convince others—through information, compelling arguments, and exemplary behavior—that they should allow us, or assist us, in helping to achieve certain ends.

Problems in Communication

Communication helps us gain control of our environment as it helps us meet our social and task-related needs. We spend a great deal of time engaged in communication and we make some attempts to improve our ability to communicate with others. Nonetheless, we face serious problems in our communication skills. Three essential causes for these problems can be identified.

1. Lack of interest
2. Lack of understanding
3. Lack of common goals and assumptions

These three causes are a result of differences in perception, which will be discussed in greater detail in chapter 2.

Lack of Interest

Communication cannot occur if one person has no interest or desire to understand or to share. While Beetle Bailey is correct when he claims the right to say what he thinks, communication is made impossible by his sergeant's obvious lack of interest.

There are many reasons for a lack of interest. People are sometimes not motivated to understand certain things or to show interest in certain people. The various subcultures in contemporary America provide numerous examples of persons

BEETLE BAILEY

or groups who blithely ignore other persons or groups. The small-town business owner in northern Minnesota may be motivated to understand the difficulties of Indians on reservations but may have no interest in the plight of inner-city blacks. Similarly, the husband whose wife cheerfully stays home may not be motivated to understand the liberated woman who is his professional colleague.

Moreover, people are sometimes suspicious, defensive, and distrustful, as well as just uninterested. The reasons for their suspicions and distrust may be complex, but the result is disastrous to effective communication. As we shall see in chapter 6, the quality of being open to others is essential to successful communication.

Lack of Understanding

Sometimes we sincerely wish to communicate with others but are unable to do so because, for one or another reason, we cannot understand them. There may be a language barrier. The barrier is obvious when one person is speaking English and the other person is speaking Spanish. It may be less obvious when one person is speaking black English and the other is speaking white English.

Even when two people share a common language and dialect, misunderstandings can still result. More subtle differences in the use of language also affect understanding. One person may use a word or phrase figuratively, only to have another interpret it literally. An example of the difference in usage is illustrated in the cartoon. The lieutenant takes the general's figurative suggestion literally.

Among the more subtle differences are also differences in our nonverbal language; one person may employ an elaborate and extensive set of nonverbal symbols in communicating with another person who is not sensitive to nonverbal communication. For example, rings, placement of key rings, specific modes of dress, particular looks, and body positioning are all used to communicate one's sexual preference, availability, and the possibilities of establishing a relationship.

BEETLE BAILEY

Communication Breakdown

You are the supervisor in an office of moderate size. Your boss phones to say that he wants the weekly report today, a day early because he is going out of town.

Ann, who generally types the report, is absent. You explain the job to John, who interrupts, protesting that it is Ann's job. You counter by telling him that you need the report today and that Ann will not return until tomorrow. After you give John all of the figures and a copy of last week's report you ask, "You do understand, don't you?" John indicates that he does and types the report.

Three hours later, John places the report on your desk. You find that, because John forgot to consider the holiday in the preceding week, all of the figures are one column out of place. When you show him his mistake, he emphatically states that he did exactly what he was told.

Sufficient time remains for John to retype the report.

1. How would you manage to have the report completed?
2. Should you take further action?
3. What problems in communication occurred?

Lack of Common Goals and Assumptions

Although we are interested in understanding another person and do, in fact, understand what he or she has to say, we may still find that we have a communication problem with that person. A third problem in communication is that we do not share the other person's goals and assumptions. All of us have heard arguments in which one person concluded, "Well, you just don't understand me," and the other person replied, "No, I understand you perfectly well, I just don't agree with you." It is difficult to recognize a problem in communication that arises because people do not share the same goals and assumptions.

Lack of common goals and assumptions are particularly abundant in our culture, which is rich with subcultural diversity. We divide ourselves in an unlimited number of ways—on the basis of our attitudes about the family, the role of women in society, the importance of working for a living, socialized medicine, and defense systems. We also form groups based on our race, sex, region of the country, size of our community, and educational background. The large number of subcultures and their constantly changing nature create many differences in the goals and assumptions of people in our society.

Differences in goals and expectations can show themselves in different ways. We can have a situation in which one person is clear about the differences but refuses to state them. For example, your goal in visiting a professor might be to gain information about tomorrow's exam. Instead of stating your goal, however, you tell her that you "just dropped in to talk." Your professor attempts to be responsive to your stated needs by discussing something of general interest. You become frustrated because the conversation does not get around to the exam. The professor becomes irritated because you do not appear interested in the conversation, even though you were the person who initiated it. When you leave the office, both of you feel dissatisfied.

When we have specific goals in mind but do not state them or share them with the person with whom we are communicating, problems occur. The term **hidden agenda** refers to a situation in which we state one goal or motive, but we actually have another goal in mind. In the example cited, your hidden agenda was to gain information about the exam. We frequently have hidden agendas. You may tell your employer that you want to discuss vacation policies, when, in fact, you are trying to get an extra day off. You may tell an audience that you want to inform them on *anorexia nervosa* when, in fact, you want to persuade them to show concern for people with this affliction. You may tell an employee that you want to share some of your feelings about the company, when, in fact, you want to conduct an appraisal interview of his work. Hidden agendas may be common in communication, but they generally destroy open and effective communication.

We also have situations in which the people involved are not clear about their differences and thus do not state them. No one has any intention of subverting the communication, but difficulties ensue just the same. For instance, if you value your college education and your parents do not share this value, you may have countless arguments and disagreements without ever discovering the reason. If you live at home, your parents might feel you should continue to join them on family outings, as you did when you were in high school, but you might want more time to study or to spend with people in your classes. You will argue about a dozen similar matters, but you are really arguing about an unrecognized and unstated difference in values and assumptions.

Summary

In this chapter, the concept of communication was introduced. Communication was defined as the process of understanding and sharing meaning. Communication begins with the self. It has a variety of forms, including intrapersonal communication, which is the understanding and sharing that occurs within a person; interpersonal communication, which is the process of understanding and sharing that occurs between oneself and at least one other person when relatively mutual opportunities for speaking and listening occur; and public communication, which is the process of understanding and sharing that occurs between oneself and a large number of other people when one person is generally identified as the speaker and others are recognized as listeners. Communication involves codes, both verbal and nonverbal, and consists of encoding and decoding, which occur simultaneously. Feedback is the verbal and nonverbal response to messages that are received and understood by the speaker. Interference in the encoding and decoding process is known as noise.

The function of communication is to help us gain control of our lives and our environment. We meet social and task-related needs through communication. Three common causes of problems in communication are a lack of interest, a lack of understanding, and a lack of common goals and assumptions.

We spend a large proportion of our time communicating, and yet many Americans report that their greatest fear is the fear of public speaking. This text is designed to help you to become more familiar with communication and to communicate more competently.

Additional Readings

Barnlund, Dean C. "Toward a Meaning Centered Philosophy of Communication." *Journal of Communication* 12 (1962): 198–202. A presentation and discussion of several axioms of communication: communication is a circular, unrepeatable, and irreversible process involving the total personality. Examines why people communicate and the nature of their communication.

Berlo, David K. *The Process of Communication*. New York: Holt, Rinehart and Winston, 1960.
Berlo's seminal work outlines the notion of communication as process. His explanation of the interaction process is thorough and recommended for advanced students who are interested in pursuing the original thought that went into communication as process.

Dance, Frank E. X., and Larson, Carl E. *The Functions of Human Communication: A Theoretical Approach*. New York: Holt, Rinehart and Winston, 1976.
A basic communication theory text. Lists over one hundred definitions of communication that have been offered by other communication researchers and offers a thorough discussion of theoretical issues surrounding communication. Students interested in understanding some of the theoretical history of communication are advised to consult this text.

Mortensen, C. David. "Communication Postulates." In *Messages,* edited by Jean Civikly. 2d ed. New York: Random House, Inc., 1977.
Mortensen develops five principles to explain the nature of communication. A good fundamental overview of the communication process, including bibliography for further reading.

Schramm, Wilbur. "How Communication Works." In *The Processes & Effects of Mass Communication,* edited by Wilbur Schramm. Urbana, Ill.: University of Illinois Press, 1971.
A discussion of several variables that affect the communication process, offering a model of communication based on those variables. Includes an explanation of messages, feedback, fields of experience, signals, and encoding and decoding.

*Smith, Raymond G. *Speech Communication: Theory and Models*. New York: Harper & Row, Publishers, 1970.
A scholarly discussion of models and their development. Smith presents several different models of communication and examines their limitations and their strengths. He also explores the nature of models in general and their uses in understanding human communication.

Watzlawick, Paul; Beavin, Janet; and Jackson, Don. *Pragmatics of Human Communication*. New York: W. W. Norton & Co., 1967.
Pragmatics, a landmark volume, precipitated a great deal of research on relational communication. The authors detail the pragmatic study of communication, which focuses on the behavior of the communicator as the fundamental component of communication. Recommended reading for advanced students of communication.

Wenburg, John R., and Wilmot, William. *The Personal Communication Process*. New York: John Wiley & Sons, 1973. Chapters 1, 2, and 3.
Chapter 1 discusses the six axioms of communication. A story illustrates communication as a process. Chapter 2 examines the contexts of intrapersonal, interpersonal, small group, public, and mass communication, and discusses how each of these arenas of communication differs. In chapter 3, the nature of models is explained, and the strengths and weaknesses of several basic communication models are discussed.

*Indicates more advanced readings.

Notes

1. Jimmy Messina, "Talk to Me," Jimmy Messina, *Oasis,* Columbia Record.
2. Charles T. Brown and Charles Van Riper, *Speech and Man* (Englewood Cliffs, N.J.: Prentice-Hall, 1966), pp. 1–2.
3. "What Are Americans Afraid Of?" *Bruskin Report* 53 (1973).
4. See, for example, Paul T. Rankin, "Measurement of the Ability to Understand the Spoken Language" (Ph.D. diss. University of Michigan, 1926) cited in *Dissertation Abstracts* 12 (1926): 847; Paul T. Rankin, "Listening Ability: Its Importance, Measurement, and Development," *Chicago Schools Journal* 12 (1930): 177; and J. Donald Weinrauch and John R. Swanda, Jr., "Examining the Significance of Listening: An Exploratory Study of Contemporary Management," *Journal of Business Communication* 13 (Fall 1975): 25–32.
5. David K. Berlo, *The Process of Communication* (New York: Holt, Rinehart and Winston, 1960), p. 24.
6. Carl R. Rogers, *On Becoming a Person* (Boston: Houghton Mifflin Company, 1961), p. 18.
7. Carl R. Rogers, *Client-Centered Therapy* (Boston: Houghton Mifflin Company, 1951), p. 483.
8. Dean C. Barnlund, "A Transactional Model of Communication," in *Foundations of Communication Theory,* ed. Kenneth K. Sereno and C. David Mortensen (New York: Harper & Row, Publishers, 1970), pp. 98–101.
9. Oliver Wendell Holmes, *The Autocrat of the Breakfast-Table* (Boston: Phillips, Simpson and Co., 1858), p. 59.
10. John Stewart, "An Interpersonal Approach to the Basic Course," *The Speech Teacher* 21 (1972): 7–14.
11. Harold P. Zelko and Frank E. X. Dance, *Business and Professional Speech Communication* (New York: Holt, Rinehart and Winston, 1965), pp. 6–7.
12. Kenneth Burke, *Permanence and Change* (Los Altos, Calif.: Hermes Publications, 1954), pp. 234–36.
13. Studs Terkel, *Working* (New York: Avon Books, 1974), p. xiv.

2

Perception

The Process
of Understanding

Objectives

1. State the differences between the view of perception as passive and the view of perception as active; describe a situation that illustrates creative meaning as opposed to inherent meaning

2. Discuss the processes of selection, organization, and interpretation as they apply to the perception of others

3. Describe an experience in which you and another person had different perceptions of the same stimuli and discuss the reasons for those differences

4. Identify the cultural roles that you play and explain the effect of those roles on your behavior

5. Give examples that illustrate the processes of organization: figure and ground, proximity, closure, similarity, and perceptual constancy

Key Terms

perception

passive perception

objective perception

inherent meaning

subjective

creative

active

cultural roles

cultural differences

subcultural differences

selection

organization

interpretation

selective attention

selective retention

selective exposure

stereotyping

figure and ground

closure

proximity

similarity

perceptual constancy

At 8:07 P.M. on March 7, 1979, a late-model blue sedan was involved in a collision with a lightweight ten-speed bicycle at 2200 College Drive. No one was injured, but the bicycle was damaged.
          Police report

Did you hear what happened last night? I didn't get all the details, but some instructor ran into a student on a bicycle. It's bad enough that those guys have to flunk us, now they're running over us!
          College student

I am sorry to report that an unfortunate accident occurred last evening. As a result of our inadequate street lighting, an automobile driven by a student was hit in the rear bumper by a faculty member on a bicycle. Luckily, no one was injured, but the front fender on the bicycle was bent.
          Dean of college

These are three descriptions of the same accident. They can be recognized as descriptions of a similar event, but they vary in all other details. The first description, from the police report, is objective, disinterested, and dry. The second, from a student, is embellished and more interesting. The dean offers an explanation for the accident and gives more details.

In none of the descriptions does the speaker claim to have witnessed the accident. But eye-witness accounts also vary greatly. Accident reports are filled with conflicting evidence. People who have seen an automobile accident, for example, will disagree about who was at fault, the number of people involved, the year, the make, and even the color of the vehicles.

Differences in **perception,** in the way people see, hear, smell, taste, or feel a specific stimulus, are common. Whether we are describing an event (say, an automobile accident), an idea (how communication occurs), or something about ourselves (how we feel about our own bodies), we encounter differences in perception. Individual experiences are not identical. Neither are individual perceptions, even of the same event.

Communication occurs only to the extent that we share perceptions. In the last chapter, we stated that communication involves two activities—understanding and sharing. In this chapter, we will consider the first of these two activities, understanding.

How Does Communication Involve Perception?

Perception is the process by which we come to understand ourselves and others. Understanding is necessary to communication. In order to make the connection more concrete, let us delineate two specific ways in which perception is related to communication.

The Process by Which We Come to Understand Ourselves

First, perception is essential to the study of communication because it is the process by which we come to understand ourselves. Communication begins with self, as we stated in chapter 1. Chapters 5 and 6 explore the role of self in communication further. At this point, it is necessary only to realize that our self-concept consists of our perceptions of ourselves. In other words, self-concept is what we understand about ourselves.

Our perceptions of ourselves affect our communication. If a person believes himself or herself to be shy, that person tends to avoid communicating; if another person believes that he or she is aggressive, that person may tend to dominate conversations and be loud and boisterous. We sometimes draw inferences about other people's self-concepts from the way they speak.

The Process by Which We Come to Understand Others

Second, perception is the process by which we come to understand others. Most communication involves other people. Chapter 7 will consider further how we understand others. At this time, we need only recognize that perception is the process by which we understand them.

We make judgments and draw conclusions about other people within a few seconds of meeting them. We use the nonverbal cues available, including the person's facial expression, vocal patterns, body language, clothes, jewelry, as well as what the person says. Our perception of the other person, including the way that person looks, sounds, and smells, provides immediate information.

The perceptions that we have of others affect our communication with them. A number of minority group people—blacks, Mexican-Americans, and handicapped persons—have related their experiences with others. Frequently, the early portion of a conversation will focus on their uniqueness—their race, their nationality, or their particular handicap. People who talk with them tend to be limited in their early perceptions. Often, the topic of conversation does not shift until these persons have known each other for some time.

What Is Perception?

In the past, people believed that perception was nothing more than sensing stimuli. It was commonly believed that people were merely cameras that recorded the events that occurred around them—**passive perception.** Sights, sounds, smells, and other stimuli were sent to them. A second implication was that people were objective. In other words, no one added or subtracted from the stimuli—**objective perception.** This point of view also implied **inherent meaning** in the object being perceived. No room for interpretation existed because the stimulus contained all of the meaning.

The contemporary view of perception is that it is **subjective, active,** and **creative.** People do add and subtract from the stimuli to which they are exposed. They blend the external stimuli and their internal states. In the contemporary view, when we perceive something, we are really "doing our own thing."

Consider the last time you were driving in the country. As you drove between the fields on the two-lane highway, your attention shifted from one stimuli to another. You did not passively absorb all of the stimuli in the environment, but you actively chose to focus on the sports car that zoomed past you and to ignore the family sedan that you followed for a number of miles. When a large van came into your vision in your rear-view mirror, you did not objectively perceive the vehicle, but instead you began to think about your truck-driver friend and you subjectively thought about the truck as a means of income. When you looked at the fields planted with corn and barley, you did not identify an inherent meaning in the plants that others would easily share, but you recognized, in your creative way, that the plants were different from those with which you are familiar.

In order to understand how the contemporary view of perception affects communication, try to remember the last week of final exams. Perhaps, as you were rushing to the exam, you noticed one of your friends coming toward you. You singled out your friend from a number of other people on the sidewalk. When you noticed him, you did not drop your glance, but you maintained eye contact to signal that you wanted to talk for a moment or two. As you began the conversation, you noticed that the rain was very cold. You began to feel uncomfortable and wondered why your friend continued to talk. Your thoughts shifted back to the exam. Your friend remarked that you seemed touchy. As he walked away, he told himself, "That's what happens when you lend people money—they try to ignore you!"

If you assumed that the older view of perception was accurate, this conversation would be difficult to interpret and understand. If you take into consideration that perception is active, subjective, and creative, your friend's misunderstanding can be explained. Barnlund's notion that every two-way communication involves six persons is also helpful in understanding this particular situation. Instead of holding that there is a single, objective view of this encounter, we recognize that at least two perspectives are possible: the way the other person views the situation and the way you view it. True, you both reacted to the same external stimuli—the sight of each other, the extended glance, and the cold rain. But your inner state, including anxiety over the upcoming exam, and your friend's inner state, including his concern about money he had lent you, produced a unique communication that could be viewed from a variety of perspectives.

Why Do Differences in Perception Occur?

We have just demonstrated a common phenomenon—different people perceive the same event in different ways. Moreover, perception is subjective, active, and creative. We now turn our attention to the factors that account for differences in perception.

Differences occur in perception for several related reasons. There are physiological reasons. There are differences due to past experience. There are differences in mood, and there are different circumstances. Let us consider these reasons in more detail.

Physiological Factors

None of us are physiologically identical. We vary in height, weight, body type, and in our senses. People can be tall or short, have less than perfect vision, and suffer from impaired hearing. Such differences in physiology alter perception. The cartoon below illustrates a simple physiological difference with which most of us are familiar. Anyone who has attempted to "get back into shape" can understand the runner's perception of the distance he ran.

FUNKY

An unfortunate experience will illustrate this point. Two small boys set out on a three-block walk to the neighborhood drugstore. As they approached their destination, they were stopped by two bigger boys who blocked their way and threatened them with a knife. The two little boys were asked if they had any money. When the bigger boys found out that they had practically no money, they ran off, leaving two frightened little boys.

Back at home, the two little boys were asked by a detective to describe the bigger boys. One boy maintained that one of the aggressors was about sixteen and the other about twenty. He thought one was about 5'6", the other about 5'10". His friend was questioned in another room. He told the detective that the two bigger boys were twenty and twenty-seven years old. He guessed their heights at 5'10" and 6'2". The detective was disappointed because the two descriptions were not the same.

A student of perception would have understood the differences in point of view. One boy was a large nine-year-old who is five feet tall. His smaller and younger friend was only six years old and just over four feet tall. Knowing this removes some of the mystery. The smaller, younger boy saw his assailants as larger and older, but even the taller boy probably exaggerated their size and age.

A second example of how physiological differences influence perception comes from Michigan State University and a 23-year-old student named James M. Renuk. Renuk suffers from cerebral palsy, and his speech is not understandable to most people. To write, he has to position himself on the floor and balance a pen against his leg. Renuk is hopeful that the artificial language department at Michigan State will perfect a group of portable machines equipped with microcomputers that will allow him and others with similar difficulties to communicate through voice synthesizers and small television screens. Although there can be no doubt that Renuk has different perceptions than other people, one of the most interesting differences is the language he uses to refer to people who are not handicapped. He and his other activist friends at M.S.U. call the rest of us TABs, Temporarily Able-Bodied. The assumption that Renuk makes in this choice of words is that we do not know how long we will be able-bodied. It is a far different assumption than we make when we refer to ourselves as "normal."[1]

Past Experience

All of us tend to pay attention to those aspects of our environment that we expect or anticipate. We also tend to expect or anticipate that which is familiar to us. A common example of this tendency occurs to most of you almost daily. You are sitting in a classroom waiting for class to begin, or you are busy doing some work. Conversations are going on around you, but you do not hear anything until someone mentions your name. At the sound of your name, you suddenly perk up and pay attention to the conversation. It really seems to make no difference if someone was talking about you or about someone else with the same name; you pay attention to one of the most familiar words you know—your name.

Differences in perception, then, are affected by physiology and also by past experience. They are also affected by cultural roles, cultural differences, and subcultural differences. Each of these factors helps explain differences in the perceptions of various groups of people.

Cultural Roles People have different perceptions and are perceived differently because of their **cultural roles,** that is, the parts that they play within a particular society. The roles that we play in our culture, including student, worker, and son or daughter, affect our perceptions of the events around us.

One of the evolving cultural roles in the United States is that of the professional or career woman. We can gain an understanding of the effect of a difference in cultural role by using the example of Dr. Elizabeth Fish, a chemist, and comparing her to Mrs. John Anderson, a homemaker. To Dr. Fish, shopping is a routine task that she shares with her husband and her teenage children. In Mrs. Anderson's life, shopping takes center stage. A great deal of time, attention, and energy goes into marketing. She spends time planning meals, writing out grocery lists, clipping coupons from magazines, checking the newspaper for specials and sales, selecting the best time and day to do the shopping, and then spends time discussing the bargains she has found or deploring the high prices. Dr. Fish perceives shopping as a necessary but relatively unimportant task; Mrs. Anderson perceives it as central to her workweek. The differences in the cultural roles of these two women account for differences in their perception of shopping.

Cultural Differences Another factor that accounts for differences in perception is our culture. In our shrinking world, we have become more aware of **cultural differences.** As the Middle East, for example, has become more visible to us, we have been especially cognizant of the differences between ourselves and people from that part of the world. Until recently, one excellent example of differences in perception between ourselves and nomadic Arabs, for example, has been the mode of transportation. Many Americans can describe automobiles in great detail—they can distinguish among makes, models, and years of cars; they discuss horsepower and gas mileage; they know a fine car from a poor one. Many Arabs, on the other hand, were knowledgeable about camels. They could distinguish among various species, predict life span and ability to work, and recognize a superior camel from an inferior one. While Arabs had a small vocabulary for automobiles, Americans can barely distinguish beyond one hump and two hump camels. The cultural difference accounted for the differences in perception of cars and camels.

Subcultural Differences Still another factor that helps explain why people perceive the same stimuli in different ways is **subcultural differences.** Such differences occur within a particular culture. Men see some things differently from women, blacks from whites, old people from young people, and so forth.

Two scholars recently found that the subcultural difference between rural and urban people had an effect on how these persons perceived communication. In their study, they found that country children are more likely to become apprehensive about communicating. Urban children have a much more positive attitude toward communication.[2]

One subcultural difference with which you are probably very familiar is the so-called generation gap. The difference in age between yourself and your parents, instructors, or classmates may significantly affect your perception of them and, consequently, your communication with them. Consider rock music, and such events as President Kennedy's assassination, the Vietnam War, and Watergate and the pardoning of Richard M. Nixon. A difference in age can affect how you hear music and perceive events, what you say about them, and the meanings that are evoked when they are mentioned in a conversation. Subcultural differences affect our perception and, thereby, our communication.

Present Feelings and Circumstances

Differences in perception also arise from different feelings and circumstances. A headache, backache, or toothache can cause us to perceive a critical comment when a friendly one is being offered. We sometimes don't see a stop sign if our thoughts are elsewhere. One of the prisoners in the cartoon feels a draft at 140° because the usual temperature is 150°. Our perceptions alter; they can become more acute, less acute, or changed by our present feelings and circumstances.

If you have ever spent a night alone in a large house, a deserted dormitory, or an unfamiliar residence, you probably understand that perceptions are altered by circumstances. Most people experience a remarkable change in their hearing. Creaking, whining, breaking, scraping, cracking sounds are heard, although none were heard in the daytime. The lack of other stimuli—including light, other sounds, and the lack of people with whom to talk—coupled with a slight feeling of anxiety, provides the circumstances that result in more acute hearing.

Similar circumstances may account, in part, for the mirages seen by lonely travelers. Commander Robert Peary encountered massive snowy pinnacles that appeared to rise thousands of feet above the plain of solid ice deep inside the Arctic Circle in 1906. Seven years later, Donald MacMillan, another explorer, verified his discovery. However, when MacMillan asked his Eskimo guide to choose a course toward the peaks, the guide explained that the spectacle was only *poo-jok* (mist). Meteorologists have explained the existence of such mirages, but have hastened to add that they are "reported infrequently because people aren't looking for them."[3] The variance in the feelings and circumstances of the many explorers may account for the difference between sighting and not sighting specific illusions.

CROCK

What Occurs in Perception?

According to the most recent information, people appear to engage in three separate activities in perception. None of us is aware of these separate processes because they occur quickly and almost simultaneously. Nonetheless, each activity is involved in our perceptions. The three activities include **selection** (we neglect some of the stimuli in our environment and focus on a few), **organization** (we group the stimuli in our environment into units or wholes), and **interpretation** (we give particular meanings to stimuli). Let us consider each of these activities in more detail.

Selection

None of us perceives all the stimuli in our environment. For example, if you drove to school today, you were bombarded with sights, sounds, smells, and other sensations during your ride. At the time, you elected to perceive some of the stimuli and you chose to disregard others. Now, you can recall some of the stimuli you perceived but you have forgotten others. In the future, you will also expose yourself to some sensations and ignore others.

Our selectivity is of three types. First, we are selective in the stimuli to which we attend. **Selective attention** means that we focus on certain cues and ignore others. On our way to school, we check our timing with the bank clock, but we fail to notice the couple walking in front of the bank. We may overhear someone gossiping about us in the next room, but not hear what one of our parents is saying in the same room.

Second, we select the stimuli we will recall or remember. **Selective retention** means that we categorize, store, and retrieve certain information, but discard other information. If you played the car radio on your way to school, try to remember

one of the songs you heard, or one of the commercials, or one of the public-service announcements. Although your attention may have been drawn to a particular song or message this morning, you may find that you cannot remember anything you heard. Your mind has discarded the sounds you heard from your radio. You may recall a criticism that your date offered last night, but have forgotten that your mother made a similar comment two days ago.

Third, we are selective in the stimuli to which we allow ourselves to be exposed. **Selective exposure** means that we perceive stimuli that we wish to perceive and disregard stimuli that we do not wish to perceive. If we have a tendency to drive slightly over the limit, we might selectively perceive other fast drivers. Selective exposure allows us to disregard many other cars that are moving more slowly. If you worry about your lack of assertiveness, you may pay special attention to advertisements for assertiveness training or workshops on interpersonal communication skills. Conversely, you may not notice similar ads for workshops on more effective parenting since you are not a parent and do not plan on becoming a parent for some time.

The relationship between selection and communication can be clarified by the concept of stereotyping. **Stereotyping** is the process of placing people and things into established categories, or of basing judgments about people or things upon the categories in which they fit, rather than on their individual characteristics. All of us stereotype to a certain extent, but particular stereotypes vary from person to person. Stereotyping involves selective attention, selective retention, and selective exposure.

A specific example will illustrate the relationship among these concepts. Suppose you perceive women to be emotional and men to be logical. In order to maintain this stereotype, you selectively attend to women who behave emotionally and ignore those who are unemotional. Similarly, you selectively attend to men who are logical, rather than to those who seem unpredictable. When you try to recall the significant men and women in your life, you find that the women were either moderately or extremely emotional and that the men were fairly rational. You have selectively retained the memory of those who fit your stereotype. Finally, as you interact with others, you find that the women you meet tend to be emotional and that the men you encounter tend to be logical. You carefully expose yourself only to those persons who fit the stereotype that you have established. Selective exposure allows you to perceive only emotional women and logical men. Selectivity in perception affects stereotyping, and stereotyping is a process by which we categorize so we can communicate with others. We will consider the processes of stereotyping, abstracting, and categorizing further, in chapter 3, when we consider verbal codes and words that we have developed and used.

Organization

All of us have a tendency to organize the stimuli in our environment. The unorganized figure 2.1 is difficult to describe if we only glance at it for a minute. When we attempt to describe it, we do so by organizing the lines we see. We might say that it consists of straight and squiggly lines, or that it has a rectangle, a triangle,

Figure 2.1   The unorganized figure.

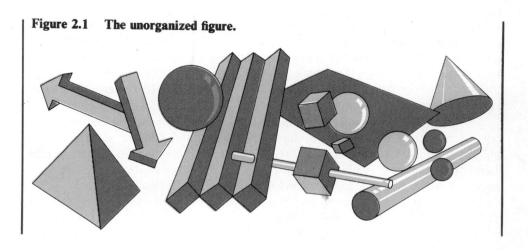

and a square, or we may categorize the stimuli in some other way. The important point is that we attempt to organize the figure as we describe it.

Gestalt psychology (the German word *gestalt* means "whole") clarified the importance of organization to perception. A fundamental principle of Gestalt psychology is that the many elements that are presented to a particular sense are perceptually organized into a whole structure. Gestaltists maintain that the structures or holistic pictures that we perceive are always the simplest possible under the conditions.

We organize stimuli in a number of ways. One method of organizing is to distinguish between **figure and ground**. In figure 2.2, some people perceive a vase while others perceive twins facing each other. People who see a vase identify the center of the drawing as the figure, and the area on the right and left as the ground, or background. Conversely, people who see twins facing each other see the center as the background and the area on the right and left as the figure.

Figure 2.3 is another illustration of the principle of figure and ground. As we first glance at the drawing we perceive nothing but ink blobs—nothing is clearly distinguishable as either the figure or the background. If we continue to look at the drawing, however, we perceive the face of Christ or of a bearded man at the top center of the picture. When we see the face, it becomes the figure; the rest of the drawing becomes the ground.

Another way of organizing stimuli was described by the Gestaltists as **closure**. We engage in closure every time we fill in things that do not exist. If someone showed us figure 2.4 and asked us what we perceive, we would probably say that it is a picture of a cat. But, as we can clearly see, the figure is incomplete. We can see a cat only if we are willing to fill in the blank areas. Additional examples of closure are given in figures 2.5 and 2.6. Most of us would identify figure 2.5 as a triangle and figure 2.6 as a circle, rather than claiming that both are simply short lines.

Figure 2.2
An example of figure and ground: a vase or twins?

Figure 2.3
An example of figure and ground: ink blobs or a bearded man?

Figure 2.4
An example of closure: ink blobs or a cat?

Figure 2.5
An example of closure: triangle or straight lines?

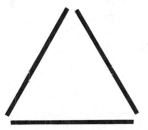

Figure 2.6
An example of closure: circle or straight lines?

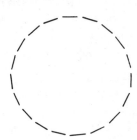

Figure 2.7
An example of proximity: three groups of lines or nine separate lines?

We also organize stimuli according to their **proximity**. The principle of proximity or nearness operates whenever we group two or more things that simply happen to be close to each other. When we group according to proximity, our assumption is that "birds of a feather flock together," even though we know that this is not always true. In figure 2.7, we tend to perceive three groups of lines of three lines each rather than nine separate lines, because of the principle of proximity or nearness.

Figure 2.8   An example of similarity: squares and circles or a group of geometric figures?

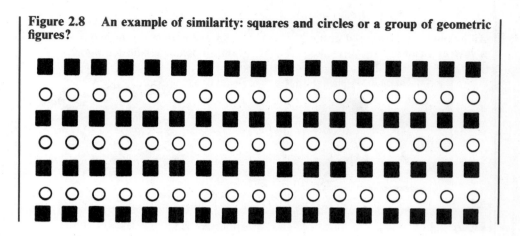

Similarity also helps us to organize stimuli. We sometimes group elements together because they resemble each other in size, color, shape, or other attributes. For example, we tend to believe that people who like the music we do will enjoy the same movies as we do. We assume that a suit that looks like one of our own is probably within the same price range. We perceive squares and circles, rather than a group of geometric shapes, in figure 2.8 because of the principle of similarity.

A final method that we use in organizing stimuli is known as **perceptual constancy**. According to the principle of perceptual constancy, we rarely change our perceptions of something once we have established a particular image of it. We are able to "see" the objects in our bedroom—even when the light burns out and the room is dark. All of us have a tendency to view things as stable and unchanging after we have formed a point of view.

In order to understand the relationship between the organizing of stimuli and communication, let us consider a typical party. When you arrive at a party, you immediately begin to organize the stimuli—the people there—into groups. You focus first on your friends and acquaintances, who serve as *figure,* and largely ignore the strangers present, who serve as *ground.* Those friends who are standing closest to you will talk with your first, because of their *proximity.* The people with whom you will spend most time are those who you perceive to be *similar* to you. The persons whom you will avoid are those whom you have previously determined to be boring, dull, or perhaps threatening. You assume that they will behave in the same way tonight because of *perceptual constancy.* Finally, you notice that two married friends, separated for a number of months and considering divorce, arrive together. As the evening progresses, they tend to stand together and to talk in an intimate way. You achieve *closure* by assuming that they have reconciled their differences. When you approach them, your mood is light and your conversation is spirited. This example illustrates how organizing stimuli—one activity of perception—affects communication. It helps to determine with whom we speak, how we speak, what we speak about, how long we speak, and the tone of voice that we use.

Interpretation

Each of us interprets the stimuli we perceive. The more ambiguous the stimuli, the more room we have for interpretation. The basis for the well-known inkblot test lies in the principle of interpretation of stimuli. Figure 2.9 is an inkblot that a psychologist might ask you to interpret. The ambiguity of the figure is typical.

In our interpretation of stimuli, we frequently rely on the context in which we perceive the stimuli, or we compare it to others. Sometimes these are helpful clues. For example, the letters and numbers are useful to us as we attempt to interpret the middle figure in figure 2.10. The context tells us it is two number 1's, rather than one H.

Nonetheless, comparisons and the use of context can be confusing. All of us are familiar with figures like 2.11 and 2.12. In these figures, we perceive differences in the lengths of the lines, and in the height of the candle and the width of the candleholder, although they do not exist.

Figure 2.9
An example of interpretation:
the inkblot.

Figure 2.10
An example of the usefulness of
context in the interpretation of stimuli.

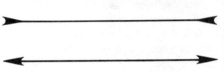

Figure 2.11
An example of interpretation:
Which line is longer?

32H23
GHI

Figure 2.12
An example of interpretation:
Is the width of the holder the same
length as the candle?

The relationship between the interpretation of stimuli and communication can be demonstrated in a situation that may be familiar to you. Women who work in large businesses or corporations more frequently serve in secretarial or clerical positions than in executive or managerial jobs. As a result, a person who is unfamiliar with a particular office may mistakenly request a cup of coffee from the lawyer instead of her secretary. The stereotype leads the visitor to an inaccurate assumption, an incorrect interpretation, which in turn leads to difficulty in communication.

Differences in Perception

Jack can see he sees
    what he can see Jill can't see
and he can see
    that Jill can't see that she can't see
but he can't see WHY
    Jill can't see that Jill can't see. . . .
Jill can see Jack can't see,
    and can't see he can't see.
Jill can see WHY
    Jack can't see,
but Jill cannot see WHY
    Jack can't see he can't see. . . .
Jack can't see he can't see
and can't see
    Jill can't see Jill can't see it,
and vice versa.[4]

R. D. Laing includes this poem in his collection *Knots*. The poem captures the complexity of perception and the difficulty of establishing common perceptions.

Discuss an experience in which you and another person attempted to reach an agreement, but could not. Identify the differences in perception, suggest reasons for those differences, and enumerate the methods you attempted to use to validate your perceptions.

Summary

Perception was discussed in this chapter. Perception is the process by which we come to understand ourselves and others, and understanding is an activity basic to communication. Perception, in the contemporary view, is considered active, subjective, and creative.

Differences in perceptions result from physiology, cultural and subcultural factors, differences in past experiences, and differences in present feelings and circumstances. Perception involves selection, organization, and interpretation.

Additional Readings

*Allport, Gordon W. *The Nature of Prejudice.* Garden City, New York: Doubleday & Co., 1958. Chapters 10 and 12.
A thorough treatment of the relationship between perceptual processes and prejudice. Allport discusses specific stereotypes of Jews and blacks as well as the effect of the mass media on the formation of stereotypes.

Carney, Clarke G., and McMahon, Sarah L. *Exploring Contemporary Male/Female Roles.* La Jolla, Calif.: University Associates, 1977.
Stereotypes are based on our perceptual processes. This book is an examination of one of the most basic stereotypes today—male and female roles. A close look at the stereotypes reveals the social patterns that foster them, the problems they cause, and the ways to create a different perception of the sexes.

Edwards, David C. *General Psychology.* 3rd ed. New York: Macmillan, 1980. Chapters 4 and 5.
Chapter 4 is a description of the psychological basis and mechanisms of perception, including organization, depth perception, and color perception. In chapter 5 Edwards discusses attention as it relates to perception, as well as the variables that affect our attention in hearing, seeing, and thinking about stimuli.

Haney, William V. *Communication and Organizational Behavior.* Homewood, Ill.: Richard D. Irwin, 1967. Pages 51–77.
Haney devotes a chapter to perception as it relates to communication, examines the problems that can be created by misperceptions and different fields of experience, and makes it easy to understand by using analogies and models.

Hastorf, Albert H.; Schneider, David J.; and Polefka, Judith. *Person Perception.* Reading, Mass.: Addison-Wesley Publishing Co., 1970.
The creative view of perception. A discussion of the factors that influence our attitudes and behavior toward other people. Granting that our perceptions are inherently subjective, the authors offer suggestions for communicating them to others.

*Korten, Frances F. "The Influence of Culture on the Perception of Persons." *International Journal of Psychology* 9 (1974): 31–44.
An investigation of the influence of various cultures on the categorization of people into groups. Korten argues that cultural needs affect the use of categories in perceiving others. The study is explained in detail and offers several possible reasons for the differences in cultural perceptions.

Rubin, Zick. "The Rise and Fall of First Impressions." In *Interpersonal Communication in Action,* edited by Bobby R. Patton and Kim Giffin. 2d ed. New York: Harper & Row, Publishers, 1977. Pages 149–67.
An interestingly written discussion of the factors that affect our impressions of others. Many good examples from sports, teaching, and politics, and a summary of some important studies of the formation and influence of first impressions.

*Triandis, Harry C. "Cultural Influences upon Perception." In *Intercultural Communication: A Reader,* edited by Larry A. Samovar and Richard E. Porter. 2d ed. Belmont, Calif.: Wadsworth Publishing Company, 1976. Pages 119–23.
Triandis presents research that suggests a connection between culture and retention, recognition, emotions, and the perception of space. Different societies interpret the same stimuli differently. A technical treatment of the topic.

*Indicates more advanced readings.

Notes

1. James M. Renuk, "A Medium for His Message," *Washington Post,* 1977.
2. V. P. Richmond and D. Robertson, "Communication Apprehension as a Function of Being Raised in an Urban or Rural Environment" (Monograph, West Virginia Northern Community College, 1976).
3. Alistair B. Fraser, "Fata Morgana—The Grand Illusion," *Psychology Today* 9 (January 1976): 22.
4. R. D. Laing, *Knots* (New York: Pantheon Books, Inc., 1971), pp. 75–76.

3

Verbal Codes
A Tool of Sharing

Objectives

1. Discuss the relationship among words, codes, encoding, and decoding
2. Discuss ways in which verbal codes can become barriers to communication and illustrate each type of barrier with examples
3. Give examples of how our verbal symbol system (English) gives us a different perception of reality than other verbal symbol systems (e.g., French, Hopi, Russian, Eskimo)
4. Discuss three ways in which we can improve our verbal skills
5. Differentiate between paraphrasing the content and paraphrasing the intent of a message
6. Discuss the relationship between the use of euphemisms and clichés and the skills of concreteness and descriptiveness

Key Terms

words
verbal
symbol
code
encode
decode
personal language
language distortion
euphemisms
clichés
culture and subculture

denotative meaning
connotative meaning
classifications
Sapir-Whorf hypothesis
operational definitions
descriptiveness
inferences
paraphrasing
concreteness
dating
indexing

Comedian Will Rogers said of President Calvin Coolidge: "He don't say much—but when he does—he don't say much."

A conservative is defined as a liberal who was mugged yesterday.

An X-rated film that I enjoy is provocative; *one that you enjoy is* tasteless; *and one that someone else enjoys is* pornographic.

These three comments demonstrate various facets of the words that we use. Words—verbal symbols—and sets of words—verbal codes—are basic to communication. However, misconceptions about words may cause them to serve as barriers, rather than as bridges, to communication.

Before we consider why words sometimes become obstacles to communication, we need to clarify some essential terminology. We define **words** as verbal symbols. **Verbal** refers to anything that is associated with or pertains to words. A **symbol** is something that stands for or represents something else, either by association, resemblance, or convention.

A word is a symbol in the same sense that a wedding ring is a symbol for marriage, a flag is a symbol for a particular country, and long hair—just a decade ago—was considered a symbol of defiance by many people. Words symbolize events,

Elements of the Communication Process

people, and ideas by agreement among the people who use them and through conventional use. They do not resemble the thing they represent; they are arbitrary representations of them. Statements like, "The word is not the thing," and "Words don't mean, people do," allude to this arbitrary nature of words.

Sets of words are verbal codes. You will recall that in chapter 1 **code** was defined as any systematic arrangement or comprehensive collection of symbols, letters, or words that are given arbitrary meaning and are used for communication. When we use verbal language to communicate, as senders we **encode,** or put the message or thought into a verbal code, and as receivers we **decode,** or assign meaning to the verbal code that we receive.

Words Can Be a Major Obstacle to Communication

We can support the argument that there are more than three billion different languages in the world. Each of us talks, listens, and thinks in a unique language (and sometimes we have several) that contains slight variations of agreed-upon meanings and that may change each minute. Our **personal language** is shaped by our culture, country, neighborhood, job, personality, attitudes, values, and mood. The possibility that even a few of us will share all of these ingredients in the same way at the same time is really quite remote.

Two experiments were used to illustrate the differences in our personal language. The photograph reproduced in figure 3.1 was shown to three people—a sophomore enrolled in a speech communication course, a Ph.D. in speech communication, and a veterinarian. Each person was asked to define or describe the picture. Their descriptions follow:

It is a deer-like animal with a white belly and horns. The ears appear relatively large and the rump is higher than the shoulders.

Student

Figure 3.1

A four-legged mammal of indeterminate size with hooves, variegated horns, large ears, elongated neck, and a two-toned torso. The rear legs are larger than the front legs as if the animal were designed for running. Its relatively large eyes are on the sides of the animal's face, so it is probably among the grazing hunted animals rather than the carnivorous hunters.

Speech communication professor

Gazella dorcas

Veterinarian

In the second experiment, the following definition of a gazelle was given to three people, who were then asked to draw the figure: "A hoofed mammal of Africa and Asia characteristically having a slender neck and ringed, lyrate horns." The drawings in figures 3.2, 3.3, and 3.4 were made by a nine-year-old boy, a woman, and a man. These experiments demonstrate something that occurs every day to each of us. Our personal verbal systems provide a barrier to communication when the messages we encode to others are decoded differently. You might try similar experiments to demonstrate this phenomenon.

Figure 3.2   **Figure 3.3**

Figure 3.4

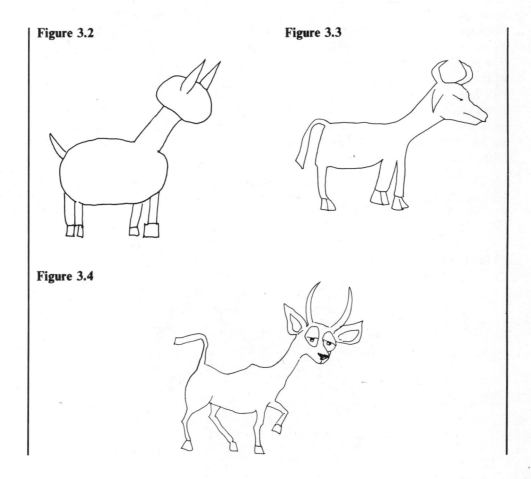

There are three reasons why words and language often hamper effective communication. People sometimes intentionally use **language distortion.** People also frequently assume that words have an inherent, intrinsic meaning that is universally understood. And people often behave as though their language is "real" in some sense. Let us consider each of these reasons in more detail.

There is probably little doubt that Jimmy Carter wished he could have withdrawn some of the comments he made to a *Playboy* interviewer while campaigning for the presidency of the United States in 1976. Carter was apparently attempting to counter the criticism that he was "holier-than-thou."

After he had used the generally unobjectionable terms *fornicate* and *sexual intercourse,* Carter demonstrated his lack of puritanism by switching to the term *shack up.* The slang synonym surprised and shocked many voters. Carter's error was two-fold—he failed to stay with the abstract terms or vague phrases that could have been interpreted to the voter's liking, and he used slang that is not used by most people in public statements.

We Intentionally Use Language to Distort or Alter Our Meaning

The lawyer in the cartoon expresses the concern of many of us who attempt to confuse ourselves and others with language. We all do it. For example, a friend asks, "How do I look?" and we respond with a compliment rather than with an honest response. People sometimes press us to state a point of view before we have had time to think it through. If pressed too hard, we may make a vague response in order to gain more time to consider the issue. We also sometimes hedge when someone asks for information that we do not have. Through ambiguity, we attempt to convey the idea that we really know more than we do.

Politicians provide abundant examples of language intentionally used to obstruct communication. People running for political office often use abstract terms and vague phrases in order to say nothing or everything. They recognize that specific and concrete terms will offend one group or another, so they seek the safety of empty and meaningless language.

Advertisers, too, often intentionally use language to confuse the consumer. Words like *better, improved, new,* and phrases like *revolutionary change, a*

THE WIZARD OF ID

taste worth smoking, a real taste, real satisfaction, more than just low tar, this is ultra-low tar, and *We're Number One* are typical. Such words and phrases, like the sign in the cartoon that advertises a *100-foot pool,* do not convey a clear message.

Politicians and advertisers are skilled in using confusing language, but they by no means have exclusive rights to this practice. Each of us uses **euphemisms,** substitute words that are considered inoffensive instead of words that are thought to be offensive, and **clichés,** words or phrases that are overused and that have lost their effectiveness because of overuse. Euphemistically, we say *rest room* for *toilet, senior citizens* for *old people,* and *lower socioeconomic status* for *poor.* Among some of the more frequently heard clichés are *as good as gold, absence makes the heart grow fonder, take it with a grain of salt, all wool and a yard wide, give them an inch, they'll take a mile,* and *you will get out of it only as much as you put into it.*

Clichés and Euphemisms

Lyle the Lion can take some comfort in Dodo Bird's use of a cliché to criticize Lyle's speech. Each of us uses a variety of clichés and euphemisms. Try to list at least five clichés and five euphemisms you use. If you have difficulty identifying clichés and euphemisms in your own language, use someone else's expressions. It is sometimes easier to identify clichés and euphemisms in other people's communication.

Clichés
1. _____
2. _____
3. _____
4. _____
5. _____

Euphemisms
1. _____
2. _____
3. _____
4. _____
5. _____

ANIMAL CRACKERS

Why do we use euphemisms and clichés? We use them to protect our-selves—to establish a healthy self-concept or to maintain a distorted self-concept, or to deny self-awareness or to gain time in order to develop self-awareness. We also use euphemisms and clichés to protect others—to help them maintain a selective view of reality or to help them distort their world, or to help them acknowledge successes or deny difficulties. A *late bloomer* does not have to admit being a decade or two older than the other students; an *underachiever* can't really expect high grades. The existence of a *word processing center* allows us to alter our perception of jobs in a typing pool. A discussion of *low rent housing* denies the real situation in the inner-city slums. Similarly, clichés like "fat people are always so jolly" and "anything worth doing is worth doing right" may allow us to maintain too much weight or may cause us to be overly methodical in those things that we attempt.

In general, the use of euphemisms, clichés, and other language to distort meaning or confuse ourselves and others should be avoided. We can establish destruc-tive patterns of talking that minimize our ability to gain self-awareness, that distort an appropriate and positive self-concept. We can easily fall into the habit of using language that prevents us from seeing social problems and weakens our sensitive perception of joy and sorrow.

Sometimes the use of language to distort is not harmful. When there is social agreement, euphemisms may be used without negative effects. Asking for di-rections to the *rest room* instead of the *toilet,* telling a friend that a new suit is *not as good-looking as it might be* instead of just plain *ugly,* and reporting that a student is *below average* rather than *stupid* may sometimes be preferable. The situation, the other people involved, and your intent must all be considered when you choose inten-tionally or deliberately to alter your message by the words that you choose.

We Assume that Words Have Universal Meaning and Are Real

Words Vary in Meaning Among Cultures   A family we know spent a summer in Europe a couple of years ago. As they traveled from country to country—sometimes crossing two or three borders in a single day—the wife noticed a striking similarity in the behavior of the Europeans they met. Although her husband is fluent in a number of European languages, the children and she are not. After successfully communicating with the husband, the European would turn to the wife and attempt to make small talk or social conversation. She would shrug her shoulders to indicate that she did not understand. The European would repeat the remark, but a bit more loudly. She would again try to say she could not understand the language. The other person would stand closer to her, use more gestures, and repeat the message very loudly. Generally, the husband intervened at this point and explained that she really did not understand the language.

This happened everywhere the family went. People in the Netherlands, France, Germany, Spain, Italy, and other countries all shared the assumption that speaking more loudly and more enthusiastically would result in understanding. This

European experience is similar to experiences that all of us have had in this country; people often assume that their words have an inherent, intrinsic meaning that is universally understood. Unfortunately they do not.

Words Vary in Meaning Among Subcultures Differences in language seem obvious when we consider different **cultures and subcultures.** The examples are more subtle within a culture. Consider differences in our own country between poor and wealthy people, older and younger people, black and white Americans, and women and men. Too often, we assume that if we "just talk louder" people from other subcultures will understand us, but *bad* means bad unless it means "very good," regardless of how loudly we talk.

People in subcultures rely on differences in language for two purposes. First, they often need a specialized language in which to conduct their business. For instance, women have traditionally been able to identify such colors as *puce, aquamarine, lavendar,* and *persimmon* and have commonly used such language. If a man were asked to purchase a scarf for a female friend that included some of these colors he might have bought a scarf that was red, white, and blue. Traditionally, women have been involved in occupations and have fulfilled jobs that required sensitivity to color. Women, rather than men, decorated their homes and chose clothing for their families. As men have become increasingly involved with professions or positions that required color knowledge, they have become increasingly aware of colors and have developed a larger vocabulary of color names. Similarly, people in the drug culture may need a large variety of terms to identify specific drugs in order to buy and sell such commodities. And researchers in the social sciences rely on jargon like "dyad," "self-disclosure," "role theory," and "neurological disorder" in order to conduct their business.

A second reason for establishing a specialized language among members of a subculture is for the subculture to maintain its identity. On a number of occasions, the black community has provided interesting terms and unique jargon that have been subsumed in the larger culture. The statement above that *bad* means bad until it means "very good" is a good example. A young Minnesotan who was about six months pregnant began teaching in an integrated high school in Columbus, Georgia. After she had been teaching in the school for about a month, one of the black males in the senior class stayed after class to tell her that he and his buddies thought she was "bad." He explained, "Mama, we think you are *so* bad—especially for a white chick." The woman was not sure if "mama" referred to her pregnant condition or what would occur now that a consensus of students had decided that she was "bad." Needless to say, the young man was attempting to compliment her on her ability to communicate with the students.

The word *bad* is no longer used in the black community. This incident had taken place in the early 1970s. When people from other subcultures began using the term *bad,* the black subculture immediately dropped the term. The same phenomenon occurs in other subcultures. For instance, the first time you heard one of your parents use the jargon of your subculture— *cool, neat, freak, boss, jerk,* or *choice*— you probably vowed never to use the word again. When other subcultures begin to use the specialized language of one group, the word no longer serves the purpose of distinguishing the subculture from others, and members of the subculture drop the word.

Two children provided a clear example of differences in subcultural usage at a dinner party not long ago. A number of adults were enjoying an after-dinner conversation in the living room while the children were supposedly asleep. In the middle of the conversation, the young boy announced, as he came down the stairs, that his sister had said five "bad" words. The dinner guests were delighted with the boy's precociousness. One of the men in the room asked the boy if he could share what his sister had said. The boy grinned, said "Sure," and then repeated "Lady, lady, lady, lady, and lady." He went off to bed, pleased with his joke.

55   Verbal Codes

In this particular home, the parents had attempted to "desex" the language and to exercise care with words that might have a degrading or negative meaning for males and females. The children knew that their parents thought that the word *lady* means a woman who is proper, who expects privileges because of her sex and her station in life, and who never commits wrong acts but may condemn others. They also knew, however, that other people use the word to show respect for women. The parents had explained to the children that some people believe that the word *lady* is tied up with the current class struggle between men and women, and that the usage of the word can cause the same reaction that the traditional "four-letter words" have caused. Thus they were able to play a safe joke on the grown-ups, based on the adults' different interpretations of a word.

Definitions

To Plato, the human was a "biped without feathers." To Aristotle, "a political animal." To Seneca, "a social animal." To Shakespeare, "a poor, bare, forked animal." To Byron, "half dust, half deity." To Emerson, "a god playing the fool." To Huxley, "an intelligence in servitude to his organs." To Mark Twain, "the only animal that blushes. Or needs to."

Each of these definitions embodies a unique way of looking at men and women, and each represents considerable thought.

Ways of viewing the word *lady* were just explained. Identify at least three words for which you have special definitions. Explain each definition in at least one page, suggesting the origin of your relationship with the word. Examples may include *mother, love, abortion, baby, war, poverty, philosophy, communication, education, ecology, money,* and *Caucasian.*

Words Vary in Meaning Among Individuals   We can demonstrate again that words do not have an inherent meaning by considering the differences among individuals within the same subculture. If, for example, you find yourself in conflict with the idea that *lady* is a sexist term, you are demonstrating a difference among individuals within a subculture. You might find yourself arguing "But I am a woman, and I don't feel that way," or "I consider myself a feminist, and I don't think that," or "I'm proud to be known as a lady." All of these statements point up the different meanings that a word can have and the idea that words vary in meaning from person to person.

A distinction is frequently made between the denotative and connotative meaning of words. **Denotative meaning** refers to an agreed upon meaning; **connotative meaning** refers to an individualized or personalized meaning. Denotative meanings are understood and shared by a large number of people. Connotative meanings are limited to a single person or to a very small number of people.

In general, people use the denotative meaning as the real meaning of a word. In addition, most of us use a dictionary, thesaurus, or other reference books to determine a word's meaning. This provides no problem for us unless we forget two principles—the meaning of words is constantly undergoing change, and the meaning printed in an old dictionary may not represent the current usage; and the connotative meaning of the word, which may well be the meaning that another person intended, is not in the dictionary.

It is unfortunate that we do not recognize the limited value of "dictionary definitions." People frequently will rely on historical, denotative definitions to defend sexism, racism, or other prejudices. For instance, a great deal of research has demonstrated that the use of man-linked words (postman, chairman, fireman) communicates that men *exclusively* are the referent and that "no women need apply." Pleas that "man" means all people, regardless of gender, are largely unheard. Nonetheless, decisions about using the term "chairman" in parliamentary procedure, a course in many speech departments, is frequently made based on the *Oxford English Dictionary* or *Robert's Rules of Order* rather than current behavioral research. Dictionaries, at best, offer an historical account of meaning among powerful subcultures.

In chapter 1 we considered the notion that communication is a *process*. We explained that communication is dynamic and always changing. One of the most obvious examples of the dynamic nature of communication lies in our verbal usage. Terms become outdated, new words or *neologisms* come into usage, and specialized language is coined. The study of language provides an interesting and informative history of our culture, and identifies those phenomena that we once felt were important, unique, or revered. Language does not stay the same from one year to the next; it is alive and filled with change.

Words Vary in Meaning Depending on the Situation and Context   Not only does the meaning of words vary in different cultures, subcultures, and to different individuals, it also varies with the same person, depending upon the situation and the context. A dictionary frequently provides us with a number of denotative meanings for a word. The *Oxford English Dictionary* provides us with twenty or thirty meanings for a number of different words. For example, the word *close* has twenty-one separate definitions and many more subtypes; the word *clear* has twenty-seven definitions and many subtypes; the word *head* has sixty-six definitions with about two to four subtypes of each; and the word *come* has sixty-nine definitions, but nearly two hundred definitions when all the subdefinitions are counted.

We gain a clue about the particular denotative meaning a person has in mind from the context in which the word is used. For example, if someone asks us for bread, we would probably hand them something to eat if we were sitting at the dinner table, but a small amount of cash if we are standing in the parking lot.

An additional problem with spoken English, not as great in written English, is the number of words that sound the same, but have different spellings and meanings. The "Peanuts" strip calls to mind *tail* and *tale*. Unless we are sensitive to the context and the situation, we can easily receive the unintended word.

PEANUTS

Words vary in meaning with cultures, subcultures, individuals, and context. They also vary as a result of factors like our work, our neighborhoods, and other subgroups to which we belong. They do not have an inherent, intrinsic meaning that is universally understood. Unless we keep this principle in mind, words can become an obstacle to communication.

Definitional Differences

In *Through the Looking Glass*, Humpty Dumpty and Alice become involved in an argument about language and meaning:

"I don't know what you mean by 'glory', " Alice said.

Humpty Dumpty smiled contemptuously. "Of course you don't—till I tell you. I meant there's a nice knock-down argument for you!"

"But 'glory' doesn't mean 'a nice knock-down argument'," Alice objected.

"When I use a word," Humpty Dumpty said, in a rather scornful tone, "it means just what I chose it to mean—neither more nor less."

"The question is," said Alice, "whether you can make words mean so many different things."

"The question is," said Humpty Dumpty, "which is to be master—that's all."[1]

Consider the arguments you have had during the last week or two. Select one that was caused by difference in definitions. For example, you may have argued with a professor about the amount of homework in a course (definitional difference concerning the *appropriate* amount of work for a three-credit college course); you argued with your husband about who should do the laundry (definitional difference about what *wife* or *husband* means); or you may have argued with a friend about dieting (definitional difference about *overweight*).

Write a two-page paper or give a short talk identifying the difference in definition, the arguments each of you gave in favor of your way of defining the term, and how you resolved the argument. Did you realize that the difficulty between you was definitional?

Words Are Not Real   We name or label things in our environment by observing them, by identifying certain characteristics or qualities about them, and by classifying them into one group or another. For example, if you are shopping for furniture and you spot a rolltop desk in the corner of a furniture store to which you want to draw your companion's attention, you would probably say "Look at that desk over there," and gesture toward it. You named it *desk* after observing it and determining that it had the essential characteristics that you associate with desks.

Language provides an important function in this regard. It allows us to order all of the stimuli that bombard us into meaningful groups or classes. If we did not have the word *desk,* for example, you might have to say to your friend "Look at that wooden object that has four legs, six drawers, a tabletop surface on which to write, about twenty or thirty small pigeonholes in which to file papers and other materials, and that is about five feet wide, four feet high, and two feet deep."

When we classify objects, persons, or situations, we are stating, in effect, that they have characteristics that are similar to other members of a particular group. We determine that the rolltop desk has sufficient essential characteristcs to call it *desk* instead of *chest,* or *buffet,* or *table.* In doing so, we neglect the differences between the object—the rolltop desk, in this instance—and other members of the class, other desks. By naming the piece of furniture *desk* we fail to take into account the pigeonholes, the size, and other unusual features.

Classifications are neither right nor wrong. Instead, the classifications we make reveal to others the criteria we are using in naming the person, object, or situation. All of us have had the experience of trying to point out a particular person to someone and of having them fail to locate the person we are describing. A conversation, as you are waiting for class to begin, might go something like this:

"Look at that woman!"

"Do you mean the blonde?"

"No, the short woman over on the right."

"Do you mean the one with the blue eyes?"

"No, she has brown eyes."

"Is it the one in the red t-shirt?"

"It looks like orange to me."

"Is she heavy?

"I wouldn't call her heavy at all."

"Now she's moving to the front of the room."

"Why didn't you say it was the instructor!"

"I guess I never thought about it."

Both of the communicators used a variety of classes into which to place the person they were discussing—sex, hair color, eye color, weight, clothing, position in the room, and, finally, occupation. This example is a particular favorite because it illustrates a phenomenon that has been experienced a number of times. Students—regardless of their age or sex—tend to classify instructors as instructors, rather than by sex, attractiveness, or other physical features.

In the conversation between the two students about the female instructor, the first student was unable to help the other student "see" the person to whom he was referring. The classification system, or language, of the two caused differences in perception. This intimate relationship between language and perception no longer seems as remarkable as it did when it was first proposed by Edward Sapir, a linguist, and Benjamin Lee Whorf, a fire-insurance expert. The **Sapir-Whorf hypothesis,** as it has become known, states that our perception of reality is determined by our thought processes and that our thought processes are limited by our language; therefore, our perception of reality is dependent upon our language.[2] To understand how the Sapir-Whorf hypothesis works, we can consider the difference in perception and language when an optometrist examines our eyes and when we look at our own eyes in the mirror. Whereas we may see our eyes only as "nice" or as "bloodshot," the optometrist might note the dilation of the pupil, the lack of perceptual acuity, the apparent distortion of the eyeball, and the accuracy of depth perception.

One of the most bizarre examples of the relationship between language and reality is contained in the story about the Charles Manson murders in the late 1960s. Manson found justification for his actions in the Bible and in the Beatles' *White Album.* Vincent Bugliosi, prosecutor in the Manson case, explains Manson's interpretation of the ninth chapter of Revelation in *Helter Skelter: The True Story of the Manson Murders,* reprinted on pages 62 to 64.

As we stated earlier, classification is neither right nor wrong, it merely reflects differences in our perception. As long as we recognize that other people may classify differently and, consequently, perceive the world differently, we have no problem. Unfortunately, most of us make the error, from time to time, of assuming that our view of reality is the only possible one. We fail to understand why someone from a different culture, subculture, or group does not use the same language as we do and does not perceive the same reality. When we behave as though the reality we create through our use of language is real, we allow language to become a barrier to effective communication.

Verbal Skills Can Be Improved

We have seen that language can become a major obstacle to our communication with others. Each of us has a unique language. Sometimes we intentionally distort meaning or attempt to confuse others. At other times, we mistakenly assume that words have an inherent, intrinsic meaning that others understand. Finally, we occasionally behave as though the reality that we have created through our use of language is real and is shared by others.

We can alter the situation so that words are not obstacles to communication. Three changes can be made in our verbal usage that will help us to become more effective communicators—we can avoid the intentional use of words to distort or confuse, we can become increasingly descriptive in our communication, and we can become increasingly concrete as we communicate with others.

Avoid Intentional Confusion

Some of the verbal patterns that we fall into have become so habitual that we no longer feel that we are intentionally confusing; rather, we believe that "everyone" speaks the way we do. We take comfort in our clichés. Edwin Newman, television news personality, talks about his own use of clichés in two recent books. Newman stated his specific motivation for writing the two books, *Strictly Speaking* and *A Civil Tongue:*

One thing that happened to me, as a reporter on the air, was that I realized I was pushing along ideas that had no substance. I was taking phrases and using them as if they had substance, and they didn't.[3]

We should strive to become increasingly sensitive to our own use of empty language, ambiguities, clichés, and euphemisms. It is often helpful to have someone else monitor our statements and point out the problem areas. After someone else has sensitized us to our confusing phraseology, we can "take the reins in our own hands." (Er, that is, do the job ourselves!) Our goal, at all times, is to keep it simple.

Confusion can also arise when we use unusual terms or if we use a word in a special way. If we suspect that someone might not understand the terminology that we are using, it is essential to define the term. We need to be careful not to offend the other person, on the one hand, and to offer a definition that is clearer than the term itself, on the other.

Operational definitions, or definitions that point to the behavior, action, or properties that a word signifies, are sometimes very useful. When Alice asked the Dodo, in *Alice's Adventures in Wonderland,* what he meant by a Caucus-race, he wisely replied by offering an operational definition: "Why, the best way to explain it is to do it."[4] We use operational definitions when we explain "For me, a good day is any day I don't have to go to classes or go to work," or when we explain outlining to a friend by writing a partial outline. Lucy provides an example of an operational definition in this cartoon.

Descriptiveness

Descriptiveness is the practice of describing observable behavior or phenomenon instead of offering personal reactions or judgments. You are being descriptive if you state "The food in the cafeteria tends to be high in cholesterol," but you are showing a lack of descriptiveness if you say "I think that cook is trying to kill us." Teachers are being descriptive when they say "You've been absent from my class six times this term," but not when they say "I know you hate this speech communication class."

We can be descriptive in different ways. We can describe shared experiences. In order to communicate effectively with another person, it is important to have a common understanding of an event that has occurred, or the definition of a particular phenomenon. We can check with another person to determine if his or her perceptions are the same as our own. We ask another person "Do you feel a draft?" or "Don't you get tired, studying and working at a full-time job?" Many disagreements occur because people do not stop to make these simple checks on their perception.

Helter Skelter
The True Story of the Manson Murders

The "four angels" were the Beatles, whom Manson
considered "leaders, spokesmen, prophets," . . . The line
"And he opened the bottomless pit . . . And there came
out of the smoke locusts upon the earth; and unto them
was given power . . ." was still another reference to the
English group, . . . Locusts—Beatles—one and the same.
"Their faces were as the faces of men," yet "they had hair
as the hair of women." An obvious reference to the long-
haired musicians. Out of the mouths of the four angels
"issued fire and brimstone." . . . "This referred to the
spoken words, the lyrics of the Beatles' songs, the power
that came out of their mouths."

Their "breastplates of fire," were their electric
guitars. Their shapes "like unto horses prepared unto
battle" were the dune buggies. The "horsemen who
numbered two hundred thousand thousand" and who
would roam the earth spreading destruction, were the
motorcyclists.

"And it was commanded then that they should not
hurt the grass of the earth, neither any green thing, neither
any tree; but only those men which have not the seal of
God on their foreheads." I wondered about that seal on the
forehead. How did Manson interpret that? . . .

"It was all subjective," Manson said, "There would
be a mark on people." Charlie Manson had never told him
exactly what the mark would be, only that he, Charlie
"would be able to tell, he would know" and that "the mark
would designate whether they were with him or against
him."

One verse spoke of worshiping demons and idols of
gold and silver and bronze. Manson said that referred to
the material worship of the establishment: of automobiles,
houses, money.

"Directing your attention to Verse 15, which reads:
'And the four angels were loosed, which were prepared for

Reprinted from *Helter Skelter,
The True Story of the Manson
Murders,* by Vincent Bugliosi
with Curt Gentry, with the
permission of W. W. Norton
Company, Inc. Copyright ©
1974 by Curt Gentry and
Vincent Bugliosi.

an hour, and a day, and a month, and a year, for to slay the third part of men.' Did he say what that meant?"

"He said that those were the people who would die in Helter Skelter one third of mankind . . . the white race."

The Beatles White Album *is a two-record set that was issued by Capitol records in 1968. Most people would describe it as consisting of thirty songs ranging from tender love ballads to pop songs to electronic noise. Manson felt it was prophecy. Bugliosi explains:*

Almost every song in the album had a hidden meaning, which Manson interpreted for his followers. To Charlie "Rocky Raccoon" meant "coon" or the black man. While to everyone except Manson and the Family it was obvious that the lyrics of "Happiness Is a Warm Gun" had sexual connotations, Charlie interpreted the song to mean that the Beatles were telling blackie to get guns and fight whitey.

According to Poston and Watkins, the Family played five songs in the *White Album* more than all the others. They were: "Blackbird," "Piggies," "Revolution I," "Revolution 9," and "Helter Skelter."

"Blackbird singing in the dead of night/ Take these broken wings and learn to fly/ All your life/ You were only waiting for this moment to arise," went the lyrics of "Blackbird." According to Jakobson, "Charlie believed that the moment was now and that the black man was going to arise, overthrow the white man, and take his turn." According to Watkins, in this song Charlie "figured the Beatles were programming the black people to get it up, get on it, start doing it." . . .

(Continued)

. . . "Revolution 9" is easily the weirdest. . . . It is a montage of noises—whispers, shouts, snatches of dialogue from the BBC, bits of classical music, mortars exploding, babies crying, church hymns, car horns, and football yells—which, together with the oft reiterated refrain "Number 9, Number 9, Number 9," build to a climax of machine-gun fire and screams. . . .

It was the Beatles' way of telling people what was going to happen; it was their way of making prophecy; it directly paralleled the Bible's Revelation 9.

It was also the battle of Armageddon, the coming black-white revolution portrayed in sound, Manson claimed.

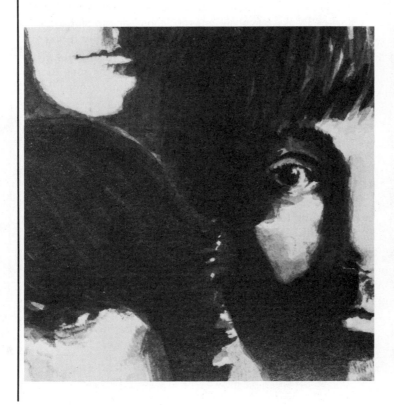

Each of us confuses **inferences**—the drawing of a conclusion from or about things that we have observed—with observations. One of the most obvious examples of this is when we walk through a dark room at night. We cannot see the furniture or other obstacles, but we conclude they are still where they were, and we walk around them without turning on the light. We have no problem with this kind of simple exchange of an inference for an observation—unless someone moved the furniture, or someone placed a new object in the room, or our memory is not accurate. Even simple inferences can be errors. Many shins have been bruised because someone relied on inference rather than observation.

Problems in communication occur when people draw different inferences from similar observations. Researchers have been known to perform the same experiment and conclude entirely different things. Lawyers have lost cases in the courtroom because none of the witnesses could agree upon critical details. Spouses face marital discord when they reach different inferences from the same observations.

In the following conversation between a young married couple, the difficulty they are experiencing arises from different inferences from the same observation.

Jane: (noticing that John has not eaten very much of his dinner) Don't you like this new recipe for chow mein?

John: No, it's fine.

Jane: Well, I get bored with the same things over and over.

John: Me, too.

Jane: It's really hard to plan meals when food costs so much.

John: I'm sure it is.

Jane: You never want to experiment. All you want is steak or pork chops every night.

John: No, I like casseroles and most of the things you make.

Jane: Maybe you should make dinner instead of breakfast. You know the breakfasts that you make are so easy anyone could make them. I can put cold cereal on the table, too! Dinner is the tough meal!

John: I would be happy to make dinner, but there's nothing wrong with your cooking.

Jane: Then why aren't you eating your chow mein?

John: (sheepishly): Well, it was one of the guy's birthdays at work and I ate two big pieces of chocolate cake at about 4 o'clock. You know how I love chocolate.

Jane: Why didn't you say so—I thought you didn't like your meal.

Difficulties in communication can also ensue when persons fail to separate their inferences from their observations. Obviously, we have to make some assumptions when we make statements about observable data. If we walk into a classroom and observe a person who appears to be about twenty-five years old, male, and Caucasian, standing at the front of the room behind a podium, we draw a number of conclusions. Most of us would assume that the living being was human, male, of an approximate age, and of a particular race. Some of us might also conclude that he is the instructor. A few people might decide that he is a graduate assistant, a boring lecturer, too formal, poor, unaware of current clothing styles, or has a host of other characteristics. All of these conclusions are inferences, but they are not all verifiable by observation to the same degree. All of the conclusions rely on assumptions. We assume that a person with relatively short hair and who is wearing a three-piece suit is a man. We assume that persons who are blond and blue-eyed are Caucasian. We assume that a certain stance, body position, and lack of wrinkles indicates a certain age. These assumptions are generally shared, and we usually agree that persons who display these characteristics are of a specific sex, age bracket, and race.

As the number of assumptions that we make increases, the likelihood that we are accurate decreases. In addition, as we move from generally agreed-upon assumptions to more questionable ones, we move from the area of observation to the area of inference. Sometimes we fail to recognize that we are drawing inferences based on many questionable assumptions and believe that we are simply stating observations that are shared by others. If you observed the person described above and concluded that he dressed in an outdated style, you might feel uncomfortable when the student sitting next to you told you how good you would look if you bought a similar suit. Agreement between you might not be possible until you both recognize that your statements reflect individual inferences based upon your separate perceptions, attitudes, values, and beliefs.

Paraphrasing

For each of the following dialogues,
identify the response as repetition,
paraphrasing of content, or
paraphrasing of intent.

Question or statement: If you had to do it over again would you do the same thing?
Response: Do you mean, would I state my disagreement to my employer?

Question or statement: Will your wife move to the new location with you if you secure this promotion?
Response: Are you asking if my wife will move with me to the new location if I get the job?

Question or statement: I'm always afraid I'm going to make a mistake!
Response: What do you mean, you feel like you're going to make a mistake?

Question or statement: I've lived here for three months, but I still don't know my way around the city.
Response: Would you like me to show you some of the principal landmarks and the main streets?

Question or statement: I really appreciate the time you have spent talking to me.
Response: I would like to encourage you to come in and see me whenever you have a problem—I understand how important it is to be able to talk to your supervisor.

A second way that we can be descriptive is to utilize descriptive feedback. *Descriptive feedback* consists of nonevaluative, nonthreatening statements about our observations of the other person and his or her communication with us. It is essential that these comments be free of evaluation and judgment. Examples of descriptive feedback include statements like "You appear to be preoccupied and unable to concentrate on what I'm discussing with you," "I perceive an edginess in your voice," and "You seem enthusiastic when you talk about him." Statements like "You're a real slob," "I don't like the way you talk to me," and "You sure could improve your relationship with your boyfriend, if you wanted to" are not appropriate descriptive feedback because of their evaluative, threatening, judgmental nature.

Descriptive feedback provides a method of indicating to the other person what we do and what we do not understand from their message. It allows the other person the opportunity to validate accurate perceptions and to correct misunderstandings. Paraphrasing—one form of descriptive feedback—allows increased understanding between two people. Simply stated, **paraphrasing** is the restatement of the other person's message. It is not merely repetition, however, since repetition only shows that you have received the words, not that you have really understood the message.

Suppose a student says "I don't understand descriptiveness." The teacher can respond by repeating "I hear you say that you don't understand descriptiveness," or "Do you mean my explanation of that skill wasn't clear?" or "Do you

Repetition   *Paraphrasing of Content*   *Paraphrasing of Intent*

mean that you would like me to explain the skill further to you?" In the first case, the teacher is merely repeating the message and has only shown that the words were heard. The second reply shows that the content of the student's message has been understood. The third reply shows the intent of the message has been understood. The first response is mere repetition; the second and third are two levels of paraphrasing. The exercises in paraphrasing on pages 66 and 67 illustrate these levels of response.

Concreteness

Concreteness is specificity of expression. A person who is concrete uses statements that are specific, rather than abstract or vague. "You have interrupted me three times when I have begun to talk; I feel as though you do not consider my point of view as important as yours" is specific; "You should consider my viewpoint, too" is not.

In the following conversation, notice that the student becomes increasingly concrete as she describes her reactions to a textbook.

Student: I don't like the book.

Instructor: What book is that?

Student: The book for this class.

Instructor: We have three required books—to which book are you referring?

Student: The big one.

Instructor: Do you mean *Speech as Fun?*

Student: Yeah, that's the one.

Instructor: Why don't you like it?

Student: Well, it doesn't say anything to me.

Instructor: Do you mean it's not relevant to your needs?

Student: Yeah, I guess so, but it's more than that.

Instructor: Could you explain why you don't like it?

Student: Well, the chapters are so long and boring.

Instructor: Do you find the examples helpful?

Student: No.

Instructor: Are there specific chapters that you find to be too long?

Student: I've only started to read the first one, but it's pretty long.

Instructor: Why do you find it boring?

Student: There aren't any cartoons, pictures, or anything but words!

Instructor: In other words, you find chapter 1 of *Speech as Fun* to be long and boring because it has so few or no illustrations?

Student: Right, I don't like the book because the first chapter is over forty pages long and has only one diagram, which is of a model of communication that doesn't make any sense to me. I like books that have short chapters and lots of illustrations that I can understand.

Concreteness is any form of more specific expression. Two of the more interesting subtypes are dating and indexing. **Dating** refers to the idea that everything is subject to change. Often we view things as remaining the same. We form a judgment or point of view about a person, an idea, or a phenomenon, and we maintain that view, even though the person, idea, or phenomenon has changed. Dating is a method of avoiding this kind of frozen judgment. Instead of saying that something is always or universally a certain way, we state *when* we made our judgment and state that our perception was based on that experience.

For example, if you had a course with a particular instructor four or five years ago, it is essential that your judgment about the course and instructor be qualified as to time. You may tell someone "English 100 with Professor Jones is a snap course," but it may no longer be true. Or, suppose you went out with a man two years ago and now your best friend is looking forward to her first evening with him. You might say that he is quiet and withdrawn, but it may no longer be accurate: the time that has passed, the person he was with, and the situation have all changed. Statements like "English 100 with Professor Jones was a snap course for me in 1975" and "Joe seemed quiet and withdrawn when I dated him two or three years ago" will create fewer communication problems.

Indexing is using the idea that all members of a subset do not share all of the characteristics of the other member of that subset. Earlier in the chapter we discussed the importance of being able to generalize and classify. Nonetheless, problems can arise when we generalize and classify. We sometimes have a tendency to assume that the characteristics of one member of a class apply to all of the members of the class. For example, you may incorrectly generalize that since your VW takes very little gas, all VWs take little gas. Or you may incorrectly believe that, since your older brother is more responsible than you, all first-born children are more responsible than their siblings.

A second problem occurs when we assume that a characteristic of one member of a group is true of another member of the same group. If you delegated the characteristics of your VW to your friend's VW, you would be making this error. Or, if you assume that somebody else's older brother is responsible because your older brother is, you would be running the risk of generalizing incorrectly.

Indexing assists us in avoiding these pitfalls. Indexing is simply recognizing differences among the various members of a group. Instead of grouping all automobiles together and assuming that a characteristic that one car has is shared by all of the others, we recognize that the car we own could be unique. Instead of assuming that all older children are alike, we exhibit openness and an inquiring attitude about older children, other than the one we know.

We are indexing when we make statements like "I have a VW that uses very little gas. How does your VW do on gas mileage?" or "My older brother is far more responsible than I. Is the same true of your older brother?" We lack an ability to index when we state, "VWs get good gas mileage—I know, I own one" or "Older children are more responsible than their younger brothers and sisters."

Concreteness

To determine if you can identify statements that are concrete from those that are not, mark the following statements *NC*, not concrete; *D*, dating; and *I*, indexing.

1. That TV program is out of date! _____

2. She never listens to anyone. _____
3. My mom is always crabby. _____
4. The president seemed so warm and friendly when he was running for office.

   _____
5. Have you seen Tom lately—he has seemed so jumpy the last two weeks.

   _____
6. Have you met the new woman in chem class? She's really stuck up—but students from the northern part of the state are all that way.

   _____

7. Who's the guy with Sue? Knowing her, he will be looking around for someone new to date soon! _____
8. Why do you want this job, Ms. Paris? You know that women just get married and quit. _____
9. When my mother died, my dad was depressed for nearly two years—he just sat in his chair night after night.

   _____
10. I was really disappointed to have a woman for my introduction to marketing course, after I had such a bad experience with the woman lecturer in geography. I decided not to prejudge her, though. Because one woman instructor doesn't work out, doesn't mean that all female college instructors are incompetent.

    _____

Summary

In this chapter we have discussed verbal codes. Words are defined as verbal symbols and languages as verbal codes. We use verbal language in communication by encoding, putting our messages or thoughts into a code, and by decoding, assigning meaning to the codes that we receive.

Words become a major obstacle to communication for several related reasons: we sometimes intentionally use language to distort and confuse; we often assume that words have an inherent, intrinsic meaning that is universally understood; and we frequently behave as though the reality we create through our language is real in some objective sense.

We can improve our use of language through three practices. We can avoid intentional confusion by defining the terminology we use and by avoiding euphemisms and clichés. Second, we can share experiences more effectively by becoming increasingly descriptive. Third, we can gain understanding through our ability to be concrete.

Additional Readings

Hayakawa, S. I. *Language in Thought and Action.* 3d ed. New York: Harcourt Brace Jovanovich, 1972.
An easily understood examination of the nature of language and the uses of symbols. Includes a discussion of verbal styles, figures of speech, language construction, inference making, and the socio-political uses of language.

*Hertzler, Joyce O. *A Sociology of Language.* New York: Random House, 1965.
Scholarly treatment of cultural and subcultural influences on language, embracing the characteristics of language, differences between languages, how languages change, and how society reflects change in its language system.

*Johnson, Wendell. *People in Quandaries.* New York: Harper & Row, Publishers, 1946.
An introduction to the principles of general semantics. Johnson shows how words can cause problems and gives suggestions about using words effectively. A classic scholarly work about verbal symbol systems.

Kramer, Cheris. "Folk-Linguistics: Wishy-Washy Mommy Talk." *Psychology Today,* June 1974, pp. 82–85.
A brief look at the differences between male and female language, including the use of adjectives, taboo words, and frequency of talking. Kramer describes some original research that indicates men talk differently than women.

*Lee, Irving J. *How to Talk with People.* New York: Harper & Row, Publishers, 1952.
On the basis of several years of observation of people in various contexts, Lee theorizes about how language can cause misunderstandings and offers suggestions for improving the effectiveness and clarity of our use of verbal symbols. Excellent application of verbal principles to human interaction.

Newman, Edwin. *A Civil Tongue.* Indianapolis: Bobbs-Merrill Co., 1976.
A humorous, tongue-in-cheek look at the uses and misuses of language. Newman warns that we are constantly bombarded with incorrect language usage by TV, radio, advertisements, political bureaucracy, and schools. He argues that the ideas we present are no stronger than the words we use to express them.

Parlee, Mary Brown. "Conversational Politics." *Psychology Today,* May 1979, pp. 48–56.
Conversational politics is defined by Parlee as "the violation of normal rules of conversation in order to assert power." (p. 48) She discusses dominating the conversation, interruptions, ignoring others, shifting the topic, and other conversational habits. Her thesis is that conversational patterns carry their own messages, separate from the content of the conversation.

Partridge, Eric. *Slang: Today and Yesterday.* New York: Barnes and Noble, 1970.
Considers the origins, uses, characteristics, and essence of slang. A brief history of English slang is included. Twenty-five different kinds of slang are considered. A very complete section on oddities includes rhyming slang, black slang, center slang, and blends.

*Indicates more advanced readings.

Pei, Mario. *The Story of Language.*
New York: New American Library
of World Literature, 1949.
Pei advances and explains several
hypotheses about the origin of
language, discusses the elements of
language, and compares several
different languages in terms of
grammar, syntax, and construction.
The social implications of language
are also explored.

*Thorne, Barrie, and Henley, Nancy,
eds. *Language and Sex: Difference
and Dominance.* Rowley, Mass.:
Newbury House Publishers, 1975.
This advanced text includes a
number of papers that view language
and sex from the perspectives of
linguistics, sociology, education, and
psychology. A very thorough
annotated bibliography provides
interested readers with a ready
reference list.

Notes

1. Lewis Carroll, *Through the Looking Glass* (New York: Random House, Inc., 1965), p. 94.
2. Benjamin Lee Whorf, "Science and Linguistics," in *Language, Thought and Reality,* ed. John B. Carroll (Cambridge, Mass.: M.I.T. Press, 1956), pp. 207–19.
3. John Barbour, "Edwin Newman Talks to Himself, but for a Good Reason," *Des Moines Sunday Register,* June 5, 1977.
4. Lewis Carroll, *Alice's Adventures in Wonderland* (New York: Random House, Inc., 1965), pp. 27–28.

4

Nonverbal Codes

A Tool of Sharing

Objectives

1. Discuss the relative importance of verbal and nonverbal codes in expressing ideas and feelings
2. Draw some conclusions about people that can usually be based on their body orientation and position
3. Discuss your own use of personal space and explain why it differs when you are with a close friend or a stranger, at home or at a party
4. Identify the factors that influence the meaning and use of touch
5. Define six characteristics of paralinguistics that can affect the meaning of a message
6. Discuss your own use of objects in communication and discuss the meaning that you think they convey
7. Identify the factors that make it difficult to interpret nonverbal behavior accurately and name some guidelines that can help you interpret nonverbal behavior more accurately

Key Terms

nonverbal code
kinesics
proxemics
territoriality
personal space
intimate distance
personal distance
social distance
public distance
tactile communication
vocal cues

pitch
rate
inflection
volume
quality
enunciation
paralanguage
objectics
double bind
descriptive feedback

There is a space between us which we cross to touch each other softly and so make up for our loss.[1]

Carole King and Toni Stern

Sometimes silence is best. Words are curious things, at best approximations. And every human being is a separate language. If the knowledge of that paralyzes you, withdraw for a little. Silence is best.[2]

The unconscious parental feelings communicated through touch or lack of touch can lead to feelings of confusion and conflict in a child. Sometimes a 'modern' parent will say all the right things but not want to touch his child very much. The child's confusion comes from the inconsistency of levels: if they really approve of me so much like they say they do, why won't they touch me?[3]

William Schutz

These three excerpts illustrate the importance of nonverbal communication. The first excerpt, lyrics from a song that was popular in the 1970s, emphasizes the use of space in human communication. The second concerns the importance of facial expression and bodily movement. The third quotation emphasizes the role of touch. Each of these excerpts suggests that communication can and does occur without words.

Importance of Nonverbal Codes in Communication

The little boy in the cartoon is well aware of the importance of nonverbal communication. Although his sister may scoff, his conclusion is borne out in research on nonverbal communication. A number of researchers have investigated the percentage of a message that is transmitted nonverbally, as opposed to verbally in interpersonal communication. Birdwhistell determined that only 35 percent of the meaning in a situation is transmitted verbally and that 65 percent is transmitted nonverbally.[4] Another student of nonverbal communication, Mehrabian, also analyzed message transmission and found that only 7 percent of the meaning is transmitted verbally. The 93

TIGER

percent of the message that is transmitted nonverbally is divided between 38 percent vocal cues and 55 percent facial cues.[5] Although the findings vary, we can conclude that nonverbal cues are probably more important than verbal cues to the sharing of meaning in interpersonal communication.

Nonverbal Meeting

In order to understand the importance of the nonverbal in your communication, try the following:

1. Spend thirty minutes with a good friend, spouse, or child without using any written or spoken words. Instead, use bodily movement, the space between you, gestures, facial expression, and other nonverbal cues to communicate.
2. Spend fifteen minutes with an acquaintance without using any words. Again, communicate only with nonverbal cues.
3. Spend ten minutes with a person you have spoken to before, but restrict your communication to nonverbal cues.

In a short paper, discuss your reactions and conclusions. Did you find that communicating nonverbally was easier or more difficult than you predicted? Did you find it easier to communicate nonverbally with someone you knew well or with a relative stranger? Why? Do you think the other person understood the message you were trying to communicate nonverbally? Do you believe that communication would have been hindered or helped if you could also have used words? How?

Definition and Identification of Nonverbal Codes

Nonverbal codes were defined in chapter 1 as codes of communication that consist of symbols that are not words. Bodily movements and facial expression, use of space, touching, vocalized sounds other than words, and clothing and artifacts are all nonverbal codes. Let us consider each of these systematic arrangements of symbols that have been given arbitrary meaning and that are used in communication.

Bodily Movement and Facial Expression

Kinesics is the term that means the study of people's bodily movements. Kinesics includes the study of posture, gestures, and facial expression. We communicate many of our feelings or emotions in these nonverbal ways. Ekman and Friesen determined that our faces give others information about *how* we feel and that our bodies suggest the *intensity* of the particular emotion.[6]

A number of best-sellers in the 1960s and 1970s, among them *Body Talk, Body Language,* and *How to Read a Person Like a Book,* have conveyed the importance of kinesics to the average person. These popular books familiarized the public with the importance of bodily movement in communication, but they also suggested that bodily movement is relatively easy to understand. Serious students of nonverbal communication know that this is not true. Assigning meaning to human movement is actually complicated. Alterations in the meaning of a person's movement may be due to characteristics of that person, characteristics of the observer, and characteristics of the environment.

In order to make an accurate assessment of the meaning of another person's movements, we need to take into account the person's particular characteristics. We may be grimacing because we have just left the dentist. Our quick pace may be due to lateness rather than habit. A lack of gestures and hand movement might result from fatigue. The physical, psychological, and emotional characteristics of the person being observed must all be taken into account.

Our own particular characteristics must also be considered when we are observing another person. When we interpret another person's movements as unfriendly, we need to consider our own expectations. Are we expecting that person to be unfriendly, and thus perceiving what we want to perceive? If someone appears nervous to us, is it because we are feeling tension and projecting our feelings onto someone else? Our own attitudes, values, and beliefs, coupled with our current needs and goals, must be taken into account when we assign meaning to another person's movements.

Finally, we need to consider the particular characteristics of the environment. A person standing with arms crossed may feel cold. Someone who is moving around slowly might be sensitive to another person's headache and might be trying to avoid making noise. A clerk who is darting in and out of the storeroom may be waiting on customers who are hard to please. Environmental factors must be considered when we try to understand bodily movement.

Mehrabian took these variables into consideration in the research he completed in 1971. He was interested in a person's body position and orientation—the degree to which one's shoulders and legs were turned toward another person. Mehrabian found that he could draw some general conclusions about this by considering three variables: liking, power or status, and vitality or responsiveness. He found that liking was often expressed by leaning forward, a direct body orientation, greater closeness, increased touching, a relaxed posture, open arms and body, positive facial expression, and more eye contact. Consider your own body orientation and movement when you are with persons you like. You tend to sit closer to them, lean toward them, touch them more, relax physically, smile at them more, and look at them more. When you are with persons whom you do not know or do not like, you tend to sit farther away from them, you seldom touch them, you are physically tense or at least not relaxed, you smile less, and you establish only minimum eye contact.

Mehrabian found that power or status was communicated by expansive gestures, relaxed posture, and less eye contact. When you consider persons in authority whom you know, you probably can recall their large gestures, the relaxed posture of their body, and their tendency to look at you less often. Supervisors, teachers, employers, and parents exhibit such behavior.

Mehrabian also found that responsiveness or involvement with other people is shown by movement toward other people, spontaneous gestures, a shifting of posture and position, and facial expressiveness.[7] Consider those persons whom you consider highly responsive. They move a great deal, they are spontaneous in their gestures and movements, and their faces are very expressive. If we keep in mind the particular characteristics of the person we are observing, our own particular characteristics, and the particular aspects of the environment, we can use Mehrabian's findings to help us interpret the movements of other people.

Ekman and Friesen offered a classification schema that is useful in understanding different types of bodily movements. They based their five categories of nonverbal movement on the functions, origins, and meaning of the behavior. Included in their categories are emblems, illustrators, affect displays, regulators, and adaptors. Let us define and identify each of these categories.

Emblems include those nonverbal behaviors that directly suggest specific words or phrases. Among the most common emblems are the thumb and first finger held together to suggest "okay," the first two fingers on the hand held up to signal a peace sign, the thumb in the air to identify a hitchhiker, and a beckoning first finger asking another person to "come here." It is important to remember that emblems, like the verbal language we use, is specific to our culture. Asking someone to come toward you by beckoning in our culture may be an insult or a derogatory comment in another culture.

Illustrators include those nonverbal behaviors that accompany verbal messages. When you shake your head at the same time that you are saying "yes" or "no;" when you point up, down, or in the direction that you are stating; and when you draw a picture in the air at the same time that you are describing the shape of an object, you are using an illustrator. Illustrators reinforce your verbal message. They appear to have more universality from one culture to another than do emblems.

Affect displays include movements of the face that hold emotional meaning. The anger, the happiness, the surprise, or the love that we show through the movements of our eyes, mouth, and other facial muscles are included in this category. These displays may be conscious or unconscious.

Regulators are those behaviors that monitor or control the communication of another individual. Those nonverbal behaviors that we use while another person is speaking including head nods, eye contact, blinking, smiling, looking away, and making various sounds are regulators. We signal others to tell us more, to stop talking, to give us additional detail, to give us fewer specific incidents, or to continue talking in the same way.

Adaptors, the final category determined by Ekman and Friesen, are nonverbal movements that serve a specific purpose. Adaptors include movements that we may fully perform in private, but that we only partially perform in public. For example, you may scratch an area of your body extensively when you are alone, but only rub the area lightly when you are in public. You may thoroughly massage a foot that has "gone to sleep" when in private, but only make a gesture toward doing so when you are with others. Adaptors serve a useful purpose, but are generally considered inappropriate in a public setting.[8]

Bodily movements and facial expression are important to the public speaker, just as they are important to the interpersonal communicator. As evidence, consider the finding that audiences who can view the speaker and his or her visible behavior understand more of the speech than audiences who cannot see the speaker.[9] Gestures and facial expression should appear to be natural when you deliver a speech. You may find that if you are sincerely concerned about the topic of a speech, you will gesture in a way that appears natural. In addition, you can practice delivering public speeches in front of friends, classmates, or even a mirror to determine if your gestures add to an understanding of your message.

Space

Edward T. Hall introduced the importance of **proxemics**, the human use of space, in 1966, in his book *The Hidden Dimension*. Robert Sommer analyzed the topic further in 1969, in *Personal Space: The Behavioral Basis of Design*. These researchers and others have demonstrated the role that space plays in human communication.

Two concepts that have been considered essential to the study of the use of space are territoriality and personal space. **Territoriality** is our need to establish and maintain certain spaces of our own. Territoriality has been studied more in animals than in humans, but it is recognized as a human need. People stake out their territory in various ways. Students leave coats or books on a library table while they search the stacks. Faculty members arrange their offices so their own chairs are identifiable. We all use fences, "no trespassing" signs, wedding rings, and other symbols that indicate our territory. We can purchase bumper stickers that read "If you can read this, you're too close"; hotels and motels provide us with "Do not disturb" signs; and airlines offer us cards that state "Sorry, this seat is occupied." Territoriality refers to territory that is generally immovable and typically separate from a person.

Personal space, on the other hand, is the area surrounding a person that moves with the person. Personal space is the amount of physical distance you maintain between yourself and other people. We seldom think about personal space until someone invades it, but such an invasion may create stress or evoke defensive behavior.

Hall, an anthropologist, originally defined four distances that people regularly use. These categories have been found to be useful in understanding the communication behavior that might occur when such a distance is used. Beginning with the closest contact and the least personal space and moving to greatest distance, the four categories are intimate distance, personal distance, social distance, and public distance.

Intimate distance, which extends from touch to approximately eighteen inches, is used with people who are emotionally close to us. Frequently this distance is used in private, rather than in public, situations. For instance, you may use intimate distance when you are showing affection to another person, when you are offering comfort to someone who has suffered a loss, or when you are protecting a person from real or imagined danger. In circumstances where intimate distance seems inappropriate, on a crowded bus or elevator, walking on a narrow path, encountering others on a busy sidewalk, you may feel discomfort. In circumstances where intimate distance is appropriate, you will probably respond very positively to the other person.

Personal distance, which ranges from about eighteen inches to four feet, can include a variety of different encounters. When people stand together at a range of about eighteen inches, they are probably signaling that something more than a conversation is occurring. At four feet, conversations are the most likely interpersonal exchange to occur. This range of space allows intimate and nonintimate interpersonal exchanges to occur. Crowded cocktail parties, informal social exchanges, and bars frequently encourage people to stand or sit at the minimum amount of space included in this distance. Such spacing encourages more intimate conversation than probably would occur if more space were available.

Social distance, which extends from four to approximately twelve feet, is generally used by people conducting business. The closer social distances are commonly used in business settings—the boss speaking to an employee, a salesperson helping a customer, or a secretary addressing co-workers. The farther social distance is used in a more formal and less personal situation. For example, we may use seven to twelve feet to separate ourselves from a college president, a potential employer, or a person with high status.

Public distance, which exceeds twelve feet, is used primarily in public speaking situations. Your instructors probably stand twelve or more feet away from most of the members of your classes. Ministers, lawyers, and public speakers usually use public distance when they address audiences. When others choose this distance with which to communicate, you may assume that they are more interested in giving a speech than they are in having a conversation with you.[10]

Personal space varies from person to person and from situation to situation. Among the variables that determine personal space are (1) the characteristics of the individuals, (2) the relationship between them, (3) the physical setting, and (4) their cultural background. Two relevant characteristics of individuals are their size and sex. People who are larger require a greater amount of personal space, and people who are smaller—including children—require a smaller amount of space.[11] Women show the least discomfort when the space around them is small and tend to interact at closer range.[12]

The relationship between the people who are interacting is also important. Generally, we stand closer to friends and farther away from enemies.[13] We also stand away from strangers, authority figures, people of higher status, physically handicapped people, and individuals from a different racial group.

The physical setting can alter our personal space. People tend to stand closer in large rooms and farther apart in small rooms.[14] In addition, physical obstacles and furniture arrangements can affect personal space.

The cultural background of the people involved must be considered. Edward T. Hall was among the first to recognize the importance of cultural background. In 1963, he was training American service personnel for service overseas and began to recognize the importance of cultural differences in his work. Hall writes:

Americans overseas were confronted with a variety of difficulties because of cultural differences in the handling of space. People stood "too close" during conversations, and when the Americans backed away to a comfortable conversational distance, this was taken to mean that Americans were cold, aloof, withdrawn, and disinterested in the people of the country. USA housewives muttered about "waste-space" in houses in the Middle East. In England, Americans who were used to neighborliness were hurt when they discovered that their neighbors were no more accessible or friendly than other people, and in Latin America, exsuburbanites, accustomed to unfenced yards, found that the high walls there made them feel "shut out." Even in Germany, where so many of my countrymen felt at home, radically different patterns in the use of space led to unexpected tensions.[15]

Cultural background can greatly alter the human use of space and the interpretation, by others, of that use of space.

Touching

Tactile communication is the use of touch in communication. Touch may be viewed as the most extreme form of invasion of personal space. Nonetheless, touch is essential to our growth and development. Studies have shown that an insufficient amount of touching can result in health disorders such as allergies and eczema, speech problems, symbolic recognition, and even death.[16] While it may be difficult to believe, researchers have found that untouched babies and small children grow increasingly ill and even die.

Touch is one of the most powerful ways we have of communicating with others. The pleasure that touch causes originates in infancy. For most people, touching is positive and enjoyable. The interpretation of the meaning of a particular touch depends, of course, on the type of touch, where a person is touched, and the cultural background of the people involved. Still, in most cultures, touch is associated with positive attitudes and lack of touch is associated with negative attitudes. Touch is one of the clearest indications that we like and accept others and that they like and accept us.

Elements of the Communication Process

Men and women do not touch each other to the same degree nor are men and women touched to the same extent. Most studies indicate that females are touched by others more than males. From about the age of six months, mothers tend to touch their female children more than their male children.[17] College students reported the extent to which they are touched and the areas of their body that are touched. Female students reported far more touching and reported that more areas of their body were accessible to others than did male students.[18] In a final study, which investigated touching among fathers, mothers, daughters, and sons, it was found that fathers and sons touched each other less than any other combination.[19]

Men touch others more than women touch others. The rationale for this sex difference has traditionally relied on the difference in sexual agressiveness on the part of men in our culture. Men generally have initiated and demonstrated sexual interest; therefore, they have tended to touch others more. Recently, Henley suggested that the greater touching exhibited by men may be an indication of power and dominance.[20] She explains that touch is not a reciprocal act; that is, that men have access to women's bodies, but women do not have the same access to men's bodies. Touching may be seen as a method of exerting power over another person as it represents an invasion of personal space. The statement that is made by men invading women's space without the reciprocal invasion of men's space by women is that men have more status or power than women.

Henley's interpretation of the differences in touching behavior by men and women may be more clear if we consider the differences in touching exhibited by subordinates and superordinates. The boss can put his hand on his secretary's shoulder, the teacher can pat the student's arm, and the doctor can touch the patient almost anywhere. Conversely, the secretary cannot put her arm around her boss, the student cannot hold the teacher's hand, and the patient is seldom allowed anything but a handshake with a physician. Persons with higher status are allowed the opportunity of touching others and the opportunity is not reciprocal. Touch may be a sign of liking or it may suggest status differences.

Vocal Cues

In chapter 1, we distinguished between nonverbal and nonoral communication. While nonverbal codes include the nonoral or nonvocal codes such as bodily movement and the human use of space, they also include pitch, duration of sound, rate of speech, and nonwords such as *eh* and *ah*. Nonverbal codes are all codes that do not consist of words. When we consider **vocal cues,** we include all of the oral aspects of sound except the words themselves.

We can categorize vocal cues into (1) **pitch**—the highness or lowness of a voice, (2) **rate**—how rapidly or slowly a person speaks, (3) **inflection**—the change or lack of change in the pitch of a person's voice, (4) **volume**—the loudness or softness of a person's voice, (5) **quality**—the pleasant or unpleasant characteristics of a person's voice, including nasality, raspiness, and whininess, and (6) **enunciation**—a person's pronunciation and articulation. In addition to these cues, specific sounds such as *uh-huh, ah,* and *mmh,* as well as silences, comprise the elements taken into consideration in **paralanguage,** that which comes with language.

Paralanguage, as we said earlier in this chapter, conveys about 38 percent of a message. The vocal aspect of nonverbal communication frequently conveys a speaker's personal attributes and provides information about the speaker's current emotional state. Among the personal attributes that are often communicated are the speaker's age, height, overall appearance, body type, status, credibility (which will be discussed further in chapter 11).[21]

A number of studies have related various emotions to specific vocal cues. Joy and hate appear to be the most accurately communicated emotions, while shame and love are the least accurately communicated.[22] Emotions like joy and hate appear to be conveyed by fewer vocal cues, which makes their interpretation less difficult than the complex sets of vocal cues that identify emotions like shame and love. Research has shown that "active" feelings like anger and joy are associated with a loud voice, a high pitch, a blaring timbre, and a rapid rate. Conversely, our "passive" feelings, which include affection and sadness, are communicated with a soft voice, a low pitch, a reasonant timbre, and a relatively slow rate.[23]

Personality characteristics, too, have been related to vocal cues. Dominance, social adjustment, sociability, and tension have been clearly correlated with specific vocal cues.[24] While the personality characteristics attributed to individuals displaying particular vocal cues have not been shown to accurately portray the person, as determined by standardized personality tests, our impressions affect our interactions. In other words, while we may perceive a loud-voiced, high-pitched, fast-speaking individual to be dominant, he or she might not be measured as dominant by a personality inventory. Nonetheless, in our interactions with such an individual, we may become increasingly submissive because of our perception that they are dominant. In addition, the other person may begin to become more dominant as he or she is treated as though he or she has this personality characteristic.

Sex differences are also related to paralinguistics. Women tend to speak in higher pitched voices than do men. Men generally speak with greater intensity than women. Last, men and women demonstrate different intonational patterns. For instance, women tend to state even declarative sentences with an upward inflection to suggest a question rather than a declaration.[25]

Vocal cues can help a public speaker establish credibility with an audience and can clarify his or her message. Pitch can be used to make the speech sound aesthetically pleasing, to accomplish subtle changes in meaning, and to tell an audience whether you are asking a question or making a statement, being sincere or sarcastic, being doubtful or assertive. A rapid speaking rate may indicate that you are confident about speaking in public or that you are nervously attempting to conclude your speech. Pauses can be used in the public speech for dramatic effect and to arouse audience interest. Vocalized pauses—the ahs, uh-huhs, ums, etc.—are not desirable in public speaking and may distract the audience. Variations in volume can be used for emphasis or to create suspense. Enunciation is especially important in public speaking because of the increased size of the audience and the fewer opportunities for direct feedback, when compared with interpersonal communication.

Clothing and Other Artifacts

Objectics, or *object language,* refers to our display of material things. Object language is comprised of hair styles, clothing, jewelry, cosmetics, and so forth. Our clothing and other adornments communicate our age, sex, status, role, socioeconomic class, group memberships, personality, and our relation to the opposite sex. Dresses are seldom worn by men, low-cut gowns are not the choice of shy women, bright colors are avoided by reticent people, and the most recent Paris fashion is seldom seen in the small towns of mid-America. These cues also indicate the time in history, the time of day, and the climate. Clothing and artifacts provide physical and psychological protection and are used for sexual attraction and to indicate self-concept.

Many studies have established relationships between an individual's clothing and artifacts and his or her characteristics. In an early study, the personality traits of conformity, sociability, and nonintellectualism were positively correlated with *decoration* in dress; self-control and extroversion were positively correlated with *comfort;* compliance, stereotypic thinking, social conscientiousness, and insecurity were positively correlated with *interest;* social conformity, restraint, and submissiveness were correlated positively with *conformity* in manner of dress; and, finally, characteristics including responsibility, alertness, efficiency, and precision were highly correlated with *economy* in dress.[26] A more recent study confirmed these results; conforming to current styles was correlated with an individual's desire to be accepted and liked.[27] In addition, another study showed that individuals felt that clothing was important in forming first impressions.[28]

Perhaps of more importance are the studies that consider the relationship between clothing and an observer's perception of that person. In an early study, clothing was shown to affect others' impressions of status and personal traits.[29] We also seem to base our acceptance of people on the clothing and artifacts that they present. Women who were asked to describe the most popular women they knew used clothing as the most important characteristic.[30] Finally, brightly colored clothing is associated with sophistication, immorality, and physical attractiveness.[31]

The importance of clothing and other artifacts on our perception of others cannot be overrated. A few years ago, the students in a female instructor's class told her that clothing was a form of communication only among older people—like herself. They argued that young people make no judgments about other people's clothing, and seldom even noticed other people's clothes, and her arguments to the contrary fell on deaf ears.

The next semester, again lecturing on object language, she told her new students about that previous discussion—but while she talked, she slipped off her jeans and sweater to reveal a leotard and tights. At the end of the hour, she gave a quiz on the material covered during the period. Not surprisingly, the students successfully answered the items on the material covered before she disrobed, but did a poor job on the questions about material she covered afterward. These students agreed—they were distracted by her unusual and provocative attire and had difficulty concentrating on the lecture. The importance of clothing as a means of nonverbal communication, to young as well as older people, was established, at least in that second class.

Clothes Communicate!

Our clothing communicates who we are, what we value, how we see ourselves, and it conveys a number of other messages. Consider the clothing and jewelry you wear and what it might communicate about you. Keep a record for three or four days of all of the clothing, jewelry, and other adornments that you wear. Record changes in clothing within the day. After you have compiled this record, suggest why you made these choices, and what these particular clothes might communicate to others. Finally, ask two friends or acquaintances what your clothing communicates to them. Consider the similarities or differences in the perception you have of your clothing and the perceptions that your friends or acquaintances have.

Interpretation of Nonverbal Cues

Problems of Interpretation

Considering the importance of nonverbal codes, it is not surprising that they provide the basis for much of the misunderstanding that occurs in communication. We have difficulty interpreting nonverbal cues for several reasons. We use the same cue to communicate a variety of different meanings; we use a variety of cues to communicate the same meaning; and we use conflicting verbal and nonverbal cues in our communication.

The Same Cue Communicates a Variety of Different Meanings Raising your right hand may mean that you are taking an oath, you are demonstrating for a cause, you are indicating to an instructor that you would like to answer a question, that a physician is examining your right side, or that you want a taxi to stop for you. We may also use the same cue to communicate different things in other nonverbal codes. We may stand close to someone because of a feeling of affection, because the room is crowded, or because we have difficulty hearing. We may speak softly because we were taught it was the "correct" way for us to speak, because we are suffering from a sore throat, or because we are sharing a secret. We may wear blue jeans because they are the acceptable mode of dress, because they symbolize our rebellion against higher-priced clothing, or because they are the only clean clothes we have that day.

A Variety of Cues Communicate the Same Meaning The "Peanuts" cartoon shows an inappropriate way of communicating meaning. Yet, those of us who are parents or have younger siblings are familiar with the tendency of young children to express affection or attraction through physical aggression. As the child grows, he or she begins to experiment with more appropriate nonverbal indications of affection.

Adults have many nonverbal ways to express love or affection. We may choose to sit or stand more closely to someone we love. We might speak more softly, use a different vocal intonation, and alter how quickly we speak when we communicate with someone for whom we have affection. We often dress differently if we are going to be in the company of a person we love.

Verbal and Nonverbal Cues May Conflict   We may have a positive feeling about the verbal message but a negative feeling about the nonverbal statement. We can all think of times when other people have said that they felt a certain way but told us nonverbally that they felt differently. Instructors have this experience when students tell them that they particularly enjoy their class but do not attend regularly. Students experience this form of conflict when instructors invite them into their office to talk but spend the entire time looking through memos and papers.

Bateson and his colleagues initially identified this situation as a **double bind**.[32] The conflict between two contradictory messages creates a difficult situation for the person who is attempting to respond appropriately to the given cues: "He is damned if he does, and damned if he doesn't." It is particularly difficult when some of the cues are verbal and others are nonverbal.

Verbal cues can conflict with cues from any of the nonverbal codes. We may find it difficult to believe that people really care for us if they never touch us or move toward us. A person may deliver a message of anger, but in an even-toned, quiet voice. We question the credibility of people who say that money means little to them if they continually flash expensive jewelry and dress in ostentatious, costly clothing.

89   Nonverbal Codes

Solutions to Problems of Interpretation

It may appear from our discussion that the difficulty of interpreting nonverbal cues is insurmountable. The problems in interpretation are serious, but they can be minimized if we make use of three sets of information. First, we need to be sensitive to all of the variables in the communication situation. Second, we should attend to all of the verbal and nonverbal cues. Finally, we should use descriptive feedback to clarify unclear cues.

Consider All of the Variables in the Communication Situation   Other people's nonverbal communication is only a small part of a communication situation. We must also consider other aspects of other persons—ability to use words, intentions, immediate and past history, and so forth. We also need to consider ourselves, and how our presence might affect the behavior of others. We should also take into account the relationship between ourselves and others. Finally, we should consider the context—the reason for the conversation.

Consider All Available Verbal and Nonverbal Cues   Rather than focusing on another person's clothing or a specific facial expression, take into consideration other nonverbal cues as well. Do not forget to listen to the verbal message. If you find contradictions between the verbal and nonverbal messages, recall the person's past communication behavior. When contradictions in verbal and nonverbal cues occurred in the past, what was the intended message? Is it likely that this is the intended message now?

Utilize Descriptive Feedback   One of the most accurate ways of solving the difficulty of interpreting nonverbal cues is to use **descriptive feedback.** By simply describing to the other person the conflict you find or suggesting the meaning you understand, you can clarify things. The other person can suggest reasons for the inconsistencies or supply the intended meaning. You can continue to request clarification until you understand and share the same message.

Summary

In this chapter we have considered the role of nonverbal codes in communication. We explained the importance of nonverbal codes and defined them as all codes that consist of symbols that are not words. Bodily movements and facial expression, personal space, sounds other than words, and clothing and artifacts are nonverbal codes. Kinesics is the study of people's bodily movements, including posture, gestures, and facial expression. Proxemics is the human use of space; included in a study of proxemics are territoriality and personal space. Tactile communication is the use of touch in communication. Vocal cues include pitch, rate, inflection, volume, quality, and enunciation. Objectics, or object language, is our display of material things, including hair styles, clothing, jewelry, and cosmetics.

We have difficulty in interpreting nonverbal cues because we use the same cue to communicate a variety of different meanings, because we use a variety of cues to communicate the same meaning, and because we use conflicting verbal and nonverbal cues. We can solve some of our difficulties if we consider all of the variables in the particular communication situation, if we consider all of the available verbal and nonverbal cues, and if we use descriptive feedback to minimize misunderstanding.

Additional Readings

Birdwhistell, Ray L. *Kinesics and Context.* Philadelphia: University of Pennsylvania Press, 1970.
Birdwhistell is an acknowledged expert in the area of body language. This book includes a thorough analysis of bodily movement and two systems for recording observed movement. Birdwhistell views communication as a process in which all participants interact with messages of varying, overlapping lengths. This book is recommended for the advanced student of nonverbal communication.

Burgoon, Judee K., and Saine, Thomas. *The Unspoken Dialogue: An Introduction to Nonverbal Communication.* Boston: Houghton Mifflin Company, 1978.
Most contemporary textbooks treat nonverbal communication as a composite of various nonverbal codes in a manner that is similar to the treatment of nonverbal communication in this chapter. Burgoon and Saine offer a different perspective as they consider the components of nonverbal communication and the functions they serve. Included among the functions they consider are first impressions, relational messages, affection, regulation of interaction, presentation of self, and the manipulation of others. This book can be understood by the beginning student of nonverbal communication, but its unique point of view allows insight for the advanced student.

*Ekman, Paul, and Friesen, Wallace V. *Unmasking the Face: A Guide to Recognizing Emotions from Facial Cues.* Englewood Cliffs, N.J.: Prentice-Hall, 1975.
A research-oriented look at what feelings and emotions are communicated by facial expressions, and how they do it. Systematic description of specific facial movements that help to determine meaning. Some excellent illustrations help to clarify the myriad of facial expressions that we use to convey our feelings.

Hall, Edward T. *The Silent Language.* Greenwich, Conn.: Fawcett Publications, 1959.
Hall compares nonverbal uses of space, time, and movement in different cultures, emphasizes the influence of culture on our behavior, and discusses the impact of cultural factors on our perception and communication. An indepth discussion of concepts, written in an easy-to-understand style.

*Henley, Nancy M. *Body Politics, Power, Sex and Nonverbal Communication.* Englewood Cliffs, N.J.: Prentice Hall, 1977.
Henley is well known for her work on male/female differences. In this book, she relates the variables of body politics, power, and sex to nonverbal communication. Henley discusses the differences in the use of nonverbal communication by men

*Indicates more advanced readings.

and women and suggests that they are linked to powerful and powerless communication in our culture. The concept of power is a unifying theme that holds this book together. This book may provide some insights into male/female communication problems as well as a different perspective from which to examine nonverbal communication.

Knapp, Mark L. *Nonverbal Communication in Human Interaction.* New York: Holt, Rinehart, and Winston, 1972. A summary of the research on nonverbal behavior, including appearance, use of space, movement, eye contact, and vocalics. Easy to understand, with good examples and illustrations to clarify major nonverbal principles.

*Mehrabian, Albert. "Communication without Words." *Psychology Today,* September 1968, pp. 53–55. Mehrabian explains the relative contributions to meaning of verbal, vocal, and facial cues. He describes his research and the implications of his finding that nonverbal cues are primarily responsible for our likings, feelings, and attitudes.

Notes

1. "Feeling Sad Tonight," words and music by Carole King and Toni Stern. Copyright © 1972 by Colgems Music Corp., 711 Fifth Avenue, New York, N.Y. 10022
2. Reprinted from "Every Human Being Is a Separate Language" by Pat Hardman in *The Salt Lake Tribune,* September 3, 1971.
3. William C. Schutz, *Here Comes Everybody* (New York: Harper & Row, Publishers, 1971), p. 16.
4. Ray L. Birdwhistell, *Kinesics and Context* (Philadelphia: University of Pennsylvania Press, 1970), pp. 128–43.
5. Albert Mehrabian and Susan R. Kerris, "Inference of Attitude from Nonverbal Communication in Two Channels," *Journal of Consulting Psychology* 31 (1967): 248–52.
6. Paul Ekman and Wallace V. Friesen, "Head and Body Cues in the Judgment of Emotion: A Reformulation," *Perceptual and Motor Skills* 24 (1967): 711–24.
7. Albert Mehrabian, *Silent Messages* (Belmont, Calif.: Wadsworth Publishing Co., 1971), pp. 113–18.
8. Paul Ekman and Wallace V. Friesen, "The Repertoire of Nonverbal Behavior: Categories, Origins, Usage, and Coding," *Semiotica* 1(1969): 49–98.
9. Edward J. J. Kramer and Thomas R. Lewis, "Comparison of Visual and Nonvisual Listening," *Journal of Communication* 1(1951): 16–20.
10. Edward T. Hall, *The Hidden Dimension* (New York: Doubleday, 1966).
11. Michael Argyle and Janet Dean, "Eye-Contact, Distance, and Affiliation," *Sociometry* 28 (1965): 289–304.
12. B. R. Addis, "The Relationship of Physical Interpersonal Distance to Sex, Race, and Age" (Master's thesis, University of Oklahoma, 1966).
13. Carol J. Guardo, "Personal Space in Children," *Child Development* 40 (1969): 143–51.
14. Robert Sommer, "The Distance for Comfortable Conversation: A Further Study," *Sociometry* 25 (1962): 111–16.
15. Edward T. Hall, "Proxemics—The Study of Man's Spatial Relations and Boundaries," *Man's Image in Medicine and Anthropology* (New York: International Universities Press, 1963), pp. 422–45.
16. Ashley Montagu, *Touching: The Human Significance of the Skin* (New York: Harper & Row, Publishers, 1971), p. 82; J. L. Desper, "Emotional Aspects of Speech and Language Development," *International Journal of Psychiatry and Neurology* 105 (1941): 193–222; John Bowlby, *Maternal Care and Mental Health* (Geneva: World Health Organization, 1951), pp. 15–29; Ronald Adler and Neil Towne, *Looking Out/Looking In* (San Francisco: Rinehart Press, 1975), pp. 225–26.
17. V. S. Clay, "The Effect of Culture on Mother-Child Tactile Communication," *Family Coordinator* 17 (1968): 204–210

and S. Goldberg and M. Lewis, "Play Behavior in the Year-Old Infant: Early Sex Differences," *Child Development* 40 (1969): 21–31.

18. Sidney Jourard, "An Exploratory Study of Body Accessibility," *British Journal of Social and Clinical Psychology* 5 (1966): 221–231.

19. Sidney Jourard and J. E. Rubin, "Self-Disclosure and Touching: A Study of Two Modes of Interpersonal Encounter and Their Inter-Relation," *Journal of Humanistic Psychology* 8 (1968): 39–48.

20. Nancy Henley, "Power, Sex, and Nonverbal Communication," *Berkeley Journal of Sociology* 18 (1973–1974): 10–11.

21. Ernest Kramer, "The Judgment of Personal Characteristics and Emotions from Nonverbal Properties of Speech," *Psychological Bulletin* 60 (1963): 408–20.

22. James C. McCroskey, Carl E. Larson, and Mark L. Knapp, *An Introduction to Interpersonal Communication* (Englewood Cliffs, N.J.: Prentice-Hall, Inc., 1971), pp. 116–18.

23. Kramer, pp. 408–20.

24. Gregory Bateson, D. D. Jackson, J. Haley, and J. H. Weakland, "Toward a Theory of Schizophrenia," *Behavioral Science* 1 (1956): 251–64.

25. Barbara Westbrook Eakins and R. Gene Eakins, *Sex Differences in Human Communication* (Boston: Houghton Mifflin Company, 1978), pp. 99–103.

26. L. R. Aiken, "The Relationship of Dress to Selected Measures of Personality in Undergraduate Women," *Journal of Social Psychology* 59 (1963): 119–28.

27. L. C. Taylor and N. H. Compton, "Personality Correlates of Dress Conformity," *Journal of Home Economics* 60 (1968): 653–56.

28. S. H. Hendricks, E. A. Kelley, and J. B. Eicher, "Senior Girls' Appearance and Social Acceptance," *Journal of Home Economics* 60 (1968): 167–72.

29. H. I. Douty, "Influence of Clothing on Perception of Persons," *Journal of Home Economics* 55 (1963): 197–202.

30. M. C. Williams and J. B. Eicher, "Teenagers' Appearance and Social Acceptance," *Journal of Home Economics* 58 (1966): 457–61.

31. P. N. Hamid, "Some Effects of Dress Cues on Observational Accuracy, Perceptual Estimate and Impression Formation," *Journal of Social Psychology* 86 (1972): 279–89.

32. Bateson, pp. 251–64.

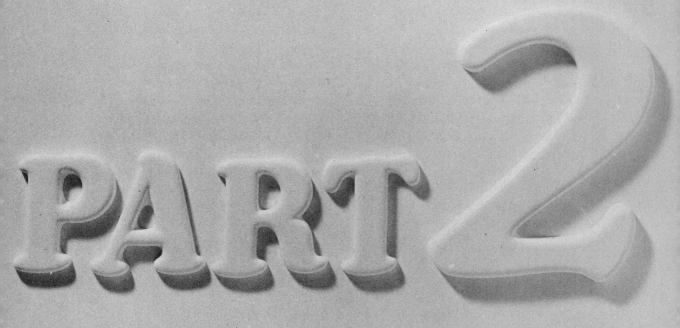

PART 2

Intrapersonal and Interpersonal Communication

Intrapersonal communication is the process of understanding and sharing that occurs within a person. Interpersonal communication is the process of understanding and sharing between at least two persons. These two communication situations are highlighted in this section of the text. The roles of self and other in communication are explored.

We begin our consideration with the components of understanding and the role of self in chapter 5, "Understanding Yourself." The importance of self-awareness and self-concept are discussed, and journal writing is explained as an activity to increase self-awareness and improve self-concept. Sharing with another is the subject of chapter 6, "Sharing Yourself." This chapter includes a definition of self-disclosure, suggests the importance of self-disclosure, identifies the attitudes that interfere with self-disclosure, and concludes with five guidelines for self-disclosure. We return to the problem of understanding, but focus our attention on the other person in chapter 7, "Understanding Another." In this chapter, the two basic skills involved in understanding another person, listening and empathy, are defined and discussed. Chapter 8, "The Interview," begins with questioning and includes the organization and purposes of interviews. We conclude the subject of intrapersonal and interpersonal communication with chapter 9, "The Small Group Discussion," which describes and analyzes a common type of communication.

5

Understanding Yourself

Objectives

1. Discuss why self-awareness is important; suggest some of the barriers to self-awareness

2. Identify the factors that inhibit change of self-concept; give an example of how your self-concept has changed in the last few years

3. Define your self-image and self-esteem

4. Show that self-concept is a process by describing how your self-concept differs in different situations and at different times

5. Explain the relationship between the self-fulfilling prophecy and the formation of self-concept

Key Terms

self-awareness

Maslow's "hierarchy of needs"

self-control

self-expression

self-concept

self-image

self-esteem

roles

self-consciousness

self-fulfilling prophecy

defensiveness

assertiveness

communication apprehension

journal

self-improvement

I really feel great! I started jogging about a month ago and I've lost four pounds and I feel so much better.

I can't take speech—I really freeze up when I have to speak to a large group of people.

Who am I? Just another student trying to make it through school.

These typical statements from our everyday conversations confirm the importance of how we feel about ourselves. All of us reveal ourselves in many different ways: when we talk to ourselves; when we talk to roommates, friends, or advisors; and when we speak in public.

In chapter 1, we stated that communication begins with oneself. Communication is viewed from one's personal perspective. In this chapter, we will explore this centrality of self to communication.

Self-Awareness

The self plays a central role in communication regardless of whether the communication is in a daydream, a journal, a small group, or at a podium. The first step in the improvement of our communication skills, consequently, is to become aware of ourselves—**self-awareness.** Unfortunately, most of us have been taught to disregard or minimize our feelings and emotions. As children we were told "Be quiet," "Don't cry," "Don't carry on so much," or "Try to act like a man (or a lady)."

If we are sensitive to children, we recognize that two universal characteristics are their spontaneity and the completeness of their responses. They respond immediately and completely to their world. Small children laugh easily and with their whole body. Frustrated youngsters respond with their entire being.

Through conditioning, children learn that many responses are inappropriate. Giggling in church is not socially approved; screaming at parents is not condoned; loud crying in public places is not rewarded. Through training and conditioning, children learn to think before they act.

Teaching children to think before they react may be essential in our culture, but we pay a high price as individuals. By analyzing the situation first, and then responding appropriately, we lose touch with our emotions. We learn to intellectualize our feelings away. Many of us become so successful at this that we are unable, as adults, to describe or even understand our own emotions.

Rediscovering ourselves is essential to our mental health and, in turn, to our ability to communicate. Abraham H. Maslow, a well-known psychologist, was one of the first to stress the importance of self-awareness or self-study. Maslow felt that people must become what they could become. In **Maslow's hierarchy of needs,** the most basic are physical, followed by the need for safety or security, social acceptance, self-esteem, and self-actualization (see fig. 5.1).[1] Physical needs include our need for food, sleep, sex, and water. Safety and security needs include our need for stability, order, predictability, and freedom from fear, harm, injury, and chaos. Among our social needs are our need to belong, to feel a part of social groups, and to feel

Figure 5.1 Maslow's hierarchy of needs.

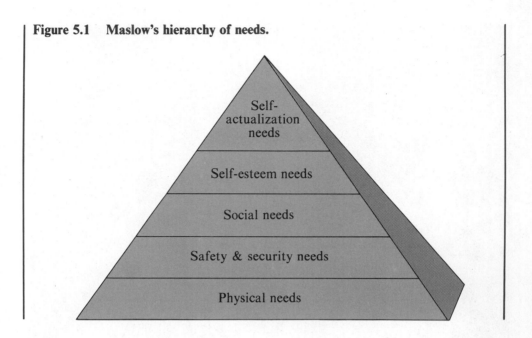

acceptance, approval, and affection. Our self-esteem needs are based on competence, confidence, and the recognition that others can give to us. Finally, our self-actualization needs include our living up to our unique potentialities and include our need for self-fulfillment.

Other psychologists have also discussed the importance of self-actualization. Carl Rogers labeled the person with this ability "the fully functioning person"; Sidney Jourard considered the "disclosed self"; Marie Johoda spoke of the "mentally healthy"; Charles Morris identified the "open self"; and Theodore Landman wrote about the "beautiful and noble person." All of these psychologists held an optimistic, empirically based view that recognized that increased self-awareness leads to self-actualization.

Will Schutz echoed this point of view and agreed about the importance of self-awareness. In *Here Comes Everybody,* Schutz considered the relationship between self-discovery and self-actualization:

Every thought, gesture, muscle tension, feeling, stomach gurgle, nose scratch, fart, hummed tune, slip of the tongue, illness—everything is significant and meaningful and related to the now. It is possible to know and understand oneself on all these levels, and the more one knows the more he is free to determine his own life.

If I know what my body tells me, I know my deepest feelings and I can choose what to do. . . . Given a complete knowledge of myself, I can determine my life; lacking that mastery, I am controlled in ways that are often undesirable, unproductive, worrisome, and confusing.[2]

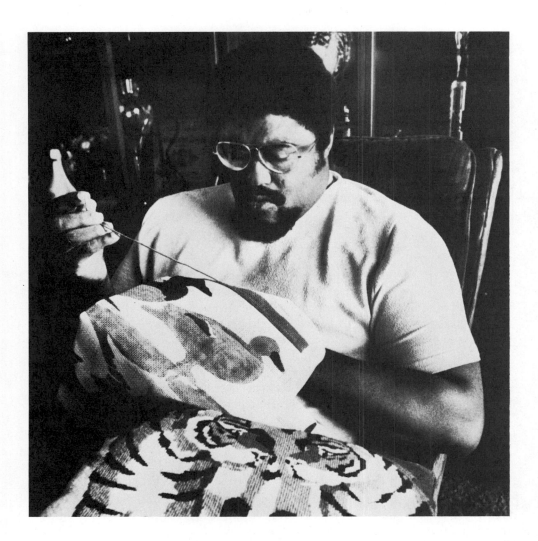

When we become aware of ourselves, our controlling agent becomes, not an outside force, but ourselves. Our self-awareness can be seen and heard in our communication behavior. People who are aware of themselves express emotions both verbally and nonverbally. They cry, they laugh, they speak in expressive tones. Their bodies communicate their fear, disappointment, joy, and pleasure.

Increasingly, people are becoming aware of the importance of self-awareness. Rosey Grier, the huge football star of the late 1960s, sang "It's All Right to Cry" on *Free to Be . . . You and Me,* an album recorded in 1972. The song, reprinted here, speaks of the importance of responding honestly and spontaneously to one's emotions. It suggests that we should not allow ourselves to rationalize our problems; instead, we should work to keep in close touch with our emotions. The price of losing close touch with our emotions is too high.

It's all right to cry
Crying gets the sad out of you
It's all right to cry
It might make you feel better.
Raindrops from your eyes
Washing all the mad out of you
Raindrops from your eyes
It might make you feel better.
It's all right to feel things
Though the feelings may be strange.
Feelings are such real things

And they change and change and change
(Sad and grumpy,
Down in the dumpy,
Snuggly huggly,
Mean and ugly,
Sloppy slappy,
Hoppy happy)
Change and change and change . . .
It's all right to know
Feelings come and feelings go
And it's all right to cry
It might make you feel better.[3]

Rosey Grier is unusual. Many American men—especially men like Rosey Grier—have difficulty expressing their feelings. Sorrow, fear, anxiety, and loneliness appear to be particularly difficult for men to express. But communicating these feelings to others is psychologically healthy. Our interpersonal relationships can be enhanced by a fuller and more complete expression of our feelings.

Many adults who have learned to deny their feelings are making attempts to rediscover themselves. Warren Doyle, a Ph.D. from the University of Connecticut, approached self-discovery by backpacking alone. Doyle set two records for hiking the 2,040-mile Appalachian Trail. He reported,

There's a theory that most people have high self-concepts that crumble in situations of crisis or adversity. Many of us never have a chance to find out who we really are. . . . I was alone for 66 days. I lost my physical fat and my emotional fat as well. I saw myself as I really was.[4]

We may not be able to go hiking alone, but we can all make some moves to increase our self-awareness. We can focus on our bodies, our feelings, our emotions, and the present. We can concentrate on how we feel about something rather than on the way we think we are expected to feel. We can look to ourselves rather than to others for solutions to problems. We can take responsibility for our own point of view as well as our own behavior. We can try to identify what we want to do and then work hard to do it well.

Self-awareness is essential to successful communication, even though our culture stresses **self-control** more than **self-expression.** Too much self-control can result in an avoidance of communication, on the one hand, or aggressive communication, on the other. Overly self-controlled people avoid being expressive and stating their own feelings, emotions, and opinions. Or, they may rebel and behave aggressively, trying to control and manipulate others through communication.

Consider Jim, an unassertive speaker. Jim was bright, the oldest of four children. His parents reminded him and others that "Jim always does what's right." When he was small he was praised for "not being lippy" and for "not talking back."

When he became a man, people complimented him for "being such a good listener." Jim learned self-control. Now he complains, "No one knows who I am—not even me."

Marcia was taught to be "seen and not heard." She expressed herself when she was a child, but she soon learned the power of disapproval. Her parents, who tried to control her, succeeded only in making Marcia attempt to control her younger brother. Marcia monitored her brother's every expression. Now, Marcia is viewed as very domineering and unpleasant. She writes, "I know people don't like me, and I don't blame them. I don't like myself."

In order to function more fully and to communicate more effectively, we need to learn how to gain more awareness of ourselves. Self-control, like control by others, can result in a lack of self-expression. As a result, we may find that we are not sensitive to others with whom we would like to talk. We are not even aware of the topics about which we would enjoy speaking and the situations in which we would find communication pleasant. Or, we may find that we are reticent or aggressive toward others.

Kampf Um Dein Leben

Kampf um dein leben is German for "fight for your life." e. e. cummings expressed the importance of this sentiment when he wrote, "To be nobody—but—yourself in a world which is doing its best, night and day, to make you everybody else means to fight, and never stop fighting."

Explain the significance of cummings's statement. From your own life, describe situations that illustrate the difficulty of self-awareness and self-actualization. How is the fight to be yourself evidenced in your communication with yourself and with others?

Self-Concept

Self-concept is each person's consciousness of his or her total, essential, and particular being. Included in self-concept are all of our physical, social, and psychological perceptions about ourselves. These perceptions are a result of our past, present, and projected experiences and interactions with our environment—including the people in our environment.

Two Components of Self-Concept

Researchers tell us that self-concept is composed of two parts. Your **self-image** is the picture you have of yourself, the sort of person you believe you are. Included in your self-image are the categories in which you place yourself, the roles you play, and other similar descriptors that all of us use to identify ourselves. If you tell an instructor that you are a married woman with three children and "only" a part-time student, you are calling attention to several aspects of your self-image—the roles of wife, mother, and part-time student.

Consider what you say about your academic status. Do you tell people that you are a "part-time student," a "commuter student," a "community college student," a "dormie," a "college student," a "university student," or simply "a student"? The label that you use to identify yourself indicates your self-image and, to some extent, affects your communication.

Our self-image is originally based on categorization by others. Other people categorize us by role: husband, father, wife, mother, boss, student. Others categorize us by personality traits—intelligent, happy, enthusiastic, shy, neurotic, superstitious—or by physical characteristics—fat, tall, beautiful, heavy, wiry. A study a few years ago showed that family roles are used most often in the categorization of other people, followed by occupation, marital status, and religious affiliation.[5]

The roles we play directly influence the way we communicate. The role of parent calls for a kind of communication that is different from a student's. What you say, how you say it, to whom you speak, and how frequently you speak are largely determined by the roles you play.

Self-esteem is the other component of self-concept. **Self-esteem** is how we feel about ourselves, how well we like ourselves. A professional woman shares her self-esteem when she explains that she really enjoys being both a mother and a college professor and seldom feels any conflict between the two roles. You share your self-esteem when you say how excited you are about the prospect of a career in retail sales or industrial management, and how eager you are to begin your work.

Our self-esteem is usually based on our success or failure. If you have a favorable attitude toward yourself, you are said to have "high self-esteem"; if you have unfavorable or negative attitudes toward yourself, you have "low self-esteem." Our self-esteem—whether high or low—is easily observed when we communicate with other people. The way they communicate to us, in turn, affects our own degree of self-esteem.

Excessive concern over self-esteem, however, is often associated with **self-consciousness**. People who are self-conscious are usually shy, easily embarrassed, and anxious in the presence of other people. Most of us are sometimes shy, embarrassed, or anxious. Nearly all public speakers experience stage fright from time to time. A self-conscious person, to make it clearer, suffers stage fright in all situations, to the point of being unwilling to even try to speak before any group. Self-conscious people experience shyness, embarrassment, and anxiety regularly.

Self-Concept in Process

If someone asks you who you are, you might respond in a variety of ways—depending upon the situation, the other person, and the way you feel at the moment. If you are applying for a job and the person requesting information is the prospective employer, you might identify yourself in terms of specific work experience or educational background. If the situation involves an intimate friend or spouse, you would probably respond with far different information—perhaps with more emphasis on your feelings than on your specific experiences.

When we say that one's *self-concept is in process,* we mean that it is not the same in all situations, with all people, and at all times. The view of yourself that you share in class is different from the view of yourself that you share at a party. The self that your employer knows is not the same person your family knows. The stumbling adolescent you once were has become a young adult.

In considering the notion that self-concept changes, we should also consider how it was originally formed. In essence, our self-concepts are determined by the treatment we receive from others and the relationships we have with them. Our self-image, as we have stated, occurs as a result of our being categorized by others. Our self-esteem depends on whether we have been rewarded or punished by others, and for what.

From the moment we were born, and some scholars believe even earlier, the treatment we received from others has influenced who we believe we are. As babies, we responded to the nonverbal messages of hugging, kissing, cuddling, and touching. As we began to understand language, we responded to verbal messages as well. Early verbal messages—"Big boys don't cry," "Little ladies don't make messes," and "Daddy thinks you're the best baby in the whole world"—influenced our self-concept.

Small children are trusting, and they have little experience on which to draw; consequently, they believe what other people tell them. Parental evaluation—verbal and nonverbal—has a particularly strong effect on the development of the child's self-concept. And what the parents believe about the child has a tendency to become a self-fulfilling prophecy.

Dorothy Law Nolte's poem, "Children Learn What They Live," frequently seen in elementary schools and day-care centers, suggests the importance of other people in the perception we hold of our self:

If a child lives with criticism
   he learns to condemn.
If a child lives with hostility
   he learns to fight.
If a child lives with ridicule
   he learns to be shy.
If a child lives with shame
   he learns to feel guilty.
If a child lives with tolerance
   he learns to be patient.
If a child lives with encouragement
   he learns confidence.
If a child lives with praise
   he learns to appreciate.

If a child lives with fairness
   he learns justice.
If a child lives with security
   he learns to have faith.
If a child lives with approval
   he learns to like himself.
If a child lives with acceptance
   and friendship
he learns to find love in the world.[6]

Select two of the predictions Nolte makes and illustrate their truth or falsity by your own way of communicating. If, for example, your parents were very critical of you, have you, in turn, learned to condemn others? If you are self-confident, does it have anything to do with the encouragement you have received from others?

The **self-fulfilling prophecy** is the tendency to become what people expect you to become. In the book *Pygmalion in the Classroom: Teacher Expectation and Pupils' Intellectual Development,* Rosenthal and Jacobson spoke of the importance of the self-fulfilling prophecy. These two researchers summarized a number of studies of academic performance that show that students who are expected to do well actually do perform better. Rosenthal and Jacobson conclude:

To a great extent, our expectations for another person's behavior are accurate because we know his past behavior. But there is now good reason to believe that another factor increased our accuracy of interpersonal predictions or prophecies. Our prediction or prophecy may in itself be a factor in determining the behavior of other people.[7]

The self-fulfilling prophecy is relevant to self-concept. Our concepts of ourselves originated in the responses we received when we were young, but it is the

self-fulfilling prophecies that maintain them. Apparently, we attempt to behave in a way that is consistent with other people's expectations, regardless of whether those expectations are positive or negative. Suppose a small girl is complimented by her family for being quiet, praised by her elementary school teachers for her lack of assertiveness, and encouraged by cultural constraints not to speak up. The result can be a reticent young woman who is afraid to make a speech. On the other hand, suppose a child is praised for talking, is encouraged to put her ideas into words, and is congratulated for winning debates. The result might be a young woman who truly enjoys talking. The self-fulfilling prophecy affects our self-concept, which, in turn, affects our communication with others.

Self-Concept Affects Communication

The way we feel about ourselves and define ourselves affects our communication behavior. Three negative communication behaviors are related to a poor self-concept. If we feel insecure about ourselves we may be overly *defensive;* if we are unsure of our own responses and believe that others are superior to us, we may be *unassertive;* and if we do not trust our interactions with others, we may experience extreme *communication apprehension.* Let us consider each of these behaviors in more detail.

Defensiveness, the tendency to protect ourselves against danger or injury, may occur because we believe that the kind of person we are is not consistent with the kind of person we are supposed to be. In other words, our "real" self is discrepant from our "idealized" self. The difference between these two "selves" causes us to feel uneasy because we are concerned that we will show others our "real" self and be discounted.

Table 5.1 Defensive Versus Supportive Communication Behaviors

Defensive Behaviors	Supportive Behaviors
1. Evaluation	1. Description
2. Control	2. Problem orientation
3. Strategy	3. Spontaneity
4. Neutrality	4. Empathy
5. Superiority	5. Equality
6. Certainty	6. Provisionalism

Six behaviors have been identified as contributing to defensiveness in individuals. These behaviors and their counterparts listed in table 5.1 lead to a supportive communication climate. Let us consider each of these categories in more depth.

Evaluation refers to comments or statements that tend to be judgmental in tone. For instance, "I wouldn't wear my hair like that!" "I never wait until the last minute to study for an exam like you do," and "I don't think people should worry about their future, do you?" are examples of evaluative statements. *Descriptive* statements are not evaluative, but merely reflect the speaker's perceptions. "That hair style is attractive on you; but I couldn't wear it because my face is so long and narrow," "Some people seem to study better under pressure; I find that I do my best work when I am done far in advance," and "I haven't spent much time worrying about the future" replace the evaluative statements above.

Control refers to statements aimed at controlling behavior. For instance, statements like "If you would get up a half an hour earlier you would be better able to start the day with breakfast," "Don't you think you would be a lot happier if you became a speech major like I am?" and "This is a good movie for our tastes, isn't it?" tend to be controlling statements. At the other end of the continuum from control is *problem-orientation,* which suggests that the speaker does not have the one best solution in mind when he or she speaks. Instead, the speaker suggests that the two communicators attempt to find a solution together. Examples of problem-oriented statements are "How do you think you should start the day?" "What major do you think would make you happy?" and "Does this movie fit your tastes?"

Strategy refers to statements that attempt to manipulate the other person into behaving in certain ways. If you tell a friend that you will go shopping with them, but then ask them to make three or four stops on the way so you can take care of some business or academic matters, they may feel that you have manipulated them into driving you around the city. *Spontaneity* refers to honest expression of your current feelings. It is not preplanned or considered in terms of its potential effect. Spontaneous expression leads to supportiveness while strategic expression leads to defensive communication.

Neutrality is contrasted with *empathy* in chapter 7. Neutrality refers to lack of interest or lack of concern for another person and is exemplified in such statements as "I don't care what you do," "I'm not interested in what happened to you," and "Your problems are none of my concern." Empathy, discussed in detail in chapter 7, is trying to understand a situation from the other person's perspective and is demonstrated in such statements as "I understand how you feel," "You know I am interested in helping you in any way that I can," and "Your problems are important to me, too."

Superiority refers to those comments that suggest that one person feels superior to the second and that he or she wants to relate in a superior-subordinate relationship. Comments like "Well, it's about time you realized how our company works," "I guess you're finally growing up," and "Perhaps when you have had more experience you will begin to understand" suggest superiority from the speaker. Conversely, comments like "I don't always understand how this company works either," "We all have more to learn," and "No matter how much experience we have, we can be surprised with the way that things turn out" suggest *equality* between the two communicators.

Certainty is reflected in statements that suggest that the speaker has all of the answers; *provisionalism* suggests that the speaker may not even know all of the answers. An example of certainty is when you assert that someone is a failure at communicating with you, that they will never improve, and that future interactions are out of the question. On the other hand, an example of provisionalism is when you suggest that you and another person appear to be having communication problems and would like to investigate some means of resolving them.[5]

Defensiveness may be a regular response pattern resulting from strong negative feelings about self or it may be a function of current statements from others. Occasionally feeling defensive as a result of people making evaluative, controlling, strategic, neutral, superior, or certainty statements is a natural response. However, recognizing that you respond defensively may assist you in altering your behavior in these occasional circumstances.

We may dismiss occasional defensiveness on the basis that it occurs on rare occasions, that it occurs in response to another person's comments, or on the grounds that it is not overly destructive to effective communication. Regular defensiveness, however, can be a problem. Never being open and honest in communication can lead to shallow interpersonal relationships and a distrust of others. In the next section on "Improving Self-Concept," we will discuss methods of altering the way we view ourselves. If you feel that you use defensiveness as a regular response to others, you may want to consider ways to overcome your negative feelings about yourself to be free of the potential negative effects of defensiveness in your communication behavior. Before we consider how we can improve our self-concept, let us consider the relationship between another communication variable and our self-concept.

Assertiveness, the ability to communicate your feelings, attitudes, and beliefs honestly and directly, is a communication skill associated with positive self-concept. Nonassertive people, conversely, probably suffer from negative self-concept. They do not stand up for their own rights or, if they do stand up for self, it is in a dysfunctional way. Nonassertive people do not acknowledge self. They do not accept the notion of personal rights and are inhibited in the expression of feelings, attitudes, and beliefs. Nonassertive people rarely achieve their own goals and may often be hurt by other people. Perhaps nonassertive people feel that their goal in life is to appease others or to serve others. While they may gain some satisfaction out of caring for another person, their joy may be shortlived if they do not enjoy a reciprocal relationship of having their own needs met.

Assertiveness is different from aggressiveness. Aggressiveness involves standing up for our own rights at the expense of others. We care little about anyone's needs, other than our own. Aggressive people strive to win, regardless of the cost to others. People who interact with aggressive persons often feel a great deal of frustration. As a consequence, the victory of the aggressive person may be only temporary because they lose their friends and do not develop meaningful relationships with others. Aggressive people, too, probably suffer from a negative self-concept. They may feel insecure or unworthy of acceptance and feel that they must compete in order to be accepted by others. Unfortunately, their intense competitiveness often denies them the acceptance they seek.

Assertiveness falls between aggressiveness and nonassertiveness. Assertiveness, as we pointed out above, is probably associated with a positive self-concept. People who are assertive are concerned with their own needs and rights as well as the needs and rights of others. Assertive individuals trust themselves and their responses. They are able to create a supportive communication climate that is marked by openness and honesty. The acceptance of personal rights and the lack of inhibition surrounding self-expression on the part of the assertive communicator encourages effective communication.

A third communication behavior related to negative self-concept is **communication apprehension.** Communication apprehension is defined as the generalized fear of communication regardless of context.[9] People who suffer from communication apprehension may fear communicating in a public speaking situation, an interview, a small group setting, or even in a conversation with one other person. Communication researchers have found that communication apprehension is negatively correlated with self-esteem and self-acceptance.[10] In other words, people who fear communicating with others may also have negative feelings about themselves. If you believe that you have high communication apprehension, you may wish to talk with your speech instructor about specific diagnosis and treatment. In chapter 10 we discuss communication apprehension in more detail, particularly as it applies to the public speaking context. If you feel that you demonstrate defensiveness, nonassertiveness, or communication apprehension, you may find the next section of this chapter helpful.

Improving Self-Concept

There are numerous recent examples of people who have made dramatic changes in their life-style, behavior, and, in turn, their self-concept. Patricia Hearst confused everyone in 1975 and 1976, when she behaved first like a wealthy socialite who was also a college student, then like the victim of a political kidnapping, and later like a member of the political underground.

Abbie Hoffman, one of the Chicago Seven, underwent a similar alteration when he went underground in 1975. Hoffman made numerous changes in his outward appearance and explained, to a *Playboy* interviewer, that he had altered the way he thought about himself. Hoffman said, "Your face changes, you have to be different all the way through."[11]

Charles W. Colson, special counsel to former president Richard M. Nixon, also underwent a profound change. Colson, a "hatchet man" in the Watergate scandal, was tried, found guilty, and sent to prison. When he came out of prison, he professed a deep faith in Jesus Christ and was labeled a "born-again Christian."

Dramatic changes do occur in people. Although none of us might choose to follow the paths of Hearst, Hoffman, or Colson, we can see, in these three people, the possibility of change. If others can change so much, we can at least hope to make small alterations in our own perception of ourselves.

Altering one's self-concept is not a simple matter, however. The "Animal Crackers" cartoon exemplifies the difficulty of change and suggests one of the factors that make change difficult. The people who know us expect us to behave in a certain way. In fact, they helped to create and maintain the self-concept that we have. These people will continue to insist that we maintain a particular self-concept, even when we are attempting to change.

This point can be clarified with an example that may be familiar to you. If your family believes that you are hard to get along with in the morning, you might establish a self-concept that includes being temperamental before 9 A.M. When you attempt to alter your behavior, your family tells you that you remain difficult to deal with at breakfast. Now it is almost impossible to convince yourself that you are the even-tempered person you wish to be, when your family continues to tell you otherwise. Similarly, you may find that ridding yourself of defensive responses is not an easy task since others have learned to expect them from you and may interpret any remark you make as a defensive response.

Sometimes we find ourselves working against ourselves when we try to change our self-concept. For instance, you may see yourself as a procrastinator. Even when you set out to do things on time, you may find that you never quite finish them until it is almost too late. You may be behaving this way because it fits in with another

ANIMAL CRACKERS

element of your self-concept: "responds to pressure," "does magic overnight," or "never lets his friends or family down." We can alter one aspect of our self-concept only to the extent that it is in line with the others. If your nonassertiveness fits with your self-concept of being warm and supportive of others, you may find that it is difficult to become more assertive unless you are also willing to be less supportive on some occasions.

Another problem occurs even when we have changed and others recognize that we have changed. Sometimes we hamper the development of our concepts of ourselves. For example, if you were overweight as a youngster but have now lost the extra poundage, you may properly think you are average weight. Others agree. And still, you may continue to worry about being fat. We must learn how to change our self-concepts and then how to allow the process to occur.

If we wish to change our self-concept in order to improve our ability to communicate with others, at least two steps are essential. First, we need to become aware of ourselves; then we need to establish a positive attitude toward ourselves and, thus, toward others. The first step is not an automatic, natural process, as we said at the beginning of this chapter. We are conditioned to be out of touch with ourselves. We need to develop sensitivity to our own feelings and our own thoughts.

It is essential that we acknowledge *all* our feelings. We are all more familiar with certain aspects of ourselves than others. If we have low self-esteem, we probably focus on those aspects of ourselves that we see as problems or deficiencies. If we have a high self-esteem, we probably ignore our liabilities and focus on our assets. All of us have negative as well as positive characteristics, and it is important that we recognize both of these aspects of ourselves.

Let's take the study of communication as an example. Some people feel that studying communication is a waste of time because they are experienced public speakers. Others feel that they have been successful in small group discussions. Still others feel that they have successfully communicated—with one other person at a time—and that is all they need.

On the other hand, another group of people feels that the study of communication is useless to them because they suffer from communication apprehension. They may feel that they simply cannot give a speech, or that they cannot talk to a member of the opposite sex and never will, or that communication is just frustrating to them, regardless of the communication situation.

The second group, people who suffer from low self-esteem, generalize from one type of communication situation, in which they feel they fail, to all other communication situations. The first group, people who enjoy high self-esteem, generalize from their successes to all other communication situations. It is essential to our understanding of ourselves that we acknowledge all of our abilities and failings and do not make the error of generalizing from one or two specific cases. Few people are competent in every communication situation; fewer still are incompetent in all communication situations.

It is also necessary that we focus on ourselves rather than on others. Instead of using your parents' perception of you, try to establish your own view. Rather than deciding "who you are" on the basis of cultural standards and norms, attempt to make your assessment on the basis of your own standards and norms. No one else knows us as well as we do—it is important that we use the best source available to us.

One woman, Alice, can illustrate the importance of focusing on ourselves instead of on others. She attended an assertiveness training workshop because she was unable to talk to her husband about family finances. She was sure that her husband felt that he should be the family financial expert; yet during the ten years of marriage, Alice witnessed countless near-crises of a financial nature. Every time she tried to talk to her husband, he acted sullen and withdrawn. His responses encouraged her to keep her ideas about finances to herself. Alice found herself in a vicious circle. She believed that he was not competent to handle money and she was unassertive in talking about it.

As Alice worked through her communication problem, she made a number of discoveries. Confronting her husband with the situation, Alice found that he did not really want to handle the money and preferred that she handle the finances. He had only seemed sullen and withdrawn because he was embarrassed by his ineptitude in economics and simple math. Alice also found that she was more capable of balancing the checkbook, budgeting the family resources, and making investigations into investments. She finally realized that she had been taking her cues from her husband rather than herself. Focusing on ourselves, rather than on others, is essential in becoming aware of who we are.

The second step, establishing a positive attitude toward yourself and others, is more difficult. If we are to alter our self-concept, we must strive for the situation in which we believe that we, and other people also, are worthy of liking and acceptance. We need to reject highly critical attitudes both of ourselves and of others. We need to develop the belief that we, and others, have potentialities worthy of respect. We need to free ourselves of anxiety, insecurity, cynicism, defensiveness, and the tendency to be highly evaluative. Our goal should be to free ourselves so we can establish meaningful relationships with ourselves and with others.

It was very important that Alice did not verbally attack her husband for his nonverbal behavior. When she approached him about the problem, she did so in a clear and straightforward way. She did not criticize his inability to handle the finances or his inability to talk to her about his problem. Instead, she tried to communicate her respect for him, while, at the same time, she discussed a problem. She showed her concern about their family's problem while maintaining her love for her husband.

Alice exemplifies the kind of respect that we should feel for everyone. We may not accept another person's behavior, but we need to maintain an appreciation for his or her potentialities that goes beyond the immediate situation. This kind of respect or appreciation of other people allows us to become the kind of person we truly wish to become.

In the album notes for *Sharepickers,*
Mason Williams wrote the following:

Here I Am Again

One night after a concert with a symphony orchestra, I was sitting by myself in my room, wondering what a super-duper love star like me is doing all alone, and I began to feel sorry for myself. I started thinking about where I was and how I had got here. I felt like I was going to cry, so naturally I grabbed my guitar to catch the tears and wrote this song, which is about living a way of life and writing songs off to it beyond the need to.

I realized I was just another blues singer with nothing to be blue about except being stuck having to sing the blues, trapped by the truth—it's not what you don't do that holds you back, it's what you do well that gets you. It seems like if you're successful at something and it comes easy, you always try to free ride it past the right point. I've met a lot of people who are stuck in spiritual ruts because they'd latched onto a magic and tried to ride it too far. Good luck turns bad on you after awhile; you have to learn where to get off. I realized I'd missed my stop. Here I was alone again writing another lonely song about being alone again, instead of really being with a friend. I had used music, God bless it, just to get to the top. It was only a ticket, and here I was fondling my ticket in a hotel room in Hartford, Connecticut, way off the track.

I realized that all my life I'd been afraid—afraid to ask for what I wanted—because of what I wanted. I realized that I had become rich and famous, a star, just so everything would come to me—even more than I could use—and I could take my pick from it without risking rejection. Suddenly it struck me that that's probably why most successful people are unhappy. They get

themselves into a position where they don't have to ask for things, without realizing that if they don't practice asking for what they want from others, they're not good at asking for what they want from themselves—which means they don't know what they want. And you know, you never can satisfy somebody who doesn't know what he wants.

You have to practice asking to be a good asker. What's more, you have to practice *true* asking. You've got to ask for what you really want and not what somebody else wants you to ask for or what you think is right to want. Practice doesn't make perfect unless you practice perfectly.

That's what praying is all about, my friends. To pray is to practice asking, and if you're not really asking, you're not really practicing. A person could spend the rest of his life afraid to ask for what he wants, because of what he wants, whether he really wants it or not.[12]

Williams lends support to the idea that it is essential to know ourselves and our needs in order to be satisfied. Suggest needs of your own that must be fulfilled in order for you to be satisfied. Is it necessary for you to alter your self-concept in order to meet these needs? For instance, if you feel that you need a full-time career in teaching in order to satisfy your desire to serve others, you might have to change your view of yourself as someone who is too busy with a family to pursue a career. If you need a certain amount of time alone each day, you may have to alter your view of yourself as a person who always has time for everybody.

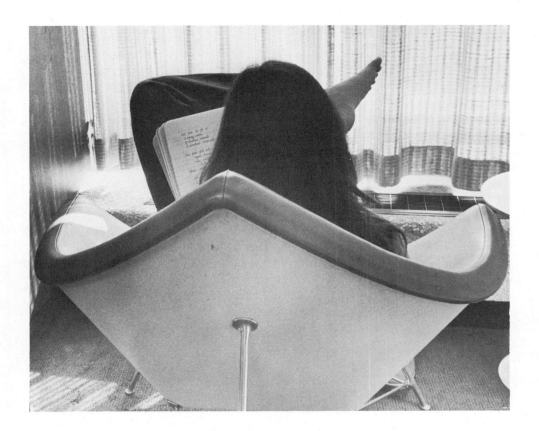

Journal Writing

Journal writing has a long and varied history. The journal has been known as a diary, a memoir, a personal journal, an autobiography, a personal notebook, and a private chronicle. Recently, the journal was discussed in the novel by Erica Jong entitled *How to Save Your Own Life*. Jong suggests that the journal is a way for a person to understand his or her own life. Essentially, the **journal** can be defined as a daily or periodic record of personal experiences and impressions.

In the past, journals have served a variety of functions, including the recording of the events of the day when other means were unavailable, the preservation of the truth as someone perceived it, or the satisfaction of egotistical needs. Journals serve all of these needs today.

The journal is introduced in this chapter because it allows a person to increase his or her self-awareness and improve his or her self-concept. The journal can increase self-awareness by encouraging self-assessment and self-understanding. The journal can improve self-concept by assisting in self-improvement, by providing an outlet for emotional expression, and by offering the possibility of celebrating a person's selfhood. The journal allows us to communicate with ourselves while helping us to improve a basic skill, the ability to communicate.

The following example from a student's journal illustrates the benefits of journal writing.

I'm really surprised by what happened today. Ever since the quarter began—about five weeks ago—I have been upset with my English teacher. He never stops lecturing until ten minutes after the class has ended. Then, he gives assignments, collects papers, and makes announcements. As a result of his lateness, I have to rush across campus and am regularly late for chem lab. The lab instructor has given me hostile looks and I believe she doesn't think I care about the class. I have felt uncomfortable in the lab as a result. Last week we talked about assertiveness in my interpersonal communication class and I decided I would see if it would help me. Today I had an appointment to see my English professor. I told him that I was constantly late for chemistry because I did not have enough time to get to class when we were excused late. It turns out that he didn't realize that morning classes are to be concluded at ten minutes before the hour because afternoon classes end at the hour. He had been following the morning schedule for his afternoon classes. He was really grateful that I had clarified his misunderstanding. When we had class this afternoon, we got out of English on time and I got to my lab. I can't believe it! I could have saved five weeks of being upset if I had only talked to the English professor earlier!

Increasing Self-Awareness

The journal allows people to become increasingly aware of themselves as they assess their characteristics and behavior and as they attempt to understand themselves. One student recognized this function of journal writing after she had written a journal. She commented, "A lot of the factors that have shaped my life seem more clear to me now and I feel more aware of my strengths and weaknesses than before."

Another student was able to relate some of her feelings and thoughts to those she perceived in others. She wrote,

The most surprising thing that I realized while writing this journal is that I'm not alone in my feelings and thoughts. I'm like everyone else in some aspects and unique in others. But, basically, I realized that my problems aren't so different from other people's problems. Right now, I'm really relieved about that. That's not to say that I didn't know it before. I just never sat down and talked about it before and really thought about it.

The principal function of the notebook in Erica Jong's book was to increase her self-awareness and to find patterns in her life. Other authors also emphasize this function of the journal. John Powell, author of *Why Am I Afraid to Tell You Who I Am?* and *The Secret of Staying in Love,* discussed the importance of journal writing in *Fully Human, Fully Alive:*

If people were regularly to practice this kind of gentle but persistent self-examination of their vision, I am sure they would find, as I have, many new insights and an immediate change in the emotional patterns of their lives. Obviously, the more precise and vivid the verbalization in writing of this kind, the greater the likelihood that misconceptions will surface for recognition.[13]

Improving Self-Concept

Journal writing can result in an improvement of a person's self-concept as well as in increased self-awareness. Writing a journal can help you to identify problems in your life and alter your behavior so you can have better relationships with others. You can also rid yourself of strong, negative emotions by putting them on paper. And, in a journal, you can celebrate your joys and successes. An improved self-concept can easily result.

Self-improvement, a worthy function of the journal, can occur in a number of ways. You can review your journal entries to determine if the difficulties you encounter form some kind of pattern. You can confront your problems more directly when you write about them than when you are just thinking about them. This direct confrontation can cause you to consider alternative behavior. Moreover, recording negative experiences is uncomfortable. Rather than deceive yourself by ignoring them, you may choose to change your behavior to minimize such experiences.

The second way that a journal can help you to improve your self-concept is by providing an outlet for your strong emotions. All of us feel anger, bitterness, resentment, impatience, and other emotions that often result in unhappiness if we express them to others. The journal is a ready listener for such emotions, and it will not judge you. One student noted that her journal served as an outlet for her emotional expressions. She discussed her "emotional traumas" and stated that "it is nice to get them on paper. I need to tell someone to relieve my distress and the paper is a patient listener—[I have found] an outlet for my emotions."

A number of writers talk about this function of the journal. In her book *Widow,* Lynn Caine entitles one chapter, "Dear Paper Psychiatrist," and in it discusses the journal she kept after the death of her husband. She considers the various ways that the journal helped her to record the events of her life and her emotional reactions to them. John Powell, in *Fully Human, Fully Alive,* shares an excerpt from his journal and then advises, "I would strongly recommend the use of such a journal every day but especially on those days when emotions have been vibrating uncomfortably."[14]

Your self-concept can be improved in yet another way because journal writing offers you the opportunity to celebrate yourself. One student who appreciated the journal assignment said that she had never before been given credit in college for focusing on herself. Another wrote, "The fact that I was writing about my favorite subject—myself—I found that writing this journal was interesting and enjoyable; I found myself to be deep and interesting."

Throughout history, journal writers have found that the journal allows a celebration of self. Fothergill discusses this motive for writing a journal. He considers the journal of the eighteenth-century English figure, James Boswell, and concludes,

Boswell discusses with himself his purposes in keeping so energetic a journal. . . . Two themes run through his formulations on the subject. One is the conventional rationale in terms of self-knowledge and self-improvement, the other a sheer and unabashed celebration of his own personality. . . . It is a book of the self in the fullest sense, the book of Boswell, intended for readers who love a parade.[15]

Summary

In this chapter we discussed the importance of self in communication. We discussed self-awareness and considered the parental and social conditioning that reinforces our lack of self-awareness. We stated that self-awareness is essential to our mental health and to our ability to communicate competently.

Self-concept was defined as each person's consciousness of his or her total, essential, and particular being. Self-concept consists of self-image and self-esteem. Self-images are the pictures we have of ourselves or the sort of persons that we believe we are. Included in our self-images are the categories in which we place ourselves, the roles we play, and the other ways in which we identify ourselves.

Self-esteem is how we feel about ourselves, or how well we like ourselves. To have a high self-esteem is to have a favorable attitude toward yourself; to have a low self-esteem is to have an unfavorable attitude toward yourself. Self-consciousness is excessive concern about self-esteem; it is characterized by shyness, embarrassment, and anxiety in the presence of others.

Self-concept is in process. Our self-concepts change with the situation, the other person or people involved, and our own moods. One's self-concept is originally formed by the treatment received from others and one's relationships with them. It is maintained largely as a self-fulfilling prophecy. The self-fulfilling prophecy is the tendency to become whatever people expect you to become.

Our self-concept affects our communication behavior. We considered the negative self-concept that results in behavioral communication apprehension, defensive communication behavior, and in a lack of assertiveness. These behaviors may persist until we are able to establish more positive feelings about ourselves.

Self-concept can be improved. We considered the difficulty, but possibility, of altering our concepts of ourselves. The two essential steps in changing self-concept are becoming aware of ourselves and establishing a positive attitude toward ourselves and others.

In the final section of this chapter, we considered journal writing. The journal was defined as a daily or periodic record of personal experiences and impressions. Although the journal can serve a variety of functions, it is introduced in this text to help you increase your self-awareness through self-assessment and self-understanding. It allows us to improve our self-concepts through self-improvement, by providing an outlet for emotional expression, and by affording us the possibility of celebrating ourselves.

Additional Readings

Adler, Ronald B. *Confidence in Communication: A Guide to Assertive and Social Skills*. New York: Holt, Rinehart and Winston, 1977.
Adler views assertiveness as a communication variable. He discusses the background and theory of assertion, the basic steps involved in becoming more assertive, and particular applications of assertiveness in a person's life. While this book was originally written as a textbook for a course in assertiveness training, an individual could use it to construct his or her own self-modification program.

*Gergen, Kenneth J. *The Concept of Self*. New York: Holt, Rinehart and Winston, 1971.
A research approach to the definition and development of self-concept. Describes the influence of self-concept on our behavior and summarizes research findings about factors that affect our self-concept.

Goffman, Erving. *The Presentation of Self in Everyday Life*. Garden City, N.Y.: Doubleday & Co., 1959.
Goffman discusses the intentional and unintentional, the honest and the deceitful ways in which we tell others and ourselves who we are. By using the analogy of the theatre, the author explains how we present and maintain masks in our interactions with others.

*Horrocks, John E., and Jackson, Dorothy W. *Self and Role: A Theory of Self-Process and Role Behavior*. Boston: Houghton Mifflin Company, 1972.
A scholarly discussion of the definition, development, and presentation of self, including the factors that influence the self and ways in which the self influences our thinking, perception, and communication.

Jourard, Sidney M. *The Transparent Self: Self-Disclosure and Well-Being*. New York: Van Nostrand Reinhold Company, 1964.
The skill of self-disclosure: how to develop an honest and open self, barriers to effective self-disclosure, and the role of self-disclosure in improving interpersonal relationships.

Lair, Jess. *I Ain't Much Baby, but I'm All I've Got*. New York: Doubleday & Co., 1972.
Advice on how to become a genuine, real person by understanding and controlling your behavior. Lair believes that trust and love stem from an honest knowledge and acceptance of yourself. Written from personal experience in an interesting and stimulating manner.

Powell, John. *The Secret of Staying in Love*. Niles, Ill.: Argus Communications, 1974.
Powell focuses on the fundamental human need for a "true and deep love of self," explores the problems of loving, the nature of love, and ways to find and maintain a high self-esteem. Written in a direct and personal style that holds one's attention.

Prather, Hugh. *Notes to Myself*. Moab, Utah: Real People Press, 1970.
An easy-to-read highly thought-provoking collection of ideas tracing one man's struggle for self-awareness. Insightful, nontheoretical treatment of self-concept, self-awareness, and self-expression.

Zimbardo, Philip G. *Shyness: What It Is and What to Do About It*. Reading, Mass.: Addison-Wesley Publishing Co., 1977.
Zimbardo is a psychologist who has done extensive research and writing

*Indicates more advanced readings.

on the subject of shyness. This book is divided into two major sections—what shyness is and what we can do about shyness. Zimbardo suggests methods for building self-esteem, developing social skills, helping others overcome their shyness, and preventing shyness in our society.

Notes

1. Abraham H. Maslow, "Hierarchy of Needs," in *Motivation and Personality,* 2d ed., New York: Harper & Row, Publishers, 1970), pp. 35–72. Copyright © 1970 by Abraham H. Maslow.
2. Will Schutz, *Here Comes Everybody* (New York: Harper & Row, Publishers, 1971), p. 1. Reprinted by permission.
3. "It's All Right to Cry" by Carol Hall, from *Free To Be . . . You and Me* published by McGraw-Hill. Copyright © 1972 Free To Be Foundation, Inc. Used by permission.
4. Jane Anderson, "Discover Yourself: Go Hiking Alone," Fort Wayne *Journal-Gazette,* March 21, 1976.
5. Michael Argyle, *Social Interaction* (New York: Atherton Press, 1969), p. 133.
6. Dorothy Law Nolte, "Children Learn What They Live," 1954.
7. Robert Rosenthal and Lenore Jacobson, *Pygmalion in the Classroom: Teacher Expectation and Pupils' Intellectual Development* (New York: Holt, Rinehart and Winston, 1968), p. vii.
8. Jack R. Gibb, "Defensive Communication," *The Journal of Communication* 11 (1961):141–48.
9. James C. McCroskey, "Measures of Communication-Bound Anxiety," *Speech Monographs* 37(1970):269–70.
10. James C. McCroskey, John A. Daly, Virginia P. Richmond, and Raymond L. Falcione, "Studies of the Relationship between Communication Apprehension and Self-Esteem," *Human Communication Research* 3(1977):269–77.
11. "Playboy Interview: Abbie Hoffman," *Playboy* (May 1976): 64.
12. Mason Williams, "Here I Am Again," liner notes from *Sharepickers.* Copyright by Mason Williams. Used by permission. All rights reserved.
13. Reprinted from John Powell, *Fully Human, Fully Alive,* p. 152. Copyright © 1976 by Argus Communications. Used with permission from Argus Communications, Niles, Ill.
14. Reprinted from John Powell, *Fully Human, Fully Alive,* p. 154. Copyright © 1976 by Argus Communications. Used with permission from Argus Communications, Niles, Ill.
15. Robert A. Fothergill, *Private Chronicles: A Study of English Diaries* (London: Oxford University Press, 1974), p. 77.

6
Sharing Yourself

Objectives

1. Define self-disclosure and explain its importance
2. Discuss the relationship among trust, respect, and self-disclosure
3. Identify the factors that affect your willingness to self-disclose
4. Discuss the relationship between self-disclosure and the growth of a relationship
5. Name five guidelines to appropriate self-disclosure

Key Terms

self-disclosure
Johari Window
open area
blind area
hidden area

unknown area
positive self-disclosure
negative self-disclosure
appropriate self-disclosure
intimate self-disclosure

In order to see I have to be willing to be seen.[1]

People who need people are the luckiest people in the world.[2]

The cartoon, the portion of the poem, and the excerpt from the song all serve to introduce us to the specific topic of this chapter. Understanding and sharing form the basis of communication. In chapter 5 we talked about understanding ourselves. In this chapter we will focus on sharing ourselves with others. Sharing ourselves requires multiple skills. It is important that we understand our verbal and nonverbal language choices as discussed in chapters 3 and 4; it is essential that we are able to defend ourselves when necessary and to take responsibility for our own feelings, attitudes, and behaviors as discussed in chapter 5; and finally, we must seek clear and specific feedback, which will be discussed in greater detail in chapter 7. In this chapter we will focus on self-disclosure, which is synonymous with sharing ourselves with other people.

Definition of Self-Disclosure

The term that is most frequently associated with a person's ability to share himself or herself with others is **self-disclosure.** The current definition of self-disclosure is broad—it includes any statement a person makes about himself or herself. A few researchers have narrowed this definition to include only statements that are intentional, conscious, or voluntary. Other writers have suggested that the term *self-disclosure* should be reserved for statements about oneself that another person would be unlikely to know or discover. Because we are more interested in intentional communication, rather than in random and unplanned statements, and because we are more interested in those statements about ourselves that others are unlikely to discover through observation, we will focus on the most limited definition of self-disclosure. For our purposes, self-disclosure consists of those statements about oneself that are intentional and that the other person is unlikely to know. Self-disclosure can be as unthreatening as saying how you feel about a particular movie or how much studying you have been doing, or it can be as difficult as telling someone that her use of obscenity makes you feel uncomfortable or that you have allowed your baby to be adopted.

Importance of Self-Disclosure

Self-disclosure is important for a variety of reasons. When we talk about ourselves, about our feelings and perceptions, we develop a greater understanding and awareness of ourselves. Self-disclosure can also result in self-improvement. As other people provide feedback to us, we can identify some of the problems we face and some mistakes we are making. However, others cannot provide accurate or helpful feedback unless we self-disclose.

Self-Disclosure Allows Us to Develop a Greater Understanding of Ourselves

In order to understand the degree of self-understanding and self-improvement that is possible through self-disclosure, consider the **Johari Window** depicted in figure 6.1. This diagram, created by Joseph Luft and Harrington Ingham, depicts

Figure 6.1 The Johari Window.

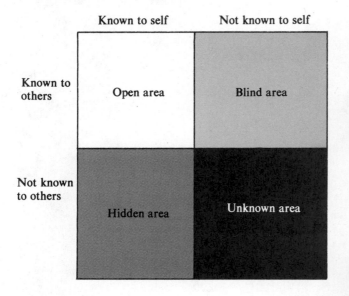

Known to self Not known to self

Known to others

Open area

Blind area

Not known to others

Hidden area

Unknown area

Figure 6.2

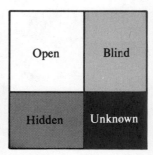

| Open | Blind |
| Hidden | Unknown |

Figure 6.3

| Open | Blind |
| Hidden | Unknown |

four kinds of information about a person. The **open area** consists of information that is known to you and known to other people. It includes such information as your height, your approximate weight, and your sex—obvious to an observer—as well as information you freely disclose, such as the courses in which you are enrolled, your major, and your home town. The **blind area** consists of information that is known to others, but unknown to you. Included in this area are personality characteristics—you are temperamental in the morning, you are assertive, or you are cynical—that others perceive but that you do not recognize or acknowledge. The **hidden area** includes information that is not known to other people, but that is known to you. It includes any information that you choose not to disclose to others. The **unknown area** includes information that is unknown to you and to others. Any characteristics or potentialities that you may have that have not been considered by yourself or by others is included in this area.

The Johari Window does not consist of four areas that are unchanging in size, nor of four necessarily equal areas. The four areas differ dramatically from person to person and vary within the same person and in the same relationship. Figure 6.2 might represent your Johari Window now, and figure 6.3 might better depict your Johari Window when you were in high school. As the size of one of the areas changes, the size of the other areas also changes.

Self-Disclosure Can Result in Self-Improvement

Self-disclosure allows you to increase the size of the open area and to decrease the size of the other three areas. In talking about a number of happy experiences you have had, you may suddenly realize why they were all happy. In learning more about yourself, you decrease the unknown area and increase the open area. In discussing clothes with a friend, you may discover that others view you as a style setter. Since others share this perception of you, and you have been unaware of it, you reduce the blind area on the Johari Window and increase the open area. The Johari Window illustrates that increased self-disclosure can result in greater understanding and awareness of ourselves and can result in self-improvement.

Self-Disclosure Allows Us to Establish More Meaningful Relationships with Others

Self-disclosure, which makes us more open, often generates self-disclosure from others. In this way, we can all become more open to ourselves and to others. Both self-knowledge and knowledge of others increases.

Consider your communication with the person to whom you feel closest. Have you engaged in a great deal of self-disclosure? Now consider what you say or write to someone with whom you have only an acquaintanceship. How does your self-disclosure differ? Self-disclosure is offered most frequently and regularly to close friends. Self-disclosure allows relationships to grow in depth and meaning.

An inability to self-disclose, on the other hand, can result in the death of a relationship. One of the common explanations for divorce given by women is their need to self-disclose. Divorced women are increasingly identifying their own lack of opportunity to express who they are as the cause of the breakup of their marriages. Without opportunities for self-disclosure, relationships appear to be doomed to shallowness, superficiality, or death. A more humorous example of the way that self-disclosure encourages relationship development is provided in this cartoon. Dagwood's disclosure of his feelings are interpreted appropriately by his friends in the pool hall.

BLONDIE

Self-Disclosure Allows Us to Establish More Positive Attitudes toward Ourselves and Others

In an article entitled "Shy Murderers," Lee, Zimbardo, and Bertholf discuss the person who is overcontrolled and shy and, because of his frustration, attacks others. They suggest that this kind of person needs to learn how to express feelings directly to others. They continue:

The social skills we've outlined should be learned by every child as a normal part of socialization. Children should be encouraged to express their feelings and to like themselves. They should come to see other people as sources of positive regard and interest, not as critical, negative evaluators who might reject them. They, and we, must be seen *and* heard.[3]

Both **positive and negative self-disclosure** can result in more positive attitudes about ourselves and others. If we disclose positive information about ourselves, we share the joy that we feel about ourselves. When we tell others about our hopes and dreams, when we share happy moments, and when we recall exciting experiences, we feel encouraged. Others reinforce our feeling by offering their support, enthusiasm, and encouragement.

Although it may seem paradoxical, negative self-disclosure can also result in more positive attitudes about ourselves and others. When we are able to expose our negative qualities, our mistakes, our failings, and our shortcomings, and when others are able to do the same, we can recognize that we are all fallible, that no one is perfect. We become more understanding and forgiving and we develop more positive attitudes about all humankind by sharing negative disclosures.

One student wrote that she originally had not seen the importance of self-disclosure in interpersonal communication, but during the course of the quarter, she learned its significance. She wrote:

I always thought that interpersonal communication would be like the required English courses that I took. It might be interesting, but it would not be applicable in the real world. As I sat listening to the professor's lecture on self-disclosure, I recall thinking, "How nice, but does it really matter? Does your interpersonal communication really improve when you are aware of your own feelings and are able to communicate them to others?"

Like many times in my life before, I found I was wrong. The amazing thing was, I proved myself wrong, not in class, but in a real life situation, in the bar where I work as a waitress. One night, two girls were holding hands and another waitress told me about it. As I always had, I just said, "If that's their bag, it doesn't bother me."

Many of my customers commented on the girls, especially after they got up and slow-danced together. The remarks ranged from "Isn't that sickening?" to "I think I need a double." I just repeated to each of them what I had told the waitress who first pointed them out to me, "If that's their thing, then I don't mind."

After about twenty minutes, the girls got up to leave. I had my back to them as they were walking out, but I saw them out of the corner of my eye. As they passed, one of the girls slapped my bottom. In a rage of anger, humiliation, and indignation, I whirled with clenched fists to strike her. Fortunately, as it later turned out, they were out the door before I could get to her. I ran to the bar manager, practically in tears and shaking like a leaf, and yelled at him that if they came back in again and one of them touched me, he'd better call an ambulance because I would kill her.

They did return a few minutes later. To my embarrassment, the band stopped playing. One of the girls announced that she and her friend were anthropology majors at the university and were completing a term project. She asked for any feedback and reactions that the crowd had.

I did not talk to them, mainly because I was too confused, and too surprised by my own reaction. That night, in bed, I ran the incident over and over in my mind and tried to examine my true feelings. By examining my reaction, I came to many conclusions about myself that I had never realized before.

First, my statement, "Let them do their own thing," was far from my true feeling—so far off that it surprised even me when I admitted it. I really felt hatred for these people because they dared to break a norm. I felt threatened by them.

Second, my reaction to the two women was similar to other statements I had made, but didn't really feel. I guess that a lot of the statements I make are because I want to seem better than everyone else. I want to appear as though I can accept things that others can't.

If the anthropology majors learned nothing from their experiment, I learned a great deal. Since then I have tried to think about how I really feel before I say anything. I still catch myself saying things that I don't really mean, but at least now I realize it afterwards. I'm glad I enrolled in interpersonal communication—if nothing else, I learned the importance of genuine self-disclosure.

Interference with Self-Disclosure

If self-disclosure is an aspect of interpersonal communication that is important to the way we view ourselves and others, we should consider why we are often unwilling to self-disclose to others. In general, we can say that people are reluctant to self-disclose because of their negative feelings about themselves or their negative feelings about others. In other words, they do not respect themselves, they do not trust others, or both.

The Risk of Self-Disclosure

Franz Kafka wrote the following short story, entitled "Give It Up!"

It was early in the morning, the streets clean and empty, I was going to the train station. When I compared a tower clock with my watch, I saw that it was already much later than I had thought. I had to hurry, the terror over this discovery made me uncertain as to the way. I did not know this city very well yet. Fortunately, a police officer was nearby. I ran to him and asked him breathlessly for the way. He smiled and said: "You want to know the way from me?" "Yes," I said, "since I can't find it myself." "Give it up, give it up," he said and turned away with a wide sweep, just like people who want to be alone with their laughter.[4]

It is unclear why the police officer answered as he did and it is unclear what he meant by his answer. It is clear that he failed to respond to the first person's negative self-disclosure—that he was unable to find his way. Suggest explanations for his answer. What response would have been appropriate to such an answer? Could the first person have asked his first question in a different way in order to elicit a different answer?

Two contemporary writers have discussed the risk involved in self-disclosure. In *The Shoes of the Fisherman,* Morris L. West wrote:

It costs so much to be a full human being that there are very few who have the enlightenment or the courage to pay the price. . . . One has to abandon altogether the search for security, and reach out to the risk of living with both arms. One has to embrace the world like a lover. One has to accept pain as a condition of existence. One has to court doubt and darkness as the cost of knowing. One needs a will stubborn in conflict, but apt always to total acceptance of every consequence of living and dying.[5]

In *Why Am I Afraid to Tell You Who I Am?* John Powell writes that he asked a number of people the question that forms the title of his book. The response of one of his friends to the question, "Why are you afraid to tell me who you are?" was to the point. He answered, "Because if I tell you who I am, you may not like who I am, and that's all that I have."[6] In essence, his friend was stating that he did not respect himself enough to trust others with the information. Frequently, our lack of positive feelings about ourselves or about others contributes to our inability to self-disclose.

Fear of situations that are not under our control and our lack of trust of other people can result in our refusal to self-disclose to others. In time, this fear and lack of trust becomes permanent and our refusal to self-disclose becomes habitual.

We are probably taught very early in our lives to avoid self-disclosure. The same kinds of responses that interfere with our self-awareness contribute also to our difficulty in self-disclosing. Our parents taught us that positive self-disclosure was bragging. Significant others responded negatively to us when we made negative self-disclosures. The message we seemed to hear was that self-disclosures should be avoided.

Guidelines for Self-Disclosure

Self-disclosure, as we have defined it, occurs when we voluntarily tell someone else about ourselves. In the many conversations that we have each day, we have the opportunity to self-disclose. In some situations, self-disclosure is appropriate; in others, it is not. The conversation that you have with your postal carrier probably does not involve self-disclosure; the exchange that you have with one of your parents probably does. Self-disclosure generally does not occur in the impersonal interactions in which you engage but it does occur within established relationships, within developing relationships, and, to a lesser extent, in deteriorating relationships. As you read this section on guidelines for self-disclosure, consider the many conversations in which you are engaged each day.

Self-disclosure reflects our present reactions to people and situations. In other words, self-disclosure is spontaneous, rather than manipulative or planned. In the student paper at the beginning of this chapter, the student wrote that she had often said things in order to appear superior to others. Those statements were not only untrue, but they lacked spontaneity and tended to be manipulative.

Self-disclosure is probably better when it is specific rather than general, tentative rather than unchanging, and informing rather than threatening. We should not self-disclose in a general, arrogant, or threatening way. Self-disclosure should help us to build relationships, rather than destroying those that already exist.

The research into self-disclosure is fairly recent, and there are few consistent conclusions. Nonetheless, the studies suggest that there are norms governing self-disclosure. These norms strongly influence the appropriateness and inappropriateness of self-disclosure in particular situations, at particular points in a relationship, for particular persons, and for specific topics. Let us consider some generalizations from the research that should guide our self-disclosure.

Self-Disclosure Should Be Reciprocal or Shared

Self-disclosure is generally not one-sided in an enduring, successful interpersonal relationship. No characteristic of self-disclosing communication is documented as well as the finding that as the disclosure of one person increases, so does the self-disclosure of the other person.[7]

131   Sharing Yourself

Two interpretations of this phenomenon have been offered. Jourard suggested that people disclose only when they feel safe and that being able to disclose is positively valued by others. As a consequence, persons self-disclose after another person has self-disclosed because they feel safe and able to do so.[8] Worthy, Gary, and Kahn used a social exchange theory—a theory that holds that we exchange communication of an equal or comparable value—to explain reciprocal self-disclosure. They suggest that people only reveal themselves to friends. And when they are the recipients of self-disclosure, they feel that they are liked or trusted. Being trusted or liked is rewarding. It also obligates the receivers of self-disclosure to reciprocate by disclosing themselves to the other person.[9]

The implication of these findings is that **appropriate self-disclosure** is reciprocal. If the person to whom you are self-disclosing refuses to self-disclose, you should stop. If a person with whom you are communicating is freely self-disclosing, you, too, should feel free to self-disclose. If you wish to self-disclose in the course of a conversation, you might try some low-risk self-disclosure to determine if the other person can, and will, make a similar disclosure.

132   Intrapersonal and Interpersonal Communication

Self-Disclosure Is Related to the Duration of a Relationship

Self-disclosure usually develops slowly, increasing as the relationship endures and becomes more stable and permanent. The only exception occurs when strangers, who expect no future interaction, meet. In such situations, self-disclosure may occur quickly.[10] In a study of **self-disclosure** that dealt with male freshman roommates, the pattern of self-disclosure that emerged seemed fairly generalizable. First, a relatively high level of ordinary information was disclosed, then intimate information was disclosed at a gradually increasing rate.[11]

Most of us have had the experience of sitting next to a stranger whom we expect never to see again, on a bus, an airplane, or in some other public place. The other person may have disclosed a great deal, or we may have disclosed a great deal about ourselves to the other person. This tendency to talk about ourselves to strangers has been demonstrated in studies. On the other hand, people do not prefer this setting for self-disclosure. In one study, it was found that people who were strangers preferred the company of those who disclosed very little rather than of those who disclosed a great deal.[12] Three other researchers have concluded that if intimate disclosures are inappropriately timed, others may perceive the person who is disclosing as suffering from maladjustment or inappropriate socialization.[13] This conclusion was verified by two other psychologists who stated, "Intimate disclosure to a stranger or an acquaintance was seen by observers as less appropriate and more maladjusted than nondisclosure."[14]

In a more recent study, two communication scholars were able to secure more specific information about the effect of the length of a relationship on self-disclosure. Gilbert and Whiteneck found that if a person were going to disclose ordinary facts, he or she would first disclose positive statements, then neutral statements, and, finally negative statements. If the person were disclosing intimate information, the likelihood of disclosure would be negative statements, followed by positive, and ending with neutral. They concluded that the duration of a relationship affected the kind of self-disclosure that seemed appropriate.[15]

Gilbert and Whiteneck's conclusion can be explained by Blau's earlier hypothesis. Blau suggested that one person's attraction to another was dependent on the anticipation and belief that the association would be rewarding.[16] In other words, we are attracted to people who seem impressive, who have attractive qualities, and who create the impression that associating with them will be rewarding. To be attractive, therefore, people should present themselves positively in the initial stages of a relationship. Disclosure of one's negative aspects should be reserved for relationships that have persisted longer.

Self-disclosure should be appropriate to the length of a relationship. You can apply this principle to your own life. You should not disclose yourself to strangers; you should reserve intimate self-disclosures for persons whom you have known for some time; and you should disclose positive information about yourself before you disclose negative information.

Self-Disclosure Should Be Appropriate for the Person to Whom You Are Self-Disclosing

In general, except for strangers whom we do not expect to see again, the research shows that we disclose ourselves most to persons to whom we feel close or toward whom we feel affectionate.[17] Jourard and Lasakow showed that the willingness of people to disclose is dependent on their relationship with the other person. Young unmarried people disclosed most to their mothers, their fathers, their male friends, and their female friends, in that order. Married people disclosed more to their spouses than to any other people.[18]

It has also been shown that the verbal and nonverbal behavior of the other person affects people's willingness to self-disclose. Researchers found that people will disclose more to persons who are perceived as warm, genuine, and understanding than to others.[19]

The Gilbert and Whiteneck study we have already cited concluded that highly negative disclosures are reserved for intimate relationships. The relationship should be intimate before you disclose highly negative information about yourself.[20]

The implications of this research are clear. You should disclose most to people for whom you have affection and to whom you feel close. You should be sensitive to the verbal and nonverbal cues that the other person transmits, particularly as they relate to that person's warmth, genuineness, and understanding. And you should reserve disclosures of highly negative information for your intimate friends or members of your family.

Self-Disclosure Is Related to the Topic under Discussion

The topic under consideration also affects self-disclosure. Taylor and Altman determined that the type of information to be disclosed influenced the level of self-disclosure.[21] Marital satisfaction was found to be affected more by the couple's satisfaction with the topics being considered and the information disclosed rather than by the amount of disclosure.[22] One researcher found that "shared activities" and "children and careers" were the only two of seventeen different topics in which disclosure was related to marital satisfaction.[23]

Because the research is limited, the implications are ambiguous. You should keep in mind, however, that the topic under discussion may affect the amount of self-disclosure that is appropriate and satisfying.

Self-Disclosure Depends on the Person Who Is Disclosing

We must consider ourselves in the process called "self-disclosure." Who we are affects our willingness and our ability to self-disclose and our willingness to engage in self-disclosive communication. But we know relatively little about what kinds of people self-disclose and what distinguishes them from people who do not. In a recent study of the role of sex in self-disclosure, Gilbert and Whiteneck found that men are more likely to disclose earlier in the development of a relationship than women; that men are less likely to make positive statements about themselves than women; but that both sexes are equally likely to make negative statements about themselves.[24] Positive statements included statements such as "I really did well on the English exam," "My wife is really helpful in my career," and "I scored sixteen points in the last basketball game." Negative statements included "I think I have to drop out of school," "My girlfriend wants to break up," and "I don't seem to be able to make any friends."

We must keep in mind, then, that in self-disclosure, we have to suit ourselves. Many factors affect our ability and our willingness to self-disclose. Our own comfort, satisfaction, and needs must be taken into account when we share ourselves with others.

Applying the Principles

The guidelines for self-disclosure are somewhat abstract. In order to test your understanding and ability to apply these guidelines to specific situations, complete the following exercise.

For each situation, determine whether the information that is disclosed is appropriate or inappropriate.

Write "Appropriate" in the blank if the self-disclosure is appropriate for the people involved, their relationship to each other, and other relevant variables. Write "Inappropriate" if one of the guidelines has been disregarded and try to identify the specific one.

Appropriate or Inappropriate

1. You are with a friend who seems distracted and you begin to talk about your marital problems.

   _____

2. You are being interviewed for a job and you tell your prospective employer that you must have the job so that you won't have to move back home with your parents.

   _____

3. You are on a bus and the woman next to you begins to tell you about her abortion.

   _____

4. You are a woman, and you walk up to a stranger in a bar and begin to tell him about yourself.

   _____

5. You tell your wife or husband that you suspect that you have lung cancer and that your fear of the disease is unbearable.

   _____

Summary

In this chapter we considered self-disclosure. We defined self-disclosure as the ability to voluntarily tell other people things about ourselves that they are unlikely to know or to learn from others.

Self-disclosure is important because it allows us to develop a greater understanding and awareness of ourselves, because it can result in self-improvement, because it allows us to establish more meaningful relationships with others, and because it allows us to establish more positive attitudes about ourselves and others. We show reluctance to disclose ourselves because we do not respect ourselves and because we do not trust others.

We can find five guidelines for self-disclosure in the research on the subject: self-disclosure should be reciprocal or shared; it is related to the duration of a relationship; self-disclosure should be appropriate for the person to whom you are self-disclosing; it should be appropriate to the topic under discussion; self-disclosure depends on the person who is making the disclosure.

We turn from this focus on the self to a consideration of the other person. Interpersonal communication involves at least two people. Self-disclosure is important, but equally important is our ability to understand others through listening and empathy, the topic of chapter 7.

Additional Readings

*Chelune, G. J. "Nature and Assessment of Self-Disclosing Behavior." In *Advances in Psychological Assessment,* edited by P. W. McReynolds, vol. 4. San Francisco: Jossey-Bass, 1978. Chelune presents a review of the current literature on self-disclosure. He defines and delineates self-disclosure as a communication construct. The measurement of self-disclosure is thoroughly considered.

Egan, Gerard. *Interpersonal Living: A Skills/Contract Approach to Human Relations Training in Groups.* Belmont, Calif.: Wadsworth Publishing Co., 1976. Self-disclosure is discussed as a prerequisite for the development of a meaningful relationship. A brief theoretical explanation of self-disclosure is offered, and a detailed list of behavioral guidelines to appropriate self-disclosure is given.

*Goffman, Erving. *The Presentation of Self in Everyday Life.* Garden City, N.Y.: Doubleday & Co., 1959. Goffman discusses self-disclosure as a method of presenting our characters to others and advises that we manage the impression of ourselves to others by wearing masks that may hinder communication.

Gordon, Chad, and Gergen, Kenneth J. *The Self in Social Interaction.* New York: John Wiley & Sons, 1968. Pages 299–308. The authors relate the need for consistency to the factors of motivation, environment, and other people that determine the way we present ourselves to others. Contains some interesting insights into why we tend to disclose certain kinds of information to others, and into some

*Indicates more advanced readings.

of the problems associated with full self-disclosure.

*Jourard, Sidney. "Healthy Personality and Self-Disclosure." In *The Self in Social Interaction,* edited by Chad Gordon and Kenneth J. Gergen. New York: John Wiley & Sons, Inc., 1968. Pages 423–34.
A synthesis of several works by Jourard, this selection is a discussion of the relationship between the ability to disclose the self and the development of a healthy self-concept. Self-disclosure is related to age, sex, interpersonal competence, personality, and interpersonal contexts.

Rogers, Carl R. *On Becoming a Person.* Boston: Houghton Mifflin Company, 1961.
A thorough discussion of trust, self-awareness, and self-disclosure as they relate to the growth of a fully functioning self. Rogers discloses the decisions and guidelines that have helped him become more effective in presenting his self-image to others. Insightful reading.

Notes

1. Hugh Prather, *Notes to Myself* (Moab, Utah: Real People Press, 1970). Used with permission.
2. From the song "People" by Bob Merrill and Jule Styne. Copyright © 1963 and 1964 by Bob Merrill and Jule Styne, Chappell-Styne, Inc., and Wonderful Music Corp., owners of publication and allied rights throughout the world. Chappell & Co., Inc., sole and exclusive agent. International Copyright Secured. All Rights Reserved. Used by permission.
3. Melvin Lee, Philip G. Zimbardo, and Minerva Bertholf, "Shy Murderers," *Psychology Today* 11 (November 1977): 148.
4. Franz Kafka, "Give It Up!" in *The Complete Stories,* ed. Nathum N. Glatzer (New York: Schocken Books, 1972), p. 456.
5. Reprinted by permission of William Morrow & Company, Inc. from *The Shoes of the Fisherman* by Morris L. West. Copyright © 1963 by Morris L. West.
6. John Powell, *Why Am I Afraid to Tell You Who I Am?* (Niles, Ill.: Argus Communications, 1969), p. 12.
7. P. C. Cozby, "Self-Disclosure: A Literature Review," *Psychological Bulletin* 79 (1973): 73–91; S. Jourard and M. J. Landsman, "Cognition, Cathexis, and the 'Dyadic Effect' in Men's Self-Disclosing Behavior," *Merrill-Palmer Quarterly of Behavior and Development* 9 (1960): 141–48; S. Jourard and J. L. Resnick, "Some Effects on Self-Disclosure Among College Women," *Journal of Humanistic Psychology* 10 (1970): 84–93; S. Jourard and P. Jaffe, "Influence of an Interviewer's Disclosure on the Self-Disclosing Behavior of Interviewees," *Journal of Counseling Psychology* 17 (1970): 252–97; H. Erlich and D. Graeven, "Reciprocal Self-Disclosure in a Dyad," *Journal of Experimental Social Psychology* 7 (1971): 389–400; G. Levinger and D. Senn, "Disclosure of Feelings in Marriage," *Merrill-Palmer Quarterly of Behavior and Development* 13 (1967): 237–49; P. Cozby, "Self-Disclosure, Reciprocity, and Liking," *Sociometry* 35 (1972): 151–60; and F. M. Levin and K. Gergen, "Revealingness, Ingratiation, and the Disclosure of Self," *Proceedings of the 77th Annual Convention,* American Psychological Association, 1969, pp. 447–48.
8. S. Jourard, *The Transparent Self,* 2d ed. (New York: Van Nostrand Reinhold Company, 1971).
9. W. Worthy, A. Gary, and G. M. Kahn, "Self-Disclosure as an Exchange Process," *Journal of Personality and Social Psychology* 13 (1969): 59–63.
10. P. T. Quinn, "Self-Disclosure as a Function of Degree of Acquaintance and Potential Power," (Master's thesis, Ohio State University, 1965).
11. D. A. Taylor, "Some Aspects of the Development of Interpersonal Relationships: Social Penetration Process," *Technical Report No. 1* (Center for Research on Social Behavior, University of Delaware, 1965).

12. S. A. Culbert, "Trainer Self-Disclosure and Member Growth in Two T-Groups," *Journal of Applied Behavioral Science* 4 (1968): 47–73.

13. C. A. Kiesler, S. Kiesler, and M. Pallack, "The Effects of Commitment on Future Interaction on Reactions to Norm Violations," *Journal of Personality* 35 (1967): 585–99.

14. A. L. Chaikin and V. J. Derlega, "Variables Affecting the Appropriateness of Self-Disclosure," *Journal of Consulting and Clinical Psychology* 42 (1974): 588–93.

15. Shirley J. Gilbert and Gale G. Whiteneck, "Toward A Multidimensional Approach to the Study of Self-Disclosure," *Human Communication Research* 4 (1976): 347–55.

16. P. M. Blau, *Exchange and Power in Social Life* (New York: John Wiley & Sons, Inc., 1964), p. 21.

17. S. Jourard, "Self-Disclosure and Other-Cathexis," *Journal of Abnormal and Social Psychology* 59 (1959): 428–31; Jourard and Lasakow, 1958; Worthy, Gary and Kahn, 1969; and Cozby, 1972.

18. Sidney Jourard and Paul Lasakow, "Some Factors in Self-Disclosure," *Journal of Abnormal and Social Psychology* 51 (1958): 91–98.

19. Jeffrey G. Shapiro, Herbert H. Krauss, and Charles B. Truax, "Therapeutic Conditions of Disclosure beyond the Therapeutic Encounter," *Journal of Counseling Psychology* 16 (1969): 290–94.

20. Gilbert and Whiteneck, 1976, pp. 347–55.

21. D. Taylor and I. Altman, "Intimacy Scaled Stimuli to Use in Studies of Interpersonal Relations," *Psychological Reports* 19 (1966): 729–30.

22. Levinger and Senn, 1967.

23. F. Voss, "The Relationships of Disclosure to Marital Satisfaction: An Exploratory Study" (Master's thesis, University of Wisconsin, 1969).

24. Gilbert and Whiteneck, 1976, pp. 347–55.

7

Understanding Another

Objectives

1. Name three common misconceptions about listening
2. Distinguish among the three kinds of listening
3. Give examples of four kinds of external distractions that interfere with listening and empathy
4. Give examples of the internal factors that interfere with listening
5. Discuss the ways in which we can overcome the barriers to effective listening and improve our ability to understand other people

Key Terms

listening

hearing

active listening

critical listening

empathic listening

empathy

neutrality

sympathy

factual distractions

semantic distractions

mental distractions

physical distractions

self-focus

defensiveness

experiential superiority

egocentrism

status

stereotypes

My younger sister goes to college in Illinois. She said that her speech department runs a contest on listening. The guy who won this year said he had an advantage over the other contestants—he's been married for twelve years!

My husband says I don't understand him. How can I understand him? With two kids, a baby, and a dog all making noise at the same time, I can't even hear him!

The Indians who live in the part of the country I come from had a belief that really made a difference in their behavior. They said that if someone wanted to understand someone else, they had to walk in the other person's moccasins for a fortnight.

In the last chapter, we discussed the importance of sharing ourselves in interpersonal communication. We will now turn our consideration to the other person. We suggest that a basic skill must be practiced if our goal is to understand another person. Listening—as suggested in the introductory statements—is the focus of this chapter.

A Basic Skill in Understanding Another

When we think about communication, we usually focus on the speaking, or sending, aspect. If someone says he is enrolled in a speech class, we ask how many speeches he has to make. If he says he had a talk with his family, we ask him what he said. The other activity involved in communication—listening—should be given equal consideration. **Listening** is the process of receiving and interpreting aural stimuli.

There are a number of popular misconceptions about listening. Most people assume that they are already good listeners, that they cannot be taught how to become better listeners, and that listening and hearing are the same thing.

Ask people you know if they listen well. Most likely, they will say that they do. Most of us believe that we listen well. Unfortunately, a number of studies demonstrate that our perceptions of our ability to listen are inaccurate.[1]

Ralph Nichols and his associates at the University of Minnesota tested the ability of thousands of students and hundreds of business and professional people to understand and remember what they heard. His research led to two conclusions— on the average, people remember only about half of what they have heard, even when they are tested immediately, and no matter how intently they believed they were listening. Then, two months later, they only remember 25 percent of what they heard.[2] These test results demonstrate our inability to hear and retain a message.

A misconception most of us have is that people cannot be taught to become better listeners. P. T. Rankin determined that people spend about 70 percent of their waking time in communication. Listening, talking, reading, and writing occurred in the percentages listed:

Listening	42%
Talking	32%
Reading	15%
Writing	11%

In other words, more of the time devoted to communication is spent listening than in any other single activity.[3] Television has probably increased our listening time even further. Also Rankin did not include intrapersonal communication, the communication that occurs within a person, in his study. If he had included intrapersonal communication, he might have found that we spend 100 percent of our waking time engaged in communication.

Another study, completed by D. Bird, confirmed Rankin's findings. Bird asked college women to record the amount of time they were involved in different aspects of communication. Again, 42 percent of the time spent in communication was spent in listening. These women also indicated that listening was as or more important than reading to their success in college.[4] Many other studies have documented the great amount of time we spend listening.[5]

Even though we have evidence of the central role of listening in communication and have had such evidence for over fifty years, we rarely study the subject. You have probably attended classes in reading and writing since the time you first started school. Most colleges require one or two courses in English composition and literature. You may have had one or more formal courses in speech before this one. You probably had show-and-tell or sharing time in elementary school. And yet, you probably have never studied listening or enrolled in any course that emphasized listening to any large extent. The conclusion is obvious—we assume that listening cannot be learned. If we thought it could be, our educational institutions would offer courses in listening at all levels.

Perhaps this is because we assume that listening and **hearing** are one and the same. That is untrue. Once in a while, we might have difficulty distinguishing between listening and hearing, but the two processes are generally distinct. Hearing is a natural process, and unless we suffer from physiological damage or some form of cerebral dysfunction, we cannot help hearing loud sounds. Listening, on the other hand, is a selective activity; it involves the reception *and* the interpretation of aural stimuli.

Most of us have been in situations in which another person assumed that listening and hearing were the same. We can all recall reprimands from our parents like "What do you mean you didn't clean your room? I came into the living room, where you were watching TV, and told you to do it. I know you heard me." An instructor might have said to you, "I just asked you a question. Everyone else in the room heard it. Why didn't you?" Many people incorrectly assume that listening and hearing are the same.

Listening, the process of receiving and interpreting aural stimuli, is an integral part of communication. Simply hearing, receiving aural stimuli, is not sufficient. As we said in chapter 1, both encoding, or putting messages or thoughts into codes, and decoding, or assigning meaning to codes, are essential to communication.

Three Kinds of Listening

Listening can be distinguished in terms of purpose, behavior of the listener, nature of the information under discussion, or communication setting. We will consider three kinds of listening—critical listening, active listening, and empathic listening. These three types represent the most typical kinds of listening in a variety of communication contexts.

Critical listening occurs most often in the public speaking setting and refers to that kind of listening in which the receiver attempts to discriminate among the information and ideas that are presented and to make analytical judgments about the validity and usefulness of the message. The listener who listens critically must distinguish between facts and inferences, must categorize arguments as emotional or logical, must understand lines of reasoning, must be able to determine the speaker's unique perception, and must be able to identify the key points of the message. Critical listening, as we noted, occurs most frequently in public speaking settings. It also should occur in the mass communication situation—listening to television documentaries, news programs on the radio, or when we attend a film that has a social message. Critical listening may also occur in the interpersonal context—in the persuasive interview, in a serious conversation, within the confines of conflict resolution, and in a problem-solving group discussion.

Active listening has been defined as "involved listening with a purpose."[6] Over twenty years ago, active listening was distinguished from passive listening:

In the former, the individual listens with more or less his total self—including his special senses, attitudes, beliefs, feelings and intuitions. In the latter, the listener becomes mainly an organ for the passive reception of sound, with little self-perception, personal involvement, Gestalt discrimination, or alive curiosity.[7]

Active listening is generally recommended as desirable in interpersonal communication situations, but it may also be used effectively in the public speaking setting. Active listening requires activity on the part of the listener. He or she does not lethargically sit or stand while another speaks; instead, active listening is characterized by movement, change, and responsiveness on the part of the listener.

One of the distinguishing characteristics of active listening is that *feedback* is offered to the speaker. Feedback was defined in chapter 1 as the verbal and nonverbal responses to a message that are received and understood by the speaker. Feedback allows us to monitor our communication with others. The effective use of feedback and the sensitive reception of it allows us to avoid many misunderstandings.

Speakers can alter, correct, or enforce their original messages as they observe and interpret the feedback that is offered to them. They may add additional examples or speak more concretely if the other person does not appear to understand the point they are making. They may retract what they have said or apologize for their position if they believe the other person is disagreeing with them. Finally, they may embellish their message and even take a more radical stand if they recognize agreement coming from the other communicator.

Feedback can be distinguished along a number of lines, but we will limit our discussion in this chapter to the difference between positive and negative feedback. Positive feedback includes such nonverbal behaviors as positive facial expression, smiling, laughing, forward body lean, increased touching, and movement toward the other person. Verbal examples of positive feedback are statements like "I see," "I understand," "Yes," "I agree," and "Why don't you tell me more?" Positive feedback results in the speaker increasing the length of his or her message, decreasing linguistic errors or nonfluencies, and decreasing his or her feelings of defensiveness.

Negative feedback is characterized by frowns and other negative facial expression, movement away from the other person, decreased touching, focus on people other than the communicator, decreased eye contact, and general nonresponsiveness. Statements like "I don't know what you're talking about," "I don't agree with you," "Who cares?" and "I don't want to hear any more" are extreme examples of negative verbal feedback. Negative feedback results in a decreasing message, an increasing number of linguistic errors, an increasing number of nonfluencies, and an increasing feeling of defensiveness on the part of the speaker.

Empathic listening is a third kind of listening. Empathic listening occurs when we attempt to understand another person. **Empathy** is the ability to perceive the other person's view of the world as though it were our own. When we talk about "putting ourselves in someone else's shoes," as Wellington literally does in the cartoon, we are alluding to empathy. Empathic listening is the type of listening that has total understanding of the other person as its goal.

Most of us assume that other people perceive things the way we do. But, as we said in chapter 2, great variations in perceptions exist. If we wish to be more understanding of others, we need to recognize that such differences occur and that we should attempt to determine what other people's experiences are. Bochner and Kelly, two communication scholars, wrote that empathy is "the essence of all communicative process."[8]

Empathy is distinct from neutrality and sympathy. We exhibit **neutrality** when we show indifference to another person. We show **sympathy** when we share the feelings of others—their pain or sorrow, their joy or happiness. When we sympathize with others, we may show that we care by expressing the same emotional response to a situation that they have made. It is possible that sympathy will not be helpful since we may find ourselves limited by the strong emotions of the moment. It can be difficult to be supportive of others when we are laughing or crying or shouting with them.

WEE PALS

Neutrality is harmful because it indicates that we do not have respect or positive regard for the other person. Sympathy may also be destructive when it connotes or suggests superiority. In feeling sorry for another person, we may be communicating that we are somehow better off, more advanced, or without need for sympathy ourselves. It is possible that our sympathetic responses may be regarded as patronizing and may not be appreciated by others.

When we listen empathically to others, we do not need to feel the same fear or anxiety that they are experiencing. What we communicate to them is an awareness and appreciation of their emotions. Empathic listening requires sensitivity to others and an ability to demonstrate this sensitivity. We should strive to communicate that we are with them, not because we are sharing their emotions, but because we understand their feelings.

If we fail to empathize with others, we fail to understand them. In a very real sense, we are hurting ourselves. To the extent that we do not empathize with others, we restrict ourselves to our personal experiences and feelings.

Nonetheless, empathic listening is not easy to achieve. We need to empathize with others precisely when it is most difficult for us to do it. When we disagree most with someone else, it is then that we most need to show that we understand them and their point of view. Seeing the other side is the most difficult when we do not agree with it. Our tendency in such situations is to spend a great deal of energy and time defending our own position and finding fault with the other person's point of view. We feel a need to prove that we are right, and the other person wrong.

And yet empathic listening can be a most important skill. Empathy allows us to enter another person's world as though it were our own. It implies understanding, rather than judgment. Carl Rogers has expressed the importance of empathy:

A person who is loved appreciatively, not possessively, blooms, and develops his own unique self. The person who loves non-possessively is himself enriched.[9]

Empathic listening is satisfying and enriching to both parties in an interpersonal relationship.

Who's Right?

The goal of empathic listening is acceptance of ourselves and acceptance of others. We should strive to appreciate our own points of view as well as the positions of other people. We have empathized when we can honestly say, "You're right and I'm right." But usually, when we are engaged in an argument, we say, "You're wrong and I'm right." Other positions we could take are, "You're wrong and I'm wrong," which demonstrates negative feelings about both positions and both people; or. "I'm wrong and you're right," which demonstrates a lack of confidence and perhaps a poor self-concept. In order to gain experience in empathizing, try to explain how both of the contradictory statements made by two different people might be seen as "right."

1. Abortion is the best form of birth control.

Right, because _____

_____

Abortions should be illegal—regardless of the reason for them.

Right, because _____

_____

2. Marijuana should be sold in all the same places that sell tobacco.

Right, because _____

_____

Smoking marijuana should be considered a felony.

Right, because _____

_____

3. The drinking age should be raised to 25.

Right, because _____

_____

The drinking age should be lowered to 15.

Right, because _____

_____

4. People should pass a test before they can marry.

Right, because _____

_____

Marriage laws should be liberalized so people can marry more easily.

Right, because _____

_____

5. Women belong in the home.

Right, because _____

_____

Women should be responsible for their own support.

Right, because _____

_____

6. President Reagan does an excellent job.

Right, because _____

_____

President Reagan is the poorest American president to date.

Right, because _____

_____

You probably found it relatively easy to support both sides of some of these issues. Others were no doubt more challenging. The conflicting statements that were easy for you to support probably concern issues that affect you very little; those that were difficult possibly deal with matters about which you have a great deal of concern and a specific position. We all need to develop empathy for the points of view with which we disagree.

Interference with Our Ability to Listen

The studies cited earlier show that we do not listen well. Understanding another by listening requires that we hear both their verbal and nonverbal messages; that we understand the content, the intent, and the accompanying emotions; and that we communicate our understanding to them. A number of difficulties and breakdowns in communication can occur on the way. Let us consider some of the factors that may interfere with our ability to listen.

The Message and the Occasion

A number of distractions occur both in the message itself and in the situation in which it is received—factual distractions, semantic distractions, mental distractions, and physical distractions. **Factual distractions** occur because we tend to listen for facts instead of ideas. Perhaps our educational institutions encourage this tendency. Instead of looking at the whole, we focus on the parts. We can lose the main idea or the purpose behind a message if we jump from fact to fact instead of attempting to weave them together into a total pattern. For example, a friend might relate an experience from her past in which she felt devastated by circumstances beyond her control. Friends may tell us stories about their childhood, stories of fear, frustration, or anger. We listen to the facts—he comes from a small town, she had a pet hamster—and we do not grasp the emotion.

Semantic distractions are similar, in that they are also caused by elements of the message. Semantic distractions occur when someone uses a word or phrase differently or uses one to which we react emotionally. Regionalisms, different names for similar things used in different parts of the country, can be semantic distractions. In different parts of the country, people may ask for a "pop," a "soda," a "coke," or a "tonic"—merely different names for a soft drink. Emotional reactions to words often occur when people are classified in a denigrating way—"girl" for women over twenty-one, "Polacks" for Polish people, "Jew" for anyone who tends to be thrifty.

Mental distractions occur when we engage in intrapersonal communication, in communicating with ourselves, when we are talking with others. The mental side trips, daydreams, counter-arguments, and recollections that we engage in when someone is talking to us distract us from receiving the other person's message. These side trips can be suggested by something the other person says or by our own preoccupation. Mental distractions may occur because of the great difference between the speed at which we hear and the speed at which we speak. Most Americans talk at a rate of about 125 words per minute, but we are able to receive about 800 words per minute. This discrepancy allows us great freedom to consider other matters that may be more important to us. A student can easily plan dinner while listening to a psychology lecture. Someone else can review the exciting events of the previous evening while listening to the news. We can decide whether to accept an invitation while listening to a friend's account of an argument with another friend.

Physical distractions include all the stimuli in the environment that might interfere with our focusing on the other person and his or her message. We can

be distracted by sound—a buzzing neon light, loud music, or the speaker's lisp; by visual stimuli—a poster of a nude on the wall, bright sunlight, or the speaker's beauty; or by any other stimuli—an unusual odor, an uncomfortable article of clothing, or an unpleasant aftertaste in our mouth.

Ourselves

Another set of factors that interferes with our ability to listen is related to ourselves. If we constantly focus on ourselves, we cannot be sensitive to others. In order to understand another person, we need to be open to them. **Self-focus,** or a preoccupation with thoughts about ourselves, hampers listening and empathy. As we suggested in the exercise entitled, "Who's Right?" we need to develop positive feelings about ourselves and about other people. Self-focus suggests that we have developed regard for ourselves, but that we have failed to develop the same feeling toward others. In the conversation that follows, Tom is unable to empathize with Karen because he allows his personal concerns to dominate his thinking and his communication.

Karen has just received word that her grandmother has died. Tom is the counselor at the agency where she works. Karen is extremely upset and goes to Tom because she needs to talk to someone. She has talked with him only casually in the past, but she feels he will understand because he is a trained counselor.

Karen:	Tom, do you have a minute?
Tom:	Sure Karen, come on in.
Karen:	I wanted to talk to someone for a little while.
Tom:	Fine. What would you like to talk about?
Karen:	Well, I just got a phone call from home saying that my grandmother died and I guess I just needed someone to talk to.
Tom:	Yeah, I know how you feel. I had a grandmother who died about eight years ago. She was the neatest lady I have every known. Why, when I was a kid she used to bake cookies for me every Saturday. We used to go to the park on weekends for picnics. She sure was fun to be with.
Karen:	I'm sure you had a good time, but I sort of wanted to talk about my grandmother.
Tom:	Oh, sure. Well, what was she like?
Karen:	Well, she was a good lady, but . . .
Tom:	Yeah, I guess all grandmothers are pretty good.
Karen:	I guess so, but . . .
Tom:	You know, it's been a long time since I thought about my grandmother. I'm really glad you came in today.
Karen:	Yes, well, I guess my break is about over so I'd better get back to work.
Tom:	Okay. It's been nice talking to you. Stop by anytime.
Karen:	Sure.

A number of factors may account for a person's focus on himself or herself rather than on the other person. **Defensiveness,** as we discussed in chapter 5, is a common reason. People who feel that they must defend their position usually feel threatened. They feel that, in general, people are attacking them and their ideas and they develop the habit of defending themselves. Sometimes people who are championing a specific cause—women's rights, the elderly, peace, racial equality—develop this attitude. They stand ready to respond to the least provocation and they tend to find fault with other people.

In the interview that follows, the supervisor demonstrates a defensive attitude and is consequently unable to listen to the employee. The supervisor is the director of operations in a social service agency. He has arranged this appraisal interview with the employee because he is evaluating her performance as a community organizer.

Supervisor: As you know, after sixty days we evaluate each new employee. That's why I've asked you to come here today. Here is the evaluation form I have filled out. Please read it.

Employee: *(after reading)* I don't understand why you have marked me so low in dependability.

Supervisor: Because you always ask so many questions whenever I tell you to do something.

Employee: But the reason I ask questions is that I don't understand exactly what you want me to do. If I didn't ask the questions, I wouldn't be able to perform the task because your instructions are usually not clear to me.

Supervisor: I marked you low in that area because you require so much supervision.

Employee: It's not supervision I need, it's clear instructions, and I don't feel it's fair for you to mark me low in this area when I am not.

Supervisor: It doesn't really matter what you think because I'm doing the evaluation.

Employee: Don't I have anything to say about it?

Supervisor: No. Now that you've read it, will you please sign here?

Employee: Definitely not. I feel that is unfair and inaccurate.

Supervisor: Then check the box that indicates you are not in agreement with the evaluation. All your signature means is that you have read it, not that you agree with it.

Employee: This is the most ridiculous evaluation I have ever had in my entire life.

Supervisor: That's unimportant at this point. If you don't have anything else to say, that will be all.

The defensive verbal behavior by the supervisor clearly interfered with his ability to listen to his employee. Defensiveness usually interferes with our ability to listen.

Another reason for self-focus is known as **experiential superiority.** People who have lived through a variety of experiences sometimes express this attitude toward people who have had less experience. Professors often cannot listen or empathize with students who are explaining why an assignment was not completed on time; they assume that the particular student will offer an excuse they have heard before. Parents sometimes fail to listen to their children's problems or to empathize with them; they feel that from their own experience with a similar problem, they can just give a pat answer.

A variation of experiential superiority occurs in long-term relationships. People have a good deal of experience in the relationship and feel they can predict the other person's statements. Husbands may respond with an occasional "uh-huh" over the newspaper at breakfast; wives may repeat, "Sure, honey," while daydreaming about other matters. The characters in the Hagar cartoon on page 153 typify people who no longer listen to each other—probably as a result of a long relationship.

Another reason people focus on themselves is simple egocentrism. **Egocentrism** is the tendency to view yourself as the center of any exchange or activity. An egocentric person is overly concerned with himself or herself and pays little attention to others. This person appears to be constantly asking "How do I look? How do I sound? How am I coming through to you?" instead of responding to how the other person looks, sounds, and is coming through.

One place you can observe egocentric people is at a party. Egocentric people usually make a number of attention-getting moves that place them at the center of the stage. They may arrive late, talk loudly, dress flamboyantly, and stand in the center of the room to make others focus on them. They also move from person to person or group to group, but they do not give their full attention to the people with whom they are talking. They look around the room, glancing from one person to another. Rarely do they focus on anyone for more than a moment and, even then, they do not concentrate on the other person's message.

Our Perception of the Other Person

A third set of factors involves our perception of the other person. Preconceived attitudes—such as status or stereotypes—interfere with our listening to another person. If we believe that the other people have **status,** we accept what they say easily, rather than listening carefully and critically. We usually do not listen carefully or critically when the speaker is an M.D., a professor, a Supreme Court justice, or a visiting expert. If we think that the other person has low status, we often do not listen to their statements at all, nor do we retain their messages. Seniors seldom listen to freshmen about study habits, and attractive people rarely take advice from people they consider unattractive. We dismiss statements made by people of lesser status. Thus, we do not listen carefully to persons whom we perceive to have either a higher or lower status than we.

Our **stereotypes** also affect our ability to listen. If another person belongs to a group we respect—Democrats, beer drinkers, Volvo owners, or joggers—we believe what they say. If they belong to a group of people for whom we have little regard— highbrows, college dropouts, football players, or flirts—we reject their messages.

Status and stereotypes affect our ability to listen. In order to demonstrate this for yourself, ask two people what they make of a presidential address or of a statement made by a labor leader, a member of Congress, or the governor. If you ask two people who have different perceptions of the status of the person and different stereotypes of the groups the person belongs to, you will probably end up with two entirely different versions of the same address or statement.

153   Understanding Another

Sources of Interference with Listening

In order to determine if you understand the various types of interference with listening, complete the following exercise. Mark each of the statements as follows:

M & O—FD	Message and occasion—Factual distraction
M & O—SD	Message and occasion—Semantic distraction
M & O—MD	Message and occasion—Mental distraction
M & O—PD	Message and occasion—Physical distraction
S—D	Self—Defensiveness
S—ES	Self—Experiential superiority
S—E	Self—Egocentrism
O—S	Other—Status
O—St	Other—Stereotype

1. I guess you're right; after all you're a teacher. _____

2. I know that my point of view is correct. If you don't like the way I handle things, you can look somewhere else for a job. _____

3. I know what you're going to say—I was a student once, too, you know. _____

4. Did you use the term *late bloomer?* You know, I really think people use that term carelessly, and often inaccurately. _____

5. I'm sorry I didn't hear what you said. By the way, what do you think of my hair? _____

6. If you think you've got problems, let me tell you what it was like when I was your age! _____

7. Did you use the word *gargoyle?* _____

8. What did you say? I was thinking about the guy I went out with last night. _____

9. It was really difficult to hear the lecture—the plumbers upstairs were making so much noise. _____

10. I know you said I should get my hair cut shorter, but you're my mom. No offense, but mothers always say that. _____

11. You don't have to say one word. I know just what you're going to say. _____

12. Those were interesting statistics, Dr. Forman, but what was the point of today's lecture? _____

13. I'm so worried about my finals that I didn't hear you. What did you say? _____

14. Yes, I guess that—Oh no, I broke a nail. That really looks bad, doesn't it? What were you saying? _____

15. I know that you don't agree with me, but I have a reputation to protect. If you only wish to attack my decision, I'm afraid our discussion is over. _____

Improving Our Ability to Listen

Just as we can identify factors that interfere with our ability to listen, we can also identify ways of improving those abilities. Let us consider the three sets of factors that interfere with our listening and suggest methods of overcoming each. The distractions that occur in the message and in the environment are factual, semantic, mental, and physical.

We can remove factual distractions by *focusing on the main ideas* that the other person is presenting, remembering that we can ask later for facts and details. It is far less offensive to another person to be asked for particular numbers, specific locations, or to spell a particular name than it is to be asked "What in the world are you talking about?"

Semantic distractions can be minimized if we keep in mind that *words are arbitrary symbols*. They have no inherent or natural meaning that is shared by everyone. If another person uses a word that confuses us, the appropriate response is to ask the meaning of the word or to ask how she or he is using the word. If we cannot overcome our emotional reaction to a specific word, it is essential that we explain the word's negative associations to the person using it.

Instead of allowing mental side trips to distract us from other people's messages, we should use the time to *focus on their intent, as well as the content of their message*. By refusing to consider unrelated matters, we will find that our listening and our understanding can be greatly increased.

Physical distractions like noise, bright lights, unusual odors, or provocative surroundings can usually be handled easily. In most cases, a simple *move to another room or another location* will solve the problem.

The distractions that result from self-focus are created by defensiveness, experiential superiority, and egocentrism. The habit of focusing on ourselves rather than on the other person is difficult to break, however. Nonetheless, we need to alter this behavior if we hope to listen to someone else, and, in turn, understand that person.

Focusing on the meaning and experiences that we share is helpful if we find that we usually react defensively to other people's messages. Other people may be attacking one of our pet beliefs or attitudes, but they may also be defending it from another perspective. Regardless of their point of view on the single issue, we can find a number of points of agreement. Maximizing our shared attitudes, values, and beliefs and minimizing our differences results in improved listening and better communication. In addition, if we do not react defensively to other people's disagreements with us, we may find ourselves being persuasive and encouraging them to agree with us.

If experiential superiority is the problem that interferes with listening and empathizing, *give the other person a full hearing.* Impatience with a person who has no experience with a particular problem and the poor listening that accompanies this attitude can result in a breakdown in communication. Listening to and empathizing with them will result in improved communication. You may even learn something new.

People who are continually concerned with their self-image and how that image is perceived by others have difficulty listening and empathizing. Egocentrism is an ingrained attitude that is extremely difficult to change. Perhaps the wisest suggestion to a person with this problem is *attempt to concentrate on the other person.* There are advantages to concentrating on the other person that should appeal to someone who is egocentric. Concentrating on other people when they are speaking will probably cause them to focus on you when you are speaking. Even more important, you will "come across" better if the other person perceives you to be a good and empathic listener. No amount of makeup, clothing, or other adornments will make you as attractive to others as the ability to listen and to empathize.

In order to overcome problems related to our preconceptions of other people, we need to *learn how to suspend judgment.* Rather than assuming that their messages are acceptable or unacceptable without listening to them, we need to wait until we have heard them out. As we saw in chapter 3, we can make grave errors by assuming that a person who belongs to a particular group is like all of the other members of that group. Bernard Gunther said, "Take a chance on getting slapped, you might get kissed!"

We can also overcome these problems if we *focus on the other person as a source of feelings and thoughts, ideas, and information.* When we categorize other people, we can easily dismiss them. When we view them respectfully as valuable human resources, we find that our listening and our empathizing improve.

Paraphrasing

Try this exercise to improve your ability as a listener. With a small group of people, discuss a controversial topic. Before each person can speak, he or she must state, without using notes, what the person who spoke just before said—and to that person's satisfaction. If the summary is inaccurate or incomplete, the previous speaker is asked to clarify the message. The next person to speak must again attempt to state the previous speaker's message.

When your group becomes successful at stating the content of the previous speaker's message, have each person state the previous speaker's intent. Now each person is explaining what the previous person said and what was intended by the remarks. Again, the previous speaker must agree that the content and the intent are accurate and complete before the discussion can continue.

Did you find that your task was easier or more difficult than you anticipated? Were particular people better able to restate another person's ideas? Why were they successful? How can you improve your own ability to listen for understanding?

Behavioral Components of Effective Listening

With the general guidelines for improving our ability to listen understood, we can specify specific verbal and nonverbal behaviors that are associated with effective listening. You may want to consider your own listening behavior to determine which of these behaviors you regularly demonstrate and which of these skills you may want to add to your repertoire.

Provide clear verbal responses. Do not provide ambiguous, complex, or overly simple verbal responses. Providing cliché responses like "That's the way it goes," "I guess that's the way the cookie crumbles," and "You only get out of it what you put into it" adds little clarity. Be as specific and detailed as you can in the verbal feedback you offer.

Rely on descriptive statements. Evaluation leads to defensiveness as discussed in chapter 5. Descriptive feedback leads to a supportive communication climate. Descriptive comments add clarity and can suggest areas of disagreement without offending or insulting the other person. For example, the statement, "I understand your position on Iran, but I can also understand those who have the opposing view," does not threaten the other person.

Provide reflective statements. In order to provide a check on the accuracy of your understanding, you might try reflective statements. Paraphrasing the content of a person's message or its intent provides information on your understanding of what that person said.

Demonstrate bodily responsiveness. A lack of movement suggests lethargy or a lack of interest; bodily movement and gestures suggest concern and interest.

Alter your facial expression, the placement of your legs, arms, and head in appropriate response to the message of the other person. Use touch to show your concern or your affection for the other person.

Use a sincere, warm voice. Avoid harshness, hostility, or aggressiveness in your voice. Vocal patterns, pitch, quality of the voice, loudness, and other vocal characteristics can interfere with the most concerned verbal message. Speak slowly, with a moderate pitch and an even tone to express your interest in the message of the other person.

Establish eye contact. Direct eye contact allows you to observe the other person more carefully. We discussed the importance of nonverbal communication in chapter 4. When you observe the other person, you are able to receive the fullness of his or her message—the nonverbal as well as the verbal elements. In addition, eye contact suggests that you are focusing on the other person rather than being distracted by other sights in the room.

Summary

In this chapter we considered the importance of understanding other people when we communicate with them. By improving our ability to listen, we can increase our understanding of another person. Listening was defined as the process of receiving and interpreting aural stimuli. Three kinds of listening—critical, active, and empathic— were considered.

A number of factors interfere with our ability to listen and to empathize. These factors fall into three categories—those related to the message and the occasion, such as factual, semantic, mental, and physical distractions; those related to ourselves, including defensiveness, experiential superiority, and egocentrism; and those related to the other person, such as status and stereotypes.

We can overcome these obstacles, however, and improve our ability to listen to others. Among the suggestions made were focusing on the main ideas; keeping in mind that words are arbitrary symbols; focusing on the intent, as well as the content, of a message; moving when physical factors interfere; focusing on the meaning and experiences that are shared; giving the other person a full hearing; concentrating on the other person; suspending judgment; and focusing on the other person as a source of feelings and thoughts, ideas, and information. Six behavioral components of effective listening were offered. They include providing clear verbal responses, relying on descriptive statements, providing reflective statements, demonstrating bodily responsiveness, using a sincere, warm voice, and establishing eye contact. Understanding another person is a difficult but worthwhile goal for each of us.

Additional Readings

Barker, Larry L. *Listening Behavior*. Englewood Cliffs, N.J.: Prentice-Hall, 1971.
Provides a complete treatment of the listening process including the importance of listening, the variables that affect listening, and problems in listening. Students may find assistance in solving specific problems in their listening behavior. Barker includes a consideration of listener feedback.

Brooks, William D., and Emmert, Philip. *Interpersonal Communication*, 2d ed. Dubuque, Ia.: Wm. C. Brown Company Publishers, 1980.
Presents an introduction to interpersonal communication. The chapter on feedback details six categories of feedback: positive and negative, immediate and delayed, internal or external, indirect or direct, verbal or nonverbal, and reinforcement or correction. This chapter would be useful for students who want more information on feedback.

Danner, Jack. *People-Empathy: Key to Painless Supervision*. New York: Parker Publishing Co., 1976.
The thesis of this book is that empathy can be profitable. Each chapter identifies a strategy in using empathy to the advantage of the supervisor. The book is replete with examples that clarify the ideas. By some interpretation, each of us provides some management of others; for this reason, the book has general appeal.

Egan, Gerard. *Interpersonal Living: A Skills/Contract Approach to Human Relations Training in Groups*. Belmont, Calif.: Wadsworth Publishing Co. Inc., 1976.
A detailed discussion of communication skills necessary for effective interpersonal relationships.

Empathy, feelings and thoughts, self-disclosure, concreteness, and descriptiveness are discussed in depth; each skill is broken into specific, easily understood behavior. Excellent introduction to the effective application of communication principles and concepts to actual behavior.

*Fromm, Eric. *The Art of Loving*. New York: Harper & Row, Publishers, 1956.
Though written over twenty years ago, the ideas presented are far from out-of-date. Fromm discusses the love of self and others as an active process involving the whole personality and tells us that love must be practiced by developing a sensitivity to ourselves and to others.

Morris, Jud. *The Art of Listening*. Boston, Mass.: Farnsworth Publishing, 1968.
This book is straightforward and easy to understand. Morris defines and explains ten blocks to effective listening, offers solutions to these basic problems, and suggests methods for improving listening skills. The book is useful for the beginning student of listening.

Nichols, Ralph G., and Stevens, Leonard A. *Are You Listening?* New York: McGraw-Hill Book Company, Inc., 1957.
Listening is considered in both the interpersonal communication setting and the public speaking setting. Nichols and Stevens discuss the types of listening that people engage in at school, work, and home. They consider bad listening habits and offer suggestions on improving listening skills. An excellent book by researchers on listening.

*Indicates more advanced readings.

Rogers, Carl E., and Farson, Richard E. "Active Listening." In *Readings in Interpersonal and Organizational Communication,* edited by Carl E. Rogers and Richard E. Farson. Boston: Holbrook Press, 1969.

A detailed discussion of the techniques and benefits of active listening, the book provides guidelines for developing active listening skills and ways to overcome barriers to active listening. A concise and easily understood discussion.

Notes

1. See, for example, Edward J. J. Karmar and Thomas R. Lewis, "Comparison of Visual and Non-Visual Listening," *Journal of Communication* 1 (November 1951): 16–20; James I. Brown, "The Objective Measurement of Listening Ability," *Journal of Communication* 1 (May 1951): 44–48; Paul W. Keller, "Major Findings in Listening in the Past Ten Years," *Journal of Communication* 10 (March 1960): 29–38; S. Duker, *Listening Bibliography* (New York: Scarecrow Press, 1964); and S. Duker, ed., *Listening; Readings* (New York: Scarecrow Press, 1966).
2. Ralph Nichols and Leonard Stevens, "Listening to People," *Harvard Business Review* 35 (1957), no. 5.
3. P. T. Rankin, "The Measurement of the Ability to Understand Spoken Language," *Dissertation Abstracts* 12 (1926): 847.
4. D. Bird, "Teaching Listening Comprehension," *Journal of Communication* 3 (1953): 127–30.
5. See, for example, Miriam E. Wilt, "A Study of Teacher Awareness of Listening as a Factor in Elementary Education," *Journal of Educational Research* 43 (1950): 626; D. Bird, "Have You Tried Listening?" *Journal of the American Dietetic Association* 30 (1954): 225–30; and B. Markgraf, "An Observational Study Determining the Amount of Time that Students in the Tenth and Twelfth Grades Are Expected to Listen in the Classroom" (Master's thesis, University of Wisconsin, 1957).
6. Larry L. Barker, *Listening Behavior* (Englewood Cliffs, N.J.: Prentice-Hall, 1971), p. 10.
7. D. Barbara, "On Listening—the Role of the Ear in Psychic Life," *Today's Speech* 5 (1957): 12.
8. Arthur P. Bochner and Clifford W. Kelly, "Interpersonal Competence: Rationale, Philosophy, and Implementation of a Conceptual Framework," *Speech Teacher* 23 (1974): 289.
9. Carl R. Rogers, *Freedom to Learn* (Columbus, Ohio: Charles E. Merrill Publishing Company, 1969), p. 237.

8

The Interview
An Application of the Principles of Interpersonal Communication

Objectives

1. Define and give examples of open and closed, neutral and leading, and primary and secondary questions
2. Distinguish the purpose of the informational, persuasive, and employment interview
3. Prepare and conduct an informational, persuasive, and employment interview

Key Terms

interview
dyadic communication
open question
closed question
primary question
secondary question

neutral question
leading question
informational interview
persuasive interview
employment interview

Interviewer: I am here to get some background information on you for the local newspaper. I am writing an article on the shows that will be presented this season here at the Cumberland County Playhouse. Do you have about five minutes?

Interviewee: Sure, what do you want to know?

Interviewer: Well, how did you get into acting?

Interviewee: I was a theatre major in college and I always enjoyed acting.

Interviewer: Where do you come from originally?

Interviewee: A small town in northeastern Ohio.

Interviewer: Alright, could we turn now to the shows in which you will be performing this season?

Interviewing is very much like piano playing—a fair degree of skill can be acquired without the necessity of formal instruction. But there is a world of difference in the craft, in the technique, and in the finesse between the amateur who plays "by ear" and the accomplished concert pianist.[1]

The cartoon, the excerpt from an informative interview, and the analogy between interviewing and piano playing all introduce us to one type of interpersonal communication—the **interview.** Each of us participates in interviews from time to time. We are interviewed by employers, doctors, instructors, friends, counselors, parents, and people taking surveys. We interview our peers, our customers, and our neighbors.

In this chapter, we will consider the interview as one type of interpersonal communication. The same principles of effective interpersonal communication that we have identified in previous chapters are essential to our success in the interview. In addition, we must understand the specific features of this form of interpersonal communication if we want to be competent interviewers or interviewees. We will focus on some of the unique characteristics of the interview in this chapter.

Interviewing is more formal than the conversations in which we engage, but less formal than other types of communication—small group discussions and public speaking. Interviews are generally planned, they are not spontaneous occurrences as are many of our conversations with others. Interviews usually have a specific purpose—to gain information, to provide information, to persuade another person, to get a job, to make a judgment about the work of another person, or to provide counseling.

Interviews are usually organized into an opening, body, and closing just as public speeches are typically organized into an introduction, body, and conclusion. Almost all interviews involve the asking and answering of questions. Indeed, questions generally form the basis of the interview. Most often, interviews occur between two people and are thus defined as **dyadic communication.** The term interviewing may be defined as "a process of dyadic communication with a predetermined and serious purpose designed to interchange behavior and usually involving the asking and answering of questions."[2]

Questions and Questioning

Nearly all interviews involve the asking and answering of various types of questions. In planning an interview, the interviewer must determine the most appropriate kinds of questions for the purpose. Questions fall roughly into three categories—open or closed, primary or secondary, and neutral or leading; that is, every question is either open or closed, primary or secondary, *and* neutral or leading.

Open or Closed

Open questions are broad and generally unstructured. They often simply suggest the topic under discussion. The respondent, or interviewee, is offered a great deal of freedom in answering. Examples of open questions are "How do you feel about Ronald Reagan?" "What is Chicago really like?" "What are your feelings on reverse discrimination?" and "What is your problem?"

Open questions do not allow for a yes-or-no answer. They allow other people to see that you are interested in them. They generally create a supportive communication climate and allow the interviewer to establish good rapport with the interviewee.

Closed questions are restrictive. They offer a narrow range of answers; often, all of the possible answers are included in the question. Sometimes, the possible answers are limited to yes and no. Examples of closed questions include "Do you attend the university at this time?" "Do you plan to drop out of school if you get this job?" "What is more important to a social worker—the ability to relate to people or the administrative experience that allows her to handle a large number of cases?" and "Have you the time to do the work necessary to complete this class?"

Closed questions are useful if you want a specific response. If the closed question is threatening, the interviewee may become defensive; if it is without threat, a short answer is easy to give. Closed questions are appropriate when the interviewer has sufficient information about the respondent and the respondent's point of view, when the question contains or permits an appropriate response, and when the respondent has information, an opinion, or a point of view about the matter under discussion.

Primary or Secondary

Primary questions introduce a topic or a new area within a topic under discussion. Examples of primary questions include "Shall we turn to the topic of summer employment?" "Could we begin the interview by discussing your experience in welding?" and "Let's go back to your grades for a minute—how's your algebra?"

Secondary questions are used to follow up primary questions. When an interviewee does not answer fully or completely, the interviewer asks another question to secure the desired information. Secondary questions are often short: "Shall we go on?" "Can you tell me more?" "How did you feel then?" and "Is there anything you would care to add?"

Neutral or Leading

Neutral questions do not contain any correct or preferred answer. They do not suggest any particular response or direction. They are usually open. Examples of neutral questions are "What did you do last summer?" "How did you like your last job?" "What kind of music do you listen to?" and "How do you spend your weekends?"

Leading questions suggest a preferred answer—they ease the way for one answer and make any other answer difficult. Examples of leading questions created from the neutral questions above are "I suppose you worked last summer. What at?"

"Even if you liked your last job, there's no harm trying to better yourself, is there?" and "I guess you play a lot of ball on weekends, like most young men. What is your game?"

Leading questions are very useful in persuasive interviews, as when you are attempting to convince people that they do want an additional insurance policy, that they do want to enroll in a particular course, or that they are prepared to accept your religious beliefs. But leading questions can create a defensive climate when the interviewer is not attempting to persuade the interviewee and assumes an inaccurate response. For example, you and your wife expect to go bowling, but you meet a friend who says "You and your wife would like to go to the symphony tonight with me and my husband, wouldn't you?" Or you go to your professor's office to drop the class, but before you can ask, you hear "You really do enjoy my class, don't you?" Both the friend and the professor make you defensive by asking a leading question instead of a neutral question.

Types of Questions

To determine whether you understand the three categories of questions, complete the following exercise. Mark each question in this interview *O* or *C* for open or closed, *P* or *S* for primary or secondary, and *N* or *L* for neutral or leading.

		Open/ Closed	Primary/ Secondary	Neutral/ Leading
Interviewer:	Hi, I was wondering if you could help me out?	_____	_____	_____
Interviewee:	Sure, what do you need?			
Interviewer:	I'm looking for a good running shoe; what do you suggest?	_____	_____	_____
Interviewee:	For jogging, a thicker sole will give you longer wear and more comfort.			
Interviewer:	Would Adidas or Pumas be better?	_____	_____	_____
Interviewee:	I'd recommend the Adidas.			
Interviewer:	But Pumas are good shoes, aren't they?	_____	_____	_____
Interviewee:	Yes, but their thinner soles make them better for racing than for recreational jogging.			
Interviewer:	Let me get this straight, the thicker soled Adidas are better for jogging and the thinner soled Pumas are preferred for racing?	_____	_____	_____
Interviewee:	Right!			

Answers and Answering

Typically we focus on the questions that are asked in the interview rather than the answers that are given. This is no different than our focusing on what is *said* in a conversation rather than what is *heard*. Nonetheless, the skill of answering questions is as important as the skill of asking questions. In some situations, the employment interview for example, you may be more interested in learning how to answer questions than in learning how to ask them. The role of the interviewee in the employment interview will be considered in more detail later in this chapter, but we feel that it is important to suggest some general guidelines at this point.

There are five guidelines that are useful in considering effective answers in the interview setting. First, interviewees are advised to always answer the questions that are asked of them. Communication theorists point out that people, even when they do not say anything, are communicating some messages. For example, they may be suggesting that they are bored, uninterested in the other person, or confused. Similarly, in the interview, interviewees who do not answer a question suggest that they are embarrassed, do not know the answer to the question, are confused by terminology, are fearful of communicating, have something to hide, are dishonest, or are attempting to fabricate an elaborate answer. None of these impressions is desirable for interviewees. If you are confused by the language that the interviewer uses, do not understand the importance or relevance of the question, or believe that the question is not within the legal guidelines recommended by the Equal Employment Opportunity Commission, you should explain your reluctance to answer or ask for further clarification. Your open, straightforward response will be viewed more positively than hesitation, a reluctance to answer, or complete silence.

Second, interviewees should not provide inaccurate or distorted answers. Stating that you have completed your college education when you are really in the last term, explaining that you already own a set of encyclopedias to a salesperson when you do not, or pretending to understand all of the ramifications of a recent constitutional amendment will only lead to trouble. If you do not know what a term or concept means, ask for explanation. If you know that a job description included specific qualifications that you do not have, be straightforward in stating those qualifications that you do not have. If you do not want to make a purchase or be persuaded by a persuasive interviewer, state directly and honestly why you do not want his or her product or service. Honesty is an ethical consideration and one that will make you a more effective interviewee.

Third, interviewees should provide complete answers. This guideline may be related to the honesty and accuracy of your response. Do not provide half of the picture when it allows the interviewer to gain a distorted view of your reality. Explain your position, your background, or your experience fully and completely. Occasionally, a factor that you may feel is less important will be perceived as highly important to the interviewer. This guideline does not mean that you should tell an interviewer every detail about yourself. You can also err by saying too much. Be aware of the tendency to say far too little or to provide incomplete answers.

Fourth, specific, concrete responses are desirable by the interviewee. Speaking in platitudes or using a large number of clichés or euphemisms will only distort your messages. You may want to review chapter 3 in order to determine how to avoid ambiguity and to be increasingly concrete and descriptive in your responses as an interviewee. Ambiguous language is confusing and may suggest that you are attempting to be dishonest.

Fifth, relevant answers are appropriate. If you are asked about purchasing a new cologne, you should not respond with a comment about foreign automobiles. If you are asked about your background in accounting, you should not detail all of the courses in speech communication that you have taken. If you are asked about your feelings on the mandatory helmet laws for motorcycle drivers, you should not talk about the rights of the unborn child. Offering a *non sequitor* may suggest that you are confused, that you have difficulty concentrating, or that you are unwilling to answer the question that was asked. If you are unwilling or unable to answer a question, you should explain your reluctance or your position rather than sureptitiously attempting to avoid the question.

In the exercise below identify the specific guideline that has not been followed. Mark the answer for each question *N* for no answer, *I* for inaccurate answer, *C* for incomplete answer, *A* for ambiguous answer, and *R* for irrelevant answer.

1. Interviewer: How did you happen to find out about our company?
   Interviewee: (Looking around, appearing nervous, and not responding)   _____

2. Interviewer: Well, why are you interested in sales?
   Interviewee: Because I'm a real go-getter. I don't mind working for what I get. You only get out of life what you're willing to put into it!   _____

3. Interviewer: Do you have any background in sales?
   Interviewee: (sold Girl Scout cookies as a youngster) You bet. I've sold door to door for three years. During the first year, I sold more than anyone else in my group.   _____

4. Interviewer: How would you feel about traveling in a five state area?
   Interviewee: Okay.   _____

5. Interviewer: Have you done much traveling?
   Interviewee: Some employers don't offer very good travel budgets.   _____

6. Interviewer: Our company has a good record of meeting our employees' travel expenses. Where have you traveled to in the United States?
   Interviewee: All over.   _____

7. Interviewer: You've been in every state?
   Interviewee: No, but I've traveled a lot. A rolling stone gathers no moss, you know.   _____

8. Interviewer: Yes, well we'll get in touch with you if we are interested in pursuing your application further.
   Interviewee: Don't take any wooden nickels!   _____

Purposes of Interviews

People engage in interviews for a variety of purposes. The most common reasons are to collect information, to persuade someone to buy or believe something, or to find employment. We will consider the informational interview, the persuasive interview, and the employment interview.

Informational Interviews

We enter into **informational interviews** when we are collecting information, opinions, or data about a specific topic. The following are two examples of informational interviews.

The first interview, which follows, was conducted in order to gain initial knowledge about a small local business. The interviewer wants to know how the business was started, learn about the personnel, and gain some preliminary accounting information as the basis for an in-depth study later. The interview is moderately scheduled. Each question is categorized as open or closed, primary or secondary, and neutral or leading. You will notice that the interview includes many closed questions. Earlier the interviewee told the interviewer that he had very little time to discuss his business with her, so she attempted to adapt her interview to the limited time.

Opening: Good afternoon, Mr. Williams. My name is Kris Cook. I spoke with you a few days ago about doing an accounting systems analysis of your business. I will need to work with your accounting personnel, but I need about fifteen minutes of your time to find out some preliminary information.

Objective: To find out the history of the business	**Type of question**		
1) How was the racquet club started?	Open	Primary	Neutral
2) When was it opened?	Closed	Secondary	Neutral
3) It has been a fairly successful business venture, hasn't it?	Closed	Primary	Leading
4) How is it owned—sole proprietorship, partnership, corporation?	Open	Primary	Neutral
5) If it is a partnership or corporation, who owns the club?	Open	Secondary	Neutral
Objective: To find out about the staff			
6) What is the make-up of the staff and their responsibilities?	Open	Primary	Neutral
7) What is the make-up of the staff during odd hours—after 5:00 and on weekends?	Open	Secondary	Neutral
8) What portion of these are full-time and what portion are part-time?	Open	Secondary	Neutral
9) Are employees screened and trained for positions?	Closed	Secondary	Neutral
10) Are the employees who do accounting work bonded?	Closed	Secondary	Neutral
11) Are employees required to take vacations or rotate jobs?	Closed	Secondary	Neutral
12) How often are appraisal interviews held to evaluate employee progress and resolve any problems?	Open	Secondary	Neutral

13) Do you have an organizational chart?	Closed	Primary	Neutral
14) If not, could you describe the organizational structure?	Open	Secondary	Neutral

Objective: To find out about the basic accounting structure

15) What are the main sources of receipts?	Open	Primary	Neutral
16) How do these rank in terms of income generated?	Open	Secondary	Neutral
17) Are the records for the pro shop kept separate from the other records?	Closed	Primary	Neutral
18) Do you use an accrual or a cash accounting system?	Closed	Primary	Neutral
19) How often are budgets prepared?	Open	Primary	Neutral
20) How often are audits done?	Open	Primary	Neutral

Closing: Thank you, Mr. Williams. I will be in touch with your bookkeeper next week to complete my field study.

In the second informational interview, which follows, the interviewer is seeking information about job satisfaction at a particular company. The interview begins with an open question, switches to a series of closed questions, and concludes with the same open question with which it began. The notation in the left-hand column indicates whether each question is open *(o)* or closed *(c)*, primary *(p)* or secondary *(s)*, and neutral *(n)* or leading *(l)*.

Interviewer:
c/p/n
We are conducting a study of job satisfaction at this company. We are particularly interested in why people came to work here originally, and why they stay for such a long time. How long have you been with us?

Interviewee: About four years, I guess.

Interviewer: Why did you choose this company?
o/p/n

Interviewee: Gosh, that was quite a while ago. Let me think.

Interviewer: Yes, it was some time ago. Who were you working for before you joined
c/p/n us?

Interviewee: Midwest Machines.

Interviewer: Why did you leave that company? Were you dissatisfied?
o/p/n
c/s/l

Interviewee: It really wasn't a very pleasant place to work.

Interviewer: Did they offer a pension plan, a job rotation plan, training for auto-
c/p/n mation, a family health plan, or any other special benefits?

Interviewee: No, they didn't have any of those things.

Interviewer: Did your wife think that you should continue to work for Midwest
c/p/n Machines?

Interviewee: No, she was the one who suggested I try to get another job.

Interviewer: Did you hear about our plant through the paper or from someone you
c/p/n knew?

Interviewee: I spent a lot of time looking at the ads in the paper.

Interviewer: Why did you finally choose us?
o/p/n

Interviewee: It is a progressive company. It has a lot of personnel policies that I like.
My wife is satisfied that it's the best job for me.

The importance of asking effective questions is apparent in the lines spoken by the interviewer. Because the interviewer's intention is to find out whether the employee is satisfied with the company, the questions focus specifically on why the employee may or may not be satisfied. The employee's answers are nearly all declarative, but in an informational interview, the interviewer has to be careful not to invite the desired answers. In this interview, for instance, the interviewer may be perceived by the interviewee as part of the company's management. The interviewee may know at the outset that employees are being questioned about their job satisfaction or he may get the drift of the interview by listening carefully to the questions. Reporters, government employees, survey takers, and others who interview other people regularly should realize that many interviewees will simply tell them what they think they want to hear. Is there any way that we could determine, for instance, that the employee being interviewed in the excerpt above was worried about his job and was simply giving the interviewer the answers that he thought were the "right" ones? In other words, is it possible that the interviewee interpreted as leading questions some that we coded as neutral?

In-Class Informational Interview

Write down a number of topics in which you are interested or about which you have some knowledge. Exchange this list with a classmate. Select one of your classmate's topics and prepare a list of objectives and questions that will allow you to meet those objectives. At the next class meeting, interview the other person about his or her topic for approximately five minutes. Then, exchange roles and be prepared to answer the questions the other person has prepared for you. Discuss this exercise. Did you meet your objectives? Could you have improved upon your objectives?

Persuasive Interviews

We engage in **persuasive interviews** when our objective is to sell a particular idea, product, or service, or when someone else is trying to sell us something.

In the short persuasive interview that follows, a person is trying to persuade a friend to join a book club.

Interviewer: Did you know there's a sale on books through the Read-A-Book Club?

Interviewee: No, I'm not a member of it.

Interviewer: I've been a member for over two years and I've really enjoyed it. You have no minimum number of books to buy, they never send you a book that you don't order, and you can quit at any time.

Interviewee: What's the catch?

Interviewer: There is no catch. As a matter of fact, you receive three free books just for joining. Not only that, but I receive two free books if I get another person to join.

Interviewee: Well, I don't know.

Interviewer: I'll tell you what, if you find that you are dissatisfied with the first book you buy, I'll buy it from you for the full price.

Interviewee: I don't know how I can say "no."

Interviewer: Great!

The reliance on logical appeals—primarily, saving money—is evident in this interview. Although the interviewer used statements as frequently as he or she used questions, the first question, which is closed, is typical of the persuasive interview. Closed and leading questions are the tools of the persuasive interviewer.

Persuasive Interview Role-Play

Select a topic about which you feel very strongly—gun control, premarital sex, fundamentalist religion, environmental conservation, saving the whales, women's rights, required courses in college, intercollegiate athletics, gay rights, the use of oil and oil products, vegetarianism, junk food, jogging, abortion, open marriage, military draft, etc. Find a classmate who has chosen the same topic, but takes a position that is dissimilar from your own. The more diametrically opposed the position of the other person is, the more interesting this role-play will be. Use logical and emotional appeals and attempt to persuade your classmate to alter his or her position. Keep in mind that you probably will not alter his or her beliefs completely, but you may move them slightly. Be aware of the role of active listening and empathic listening on the part of the persuader. How well did you do in persuading your classmate? How could you have been more effective? What did you learn about persuasion in this exercise? (Keep these principles of persuasion in mind when you study the persuasive speech later in this book.)

After you have served as the interviewer in this assignment, exchange roles with the same person or with another classmate. After you have had the opportunity to serve as the interviewer and the interviewee, what conclusions can you draw? Have you retained your perspective on persuasion that you determined when you were the persuader? Does serving as the persuadee alter your perception? Which role do you prefer? Why? Have you learned anything about yourself as a communicator or the role of persuasion in communication?

Employment Interviews

The purpose of **employment interviews** is to select people for employment and to place them in certain positions or jobs. In the past, employers may have selected people because of their personality characteristics, their style, or their sex. Today, guidelines from the federal and state levels and recommendations from experts in the area of employment interviewing[3] suggest that such criteria are illegal or irrelevant. The Equal Employment Opportunity Commission (EEOC) has developed strict guidelines for interviewing and testing applicants. The five major provisions in the EEOC guidelines are: (1) discrimination on the basis of race, sex, or ethnic group cannot occur, (2) no one part of the interview may affect the evaluation of the whole, (3) validation of decisions must be demonstrated, (4) documentation must be provided, and (5) affirmative action should be taken to enact the guidelines. Both employers and employees should be familiar with the federal guidelines as well as state laws that govern hiring and firing.[4]

Planning is essential for a successful employment interview. A recent article portrayed two distinct models of the employment interview: the ideal and the dysfunctional. The ideal model assumes that the employment interviewer is prepared for the interview, conducts it in an unhurried and uninterrupted manner, and devotes his or her full attention to the employment candidate. The dysfunctional model includes a recruiter who has not read the candidate's resume before the interview, who allows interruptions, glances at his watch and other distractions, and generally makes the candidate uncomfortable.[5]

Thorough planning by the employment interviewer can insure a legal, effective interview. One method of planning includes the creation of an employment interview guide. This guide can be used in the actual interview, although the interviewer might want to deviate from it slightly depending upon the answers of the interviewee. The employment interview guide should consist of a general purpose, an opening or introduction, a schedule or list of questions, and a closing or summary. The general purpose identifies the objective of the interview, such as finding a manager of a local fast-food restaurant.

The opening or introduction should be brief but should introduce the employment interviewer, develop a congenial atmosphere, and provide an orientation for the interview. The early questions in the opening should be relatively easy to answer and should serve to put the interviewee at ease. An example of an opening follows:

Interviewer: Good afternoon. You're John Anderson, right? May I call you John? I'm Betty Wright, the owner of "Happy Hamburgers." Feel free to call me Betty, if you wish. Please sit down. I appreciate your being free at this time to talk with us about the possibility of managing our local store. I'd like to begin the interview by talking to you about your interests and background. Then we will proceed to what managing our store has to offer, and finally, I will answer any questions you may have. Please feel free to ask any questions about the position.

John, I see that you were a fry cook and a cashier for two other similar restaurants. I am not sure how they operate. Please tell me about the general operation at each of the two restaurants. What were your specific responsibilities at each?

The body of the interview includes questions designed to measure the individual's qualifications for the position. The employment interviewer should examine the responsibilities that the person will have and then determine the qualifications necessary for the job. Responsibilities for the management position at "Happy Hamburgers" include hiring counter personnel, insuring a particular level of quality in service and food, and suggesting promotional campaigns. Qualifications include being responsible, being organized, being creative, and relating well with people.

After the employment interviewer has determined general qualifications, he or she should determine more precisely what he or she needs by operationalizing the qualifications. For instance, being creative may be defined as "someone who can use language in a thought-provoking way for advertisements and promotional slogans." The operationalization of this definition would be "knows how to write jingles, rhymes, or alliterated phrases" or "knows currently used jargon that could be incorporated into a successful slogan."

Next, the employment interviewer creates sets of questions to help him or her obtain information to determine if the potential employee can meet the needs of the firm. In this example, questions might include "Have you ever written advertisements, slogans, or other promotional materials?" "What kinds of words do you associate with a *good* hamburger?" or "Can you think of some ways that 'Happy Hamburgers' could be marketed more successfully?"

The employment interviewer should also inform the applicant about the company. Before he or she proceeds, it is wise to ask the applicant if he or she has any information already. A direct question, "What do you know about 'Happy Hamburgers'?" is usually most successful in determining the applicant's level of knowledge.

Finally, you should allow the applicant the opportunity of asking questions about the position. Again, a simple request such as "What questions do you have?" or "Do you have questions about this position that have not been answered?" is sufficient.

The closing of the interview should maintain a positive climate and provide the employment interviewee with information about what will occur next. An example of a closing follows:

Interviewer: Thank you for interviewing with me. The information that I obtained will be very useful in making a decision. We have two more applicants to interview, and we will be finished with the interviewing process at the end of this week. I will call you on Monday of next week to let you know our decision. If you have any questions, don't hesitate to call. Also, if you have another offer or a change in your plans, please let us know. Thanks again for coming in to interview today.

Remember that, during the interview, the objectives should always be clearly stated, specifically defined and operationalized, relevant to the job, and ordered in terms of importance. The questions should be within the EEOC guidelines, should be designed to seek information specified in the objectives, should utilize information that is already available on the resume or application form, and should be sufficient in number to accurately assess applicant qualifications.

In addition to preparing an employment interview guide, the employer should demonstrate good communication skills in the interview. He or she should listen carefully and maintain eye contact, should word comments and questions in a careful manner, and should encourage the interviewee to answer freely.

The employment interview may be viewed from the perspective of the employment interviewer, as above, or from the perspective of the employment interviewees, or applicants. Applicants can do a great deal to make the employment interview a positive experience. Galassi and Galassi suggest that the interview preparation process can be divided into four phases. First, interviewees should develop realistic expectations about the particular job. Second, they should develop interviewing skills. Third, they should be able to demonstrate their skills and assess how they meet the needs of the job. Finally, the interviewee should be prepared for rejection. Most interviews do not conclude with the applicant being hired.[6]

Employment interviewers frequently complain that the interviewees demonstrate poor communication skills, that they appear ill-prepared for the interview, that they express only vague interest, that they lack motivation, and that they hold unrealistic expectations. Poor communication skills include long, rambling responses, lack of description, nervousness, and talking too much or talking too little. A recent study demonstrated that poor communication skills could be perceived as dishonesty. Interviewees who used short answers with long intervals between answers, vagueness, constant smiling, postural shifting, and grooming behavior were perceived as lying.[7]

Interviewees are perceived to be ill-prepared for the interview when they have no information about the company with which they are interviewing and if they have no questions to ask the interviewer during the interview. Lack of concern or lack of commitment are suggested by the interviewee who has not done the necessary homework before the interview.

Vague interests by applicants are demonstrated when they are not clear about their lifetime goals or when they cannot specify their career goals. Applicants who offer vague or ambiguous responses to questions about where they see themselves in ten years or how they expect their career to progress are viewed as holding unclear interests.

Lack of motivation is sometimes expressed by applicants for jobs. In a recent interview, a woman who was graduating from college was asked why she enjoyed her previous part-time employment and she responded, "Because that job was close to home and it started late in the day. It was easy to get to and didn't interrupt my sleep." The woman did not get the job because "She didn't seem to have any motivation—she seemed to want something that was easy and that would meet her own particular schedule." Lack of motivation can also be shown by lack of enthusiasm, lack of interest, and apathy. In addition, the applicant who is *too* agreeable may also be perceived as lacking in motivation. For instance, if you are willing to take low pay, poor working hours, bad working conditions, and no security, an employer might wonder about your ambition.

Finally, some employment interviewers have criticized interviewees for holding unrealistic expectations. The beginning college professor who expected a private secretary, the new clerk-typist who expected a private office, and the young physician who refused to work at night or on the weekends all serve as examples. Interviewees who are overly concerned with salaries or expect luxurious offices may be rejected because they lack realistic expectations.

The employment interview is worth time and preparation. The average person spends about two thousand hours each year at work. In forty years, the average length of time that most people work, he or she will have spent over eighty thousand hours at his or her chosen profession. Our time commitment to our employment warrants adequate preparation for the employment interview. Three essential steps in preparation include—knowing yourself, knowing about employment opportunities in general and especially at the specific company with which you are interviewing, and knowing the steps involved in getting a job, including the development of successful interviewing skills.

Knowing yourself is the first step to success in the employment interview. It is important to assess your own skills, knowledge, and experience. It is sometimes helpful to list each of these and rank them in terms of importance to you and in order of enjoyment. You might want to consider your *wants*—those things you would like to be able to obtain in a position—and your *musts*—those things that are imperative before you accept an offer. A review of chapter 5 on understanding yourself may be useful.

Second, you should know about employment opportunities in general and at the specific company with which you are interviewing. Many people consider only a relatively small number of occupations. A thorough search of potential positions might surprise you. Over twenty thousand jobs are currently available in the United States. A visit with your local placement office or an examination of the book, *Career Guide to Professional Occupations,* may provide you with useful information. Other opportunities available on many campuses such as internships, externships, cooperative positions, and summer work may also be beneficial.

You will impress an employment interviewer if you do a little homework before the interview. You can learn about the particular company with which you are interviewing from a variety of sources, including placement offices, the Better Business Bureau, the Chamber of Commerce, Dunn & Bradstreet, or you can write to the Security Exchange Commission for an Annual Corporate Report or a 10-K, which outlines the financial situation of corporations. A little knowledge about the position will demonstrate your interest and commitment.

You should know the process of getting a job with a particular company. Are you required to send a resume, send a letter of application, complete an application form, have references, send letters before the interview, participate in role-playing situations, complete personality inventories, participate in screening and selection interviews, or provide a copy of your portfolio? The steps that are involved and the order of these steps vary from company to company. You should know the basic steps that generally occur and learn about unusual procedures.

Finally, you should develop good communication skills that will be useful to you in the interviewing situation. Providing unambiguous nonverbal cues, self-disclosing appropriately, demonstrating empathy and active listening, and being descriptive and clear in your verbal comments are all important. In addition, you should rehearse your answers to some possible questions in order to be thoroughly prepared. A recent article lists the twelve questions that are asked most frequently by employers. They include the following:

1. What brings you to this agency?
2. What sort of job are you looking for?
3. What other efforts have you made to find a job?
4. Why do you want to leave your present job?
5. What percent of college expenses did you earn yourself?
6. What do you think of your present job?
7. What makes you think you would be good at the new job?
8. This question is unspoken. You simply fall silent, a device to test the applicant. Some applicants feel they must keep the ball rolling.
9. What sort of money are you looking for?
10. What do your parents do?
11. What are your best qualities?
12. Since no one is perfect, what are your worst qualities?[8]

Your placement office may be able to provide other typical sample questions that employers will ask. Some of the more common include the following:

What are your future vocational plans?
Why do you think you would like to work for our company?
What jobs have you held?
Why did you leave your previous jobs?
What courses did you like best in college (or in high school)?

Why did you choose your particular area of work?

What do you already know about this company?

What kind of salary do you expect?

What kind of person do you like to work for?

Do you like to travel?

Would you be willing to work overtime?

What special skills do you possess?

Were you involved in extracurricular activities in college?

Why did you go to college?

Do you like routine work?

Which cities seem particularly attractive to you in which to work?

Do you have an analytical mind?

Do you plan on doing any graduate work?

Do you prefer to work with others or alone?

Are you interested in research?

What kind of writing ability do you possess?

Do you believe your oral communication skills are above average?

You may wish to provide answers to these two sets of questions in order to thoroughly prepare yourself for the interview situation.

Employment Interview Preparation

For what a job or occupation are you most likely to interview? List ten questions that you will probably be asked in an interview setting, and write complete answers to each. In class, have a classmate role-play as an interviewer and ask you these or other appropriate questions. Discuss the results.

As an interviewee in the employment setting, you should effectively present your qualifications. This includes taking the initiative to present your major personal characteristics that meet the job qualifications, providing specific details about your background and qualifications, stressing skillfully, but honestly, your favorable characteristics, and treating questionable or weak factors in a tactful, positive, and candid way. By using good communication skills, you should present comments that are well organized, worded appropriately, and presented smoothly with confidence and enthusiasm; you should listen carefully; you should maintain good eye contact; and you should generally present an effective style. Your physical and mental image should include a neat, clean, conservative appearance; and you should demonstrate a thorough knowledge of yourself, including career objectives and personal goals, and a good knowledge of the potential employer and the position that is available.

In the employment interview that follows, emphasis is on the background, experience, training, and other interests that the applicant may have. In this situation, an application for the position has been previously submitted.

Interviewer: Good morning Bob; Bob Johnson, is that correct?
c/p/n

Interviewee: Yes, that's correct.

Interviewer: I'm Dave Selking, employment interviewer here at the company. Come over here and have a seat. Do you smoke, Bob?
c/p/n

Interviewee: No, thank you, I've never had the urge to start.

Interviewer: Well, I think you used good judgment in regard to your health and well-being, according to all recent medical reports. I see by your application you have some college training.

c/p/n Are you currently enrolled?

Interviewee: Yes, but only part-time now.

Interviewer: What are you studying?
c/s/n

Interviewee: Industrial management. I have twenty-one hours in the program.

Interviewer: Do you enjoy this field enough to continue and complete the program?
c/s/n

Interviewee: I enjoy the studies so far, but I met some students who are enrolled in a supervision program. I'm going into that some more because I think I would do well working with people. I'm more at ease with the human rather than the technical side of industry. And my credits would count toward a supervision degree.

Interviewer: Have you had any experience either in technical work or in a supervisory
c/p/n position?

Interviewee: Not really; I haven't been out of high school that long. However, I led a Boy Scout troop for five years and really enjoyed working with people. After becoming aware of the supervision courses, I feel that would suit me better.

Interviewer: Have you had any other leadership positions?
c/s/n

Interviewee: Not really in *leading* people, but I coach Wildcat Baseball teams every year and help to schedule the year's games.

Interviewer: Do you enjoy working in community affairs?
c/p/n

Interviewee: Yes, but I need a job, and that doesn't help me in getting one.

Interviewer: It doesn't hurt your situation any, let me assure you! Our organization, like every other industrial plant, exists in a community. We encourage our employees to participate and to show an interest in community projects.

Interviewee: In that case, I would like to point out that I helped form and organize the Decatur Youth Center and helped secure the use of the old County Building for our activities. We canvassed for funds and assistance in remodeling the interior to meet our needs. Oh, yes, I also helped organize

Interviewer: girls' softball three years ago. We had four teams then, and last summer we had sixteen full teams in the league with full sponsors. That took a lot of work, but it was rewarding. That's about all I helped to start.

Interviewer: This has been a highly informative interview. We are not hiring at present, but when we do, I assure you you'll be given every consideration. Thank you for your time, Bob. I appreciate your promptness in coming in when we called you.

The interviewer in the employment interview tries to draw out as much information as possible from the applicant. Notice how the interviewer reinforces the applicant every time he discloses additional information about his activities. The result is that the applicant feels good about telling the interviewer even more about his experience.

In general, the applicant should try to anticipate the questions. In this interview, the interviewer had to work to get the applicant to supply relevant leadership experience. Perhaps the interviewee was interpreting neutral questions as leading questions and was reluctant to disclose information that might hurt his opportunity for future employment with the company. It is essential to answer questions as openly and fully as possible in the employment interview situation.

Summary

In this chapter we explored the interview. We stated that interviews generally have a specific purpose and that they are planned and organized. Interviews are more formal than conversations and less formal than most small group discussions and public speaking. Interviews generally involve questions and are usually limited to two people. The questions can be categorized as open or closed, primary or secondary, and neutral or leading. The reasons that people engage in interviews are to collect information, to find employment, and to persuade.

Additional Readings

Beach, Dale S. *Personnel: The Management of People at Work.* 3d ed. New York: Macmillan Publishing Co., 1975. Pages 273–87.
Beach outlines the purposes and problems of the employment interview from the perspective of the employer. Good suggestions for planning the interview and communicating with the interviewee for best results.

*Dohrenwend, Barbara Snell; Klein, David; and Richardson, Stephen A. *Interviewing: Its Forms and Functions.* New York: Basic Books, 1965.
Analyzes the elements of the interview in terms of the interviewer's purpose, the interaction between interviewer and respondent,

*Indicates more advanced readings.

and the effects of questions. The book includes a discussion of the forms and the purposes of the interview, respondent participation, the question and answer process, and characteristics of interviewers and respondents. The book is recommended for beginning interviewers for its easy-to-understand style.

Fear, Richard A. *The Evaluation Interview*. New York: McGraw-Hill Book Company, 1978.
This book provides practical procedures on how to handle a job applicant from the moment he or she walks into the room until the interview is terminated. Fear's text could be useful for personnel workers and industrial managers. Two appendices include comprehensive instructions for writing the report of interview findings, samples of interview guides, rating forms, and illustrative reports of findings.

*Gordon, Raymond L. *Interviewing Strategy, Techniques, and Tactics*. Homewood, Ill.: The Dorsey Press, 1969.
Considers basic problems in interviewing and suggests techniques for attacking these problems. Interviewing strategy is discussed and examples are provided of friendly and hostile situations that might be encountered. Interviewer selection and characteristics of effective interviewers are considered. Techniques of interviewing, such as silence, and tactics of interviewing, such as chronological order of topics are included. Excerpts from interviews give this book a practical orientation.

*Kahn, Robert L., and Cannell, Charles F. *The Dynamics of Interviewing*. New York: John Wiley & Sons, 1957.
This book has an easily understood, conversational tone. It moves through the interview stages of motivating an "E," formulating objectives and questions, and probing. Nearly a hundred pages are devoted to illustrating interviews from such diverse fields as medicine, business, and social work. The dialogues in the appendices are also helpful in detecting a question that will lead to a better, more complete answer.

Pell, Arthur R. *Be a Better Employment Interviewer*. New York: Personnel Publications, 1978.
A guide for the screening employment interview. Among the topics considered are evaluating the resume and employing the physically handicapped. The book contains examples of job-related questions to ask when interviewing applicants in accounting, computer technologies, engineering, personnel, production, and marketing. An updated section on the legal requirements of interviewing and interviewing techniques is also included.

Stewart, Charles J., and Cash, William B. *Interviewing: Principles and Practices*. 2d ed. Dubuque, Iowa: Wm. C Brown Company Publishers, 1978.
A discussion of informative, persuasive, employment, appraisal, and counseling interviews, with insightful examples of each type. The principles of effective communication in the interview context and the writing and organizing of questions for the interview are also covered.

Thomas, Coramae, and Howard, C. Jeriel. *Contact: A Textbook in Applied Communications*. Englewood Cliffs, N.J.: Prentice-Hall, 1970. Pages 38–48.
The authors answer common questions about an employment interview: what to wear, what information to give, how to prepare for the interview, and how to behave verbally and nonverbally to make the best impression.

Zelko, Harold P., and Dance, Frank E. X. *Business and Professional Speech Communication*. New York: Holt, Rinehart and Winston, 1965. Pages 142–59.
A concise and helpful description of the procedures for conducting a successful interview. Step-by-step advice on setting up the interview, planning the questions, and conducting, recording, and closing the interview.

Notes

1. Felix M. Lopez, *Personnel Interviewing* (New York: McGraw-Hill Book Company, 1975), p. 1.
2. Charles J. Stewart and William B. Cash, *Interviewing: Principles and Practices,* 2d ed. (Dubuque, Iowa: Wm. C. Brown Company Publishers, 1978), pp. 5–6.
3. See, for example, John T. Hopkins, "The Top Twelve Questions for Employment Agency Interviews," *Personnel Journal* 59(May 1980):209–13; and Jack Bucalo, "The Balanced Approach to Successful Screening Interviews," *Personnel Journal* 57(August 1978):420–28.
4. Two recent articles that clarify the EEOC guidelines are William A. Simon, Jr., "A Practical Approach to the Uniform Selection Guidelines," *Personnel Administrator* 24(November 1979):75–79; and Robert D. Gatewood and James Ledvinka, "Selection Interviewing and the EEOC: Mandate for Objectivity," *Personnel Administrator* 24(December 1979):51–54.
5. Richard M. Coffina, "Management Recruitment Is a Two-Way Street," *Personnel Journal* 58(February 1979):86.
6. John P. Galassi and Merna Dee Galassi, "Preparing Individuals for Job Interviews," *Personnel and Guidance Journal* 57(December 1958):188–91.
7. Robert E. Kraut, "Verbal and Nonverbal Cues in the Perception of Lying," *Journal of Personality and Social Psychology* 36(1978):380–91.

9

The Small Group Discussion

An Application of the Principles of Interpersonal Communication

Objectives

1. Define small group discussion and explain the relevance of the terms cohesiveness, commitment, consensus, norms, and roles to small group discussion

2. Identify the four main principles of brainstorming; use brainstorming to create a list of topics for a small group discussion

3. Write questions of fact, policy, and value, and discuss the purpose of each type of question

4. List three ways of discovering information about a topic; state three questions that you should ask about the quality of information gained from primary sources; and state three questions you should ask in evaluating information gained from secondary sources

5. Discuss the functions, characteristics, and styles of leadership

Key Terms

small group discussion
group
small
cohesiveness
commitment
consensus
norms
roles
social function
task function
brainstorming
questions of fact
questions of value
questions of policy
primary research

secondary research
Dewey's method of reflective thinking
problem-solving discussion
communication networks
leadership
leader
emergent leadership
appointed leadership
laissez-faire leadership
permissive leadership
democratic leadership
supervisory leadership
autocratic leadership

ANIMAL CRACKERS

TUMBLEWEEDS

ANIMAL CRACKERS

These three cartoons introduce us to one type of interpersonal communication—the **small group discussion.** The first cartoon illustrates a number of small groups; the second states one purpose of small group discussion; and the third reminds us of the importance of leadership in the small group setting. We participate in small group discussions on a regular basis. Some of these discussions are about problems that we share with others and some are for sharing information. Sometimes we communicate in small groups as a sociable way to spend time.

In this chapter, we will consider the small group discussion as one type of interpersonal communication. The small group is interpersonal communication because individuals have equal opportunity to serve as listeners and as speakers. The same principles of effective interpersonal communication that have been identified in previous chapters, such as listening and self-disclosure, are essential to success in the small group discussion. In addition, we must understand the specific features of this form of interpersonal communication if we want to be competent in small group

discussions. This chapter focuses on some of the unique characteristics of the small group discussion. The context of communication in the small group will be our perspective.

Open and free discussion is essential in a free, democratic society. The complexity of our culture requires that each of us spends a great deal of time in small groups. Group discussion allows us to retain our humanity in a time that is marked by major social changes and a media-constructed reality. Small group discussion is important if we are to maintain our democratic way of life, cope with the complexities of our culture, and retain our humanity. Let us consider a definition and the basic components of the small group discussion.

Definition of Small Group Discussion

Before we define small group discussion, we need to clarify the terms we are using. **Small** alludes to the number of participants in group discussions—generally three to twenty people, most often four to seven. The word **group** is also used in a special way. In speech communication, it means a small number of individuals who share a common interest or goal, communicate with each other regularly, and contribute to the functioning of the group. We discount small numbers of people who do not have shared interests, do not communicate regularly with each other, and do not all contribute to the functioning of the group. Small group discussion is defined as communication among approximately three to twenty people who share a common interest or goal, meet regularly, and contribute to the functioning of the group.

Since small group discussion is a form of interpersonal communication, all the members have opportunities for verbal and nonverbal exchanges. The specific skills related to effective verbal and nonverbal communication in a dyad or in an interview are equally important in small group discussion. Self-awareness, self-disclosure, listening, and empathy all contribute to the success of the small group discussion.

Unique Features of the Small Group Discussion

Although the small group discussion shares characteristics with other forms of interpersonal communication, it also involves some unique features. The terms cohesiveness, commitment, consensus, norms, and roles are applied in a special way to the small group setting. The definition and application of each of these terms will be useful in understanding the small group.

Cohesiveness refers to the "stick-to-it-iveness" of the small group. Small group members must feel a sense of belonging or "groupness." This sense of unity with the group depends on the individual member's attraction to the group. Small groups sometimes are very cohesive because the members of the group feel that they have a great deal in common with the other members. They perceive their needs and interests matching the needs and interests of the others. The group may reinforce individuals for belonging to the group, which increases a feeling of cohesiveness.

Commitment is closely related to cohesiveness. Group members feel commitment to a group when the group is cohesive. Commitment to a group may arise because of interpersonal attraction among group members, because of commonality in beliefs, attitudes, and values, because of fulfillment of needs, or because of the reinforcement the group offers. Groups that meet to solve a problem or share information should also feel a commitment to their task. The lack of commitment to an assigned task can be very disruptive to the functioning of a small group.

Consensus generally results in a group that is identified by cohesiveness and commitment of the group members. Consensus refers to the general agreement among members and their support of the decisions that are made by the group. Consensus should not be confused with the situation in which people feel they cannot object to the decisions of the group. For instance, if a majority of the group members have a particular point of view and the minority feels they cannot object, consensus is not achieved. Consensus refers to genuine agreement and real commitment to the group decision. In the same way that commitment and cohesiveness contribute to consensus in the small group, consensual decision making often results in higher levels of commitment and greater cohesiveness.

Small groups establish **norms** by which to conduct their business. The norms of a group are those rules governing how members should behave and what behaviors are acceptable and unacceptable. The established norms of a group may be stated directly or only implied. The norms of a group help a group manage interaction and unify the members. Examples of norms are that group members can interrupt each other in discussion; that one member may criticize the decisions of the group, but no one else can offer evaluative comments; that the group meetings always begin ten or fifteen minutes after the appointed time to begin discussion; and that personal issues cannot be discussed.

Group members are often placed in particular **roles.** The role an individual plays in a group is her or his function in the group. The role that an individual plays is a function of her or his relationship to the other members of the group and to her or his relationship to the purpose of the group. A person may play the role of leader, of being highly task-oriented, of creating "comic relief," of organizer, of recorder, or a host of other roles. These roles may arise because of an individual's natural propensity to behave in a certain way. For example, "class clowns" play their role because of their sense of humor. Roles may also be assigned. For instance, many groups will appoint or elect someone to chair, or run, a discussion. In either case, a role is a pattern of behavior that is assumed by a member of a group.

You may find that you play one role particularly well in the small group. For instance, you may find that you are regularly the person who summarizes the other group members' contributions and moves the discussion forward. Or, you may be the person that everyone looks to for humor when the discussion is particularly difficult. It is important that we are able to identify those roles that we play most successfully and regularly in the small group and recognize the importance of our role to the success of the small group. On the other hand, it is also important to recognize that flexibility in our behavior is even more important. Playing the role of "tension reliever" when everyone else in the group is playing the same role is not useful. A group made up of "leaders" and no "followers" is probably doomed. We need to recognize that certain roles help the group achieve its goals and that we can be most effective in the small group setting by sensitively analyzing the roles that are needed and by being flexible enough to offer that particular role to the group.

The Function of Small Group Discussion

Small groups serve a variety of functions. They can satisfy the need that people have to be with each other. They can provide an emotional outlet for people who are concerned about a particular problem. Small groups allow people to meet the need they feel to belong to something. Small groups can share information or tackle important and difficult problems. In general, we can identify the function of most small groups as either social or task.

Small groups that have a **social function** include lunch groups, coffee parties, beer busts, cocktail parties, family reunions, and similar gatherings. The function of these groups is to provide time for companionship. They present an opportunity for individual interaction with a number of other people. Ritualized or ceremonial small groups, such as people at presidential teas, annual picnics, and even powwows are small social groups.

Small groups that have a **task function** include committees, church groups, community councils, task forces, book or literary clubs, parent-teacher associations, and business conferences. The task of such groups may be to share information or to solve a problem. In this chapter, we will limit our consideration to small groups that have a task to perform.

Social, Task, or No Small Group at All?

Identify each of the groups listed below as a small social group (a group that allows people time to share pleasant companionship), a small task group (a group whose purpose is sharing information or solving a problem), or as a group of people who do not fit our definition of a small group (approximately three to twenty people who have a shared interest or goal, who meet regularly, and who all contribute to the functioning of the group). Mark each statement with an *S* for a social group, a *T* for a task group, and an *N* if it does not fit the definition.

1. A group of people in an elevator   _____
2. Weight Watchers' weekly meeting   _____
3. A bridge group   _____
4. A group of Elks out for a night on the town   _____
5. The people who are riding on a city bus   _____
6. The monthly company meeting   _____
7. Four or five clerks in a department store who are gossiping about a new employee   _____
8. The people assembled in a huge stadium to hear Billy Graham   _____
9. A consciousness-raising group at a weekly meeting   _____
10. A university committee meeting   _____

The Process of Small Group Discussion: Preparation and Presentation

In the speech communication class in which you are enrolled, you will very likely be asked to present a small group discussion of an information-sharing or problem-solving nature. In order to assist you in the successful completion of this assignment, the steps essential to the preparation and presentation of the small group discussion are described. Our focus is on the discussion in a problem-solving group because it incorporates the essential elements of the information-sharing group discussion and includes additional steps. The problem-solving discussion tends to be more complex. If you are able to understand and carry out the suggestions for this form of

group discussion, you should have no difficulty adapting the suggestions to an information-sharing discussion.

Selecting a Topic   The first step in preparing for a group discussion is to select a topic. The method most often recommended is brainstorming. **Brainstorming** is a technique in which you list or name as many ideas as you can within a stated period of time. Alex Osborn, who introduced the technique nearly a quarter of a century ago, listed four rules governing brainstorming: (1) don't criticize any ideas; (2) no idea is too wild; (3) quantity is important; and (4) seize opportunities to improve or add to ideas suggested by others.[1]

Wording the Question to be Discussed   After you have selected a topic, the next task is to word the question to be discussed. The wording of the question is very important—it can lead to a fruitful or a wasted group discussion. The question clarifies the purpose of the discussion, suggests the avenues of research, and largely determines the agenda.

        Categories of discussion questions. In general, questions to be discussed can be placed into one of three categories. **Questions of fact** deal with truth and falsity. They are concerned with the occurrence, the existence, or the particular properties of something. Examples of questions of fact include "Does the United States have enough water to meet normal needs?" "Are small amounts of marijuana harmful to the human body?" "Do women have equal opportunities for employment in the United States?" and "Has Consolidated Edison New York taken measures sufficient to forestall another blackout in the next five years?"

Questions of value require judgments of good and bad. Such questions are grounded in the participant's motives, beliefs, and cultural standards. Desirability and satisfaction are often central to questions of value. Examples of questions in this category are "Is a college education desirable for everyone?" "Are older people discriminated against?" "Are beauty contests desirable?" and "Do we need to reform tax laws in the United States?"

Questions of policy concern future action. The purpose of a policy question is to determine a course of action to be taken or supported in a specific situation. The word *should* often appears in a question of policy. Examples of questions of policy include "Should rules against nepotism be dropped?" "Should seniority systems be eliminated?" "Should students be required to take specific courses?" and "Should the possession of small amounts of marijuana be legalized?"

Identify the Category of Each of These Questions for Discussion

Place the following questions into one of the three categories of discussion questions. Mark each question *F* for fact, *V* for value, or *P* for policy.

1. Does the U.S. need to import oil? _____
2. Is the U.S. facing a drought? _____
3. Should pornography be prohibited? _____
4. Do X-rays of the head or neck cause cancer of the thyroid gland? _____
5. Is a person's social standing directly related to his or her wealth? _____
6. Should we spend less money on weapons? _____
7. Should employees determine their own work schedules? _____
8. Should women retain their unmarried names when they marry? _____
9. Should saccharin be banned? _____
10. Does regular exercise lengthen your life? _____
11. Should the federal government regulate the use of energy? _____
12. Should everyone have the right to get married? _____
13. Does unemployment fall disproportionately on the young? _____
14. Are abortion laws too liberal? _____
15. Should right-to-work laws be repealed? _____

Characteristics of good discussion questions. All discussion questions should meet a minimum set of standards. Among the characteristics of good discussion questions—whether they are questions of fact, value, or policy—are that they should be simple, objective, and controversial. By *simple,* we mean that the question should be written with the fewest number of words, easily understood. The question should be understandable to all who read or hear it. The questions should be concise, not wordy. In addition, the question should be appropriate for the time available, the research available, and the persons who will be discussants. A question for discussion such as "Do most people anticipate the advent of androgyny vis-à-vis the economic structure?" does not meet the criterion of simplicity. This question is lengthy, esoteric, and obtuse.

A discussion question should be written *objectively*. It should not imply "correct" answers. Persons reading the question should be able to suggest alternative answers. The question "Should the current national tax structure, which favors the rich and discriminates against the poor, be changed?" does not meet the criterion of objectivity. The only possible answer to this leading question is "Yes."

The discussion question should be controversial. It should not be a question the answer to which has already been determined. Nor should it concern a matter for which the group has an agreed-upon solution. The question should be timely—of current international, national, or local concern; interesting to the group members; and worthwhile to those involved. The questions that follow are not suitable. "Should the E.R.A. be passed?" is out of date for many Americans. "Should homosexuals be allowed to marry?" may be irrelevant to the members of a particular discussion group. "Should students be given more course selection in their higher education?" would probably receive a unanimous "yes" from a group of college students.

Researching the Topic   After you have identified the topic of your discussion and worded the question, the next task is to research the topic. You must *discover the information,* and then you must *evaluate it.* Among the sources that you should consider for securing information are interviews with people close to the problem, surveys of the people involved, and secondary sources available in the library. Interviewing was discussed earlier in this chapter. Surveys and library research are discussed in chapter 11; read ahead to familiarize yourself with them. You may choose one or more avenues of research. The nature of your question will dictate the kind of research that is necessary.

It is equally important, in research, to evaluate the information you find. Too often, we assume that simply collecting information concludes the research task. An abundance of unevaluated information may be worthless.

Evaluating Primary Research   We evaluate **primary research**—interviews, surveys, and personal experience—differently from **secondary research**—information we

find in books, magazines, and similar sources. Three questions should be asked about our *primary research:* (1) Are eyewitness accounts confirmed? (2) Is the authority competent? (3) Is the source unbiased?

Are eyewitness accounts confirmed? In chapter 2 we discussed the role of perception in communication. We stated that people can observe the same phenomena but have greatly divergent perceptions and draw entirely different conclusions. Consensual validation—checking our observations with others—was suggested as a remedy. When we engage in primary research, we should validate the perceptions of one person with the perceptions of others.

Is the authority competent? In other words, is the person a recognized expert? Do others agree that he or she is knowledgeable and experienced about the question under consideration? We should keep in mind that people can be experts in one area, but may know little about other areas. The football player who testifies to the quality of women's clothing may be out of his league.

Is the source unbiased? Sometimes people have a vested interest in a particular point of view. They may realize some real or intangible gain if others can be convinced to see things in a certain way. For instance, a speech teacher would very likely believe that speech should be a required course. Experts in college administration or alumni would be better sources because they are less likely to be biased.

Evaluating Secondary Research A different set of questions should be asked if we are evaluating *secondary research*—information from books, magazines, and similar sources. Among them are (1) Is the information consistent? (2) Is the information current? (3) Is the information complete?

Is the information consistent? Two types of consistency are important in evaluating secondary research. Is the information internally consistent? Does the author suggest two or more conflicting conclusions? Do the conclusions follow logically from the material reviewed? Second, is the information consistent with other sources? Does it agree with other findings? Are there startling conclusions that violate previously known facts? Differences between one author's point of view and another's do not render the information inaccurate or the conclusion false, but you must consider why the disagreement exists.

Is the information current? The publication date of a source may be unimportant or crucial. In some cases, the date can resolve conflicts of evidence.

Is the information complete? The reference should be complete in two senses. The source should not take information from other sources out of context or report someone else's work only partially, in order to make a point. The reference work should be an examination of the entire problem or area under consideration, rather than a tangential view. In other words, the secondary source should include the comprehensive statement or conclusion offered by another and should cover all of the ground that is promised.

Organizing the Discussion For many years, **Dewey's method of reflective thinking** was considered the only way to organize a group discussion. Discussants followed this organizational plan:

1. *Recognize the problem.* Acknowledge that a problem exists and that the group members are concerned about that specific problem.
2. *Define the problem.* Identify the nature of the problem and define the critical terms.
3. *Analyze the problem.* Suggest the cause of the problem, the extensiveness of the problem, and the limits of the problem.
4. *Establish criteria for evaluating solutions.* Decide by which criteria a solution will be evaluated. The group determines if the solution must solve the problem entirely or whether a partial solution will be acceptable. It decides whether the efficiency of the solution is an important criterion and makes other similar decisions.
5. *Suggest solutions to the problem.* By brainstorming or other techniques, the group lists possible solutions to the problem.
6. *Select the best solution.* After many solutions have been offered, group members subject them to the previously established criteria (Step 4). They select those solutions that best fit the criteria. They consider combining two or more possible solutions. Finally, they identify the best solution.
7. *Test the solution.* The final step in the Dewey method of reflective thinking is testing the solution, which is often done by trying out the solution in practice. Decisions can then be made about the effectiveness of the solution.

More recently, authors have suggested that a strict adherence to this organizational pattern results in planned performances rather than decision-making processes. These authors have demonstrated that many questions are not susceptible to solution by Dewey's method of reflective thinking. However, you may find Dewey's method helpful in arranging your **problem-solving discussion.**

A number of alternative organizational patterns have been created for the use of small groups. Most of them include the following stages:

1. Identifying and specifying a particular question.
2. Collecting and analyzing relevant information.
3. Determining the strengths and weaknesses of various answers to the question.
4. Selecting the most appropriate answer.
5. Testing the answer.

At base, all problem-solving discussions must include two questions: (1) What is the nature of the problem? and (2) How can we solve it? Subsidiary questions can be added to this most simple organizational pattern to meet the group's needs.

A group may find that the problem it is considering requires a very loosely structured pattern. Or group members may find that they require a very prescriptive pattern of organization. The appropriate organizational pattern will depend on the nature and composition of the group as well as on the nature of the problem. Regardless of what specific organizational pattern seems appropriate, it is essential that the discussion be organized.

Interaction in the Small Group

Communication Networks

Communication in the small group is complicated by the number of individuals involved. In the dyad, the two people can only interact with each other; in the small group, interaction is possible in a variety of combinations. In order to better understand the possible interactions and the influence of these interactions on the group, the phrase communication networks has been coined. **Communication networks** refers to the pattern of communication among members. Five different possibilities have been identified. These include the chain, the Y, the wheel, the circle, and the all-channel network. These five possibilities are depicted in figure 9.1.

The chain allows each member to communicate with one or two other members, but not with everyone in the group. The chain is often present in business organizations in which the president speaks only to the vice-president, who, in turn, speaks only to senior managers, who pass information on to subordinates. The Y similarly allows communication only among two or three members.

The wheel often occurs when one person serves as the leader and is very dominant in his or her interactions with others. This person communicates with everyone else, but the others in the group have the privilege of speaking only to him or her. The dominant person is depicted by the middle position in the wheel. Group discussions, which can be depicted as wheels, are often characterized by satisfaction being demonstrated by one person (the dominant center) and dissatisfaction shown by the others. The wheel is generally faster in information flow than the other networks, but the decreased member satisfaction often outweighs this consideration.

Leaderless discussions are depicted in the circle and the all-channel networks. The circle is similar to the chain in that each person may only speak with two others rather than the entire group. The all-channel network may be the slowest interaction system of the five shown here, but it generally results in the highest member satisfaction. In the all-channel network, each person is allowed the opportunity of speaking with all others.

Figure 9.1   Communication networks: a. chain, b. Y, c. wheel, d. circle, and e. all-channel.

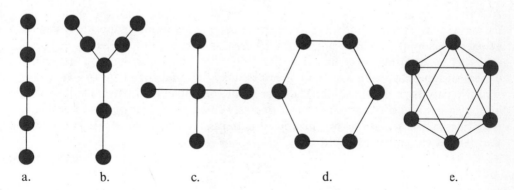

a.   b.   c.   d.   e.

Intrapersonal and Interpersonal Communication

Research on these five communication networks has resulted in some interesting conclusions. Centralized networks, which are exemplified by the chain and the wheel, appear to be superior in simple problem-solving, but decentralized networks, such as the circle and all-channel network, are clearly superior if the problem is complex. In general, the decentralized circle and decentralized all-channel network will allow faster and more accurate solutions and will also allow greater member satisfaction.[2] You may wish to examine the communication patterns of the groups in which you are involved to determine the typical interaction patterns that occur.

Participating in a Small Group Discussion

You can interact more effectively in the small group if you consider your role as a participant and if you are sensitive to the interaction patterns that occur in the group. You may be surprised that participants, like leaders of small groups, have responsibilities in the small group context. In general, you should review the earlier chapters on self-awareness, self-disclosure, and listening. A positive self-concept, an ability to share your feelings and experiences, and critical, active, and empathic listening are all important to the effective small group participant.

In addition to these general skills, you may wish to consider some other specific abilities that will contribute to the success of the small group. First, you should try to develop a sense of "groupness." We have all observed team sport players who have demonstrated a great deal of individual talent, but were unable to "play as a team" member—the basketball player who dribbles, passes, and shoots well, but refuses to hand off the ball so a team member could make a basket; and the tennis player who plays singles well, but tries to cover the entire court when playing doubles and consequently loses the game. Similarly, an effective communicator who cannot cooperate with the group, but views small group communication as an individual competitive event, will negatively affect the entire group.

Second, you should develop an openness to others and to new ideas. You need to be willing to hear other people, just as you expect them to hear you out. You may need to develop patience in dealing with specific individuals in the small group and in dealing with the sometimes seeming slowness of the small group process. You should listen carefully and thoughtfully to ideas that may seem, at first, to hold little merit. Sometimes the most successful ideas are created by combining two or more unworkable ones. Avoid premature dismissal of ideas or of individuals in the small group.

Third, be willing to communicate appropriately. You should avoid monopolizing the small group. Remember, small group communication allows *equal* opportunity for the communication of all members. However, you should also avoid becoming the "silent member." Be willing to share your ideas and make appropriate contributions, but do not do so to the exclusion of the other members.

Fourth, attempt to become sensitive to the other group members. Listen carefully to the feelings being expressed as well as the ideas. Become a sensitive observer of nonverbal communication. Do others look bored, tired, angry, confused, or frustrated? What are some of the possible causes for their reactions? How can you alter or alleviate a negative situation? How can you sustain or encourage a positive situation? Be observant to verbal and nonverbal messages and try to determine how you can react.

Finally, you should be sensitive to the context of small group communication. Consider the role of cohesiveness, commitment, consensus, norms, roles, and communication networks. How would you define them for the particular small group in which you are working? Are they operating in an effective way? Can you alter some of the patterns of communication, the roles that members are playing, the agreements that are being reached, or the rules that govern communication in your small group? Do physical features, such as the size of the room, the arrangment of tables and chairs, etc., affect the interaction in the group? What other factors that are unique to the small group setting should be considered and possibly altered? Can you initiate some of these changes? Let us turn now to the role of the person who serves a leadership function.

Leadership

In the past, this section on preparing for group discussion might have been entitled "Choosing a Leader." Earlier writers and researchers stressed the importance of identifying one person who would serve as the leader of the group rather than considering leadership as a process in which the entire group engages. **Leadership** is defined as behavior that aids in the clarification and achievement of group goals. Leadership is synonymous with influence. A **leader,** then, may be defined as an influential person, as one who helps the group to clarify and attain its goals, or as one who is selected or designated as the leader of a particular group. Leadership is generally shared by the members of a group; often, more than one person acts as the leader, depending on the definition that is used.

Leadership may emerge in a small group or it may be appointed. **Emergent leadership** occurs when no one is appointed to be the leader, but individuals with leadership ability emerge from the group. The emergent leader is the person who others in the group identify as the leader, when no leader was elected or officially chosen for the group. **Appointed leaders** are those leaders who are selected by someone outside the group, elected by the group members, or chosen in some other way. Group members respond differently to emergent and appointed leaders. In general, group members agree more with statements made by appointed leaders than they do with emergent leaders.[3] In addition, elected leaders have more freedom in their behaviors than do appointed leaders, but the group members hold higher expectations for the elected leader.[4]

One approach to leadership suggests that emergent leaders share certain qualities or traits. These characteristics are:

1. An ability to communicate clearly and effectively
2. An ability to listen for the content and the intent of the other group members' comments
3. An ability to think quickly—to follow closely what is being said and to think ahead of the group
4. Knowledge about the topic under discussion
5. Knowledge of group process

Figure 9.2   Styles of leadership.

Laissez-faire   Democratic   Autocratic

Permissive   Supervisory

Another perspective on leadership suggests that typical patterns or styles of leadership exist. One of the most common methods of distinguishing among leadership styles is to place laissez-faire leadership at one end of a continuum and autocratic leadership at the other end and the various styles between these extremes. Figure 9.2 depicts five styles of leadership. **Laissez-faire leadership** is the least directive and offers group members almost no direction. **Permissive leadership** offers some control, but is relatively free. **Democratic leadership,** the golden mean of leadership, falls somewhere in the middle of the continuum and balances control with freedom. **Supervisory leadership** falls between democratic leadership and the autocratic style. **Autocratic leadership** offers the most control and group members who have an autocratic leader find that they have no, or very little, freedom.

The type of leadership affects the group outcome. Laissez-faire leadership appears to result in the least amount of work and the poorest quality of work. Hostility and aggression often result when the leadership is autocratic, but autocratic leadership produces more work than does democratic leadership. Democratic leadership seems to be the most successful because work motivation is higher, more originality in ideas is demonstrated, and group members indicate a preference for this style of leadership.[5].

In a group discussion, the ideal situation is to have a number of people who can perform leadership functions and who are able and willing to share leadership. In addition, it is also important to identify one person as the chosen or designated leader. This person generally exhibits a number of leadership qualities, but also performs a number of procedural functions. Brilhart suggests that the functions of leaders can be categorized into "initiating, organizing, spreading participation, stimulating both creative and critical thinking, facilitating understanding, promoting cooperative interpersonal relationships, and developing the group and members."[6] While this list may sound overwhelming, these classes of behaviors are comprehensive and may be shared among members.

Initiating may include ice-breaking activities or other action by which the members of the group learn the names of the other members and are introduced to each other. During this stage, procedures, purposes, and other plans should be outlined. Opening remarks may be made and necessary arrangements, such as securing and running a tape recorder, appointing a secretary, or arranging the room, should be handled. The members should be made to feel comfortable during this initial phase.

Organizing refers to orderliness. The leader should help to keep the group moving toward its goal, summarize, make transitions, and bring the group to a conclusion at the end. When the group digresses from the topic, the leader should help the group go back to the topic; when the group repeats itself, the leader should be sensitive to the need to move on; and when the group spends a great deal of time on one aspect of the problem, the leader should remind the group of time constraints and help them to budget their time appropriately.

Spreading participation means that the group leader helps to equalize or divide participation among group members. Individuals in the group should not feel obliged or forced to speak if they have nothing to contribute, but talkative members should not be allowed to obviate the contribution of certain members. The leader should be a careful observer of members to determine if they wish to speak and an active listener to determine what points need extension or clarification. Acceptance should be shown toward the contributions of all of the members—no matter how trivial the remark. Highly evaluative verbal or nonverbal responses may serve to discourage individuals from future participation.

Stimulating both creative and critical thinking refers to encouraging both novel and unique ideas and being analytical and careful in the easy acceptance of ideas. While it is difficult to encourage both at once, both kinds of thinking are essential to the successful small group discussion. Criteria by which solutions or answers will be measured should be uniformly understood; ideas should not be dismissed until they have been carefully and thoughtfully measured against existing criteria; and new approaches should be encouraged.

Facilitating understanding means that the leader models active and empathic listening and that he or she encourages others to engage in this kind of listening as well. Pointing up areas of agreement, stressing commonalities, suggesting visualizations, and offering analogies would all contribute to understanding among members.

Promoting cooperative interpersonal relationships is another function of the leader. Tension within the group should be reduced so people can work together effectively. Disallowing conflict over personalities or personal issues is useful. The leader can encourage humor as a tension-reliever in groups that are particularly serious or have an especially difficult task. When conflict does arise, using conflict-reduction methods such as compromise, negotiation, consensus, or arbitration may be helpful.

Developing the group and its members suggests that the leader helps the group and the individuals that comprise the group to grow and change. Sometimes these goals are at cross-purposes, but usually helping individuals develop their repertoire of roles within a group or helping members learn more about a certain topic also helps the group to develop and grow. Similarly, helping the group to develop by establishing consensus and member satisfaction frequently results in individual growth in the members. Growth of the group at the cost of the individuals has short-term positive benefits. Also, helping individuals grow and develop without regard to the group's goal has limited benefit.

Effective leadership is essential to successful problem solving in the small group discussion. As we stated earlier, the leadership of a small group discussion is generally shared, but the designated leader has the responsibility of ensuring that all of the leadership functions are performed. If you are selected as the leader of a small group or if you emerge as the leader, you will want to review the functions that must be provided by leadership and ensure that someone else is fulfilling them, or you must be able to fill this role.

Summary

In this chapter we explored one form of interpersonal communication—the small group discussion. We defined a small group as consisting of about three to twenty people who share a common interest or goal, meet regularly, and contribute to the functioning of the group. Small groups serve a variety of functions, but most functions can be classified either as social, which means that the group's purpose is to share time with agreeable companions, or as task, which means that the group has the purpose of sharing information or solving a problem.

We considered the preparation and presentation of the problem-solving small group discussion in detail. Essential steps in problem solving include selecting a topic, wording the question to be discussed, researching the topic, evaluating primary and secondary research, organizing the discussion, and establishing appropriate interaction patterns. Leadership was defined and the qualities, functions, and styles of leadership were delineated. The success of the small group discussion depends on the ability of the participants to communicate with each other effectively.

Additional Readings

Bormann, Ernest G., and Bormann, Nancy C. *Effective Small Group Communication.* 2d ed. Minneapolis: Burgess Publishing Company, 1976.
A practical approach to learning the skills of effective small group communication, including task, leadership, message preparation, research, and discussion techniques. Understandable, good introductory reading.

Brilhart, John K. *Effective Group Discussion.* 3d ed. Dubuque, Iowa: Wm. C. Brown Company Publishers, 1978.
A practical approach to researching, organizing, and discussing problems in a small group. Contains specific guidelines for improving discussion and leadership skills.

*Cathcart, Robert S., and Samovar, Larry A. *Small Group Communication: A Reader.* 3d ed. Dubuque, Iowa: Wm. C. Brown Company Publishers, 1978.
An excellent collection of the important writings on small group behavior, including a discussion of models, interpersonal dynamics, leadership, conformity, and group decision making. Excellent source of material for term papers or in-depth study of small group processes.

*Davis, James H. *Group Performance.* Reading, Mass.: Addison-Wesley Publishing Company, 1969.
A report on the research into individual performance in groups, the influence of social interaction on decision making, group size, cohesiveness, and structure. Becomes a bit technical at times.

*Fisher, B. Aubrey. *Small Group Decision Making: Communication and the Group Process.* 2d ed. New York: McGraw-Hill, 1980.
Fisher asserts that communication is a process and that the small group is a social system. Thoroughly covers the group process, dimensions of the group process, structural and functional elements of group communication, behavioral standards, leadership, and status, social conflict and deviance and improvement of the effectiveness of communication in the small group.

Phillips, Gerald M.; Pedersen, Douglas J.; and Wood, Julia T. *Group Discussion: A Practical Guide to Participation and Leadership.* Boston: Houghton Mifflin Company, 1979.
"Method" and "choice" are the key concepts in the development of this text. The authors provide numerous detailed descriptions of methods that can be used to organize more effective discussions. They stress the notion that the competent small group communicator is able to analyze group conditions and to respond with appropriate alternative choices. The book is evenly divided between theory and application.

Scheidel, Thomas M., and Crowell, Laura. *Discussing and Deciding: A Desk Book for Group Leaders and Members.* New York: Macmillan Publishing Co., Inc., 1979.
A reference book that considers the components of the small group process, discusses and analyzes the steps that are involved in group discussion, and gives an annotated list of special techniques and references. Theory and research is integrated in order to create an easy-to-understand how-to-do-it book on small group discussion.

*Shaw, Marvin E. *Group Dynamics: The Psychology of Small Group Behavior.* New York: McGraw-Hill Book Company, 1971.
A classic treatment of the variables affecting small group processes. Especially good chapters on group formation, leadership, and interpersonal dynamics as they affect the group's ability to complete a task and make decisions.

*Indicates more advanced readings.

Notes

1. Alex F. Osborn, *Applied Imagination: Principles and Procedures of Creative Thinking* (New York: Charles Scribner's Sons, 1953), pp. 300–301.
2. Marvin E. Shaw, "Communication Networks," in *Advances in Experimental Social Psychology,* ed. Leonard Berkowitz, vol. 1 (New York: Academic Press, 1964), pp. 111–47.
3. Connie S. Hellmann, "An Investigation of the Communication Behavior of Emergent and Appointed Leaders in Small Group Discussion" (Ph.D. diss., Indiana University, 1974).
4. Myles T. Edwards, Edwin P. Hollander, and Barry J. Fallon, "Some Aspects of Influence and Acceptability for Appointed and Elected Group Leaders," *Journal of Psychology* 19(1977): 289–96.
5. R. White and R. Lippit, "Leader Behavior and Member Reaction in Three 'Social Climates'," in *Group Dynamics: Research and Theory,* ed. Dorwin Cartwright and Alvin Zander, 2d ed. (New York: Harper and Row, 1960), pp. 527–53.
6. John K. Brilhart, *Effective Group Discussion,* 3d ed. (Dubuque, Iowa: Wm. C. Brown Company Publishers, 1978), pp. 170–82.

Public Communication

Public communication is the process of understanding and sharing that occurs in the speaker-to-audience situation. Public communication, like interpersonal communication, is a transaction in which people simultaneously give and receive meaning from each other.

Our exploration of public communication begins with the audience. Chapter 10, "Understanding through Topic Selection and Audience Analysis," reveals how to select and limit a topic and analyze an audience for information of value to the speaker. Chapter 11, "Sharing Yourself: Source Credibility and Credible Sources," focuses on the speaker and explains what credibility is, what a speaker can do to enhance it, and how the speaker can find and use credible sources. Will credibility, for example, help change attitudes or opinions?

Chapter 12, "Sharing Your Message through Organization," is a survey of the various patterns of organization for a public speech. It deals especially with the principles of outlining. "Sharing Yourself through Delivery and Visual Aids," chapter 13, discusses the vocal and bodily aspects of speaking in public—including voice, eye contact, gestures, and movement. It also describes the use of visual aids in delivering a speech. Chapter 14 studies the informative speech and contains practical advice for developing this type of speech. Chapter 15 is a study of the persuasive speech. It discusses various topics, purposes, and appeals of persuasive speaking and describes strategies for altering the audience's attitudes and behavior.

10

Understanding through Topic Selection and Audience Analysis

Objectives

1. Employ brainstorming techniques to generate a list of possible topics for your speeches
2. Use personal inventories to find subject areas for possible topics
3. Limit your topic to fit the subject, the audience, and the time allowed
4. Analyze your audience for demographics, interest, knowledge, and attitudes
5. Deliver a speech in which you exhibit audience sensitivity

Key Terms

brainstorming	audience knowledge
personal inventory	attitude
involvement	belief
narrowing the topic	value
audience analysis	observation
captive audience	inference
voluntary audience	questionnaire
demographic analysis	adapting to an audience
audience interest	

I don't have the foggiest notion what I should talk about in my speech next Monday.
Beginning speech student

I have found a topic that I really like, but I find that I know only enough about it to fill two minutes, not five or ten. What am I supposed to do now?
Intermediate speech student

I don't know why we don't get to talk longer. Why, I had enough material to last for an hour and a half on the topic.
Advanced speech student

Choosing a topic for a speech can be a problem, unless you know what you are doing. You may have discovered that when you are assigned to write a paper or deliver a speech, the beginning step of finding something to write or speak about is difficult. You may not be able to think of a topic as soon as you hear the assignment. Instead, you may find yourself mulling over the assignment for days, sharpening your pencil, and getting water or coffee as you think, and selecting a topic after most of your time for completing the assignment has slipped away.

Most of us find that we spend too much of our time thinking of a topic. Reading this chapter will help you by illustrating two methods of selecting topics for speeches. This chapter will also help you to link topic selection to audience analysis; that is, to select topics with your particular audience in mind so the topic is appropriate for you, for your audience, and for the situation in which you are going to deliver the speech. Let us begin by examining some methods of finding a topic.

Selecting and Limiting the Topic

Brainstorming

In chapter 9, in the section "Selecting a Topic," you learned the term **brainstorming.** This technique can also be used effectively in selecting a topic for a speech. Brainstorming generates a large number of ideas, which are not being evaluated. Imagination can run riot. No one student will develop the same list as another because each will think of topics that relate in some way to himself or herself. You may end up with a list of possible topics that you can develop into speeches. You might want to try brainstorming, to find out if it works for you.

Brainstorming Exercise

Take out a pencil and paper. Give yourself five minutes to write down the ideas that come to mind. Use single words, phrases, or sentences, or any combination. The emphasis is on quantity. How many topics can you produce in five minutes? When you have completed this portion of the exercise, you may have as many as twenty-five or more ideas, or as few as five. The second step is to go over your list and select three that you find interesting enough to use for your speech. Last, select the one that appeals to you most. This can be the topic you use for your speech *if* you know enough about the topic or can find out enough through research, and *if* you can figure out how to adapt the topic to your audience.

Understanding through Topic Selection and Audience Analysis

Personal Inventory

Another way to find a topic for your speech is to do a **personal inventory** of your own reading habits. Choosing one topic from thousands of possible topics requires some self-analysis.

You make choices every time you read something. When you sit down with the newspaper, you probably do not read the entire paper. You might read the headlines, a few articles on the front page, the comic strips, and the sports page. Another person might read the wedding announcements, the opinion page, and the obituaries. Even when you read a general newsmagazine like *Time, Newsweek,* or *U.S. News and World Report,* you probably choose certain parts to read. You might read the international news and the art news but skip the sections on music and books. What you do when you read a newspaper or newsmagazine reflects your own interests. To discover your own interests more systematically, you might try completing the next exercise.

Newspaper Inventory

Take the local newspaper and note the sections you read often (+), sometimes (O), rarely or never (−).

_____ Front-page news	_____ Birth and wedding announcements
_____ Comics	_____ Home and family
_____ Sports	_____ Art and music
_____ Editorial page	_____ Books
_____ Letters to the editor	_____ Travel
_____ Obituaries	

Newsmagazine Inventory

Or, take the newsmagazine of your own choice and record the sections you actually read (+), the sections you occasionally read (*O*), and the sections you rarely or never read (−). The following sections are the ones ordinarily published in *Time* magazine, but a similar list could be compiled for any newsmagazine.

_____ Cover story	_____ Living
_____ Essay	_____ Milestones
_____ Art	_____ Nation
_____ Books	_____ People
_____ Cinema	_____ Religion
_____ Economy and business	_____ Science
_____ Energy	_____ Sports
_____ Law	_____ World
_____ Letters to the editor	

The checklist of items that you read in the newsmagazine or newspaper gives you a rough indication of your own interests. Another way is to list your hobbies or leisure-time activities, the organizations to which you belong, the books you have read recently, the movies you have seen recently, the television shows you watch most frequently, and the magazines you most enjoy. Your choice of college, major subject, and elective courses can also indicate your likes and dislikes.

After you have completed a personal inventory of your own preferences, you can more clearly identify the topics or subjects that are most appropriate for you. After you learn how to analyze an audience, you can determine whether your topic is appropriate. You are now ready to assess your personal involvement in the topic and your personal knowledge of the topic.

Involvement

After you have tentatively selected a topic area, you should evaluate the topic to see if you have the appropriate interest, knowledge, and experience to speak about that topic. The first step in evaluating the topic is to consider how important the topic is to you—**involvement.**

The first question is: How strongly do you feel about the topic you have selected? An easy test of your feelings is the question: Would you feel that an attack

Understanding through Topic Selection and Audience Analysis

on your speech is in some way an attack on you? For example, if you spoke about rock music and someone attacked the speech, would you view the critic's reaction as a personal affront? If a hypothetical attack on your speech does not make you feel defensive, that is a sign that the topic does not mean that much to you, that you are not highly involved in it.

A second question is: How much time and energy do you devote to the subject area or topic? When you are really involved in something, you usually expend time and energy on it. If you really want to become a secretary, retailer, lab technician, or forester, you will be committing your time and energy to learning the subject matter and the skills that will lead to success in that vocation. And you will probably resent any implication that your chosen field is not worthy and will defend it.

Observation of your fellow students will probably reveal which speakers are involved in their topics and which are not. People who are involved in their topics speak with more conviction, passion, and authority. They give us many indications that they care about the subject. The person who has, by chance, selected a topic from a *Reader's Digest* article the night before usually cannot convey the sense of involvement that is so important in public speaking. When the president talks on television about one of his favorite plans, when Ralph Nader talks about consumerism, and when your professors discuss their favorite subjects, they usually show that they are involved, that the topic is important to them. You can display the same kind of involvement if you choose a topic that matters to you.

Knowledge

If you select a topic in which you are involved, you will probably know more about that subject than most of your classmates. This personal knowledge is something that students often forget to consider in their speeches. Speeches do not have to consist entirely of material looked up in the library. The speech will be better, in fact, if you add your own experience.

The importance of speaking from personal experience was demonstrated to us at a large university where over seven hundred students were invited to select the best speeches made in their individual speech classes. The winners delivered their speeches in a runoff contest, and the three best speakers gave their speeches to everyone taking the course. Those three speakers, selected by their classmates, were two black males and a handicapped white female—but, of the seven hundred competitors, very few were black and even fewer were handicapped. All three spoke about topics in which they were highly involved and to which they were committed: the two black men spoke about being black students in a predominantly white university, and the woman told what it was like to be a student confined to a wheelchair.

The black men told about being stared at in class, hearing classmates constantly asking them about being black, and being misunderstood. The handicapped woman told of having practically nobody speak to her no matter where she was, of people moving to the other side of the sidewalk when she approached, and of being considered an oddity. All three students had special knowledge and experience with the topic on which they based their speeches.

You may not be able to find an aspect of yourself that is that dramatic, but you probably can find a topic about which you have personal experience. You will find that you can strengthen your speech by taking advantage of your own knowledge of the topic.

Narrowing the Topic

Brainstorming techniques and personal inventories can yield topic areas appropriate for you. However, these topics are probably too large or abstract for a brief speech. Your personal inventory may show that a speech on the topic of *welfare reform* is a good one for you because you are involved in the topic, read about it, and know about it. Unfortunately, a speech on welfare reform could take days or weeks to deliver because so much information is available on the subject. You might try **narrowing the topic** to a topic so small that at first glance it might appear that you would never be able to find enough information on the topic. The advantage in starting with a very narrow topic is that it renders much information on the subject irrelevant. Only a small amount of the available information will be pertinent to your narrowed topic. Your research on the topic will be highly focused, and you will not end up with information that you cannot use.

The most common way to narrow a topic is to make it more specific and concrete. For example, the welfare reform topic can be narrowed geographically to welfare reform in the state of New Jersey, welfare reform in Polk County, or welfare reform in Rock City. Even then the topic is broad so the category welfare reform might have to be reduced to a smaller, more manageable category such as aid to dependent children, funds for widows and orphans, or support for the disabled. After carefully considering the audience's interests in the various geographies and in the various kinds of welfare reform, you might end up delivering a speech on problems with aid to dependent children in Polk County.

One method of narrowing a topic is suggested by the process described above. Take an abstract category discovered through brainstorming or personal inventories and narrow that topic by listing smaller categories directly related to that topic. The abstract topic called *business,* for instance, might yield the following smaller categories directly related to it:

Securing a job in business
Securing a job in local businesses
Where to find jobs in local businesses
How to get job interviews with local businesses
How to get interviews for summer jobs with local businesses

Another way of viewing the same method with a slightly different approach is to take a broad category like *sports* and think of as many smaller topics as you can that are at least loosely related to that topic:

Special treatment of football recruits
Tutoring of athletes
Scholarships for athletes
Keeping score in wrestling
New opportunities for women in golf
Financing our athletic program
Is our proposed stadium worth the expense?
The track program for women
Injury: the unpublicized problem in college football
What happened to our basketball stars of the past?

The lists of more specific and concrete topics can be extended until you have a large number from which to choose.

How will you know if your topic is narrow enough? There is no easy answer to that question. Several things to consider are: how much information is available on my narrowed topic, how much information can I convey within the time limits for the speech, and will I be able to cover the narrowed topic with enough depth to keep my audience interested and to increase their knowledge? An important reason for starting with a relatively narrow topic is that it saves you considerable time. A broad topic will require more research, much of which will ultimately have to be omitted for lack of time or relevance. Finally, the narrowed topic has to be interesting both to you and to your audience so next we turn to ways to analyze the audience.

Understanding Your Audience

To begin our study of **audience analysis,** we will survey four levels of audience analysis. The categories are called *levels* because the first is relatively easy and the last is the most difficult to understand and to use. In that sense, the levels are like grade levels in school; the ideas and concepts increase in difficulty. The four levels begin with the distinction between voluntary and captive audiences.

Level I: Captive and Voluntary Audiences

A **captive audience,** as the name suggests, is an audience that did not choose to hear a particular speaker or speech. It might look like the audience in figure 10.1. The teacher of a required class addresses a captive audience. A disc jockey who broadcasts commercial announcements between the songs that you want to hear addresses a captive audience. The administrator who speaks at a mandatory orientation

Figure 10.1

session, the preacher who addresses a mandatory chapel, the student who addresses fellow students in a required speech class are all addressing captive audiences.

Why should a public speaker distinguish a captive from a voluntary audience? One reason is that a captive audience did not choose to hear from you or about your subject—you may have to motivate them to listen. Another is that captive audiences are characterized by their heterogeneity, by the wide variety of differences among the individuals. This means that the speaker must adapt the topic and the content of the speech to a wider range of information and to more disparate attitudes toward the subject. One of the advantages of a captive audience is that it gives the speaker an opportunity to present ideas to people who, under ordinary circumstances, might never have heard the information or the point of view embodied in the speech.

The **voluntary audience** chooses to hear the particular speaker or speech. The most important characteristic of the voluntary audience is that the participants have some need or desire to hear the speech. The people who go to listen to a politician are usually sympathetic to the speaker's ideas. The students who stop to hear a traveling evangelist speak on the campus lawn are usually curious about, or perhaps even committed to, the speaker's religious beliefs. The advantage is that the speaker addresses an audience that is more homogeneous. Addressing a captive audience is like attempting to attract new customers to a product; addressing a voluntary audience is like attempting to please customers who have purchased the product before. Both salesperson and speaker are helped by knowing whether the audience is voluntary or captive, because the nature of the audience affects the topic, the rationale, the approach, and the goal.

The task of determining the character of an audience is far from simple. A specific example can demonstrate its complexity. At first, you might guess that a congregation is a voluntary audience—people chose to attend that particular church to hear that particular minister. But what about the children in the congregation? Did they choose to hear the sermon or did their parents make them go to church? What about some of the husbands and wives? How many people are there because their spouses wanted them to come along? To what extent did social pressures persuade them to attend church? Did they really know what the minister was going to say, or are they captives of the message that he or she is delivering? Even this first level of audience analysis is more challenging than it appears. The minister of a congregation addresses an audience that is in some ways voluntary and in some ways captive and must adapt the message to those differences.

How can you, in your speech class, make the distinction between the voluntary and the captive audience? You may find that your audience is more captive than voluntary—the members of the audience did not enroll in the class to hear you or your speech. On the other hand, they are there to learn how to give and listen to speeches. You may have to adapt to your student audience by insuring that they know why *you* are speaking to *them* about *this* particular subject. You will actually find yourself more dependent than most speakers on the other kinds of audience analysis covered in this chapter. Most public speakers work with voluntary audiences. They know, from experience and investigation, what their audience wants to hear and what they can do. You will probably have to learn about your audience through the methods suggested in this chapter.

Captive vs. Voluntary Audiences

Can you tell the difference between a captive and a voluntary audience? Categorize the following audiences:

	Captive	Voluntary
1. An audience gathered on the grass to hear a traveling evangelist.	_____	_____
2. A troop of army privates listening to their drill instructor.	_____	_____
3. A Democratic senator speaking to a party rally in his behalf.	_____	_____
4. Employees listening to their employer at the monthly meeting.	_____	_____
5. Your classmates listening to your speech.	_____	_____

Figure 10.2

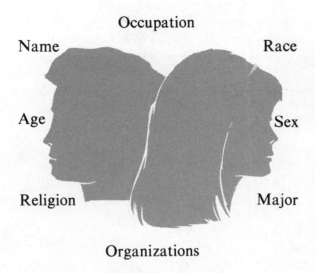

Occupation

Name

Race

Age

Sex

Religion

Major

Organizations

Level 2: Demographic Analysis

Demographics literally means "the characteristics of the people." **Demographic analysis** is based on the kind of characteristics that you write on forms: name, age, sex, home town, year in school, race, major subject, religion, and organizational affiliations. Such information can be important to public speakers because it can reveal the extent to which they will have to adapt themselves and their topics to that audience. A closer look at one item might demonstrate the importance of information about the audience. Let us see what the effect might be of your audience's majors.

Suppose you plan to speak about the cost of littering in your state. Your audience consists of twenty-two students: seven have not chosen a major subject, three are mathematics majors, four are biology majors, six are majoring in business administration, and one is an English major. This information gives you no reason to assume that any of them knows much about littering, but you can assume that from nine to thirteen have a basic understanding of numbers. The six business majors may have a better understanding of costs than the others, and the students majoring in math and science may find the cost-benefit approach attractive as well. If you add to that small bit of information more demographic information, then you can find even more to guide you. Does your college attract students who are likely to be concerned about the expense of littering? Is your audience likely to be knowledgeable about rural or urban littering? Do any students in your audience belong to organizations concerned about conservation? Whatever your topic, the demographic characteristics of your audience can imply its receptiveness to your topic.

Public speakers usually rely heavily on demographic information. Politicians send personnel ahead to find out how many blue-collar workers, faithful party members, elderly people, union members, and hecklers they are likely to encounter. They consult opinion polls, population studies, and reliable persons in the area to discover the nature of a prospective audience. Demographic analysis of your own class can serve a similar purpose—it will help you to design a speech that is better adapted to your audience.

Level 3: Audience Interest in and Knowledge of the Topic

As you move up the levels of audience analysis, the information you are asked to discover becomes more difficult to find. On level 3, your task is to find out the degree of the **audience's interest** in your topic and the **audience's knowledge** of the topic. Another way to ask the same question about interest and knowledge is: How familiar is your audience with the topic? This question is important because, if your audience is uninterested or unfamiliar with your topic, you will have to generate that interest in your speech.

One means of finding an audience's interest in and knowledge of a topic is to consider the age of the topic. Age and familiarity are closely related because the longer a topic has been around, and the more recently it has gained importance, the more likely the audience is to know about it. Your classmates may know much about a topic that has been a burning issue in the student newspaper, but they may not know about nuclear fusion, power satellites, or the latest fashions. A topic that is old to a

Figure 10.3

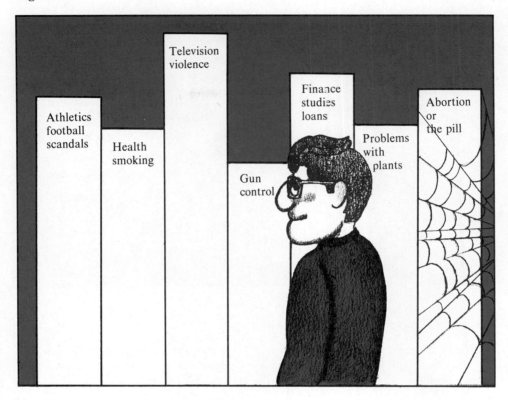

middle-aged person can be new to a nineteen-year-old student. Addressing classmates of mixed ages, you would have to adapt to those persons who are familiar with the topic and to those who are not. Fortunately, old topics have new variations. Topics, like people, live, change, and die—some have long and varied lives, while others pass quickly.

How can you gauge the audience's interest in and knowledge of your topic? One way to find out is to ask. You can ask demographic questions to help you assess audience interest in your topic. The audience members' ages, majors, year in school, and organizational memberships can suggest their familiarity with, knowledge of, and interest in your topic. Ask your fellow students before and after classes, in the hallways and in the cafeteria. Ask them in writing, through a questionnaire, if your teacher encourages that kind of analysis. You can even ask for some indication of interest during your speech, by asking your classmates to raise their hands in response to such questions as: How many of you watch TV news? How many of you have been to Washington, D.C.? and How many of you have read an unassigned book in the last three months?

Speech Topics

Consider the appropriateness of some of these subjects with your teacher and your classmates. The answers you receive will tell you a lot about your classmates' attitudes.

Gun control

Birth control

Abortion

Weapons

Secret societies

Sexual mores

Value of a college education

Marriage

Divorce

Oil prices

Swear words

Street language

Gambling

Equal rights

Gay liberation

Level 4: The Audience's Attitudes, Beliefs, and Values

An **attitude** is a tendency to respond favorably or unfavorably to some person, object, idea, or event. The attitudes of members of an audience can be assessed through questionnaires, by careful observation, or even by asking the right questions. If your audience comes from a place where many attitudes, beliefs, and values are shared, you may have an easy task analyzing that audience. A speech about birth control would be heard in some colleges with as much excitement as one on snails, but at other colleges the same speech could be grounds for dismissal. Attitudes toward politics, sex, religion, war, and even work vary in different geographical areas and

Figure 10.4

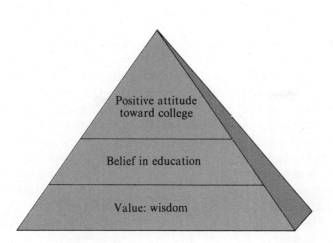

Positive attitude
toward college

Belief in education

Value: wisdom

subgroups. Regardless of the purpose of your speech, your audience's attitude will make a difference in the appropriateness of your topic.

A **belief** is a conviction. Beliefs, or convictions, are usually considered more solid than attitudes, but our attitudes often spring from our beliefs. Your belief in good eating habits may lead to a negative attitude toward overeating and obesity and to a positive attitude toward balanced meals and nutrition. Your audience's beliefs make a difference in how they respond to your speech. They may believe in upward mobility through higher education, in higher pay through hard work, in the superiority of the family farm, in a lower tax base, or in social welfare. Or they may not believe any of these ideas. Beliefs are like anchors to which our attitudes are attached. To discover them we need to ask questions and observe carefully.

Values are the deeply rooted beliefs that govern our attitudes. Our beliefs and attitudes can usually be traced to some value that we hold, sometimes unconsciously. Freedom, equality, and justice are values to many people; so are chastity, honesty, and courage. To know whether an attitude or belief is a value, you must know how it functions in a person's life. A value is an end, not a means. Money can be a means or an end—it can be regarded as something that we need to secure other things (a means) or it can be something we need to acquire for its own sake (an end). If money is a means, it is just something that we have a positive attitude toward; if it is an end, then it is one of our values.[1]

When people are asked to list their values in order of importance, they come up with suprisingly different lists. One researcher asked three groups of people to rank a list of values that included freedom and equality. One group consisted of people who had participated in political demonstrations; the second group was sympathetic to demonstrations; and the third group was unsympathetic to demonstrations. The figures below indicate how these three groups of people ranked freedom and equality.[2]

Value	Group 1 Participants	Group 2 Sympathetic	Group 3 Unsympathetic
Freedom	1	1	2
Equality	3	6	11

The people in group 1, who had been participants in the demonstrations, ranked freedom first among the values listed; their sympathizers ranked it first as well; and the unsympathetic ranked it second. All three groups ranked freedom high. But the demonstrators ranked equality third, their sympathizers sixth, and the unsympathetic group eleventh. The more unsympathetic the groups were toward demonstrations, the less they valued equality.

To gain some idea of how values affect public speeches, rank the values in the exercise below. The values held by your audience and the order in which it ranks them can provide valuable clues about their attitudes and beliefs. The speaker who addresses an audience without knowing its values is taking a risk that can be avoided by careful audience analysis.

Ranking Values

Rank these values in their order of importance to you.

If you can persuade some of your classmates, or the entire class, to do this as well, you will have information that will help you prepare your speech.[3]

Wisdom	Equality
A comfortable life	Wealth
A world at peace	Leisure
Freedom	Security
Maturity	Fulfillment

How does your ranking compare to your classmates' ? What other values might help you with your speech?

Three Methods of Audience Analysis

Method 1: Observation

Effective public speakers are often astute observers. An effective lawyer selects his or her audience by questioning prospective jurors. The lawyer asks questions that are designed to discover prejudice, negative, and positive attitudes, beliefs, and values. Later, as the witnesses testify, the lawyer observes their verbal and nonverbal behavior and decides which arguments, which evidence, and which witnesses are influencing the jurors. Evangelists know, from their many sermons, which Bible verses, which stories, and which testimonials will bring sinners to the altar. People who speak on behalf of business associations, unions, political parties, colleges, and the underprivileged have usually spent years watching others and learning which approaches, arguments, and evidence are most likely to be accepted by an audience.

You can learn to do the same thing in your speech class. For every speech that you give, you might listen to twenty or twenty-five. You have a unique opportunity to discover what your classmates respond to. Do they respond well to speakers who come on strong and authoritatively, or to speakers who talk to them like equals? Do your classmates like or dislike numbers and statistics? Do they like speeches about work, leisure, getting ahead, or getting the most out of their education? Do they respond well to stories and examples, graphs and posters, pictures and slides? Do they like a speaker to argue forcefully, or do they dislike speeches that stir them up? As a listener in the classroom, you have a unique opportunity to observe your own and your classmates' responses to a variety of speakers.

You can also observe some demographic characteristics of the audience: age, sex, race, group affiliations (athletic jackets, fraternity pins). You can see how it responds to a speaker who keeps his eyes on the audience and how it responds to one who depends heavily on notes. You can observe whether you and the audience respond favorably when the speaker is deeply involved in the speech. Every speech you hear will, in some way, indicate the speaker's attitudes, beliefs, and values, and the response of the audience.

Even though your audience of fellow students may be more captive than most, you have an advantage over most public speakers. How many public speakers have an opportunity to hear every one of their listeners give a speech? Instead of sitting back like a passive observer when you are a member of the audience, take advantage of the situation by listening actively, by taking notes about the speaker's characteristics, and by recording the audience's responses. You can analyze your audience continually during a round of speeches by careful observation.

Method 2: Inference

To draw an **inference** is to draw a tentative conclusion based on some evidence, as the woman in the "B.C." cartoon does. We draw an inference when we see someone dressed in rags, and we tentatively conclude that the person is poor. Our inferences are often accurate—we infer from his wedding band that a man is married, from the children tugging at his sleeve that he is a father, and from the woman holding his arm that she is his wife. We are basing these inferences on thin data, but they are probably correct. You can base inferences on observed characteristics in your audience, on demographic information, and on questionnaires.

Inferences may be true, accurate, or reliable, but they may also be untrue, inaccurate, or unreliable. The more evidence on which you base an inference, the more likely it is to be correct. You can draw inferences either indirectly or directly. An indirect way to draw inferences is by observation. For instance, you might be in a school where male students do not hold hands with female students (an observation). You infer that public displays of affection are discouraged by administrative edict, by custom, or by the students' own preference. You might also infer, from your limited data, that the prevailing attitudes militate against public disclosure of sexual mores, dating, courtship, and divorce.

B.C.

A more direct way to gather data on which to base inferences is to ask questions of your classmates. You could ask them, either orally or in writing: How many students in the class have part or full-time jobs? How many are married, have families, have grown children? How many plan to become wealthy? How many were raised in urban or rural settings? How many have strong religious ties? The answers to these questions provide valuable information about your audience.

To illustrate how this method works, let us examine one question, one answer, and some inferences that could be drawn from the information. The question is: How many students have full or part-time jobs? The answer is that two-thirds, thirteen out of twenty students, are employed. The inferences that can be drawn from this data include the facts that the students are probably older than the usual eighteen to twenty-one-year-olds who attend college, that the students' or their parents' income is insufficient to allow them to attend school full time, that the students are very ambitious or intelligent and can handle both jobs and classwork.

How can the inferences help you in preparing your speech? If the best-supported inference is that your classmates cannot afford to go to school full-time, then certain topics, lines of argument, examples, and approaches will be more attractive to them than others. Speeches on how to save money and how to manage time would probably be welcomed by this audience. On the other hand, speeches on yachting, owning your own racing horse, or taking a cruise might get you hooted out of the room.

Method 3: The Questionnaire

A more formal way to collect data on which you can base inferences is to ask your audience to fill out a **questionnaire** that you or others have developed. Demographic and attitudinal questions yield important information. A questionnaire can ask questions that require only that the people being questioned select the correct answer. This method of data collection makes it relatively easy to summarize the information. The questions would look like this:

_____ 1. I am   *(a)* a freshman
               (b) a sophomore
               (c) a junior
               (d) a senior

_____ 2. I am   *(a)* under 18
               (b) 18–19 years old
               (c) 20– 21 years old
               (d) over 22

_____ 3. I am   *(a)* single
               (b) married
               (c) divorced
               (d) separated

_____ 4. I have   *(a)* no children
               (b) one child
               (c) two children
               (d) more than two children

The audience members do not have to identify themselves by name to provide this information. Keeping them anonymous (no blank for the name) encourages honest answers and does not reduce the value of the information.

The second kind of information, based on attitudinal questions, can be collected in at least two ways. One way is to ask questions that place audience members in identifiable groups, as these questions do:

_____ 5. I   *(a)* am active in campus organizations
             (b) am not

_____ 6. I see myself as   *(a)* conservative
                           (b) liberal
                           (c) independent

_____ 7. I see myself as   *(a)* strongly religious
                           (b) moderately religious
                           (c) unreligious

A second method of gaining attitudinal information is to ask questions that assess people's values by asking them to rank values such as hard work, higher education, high pay, and security. The answers that people give when they rank values can suggest additional information about their attitudes and beliefs.

Finally, you can list word-concepts that reveal attitudes to assess your audience's attitudes toward specific issues. One way is to list the concepts along with an attitudinal scale like the one on the following page.

The reactions to these and similar words or phrases can provide you with information that will help you to approach your audience successfully. If most

Attitudinal Scale

Indicate, next to each word or phrase, your attitude toward it by writing in the appropriate number: (1) strongly favor, (2) mildly favor, (3) neutral, (4) mildly disfavor, or (5) strongly disfavor.

_____ a. Police	_____ h. Abortion
_____ b. Born-again Christians	_____ i. Welfare
_____ c. Gun control	_____ j. Military
_____ d. Minority groups	_____ k. Marijuana
_____ e. Divorce	_____ l. Religion
_____ f. Government controls	_____ m. Individual rights
_____ g. Professors	

persons in your audience are neutral to moderately favorable toward abortion, then your speech advocating it could be designed to raise their attitudes to moderately favorable to strongly favorable. If the responses are mixed, then you may have to work just to move your audience closer to a mildly unfavorable attitude or toward neutrality. The questionnaire will help you to learn about your audience's demographics, and its attitudes, beliefs, and values better than observation alone.

Adapting to the Audience

Analysis of an audience yields information about your listeners that enables you to adapt yourself and your verbal and nonverbal codes to that audience. A speech is not a message imposed on a collection of listeners; a speech is a compromise between speaker and audience that is designed to inform, entertain, inspire, teach, or persuade that audience. This compromise is based on your analysis of your audience.

An important question to consider in **adapting to an audience** is: How do I adapt to an audience without letting them dictate my position? The answer is that audience analysis reveals characteristics of the audience that need to be taken into account when informing and persuading. You do not analyze the audience to discover your own position but to discover theirs—how much do they know about the topic? What approach is most likely to persuade persons with their attitudes, beliefs, and values? To find, for example, that an audience is likely to be utterly opposed to your position is not an indication that you should alter your position on the issue; instead, it is an indication that you may have to adopt a more gradual approach to changing them than you would have likely used. Similarly, to discover that the audience is even more ignorant of the topic than you thought only indicates that you will have to provide more background or more elementary information than you had originally planned. In short, you have to adapt yourself, your codes, your topic, your purpose, and your supporting materials to the particular group of people you will face in your speech.

Adapting Yourself

In the study of interpersonal communication, you learned about self-concept and about how people in pairs and groups adjust to each other. In public speaking, the speaker also has to adjust to information about the audience. Just as the senior who is preparing for a job interview adapts to the interviewer in dress, manner, and language, the public speaker prepares for an audience by adapting to its expectations. How you look, how you behave, and what you say should be carefully adjusted to an audience that you have learned about by observation, experience, and analysis. As you will discover in chapter 11 on source credibility, there are ways you can help an audience perceive you as a credible person.

Adapting Your Verbal and Nonverbal Codes

The language you employ in your speech, as well as your gestures, movements, and even facial expressions, should be adapted to your audience. Does your experience, do your observations, and does your analysis of the audience's attitudes indicate that your language should be conversational, colloquial, formal, cynical, or technical? Does your analysis indicate that your listeners like numbers and statistics? Do your observations and the evaluations of your teacher and classmates indicate that you should pace the stage, or stand still behind the lectern? Does your analysis indicate that you should not use taboo words in your speech lest you alienate the group, or does the audience like a little lively language? Your analysis of your audience provides the information that you need to make these strategic choices about verbal and nonverbal codes.

Adapting Your Topic

Public speakers should be permitted to speak about any topic that fits the assignment. In the classroom, at least, you should select a topic that relates to you. But remember, you will be giving your speech to an audience of classmates. Therefore, the topic you select must be adapted to them. Audience analysis is a means of discovering the audience's position on the topic. From information based on observation, description, and inference, you have to decide how you are going to adapt your topic to this audience.

Audience analysis can tell you what challenges you face. If you want to speak in favor of abortion and your audience analysis indicates that the majority of your listeners is opposed to that position, you need not conclude that the topic is inappropriate. But you may have to adapt to the members of your audience by starting with a position closer to theirs. Your initial step might be to make the audience feel less comfortable about its present position so they are prepared to hear your position. You might choose another tactic. Audience analysis can reveal the obstacles that you face with that audience.

Your analysis might indicate that the audience already has considerable information about the subject. The analysis, then, might require that you adapt by locating information that they do not have. You may want to deliver an informative speech about the latest world crisis, but analysis indicates that the audience is not only already interested but also that it has sufficient information of the sort that you planned to offer. You can adapt your topic by shifting to an area of the subject about which they are not so well informed: What is the background of the conflict? What is the background of the personalities and the issues? What do the experts think will happen? What are the possible consequences of the confrontation? Your analysis can help you to adapt your topic to your particular audience.

Adapting Your Purpose

You should also adapt the purpose of your speech to your audience. Speech teachers often ask the student to state the purpose of a speech—what do you want your audience to know, to understand, or to do? It may help you to think of your speech as one part of a series of informative talks that your audience will will hear about your topic. They have probably heard something about the topic before, and are likely to hear about the topic again. Your particular presentation is just one of the audience's exposures to the topic.

Still, your immediate purpose is linked to some larger goal. The goal is the end that you have in mind. In the "Doonesbury" cartoon, Ms. Slade's immediate purpose is to announce her candidacy for the United States Congress; her larger goal is to be elected to office. Some examples of immediate purposes and long-range goals will illustrate the difference. In an informative speech, the immediate purposes and long-range goals might be:

Immediate Purpose	Long-Range Goal
To help the audience remember three factors in adopting nuclear power plants as a source of energy.	To increase the number of people who will read articles and books about nuclear power as an energy source.
To teach the audience six expressions that are part of the "street language" used by urban blacks.	To help the listeners understand and appreciate the language employed by some black students.

DOONESBURY

In a persuasive speech, the immediate purposes and the long-range goals might be:

Immediate Purpose	Long-Range Goal
To get the audience to remember three positive characteristics of the candidate for mayor.	To get some of the audience members to vote for the candidate at election time.
To reveal to the audience the nutritional value of two popular "junk foods."	To dissuade the listeners from eating junk food.

The more specific your purpose, the more you will be able to discover whether you accomplished it.

In this chapter, we have explored a number of ways to analyze an audience. You should employ audience analysis to help you discover whether your purpose is appropriate. Suppose half the people in your class are going into fields where knowledge of food and nutrition is important. They already know more than the average person about nutritional values, and they know about the debilitating effects of junk food. Consequently, it is probably not appropriate to deliver a speech about junk food. It may also not be wise to speak to a group of athletes about the importance of exercise. You should adapt your purpose to the audience by considering the level of their information, the novelty of the issue, and the other factors that we talked about in this chapter.

Adapting Your Supporting Materials

Your personal knowledge, your interviewing, and your library research should provide more material for your speech than you can use. Again, audience analysis helps you select materials for this particular audience. Your analysis might reveal that your classmates do not have much respect for authority figures. In that case, you might be wasting your time informing them of the surgeon-general's opinion about smoking; your personal experience or the experience of some of your classmates might be more important to them than an expert's opinion. On the other hand, if your audience analysis reveals that parents, teachers, pastors, and other authority figures are held in high regard, you may want to quote physicians, research scientists, counselors, and health-service personnel.

As a public speaker, you should always keep in mind that the choices that you make in selecting a topic, in choosing an immediate purpose, in determining a long-range goal, in organizing your speech, in selecting supporting materials, and even in creating visual aids are all **strategic choices.** All these choices are made for the purpose of adapting the speaker and the subject to a particular audience. The larger your supply of supporting arguments, the better your chances of having effective arguments. The larger your supply of supporting materials, the better your chances of having evidence, illustrations, and visual aids that the audience will respond to. Your choices are strategic in that they are purposeful. The purpose is to choose, from among the available alternatives, the ones that will best achieve your purpose with the particular audience.

Summary

The purpose of this chapter is to help you select a topic appropriate for you and for your audience. Brainstorming and personal inventories are two methods of topic selection. Involvement in and knowledge of a topic are two means of evaluating its appropriateness for you. To discover if a topic is appropriate for your audience, you have to analyze your audience. Four levels of audience analysis were examined. Level 1 distinguishes between voluntary and captive audiences. Level 2 is demographic analysis, in which the characteristics of the audience members are evaluated. Level 3 analyzes the audience's interest in and knowledge about a topic. Level 4 determines the audience's attitudes, beliefs, and values. Three methods of analyzing an audience were discussed. The first method, observation, is based on watching your audience and learning from its behavior. The second method, inference, uses incomplete data to draw tentative conclusions about an audience, conclusions that may make the audience's response more predictable. The third method of analysis is the questionnaire, which can be used to garner information about demographics, attitudes, and strength of belief. Finally, topic selection and audience analysis were discussed in an attempt to adapt to the audience through adapting yourself, your language, your topic, your purpose, and your supporting materials. In the next chapter, you will find out more about you as the source or speaker and more about how to find materials for your speech.

Additional Readings

*Becker, Samuel L. "New Approaches to Audience Analysis." In *Perspectives on Communication,* edited by Carl E. Larson and Frank E.X. Dance. Shorewood, Wis.: Helix Press, 1970. Pages 61–77.
A complex and detailed look at approaches to audience analysis and selective exposure. Becker presents a model for analysis of audience attitudes.

Clevenger, Theodore, Jr. *Audience Analysis.* Indianapolis: The Bobbs-Merrill Co., 1966.
Contains a detailed discussion of techniques of measuring audience attitudes and knowledge, with specific discussions of the construction and uses of questionnaires, attitude scales, observational techniques, and information tests.

Holtzman, Paul D. *The Psychology of Speakers' Audiences.* Glenview, Ill.: Scott, Foresman and Company, 1970.
A look at speakers and speeches from the audience's perspective. Holtzman discusses the audience's listening behavior, attitudes toward the speaker and the topic, and willingness to accept new ideas and values. He argues that the speaker must listen to the audience, i.e., audience analysis is a continuous process.

*Katz, Elihu. "On Reopening the Question of Selectivity in Exposure to Mass Communication." In *Speech Communication Behavior: Perspectives & Principles,* edited by Larry Barker and Robert Kibler.

*Indicates more advanced readings.

Englewood Cliffs, N.J.: Prentice-Hall, 1971. Pages 182–92.
Katz examines studies of selective exposure as they relate to mass communication and provides insights into the concept of captive and voluntary audiences and how selective exposure is used by an audience to select only desired messages.

Verderber, Rudolph F. *The Challenge of Effective Speaking.* 4th ed. Belmont, Calif.: Wadsworth Publishing Co., 1979.
The chapter "Selecting Topics and Finding Material" presents some alternative methods of finding topics and some information on purpose and audience analysis.

Notes

1. Daryl Bem, *Beliefs, Attitudes and Human Affairs* (Belmont, Calif.: Brooks/Cole Publishing Company, 1970), p. 16.
2. Adapted, with permission, from Milton Rokeach, *Beliefs, Attitudes, and Values* (San Francisco: Jossey-Bass, Inc., Publishers, 1968), p. 170.
3. Adapted, with permission, from a list of values cited in Robert L. Heath, "Variability in Value System Priorities as Decision-Making Adaptation to Situational Differences," *Communication Monographs* 43(1976): 325–33.

11

Sharing Yourself
Source Creditibility
and Credible Sources

Objectives

1. Recognize the four dimensions of source credibility
2. State four ways that a speaker can influence source credibility
3. State some ways that a speaker can improve source credibility
4. Find supporting materials for your speeches
5. Use supporting materials in your speeches

Key Terms

credibility

competence

trustworthiness

dynamism

coorientation

sleeper effect

example

surveys and studies

testimonial evidence

statistics

mean or average

mode

percentage

range

raw numbers

analogy

explanation

definition

Too much sun will ruin your skin.
      Little brother to sister

Too much sun will ruin your skin.
      Mother to daughter

Too much sun will ruin your skin.
      Physician to patient

The idea that *who* says something makes a difference is at least as old as Aristotle. Twenty-three hundred years ago Aristotle said that a speaker's "character may almost be called the most effective means of persuasion he possesses."[1] In all the centuries since that ancient Greek announced the importance of the source, and especially in this century, dozens of scholars have attempted to determine the importance of the source, or speaker.

Who you are can make an important difference in your speech and in how it affects an audience. What you say is equally important. In this chapter we will first explore the concept of source credibility or the importance of the speaker and then we will turn to what you say by discovering how to find information that you can use in your speech.

Who are you? What do you know that will inspire an audience to listen? What can you learn about yourself that will help you deliver effective speeches? The notion of source or speaker **credibility** refers to why an audience ought to listen, remember information, and act on what you say. People used to think that source credibility referred to a group of characteristics that led audiences to see the speaker as credible. A pope, king, or president could be such a person. But people do not necessarily find even these sources credible when they speak. A more realistic view of credibility says that certain audiences in certain situations find some persons more credible than others. A foreman or line supervisor may be credible to those who work for him; a boss may be credible to her employees; and a physician may be credible to her patients. But the same foreman or line supervisor may not be credible in his church; the boss may not be credible at her country club; and the physician may find that she cannot even get patients to quit smoking. So who is credible?

To understand the concept of source credibility you must first recognize that it is not something that a speaker possesses like a suit of clothes. Instead, the audience determines credibility; they see a speaker as credible or not. "Credibility," like beauty, "is in the eye of the beholder."[2] A speaker's credibility depends in part on who the speaker is, in part on the subject being discussed, in part on the situation, and in part on the audience. You might be highly credible to an audience about your major, your adventures, or your hobbies; but you might be low in credibility when you speak on nuclear fission, water conservation, or economics. You might be more credible in some situations than in others—you might be highly credible as a student who can achieve high grades and very low in credibility as a person who can tell others how to

   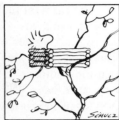

repair a car. You might be more credible to some audiences than you are to others—your classmates might find you credible and the local Teamsters Union might think that you are not. Some people are like the little bird in the "Peanuts" cartoon; they think that a certain characteristic will give them credibility. You know that the concept is more complex.

How do we gain credibility with an audience then? The answer is that public speakers earn the right to speak. They earn the right through their own lives, their own experiences, and their own accomplishments. As one sage said, "Before you express yourself, you need a self worth expressing." You may have earned the right to speak on a number of subjects. Have you worked in a fast-foods place? You may have earned the right to comment on the quality of their food and service. Have you raised children? You have earned the right to speak on the problems and pleasures of family life. Have you gone without work for a period of time? You have earned the right to give a first-hand account of what it is like to live without your usual income. Think about it. What have you experienced, learned, or lived through that has earned for you the right to speak?

Four Aspects of Credibility

What does an audience perceive that gives it the idea that a speaker is credible? If credibility is based on judgments by individuals in the audience, then what is the basis for those judgments? On what will your classmates be rating you when they judge your credibility? According to recent studies, four of the most important aspects of credibility are competence, trustworthiness, dynamism, and coorientation.[3]

Competence

The first aspect of credibility is **competence.** A speaker who is perceived as competent is perceived as qualified, trained, experienced, authoritative, expert, reliable, informed, or knowledgeable. A speaker does not have to live up to all these adjectives; any one, or a few, might make the speaker credible. The machinist who displays his metal work in a speech about junk sculpture as art is as credible as the biblical scholar who is demonstrating her ability to interpret scripture. They have different bases for their competence, but both can demonstrate competence or expertise in their own areas of specialization.

Your own competence as a speaker is conveyed by your words, your visual aids, even your air of authority. What can you build into your speech that will help the audience to see and understand the basis for your air of authority? What experience have you had that is related to the subject? What special training or knowledge do you have? How can you suggest to your audience that you have earned the right to speak about this subject? The most obvious way is to tell the audience the basis of your authority or expertise, but a creative speaker can think of dozens of ways to hint, suggest, imply, and indirectly indicate competence without being explicit, without seeming condescending, arrogant, superior, and without lying.

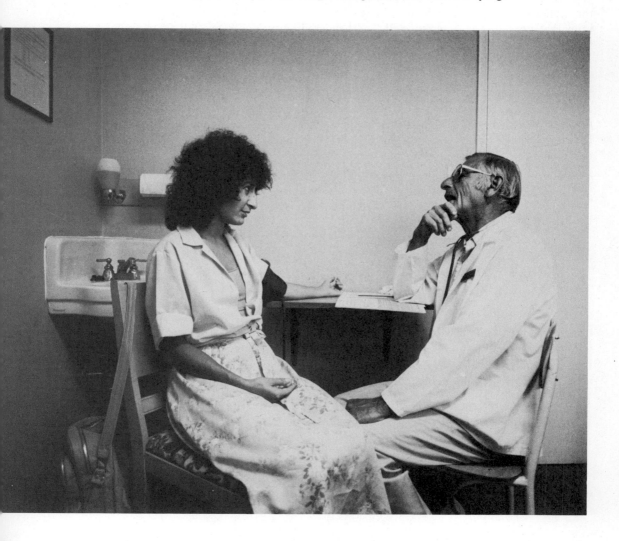

A speaker will signal competence by knowing the substance of the speech so well that the speech is delivered without reading from notecards and without unplanned pauses, vocalized pauses, and without mispronounced words. The speaker who knows the technical language in a specialized field and who can define the terms for the audience is signaling competence. The speaker who can translate complex ideas into language that the audience can understand, the speaker who can find ways to illustrate ideas in ways that the audience can comprehend, and the speaker who is familiar with people who know about the subject, and with books and articles about the subject are all signaling competence to the audience.

Trustworthiness

The second aspect of credibility is **trustworthiness.** How honest, fair, sincere, friendly, honorable, and kind does the audience find the speaker? These descriptors are also earned. We judge a person's honesty both by past behavior and present estimates. Your classmates will judge your trustworthiness when you speak before them. How do you decide whether or not other speakers in your class are responsible, sincere, dependable, or just? What can you do to help your audience perceive that you are trustworthy?

You may have to reveal to your audience why you are trustworthy. Have you held jobs that demanded honesty and responsibility? Have you been a cashier, a bank teller, a supervisor, or a foreman? Have you given up anything to demonstrate that you are sincere? The person who works his or her own way through college ordinarily has to be very sincere about education; the person who chooses a lower paying job because he or she feels a sense of public service may be showing sincerity about the job; and the person who gives considerable time to charity, politics, or religion may be demonstrating sincerity about those causes. Being respectful of others' points of view can be a sign of your fairness, and being considerate of other people and their ideas can be a sign of your kindness and friendliness. What can you say about yourself that will show your trustworthiness?

Dynamism

The third aspect of credibility is **dynamism**—the extent to which an audience perceives the speaker as bold, active, energetic, strong, empathic, and assertive. Audiences value behavior that can be described by these adjectives. Perhaps when we consider their opposites—timid, passive, tired, weak, hesitant, and meek—we can see why dynamism is attractive. People who exude energy, who exhibit strength, and who show the spirit of their convictions impress others. Observe the public speakers on Sunday-morning television—the evangelists, the ministers, and the healers—and see how dynamic they look and sound. You can learn to do the same. Evidence indicates that the audience's perception of your dynamic qualities will enhance your credibility.

Dynamism is exhibited mainly by voice, movement, facial expression, and gesture. The person who speaks forcefully, who speaks with considerable voice variety, and who speaks rapidly exhibits dynamism with his or her voice. The speaker who moves toward the audience, back behind the lectern, over to the visual aid, and

literally works while speaking is exhibiting dynamism. And the speaker who employs facial expression and gestures to make a point is providing signs of dynamism. What can you do with your voice, movement, facial expression, and gestures to show the audience that you are an energetic speaker?

Coorientation

Coorientation refers to the sharing of values, beliefs, attitudes, and interests. Audiences are drawn to speakers whose ideas are similar to their own. People flock to a speaker who can state their ideas and beliefs better than they could themselves. If our own views about a public issue coincide with his, William F. Buckley can state them better than we could. In the classroom, speakers can establish coorientation by revealing to their audience the many ways in which they share their audience's orientation toward life, toward the issues, toward the information being presented, or toward the persuasive proposition. Thus we use the word coorientation to indicate a vision possessed jointly by audience and speaker.

Some examples of speeches in which the speaker employed coorientation include speeches about student housing, dormitory food, and honors societies. The student who spoke about student housing was complaining about the use of three-person rooms in the dormitories. He knew that the majority of the students in the class had suffered through a year or two of these same living conditions, and he established coorientation by simply recounting some of his experiences in trying to study, entertain, and sleep in a three-person room. The student who spoke about the low quality of dormitory food knew that most of the audience members had tasted it. She brought in a tray of dormitory food to remind them and to establish coorientation. The student who spoke about honors societies was in an honors section full of students who had received invitations to join various honors societies. Unfortunately, most of them met only once and each honorary cost a high fee to join. She established coorientation by recounting a common experience of receiving such letters and of being uncertain whether to join. What can you do to establish coorientation with your audience?

A student reading the long list of adjectives describing the four aspects of credibility might feel that establishing credibility is beyond the capability of the beginning speaker. It is some comfort to know that you do not have to fit all the adjectives or even score well on all the aspects. Many highly credible speakers are not dynamic; in fact, all they may possess is their specialized knowledge. Some speakers may be thought to be credible simply because they exude sincerity, even though they lack knowledge and expertise and are not dynamic.

You do not have to excel in all four aspects of source credibility to be an effective speaker, but competence, trustworthiness, dynamism, and coorientation are the grounds on which your audience is likely to evaluate your credibility so you should take whatever steps you can to insure that you come across as a credible source.

To continue our examination of source credibility, we turn next to some research findings. While explaining each finding we will suggest ways in which you can apply it to your own public speaking.

Some Ways of Increasing Credibility

Credibility can be achieved before, during, or after a public speech. A speaker can have a reputation before arriving at a hall; that judgment can be altered during the presentation; and the evaluation can change again, long after the speech has ended. You might think that speaker X is a great person before you hear him. His dull presentation reduces his credibility. Then, in the weeks after the speech, your evaluation of speaker X might rise again because you discover that his message has given you new hope. In other words, credibility is not static—it is always in flux, always changing, always alterable.

Nor is credibility, we should remind you, something that a speaker always possesses. It depends on topics, audiences, and situations. That makes the concept of source credibility a challenging one to public speakers. We intend these comments about the changing nature of credibility as a caution in interpreting the findings cited below. We will examine these findings by looking at some ways of increasing credibility.

Four Aspects of Source Credibility

Examine the items below and indicate which of the four aspects of source credibility is being illustrated by the speaker's words or actions.

A. Competence
B. Trustworthiness
C. Dynamism
D. Coorientation

_____ 1. Like the rest of you, I pay tuition, pay exorbitant prices for books, and ignore my friends and family to get an education.

_____ 2. I worked for three years as a mechanic on diesel trucks, took four weeks of formal instruction at the plant where the trucks are made, and am the highest paid mechanic of the fourteen who work in our local garage.

_____ 3. I really liked Fred's speech about evolution and I found that I learned some things that I did not know before. I respect his point of view, but . . .

_____ 4. Do we want to be Number 1 this Saturday? (Speaker raises hands with palms outstretched to invite applause.) Do we support this team? (Big smile and gesture to the team seated in the front.)

A Highly Credible Speaker Will Change an Audience's Opinion More than a Speaker of Low Credibility, but the Difference Diminishes in Time

A highly credible speaker is one who is perceived by the audience as competent, trustworthy, dynamic, or cooriented. We might say that such a speaker has prestige before, during, and after the speech. Most of the studies that try to measure the effect of such a person's message on an audience indicate that highly credible speakers change opinions more than speakers whose credibility is poor.[4] At least at first, a person perceived as credible can seek more changes of opinions and achieve more changes.

This finding demonstrates the importance of working for and earning an audience's respect as a source. In the speech classroom, it should make the speaker strive to become credible during the speech, since the speech is the main source of the audience's information about the speaker. Describing the origins of your authority, revealing to the audience how you relate to the topic and how you relate to them can help you become credible.

As our statement indicates, a highly credible speaker changes opinions when a speech is delivered.[5] However, as time passes, an interesting phenomenon occurs. Apparently the source of the speech and the message become separated in the listener's mind— "I don't remember who said this, but. . . ." The result of this separation of source and message is that the effect of the credible speaker's message diminishes as the listener forgets who relayed it. The speaker with little credibility

creates just the opposite effect. As time passes, the listener forgets the source of the information and the message tends to become more effective. In one study, three or four weeks after a speech, a highly credible speaker and one with little credibility had pulled about even in respect to their ability to change opinions. Gains made by the less credible speaker are due to the **sleeper effect.**[6]

The lesson for the public speaker is that the effect of credibility is shortlived. In most speech classes, several weeks or more may elapse between your presentations. In between, your classmates are exposed to other speakers and speeches. They need reminders of your credibility. We like to think that audiences remember us and our speeches, but in fact it is sometimes difficult for students to remember a speech they heard the day before yesterday. Intelligent speakers remind the audience of their credibility. Remind your audience about your major subject, your special interest in the topic, your special knowledge, or your special experience. Credibility decays in time and must be renewed if you want to have the maximum effect on your audience.

A Speaker Can Gain Credibility by Establishing Common Ground with the Audience

To establish common ground with an audience is to emphasize what you share with it—in the present situation, in your experience, in your ideas, or in your behavior. You can establish common ground by sharing the situation that you and your classmates have in common—you all have speeches to give and exams to take. You can share ideological common ground—values, beliefs, or ideas. One way to earn an audience's trust is to point out some of the important ways that you are like the audience. Revealing shared attitudes, beliefs, and values establishes coorientation. You can address members of your audience as fellow students (common ground) or as people who believe that grades are destructive to learning or that bookstore prices are too high (coorientation).

Some studies indicate that areas of agreement should be established early in a speech for maximum effect; others say that when it is established is not important, as long as it is established sometime during the speech. All the studies agree that speakers can enhance their relationship with the audience by talking about something they have in common with the audience. Some degree of commonality with voluntary audiences may be assumed, but it is necessary to be explicit to captive audiences. In the cartoon, it was probably the defense attorney who was wise enough to see that his client's position on conservation was conveyed to the jury.

DUNAGIN'S PEOPLE

"WE FIND THE DEFENDANT GUILTY OF MURDER, CONSPIRACY, ROBBERY, ASSAULT, AND KIDNAPPING... BUT WE RECOMMEND LENIENCY BECAUSE HE WANTS TO SAVE THE REDWOODS."

Credibility Is Influenced by the Introduction of the Speaker, by the Status and Sincerity of the Speaker, and by the Organization of the Speech

The following generalizations and conclusions are based on a summary of nearly thirty years of studies of credibility.[7] *The introduction of a speaker by another person can increase the speaker's credibility.* The credibility of the person making the introduction is as important to the speaker's credibility as what is said in that introduction. A close friend introducing you can reveal information that could enhance or harm your status. To be safe, the speaker should always provide the introducer with information that could potentially increase credibility by showing the speaker's competence, trustworthiness, coorientation, or dynamism. Your introducer can make evaluative statements about you that might sound self-serving from your own mouth. Your credibility may also be enhanced if the audience believes that your introducer is highly credible.

The way you are identified by the person introducing you can affect your credibility. Students who are identified as graduate students are thought to be more competent than undergraduates. Graduate students are also seen as more fair-minded, likeable, and sincere.[8] It is possible, therefore, that your identification as a sophomore, junior, or senior might contribute to your credibility with a student audience.

The organization of your speech can affect your credibility. Students who listen to a disorganized speech think less of a speaker after the speech than they did before the speech.[9] This judgment by the audience may be based on its expectations—in the speech classroom, the students expect good organization, and when they perceive a speech as poorly organized they lower their evaluation of the speaker. The lesson from this study is relatively clear. The classroom speaker should strive for sound organization lest he or she lose credibility even while speaking.

The perceived status of a speaker can make a difference in credibility. In the study cited above, not only did audiences find graduate students more credible than undergraduates, their positive evaluation spread to several other areas as well. In another study, speakers of high status were consistently rated as more credible than speakers of low status. Even more striking was the finding that the listeners judged credibility and status during the first ten or fifteen seconds of the speech.[10] The probable explanation of this finding is that the audience receives a barrage of cues about the speaker at the very beginning of the speech: they see how the speaker is dressed; they see and make judgments about the speaker's appearance; they hear the speaker's voice; and they get an initial impression of the speaker's confidence, competence, trustworthiness, and dynamism.

Other interesting findings about credibility are related to delivery, fluency, and repetition. *A speaker whose delivery is considered effective, whose use of voice, movement, and gesture is effective, can become more credible during a speech.*[11] A payoff exists for the student who practices a speech and who learns to be comfortable enough in front of an audience to appear natural, confident, and competent. Nonfluencies, breaks in the smooth and fluid delivery of the speech, are judged negatively.

Vocalized pauses such as *like, you know,* and *ahhh* are nonfluencies. Another kind of nonfluency is the repetitive use of certain words and phrases, such as *well, then,* or *now,* at every transition. These nonfluencies decreased the audience's ratings of competence and dynamism, but did not affect the speaker's trustworthiness.[12]

Strategies for Improving Your Credibility

Below is a checklist that you can use to make sure that you have considered the possible ways to improve your credibility. Place a check in the blank on the right to indicate that you have considered the implications of the statement.

1. Have you selected a topic in which you are involved, so that you can be perceived as sincere, responsible, reputable, and trustworthy? _____

2. Have you considered the relationship between your apparent competence and your credibility by building into your speech cues that indicate your experience, training, skill, and expertise in the subject? _____

3. Have you considered the relationship between your apparent trustworthiness and your credibility by building trust through concern for your audience's welfare, through objective consideration of their needs, through friendly rapport, and through responsible and honest handling of the speech content? _____

4. Have you selected a means of delivery and content that will help the audience see you as dynamic—energetic, strong, empathic, and assertive? _____

5. Are you indicating in your speech one or more ideas, beliefs, attitudes, or characteristics that you hold in common with most of the people in your audience? _____

6. Can you ask your teacher or someone else who introduces you to say something praiseworthy about you or your qualifications? _____

7. Have you reminded your audience, descriptively, of your qualifications to speak on the subject? _____

8. Are you dressed appropriately for this audience? _____

9. Given the classroom situation, your class audience, and the topic you have selected, are you likely to be perceived as competent, trustworthy, dynamic, and interested in this audience's well-being? _____

10. Have you carefully pointed out how your topic is related to the audience, selected appropriate supporting materials, organized the content, and found a way to deliver your speech that will help your audience to learn and to retain what you say? _____

The effective speaker is constantly aware of his or her own impact on the speech and on the audience. We have examined four aspects of credibility: competence, trustworthiness, dynamism, and coorientation. We have reviewed the results of studies that indicate that a highly credible speaker has an advantage at the time of the speech, that establishing common ground can help your speech, that the introduction of a speaker can help or harm credibility, that the speaker's status, sincerity, and organization can influence credibility, and that effective delivery can enhance credibility. The credibility of your sources, or the value of the materials that you find to support what you say in a speech, also affects the success of your speeches.

Finding Credible Sources

Now that you know what audiences seem to look for in a speaker, you must find substance or content for your speech. The content of a speech usually consists of definitions, analogies, examples, illustrations, comparisons, contrasts, statistics, testimony, and descriptions when your purpose is informative and of arguments and support for those arguments when your purpose is persuasive. Typically a speech has a mixture of purposes that result in a wide array of supporting materials like those listed above. As a speaker you need to be sure that your speech employs arguments and supporting materials that will inform, convince, or persuade your audience. Where you are supposed to find these materials is the subject of this section. After discovering how to find materials for your speech, we will conclude by reviewing some of the kinds of supporting materials that are most useful in public speaking.

The first place you should look for materials for the content of your speech is yourself. Your personal experience is something that you can talk about with some authority. One student had been a "head hunter," a person who tries to find employees for employers who are willing to pay a premium for specific kinds of employees. This student gave a speech from his personal experience concerning what employers particularly value in employees. Another student had a brother who was retarded and who died at age nine. She gave a speech about retarded individuals and the way they are treated in our society. Your religion, your special causes, your military experience, your jobs, and even your family can provide you with firsthand information that you can use in your speech.

You should not, however, use your own experience uncritically. Important questions should be asked about personal experience before you employ it as proof. Is your experience typical? If you are among the very few who had an unfortunate experience with a local bank, you should think carefully before you generalize and assume that many people have been treated similarly. You can ask some questions about your personal experience that will help you evaluate it as evidence of what you plan to say in your speech:

Was your experience typical?
Was your experience so typical that it will be boring or so atypical that it was a chance occurrence?

Was your experience one that this audience will appreciate or from which this audience can learn a lesson?
Does your experience really constitute proof or evidence of anything?

Not all personal experiences can be shared with an audience. Only a limited number of them can really be used as evidence.

Another question about your experience is whether it was firsthand or the experience of someone else. If the information is not firsthand, it is usually questionable. It may have been distorted in transmission. The old game of passing a message down a line of people illustrates the problem of getting a message intact from person to person. You might find yourself passing along a falsehood to your audience unless the experience is your own.

ANIMAL CRACKERS

The second place you can look for content for your speech is to others who may know about the subject. Sometimes these sources of information are fellow students; more often, they are faculty members or people in the town or city who have special knowledge of the subject. To prepare yourself for this kind of information gathering, you should review the information in chapter 8 on interviewing, where you learned and may have even practiced the very kind of research that is suggested for the public speaker.

You are likely to derive some benefits from interviewing people for your speech. You will meet people who share an interest in your subject. You will gain information that you can use yourself as well as in your speech. You may be able to enhance your own credibility by being knowledgeable, authoritative, and responsible. And you may increase your self-confidence by addressing an audience about a subject in which you are increasingly involved. Interviewing takes planning, time, effort, and, sometimes, a little courage, but the benefits for you personally and for your speech make it a worthwhile method of research.

A third place you can look for substance for your speech is in published sources. Perhaps the quickest and most efficient way to find information in published sources is to go to the *Reader's Guide to Periodical Literature*. This multivolume work lists articles that have appeared in magazines. You can look up a topic like marijuana and find a listing of all the articles that have appeared in popular magazines on the subject. If you want to explore the topic further, you can look up "key words" in the *Reader's Guide* that will lead you to still other sources. You could explore the subject of marijuana further by looking up key words like drugs, law enforcement, international regulation, medicine, and juvenile delinquency. It would be difficult to think of a topic that is not covered in the popular literature. As a student of public speaking, you should learn how to use this reference to help you learn more about your topic.

Some additional sources frequently used by speech students for finding information include:

1. Yearbooks and encyclopedias. Some frequently used yearbooks are the *World Almanac*, the *Book of Facts, Facts on File*, and the *Statistical Abstract of the United States*. These compendia contain facts and figures about a wide variety of subjects, from population to yearly coal production. The encyclopedias contain background material about many topics, and short bibliographies. Among the popular encyclopedias are the *Encyclopedia Americana* and the *Encyclopaedia Britannica*.

2. Sourcebooks for examples, literary allusions, and quotations include Bartlett's *Familiar Quotations*, George Seldes' *The Great Quotations*, and Arthur Richmond's *Modern Quotations for Ready Reference*.

3. Biographies of famous persons can be found in *Who's Who in America, Current Biography*, and the *Dictionary of American Biography* (deceased Americans).

4. Newspaper files are useful, especially if your college has the *New York Times*, one of the few newspapers that has an index.

5. Professional journals, which are also indexed, are collected by many libraries. You can find articles about speech, communication, psychology, sociology, economics, chemistry, mathematics, and many other subjects.

6. Many modern libraries own volumes of material on microfilm. Media resource centers on campuses have lists of slides, films, and other visual materials.

7. Your reference librarian is an expert at helping you locate materials.

You can also use information from television news and documentaries, from film and microfilm, from records and newspapers. An effective public speaker becomes like a skilled debater—he or she learns rapidly where to find good supporting materials.

Still another resource important to the public speaker is the card catalog. The card catalog lists every book in the library by author, title, and subject. The books are usually cross-indexed so you can find them simply by looking at the cards collected under the subject heading. If you picked a subject in which you are involved and to which you are committed, you should not have to read a large number of books on the subject. On the other hand, if the subject is truly of interest to you, you may want to read some of them. Usually, it is sufficient to check out several of the best books on the topic and read them selectively for information that is most usable to you in your speech. As in interviewing, it is important to take good notes, to record the information accurately and precisely, and to credit the author of the book in your speech when you deliver it. An entry like the one in figure 11.1 on an index card or a separate sheet of paper will usually help. Be sure to include author, title, publisher, place of publication, date of publication, and page reference, as well as the information.

Figure 11.1 Index card: A speaker's notes from a book.

Marvin Karlins and Herbert I. Abelson, <u>Persuasion</u>
(New York: Springer Publishing Co., Inc., 1970),
pp. 128-29.
The authors state: "People are most persuaded by
a communicator they perceive to be similar to
themselves." P. 128.
They cite a study in which some discussion leaders
tried to be "liked" by their fellow discussants and
others tried to be disliked. They were more
successful in persuading the discussants when they
were liked by them. Pp. 128-29.

To assist you further in your search for information that you can use in your speech you should examine the written resources listed in figure 11.2. The indices will lead you to other sources, the dictionaries and encyclopedias will provide definitions and explanations, and the yearbooks will provide facts and statistics.

Library Scavenger Hunt

You are more likely to use reference works if you know where they are in the library and if you know what kind of information is in them. The following exercise is designed to better acquaint you with the library and its reference works.

1. From the card catalog find the author and title of one book that deals with your topic.
   Author _____ Title _____
   _____

2. From the *Reader's Guide to Periodical Literature* find the title and author of one article on your topic.
   Author _____ Title _____
   _____

3. Using the *Education Index* or other specialized index, give the author, title, and name of publication for an article on the topic you have selected.
   Author _____ Title _____
   _____Publication _____

4. Using an encyclopedia or a yearbook, find specific information about your topic. In one sentence explain what kind of information you found.
   _____
   _____
   Source _____

Figure 11.2   Printed resources for the public speaker.

Written Resources for the Public Speaker

General indexes to periodicals
Reader's Guide to Periodical Literature. 1900–. (Author, title, subject)
Book Review Digest. 1905–. (Author, title, subject)
Social Sciences and Humanities Index. 1965–. (Author, subject)
New York Times Index. 1913–. (Author, subject)

Special indexes to periodicals
Art Index. 1929–. (Author, subject)
Bibliographic Index. 1937–. (Subject)
Biography Index. 1946–. (Subject)
Book Review Index. 1965–.
Catholic Periodical Index. 1930–. (Subject)
Education Index. 1929–. (Author, subject)
Biological and Agricultural Index. 1964–. (Subject)
Engineering Index. 1884–. (Subject)
Quarterly Cumulative Index Medicus. 1927–. (Author, subject)
Index to Book Reviews in the Humanities. 1960–.
Index to Legal Periodicals. 1908–. (Author, subject)
Business Periodicals Index. 1958–. (Subject)
Music Index. 1949–. (Author, subject)
Public Affairs Information Service. 1915–. (Subject)
Technical Book Review Index. 1935–.

Specialized Dictionaries
Evans, Bergen and Cornelia Evans. *A Dictionary of Contemporary American Usage.* 1957.
Partridge, Eric. *Dictionary of Slang and Unconventional English.* 5th ed., 1961.
Roget's International Thesaurus. 3rd ed., 1962.
Webster's Dictionary of Synonyms. 1942.

Specialized Encyclopedias
Adams. J. T. *Dictionary of American History.* 6 vols. 1942.
Encyclopedia of the Social Sciences. 15 vols. 1930–35.
Encyclopedia of World Art. 1959–.
Grove's Dictionary of Music and Musicians. 9 vols. 1954. (Supplement, 1961).
Harris, Chester W. *Encyclopedia of Educational Research,* 1960.
Hastings, James. *Interpreter's Dictionary of the Bible.* 4 vols. 1962.
McGraw-Hill *Encyclopedia of Science and Technology.* 15 vols. 1966.
Munn, Glenn G. *Encyclopedia of Banking and Finance.* 6th ed., 1962.
Van Nostrand's *Scientific Encyclopedia.* 4th ed., 1968.
Worldmark Encyclopedia of the Nations. 5 vols. 1963.

Yearbooks
Americana Annual. 1923–.
The Annual Register of World Events. 1958–.
Economic Almanac. 1940–.
Facts on File. 1940–.
Information Please Almanac. 1947–.
New International Year Book. 1907–.
Statesman's Year-Book. 1864–.
Statistical Abstract of the United States. 1878–.
World Almanac and Book of Facts. 1868–.

Citing Your Sources

Often in an outline or a manuscript you may be expected to reveal where you got your information. Citing sources is a convention or common practice that makes sense when you think about it. When you give a speech or write an outline or manuscript, you cannot be expected to know all of the relevant information about the subject. Many other people have studied the issues more closely than you have. You can use their ideas and information as long as you give them credit. Citing sources is giving credit to others for their ideas or information.

There are a number of different forms that are used in citing sources. One is the footnote form used in manuscripts and outlines when you want to reveal where you found the information. The footnote typically follows the information cited and is signaled by an elevated number in the manuscript.

Bettinghaus argues that ". . . the study of *proof* is vital to the student of communication."[13]

In this case the footnote follows a direct quotation, a statement set apart with quotation marks that states the exact words used in the source. A paraphrased statement, a statement recast in your own words, is also footnoted:

Bettinghaus says that students of communication should study the nature of proof.[14]

If a direct quote is longer than three sentences, it should be indented on both the right and the left margin, stated exactly as the source states it, typed single spaced, and followed by a footnote.

As Bettinghaus says in his book, *The Nature of Proof:*

> Modes of proof have changed greatly over the centuries, but the concept of proof is recognizable over a span of two thousand years. Ancient Greeks recognized confessions obtained from the torture of witnesses as valid evidence—and perfectly good proof—in their courts. During the Roman era, a defendant was allowed to parade his weeping wife and children before the judges as proof of his innocence. During the Middle Ages, the "water test" could establish the proof of a man's guilt. The accused was thrown into a lake or pond. If he swam, he was judged guilty; if he drowned, he was believed to have been innocent.[15]

Similarly when you paraphrase a number of sentences based on someone else's idea or information, you so indicate by following it with an elevated number but without indenting.

As you might suspect, you have to do more than simply place an elevated number after a direct quotation or a paraphrased statement. The elevated number indicates that the source is cited or listed either at the bottom of the page (thus the name "foot" note) or at the end of the paper in endnotes. The footnotes or endnotes should follow a form in which you indicate your source as illustrated below.

If the footnote cites an article from a magazine or journal, you should indicate the author, the title of the article (in quotation marks), the name of the magazine or journal (underlined), the volume number, the date (in parentheses), and the page on which you found the information. For a single authored magazine article, the footnote would look like this:

[1]Meg Greenfield, "Waiting to the Last Minute," Newsweek, XCVI (November 3, 1980), 100.

Notice that the first line is indented three spaces and that the second line moves out to the left margin. Notice also that when you include a volume number you do not write "p." or "pp." before the page reference.

If the footnote cites a newspaper, you follow the same idea:

[1]Herschel Nissenson, "Time to start a new chapter in Notre Dame legend," Des Moines Sunday Register, November 30, 1980, p. 1D.

If the footnote is from a book, it looks like this:

[1]Erwin P. Bettinghaus, The Nature of Proof (New York: The Bobbs-Merrill Company, Inc., 1972), pp. 1–2.

In a footnote for a book the publication information is placed in parentheses and the pages are indicated either with a "p." for a reference from a single page or with a "pp." for material from more than one page. The name of the book, like the names of magazines, journals, and newspapers are underlined when you type, or set in italics when they appear in print.

A quotation or paraphrased material from an interview or class or TV program follows the same form except that the footnote contains slightly different information:

[1]Dr. George Kirk, Associate Professor of Anthropology, in an interview on September 23, 1982.
[2]Ronald Reagan, "Meet the Press," Sunday, November 30, 1980.

With pamphlets, the amount of information that you can provide may be quite different:

[1] "Controlling Garden Pests," U.S. Department of Agriculture Pamphlet available through State University's Agricultural extension office, p. 3.

Remember that the purpose of citing sources and writing footnotes is to provide sufficient information to lead the reader to the source for verification or for further reading.

Footnotes might be fine in written manuscripts or outlines, but what are you supposed to do about indicating your sources in a speech? The answer is oral footnotes. An oral footnote is simply an abbreviated footnote that tells the audience where you found your information. In a speech the footnotes illustrated previously sound like this:

"A recent article by Meg Greenfield in *Newsweek* pointed out how difficult it is for voters to. . . ."

"The Sports Peach revealed a story about why one coach quit coaching for Notre Dame."

"Professor Erwin Bettinghaus of Michigan State says in his book that. . . ."

"When I interviewed Dr. Kirk last week, he said. . . ."

"Ronald Reagan was on 'Meet the Press' last Sunday. In that interview he said. . . ."

In other words, in a speech the speaker indicates that the information or idea came from a magazine, newspaper, book, or interview by providing some signal to the audience that the material came from some other source than his or her own head. Now that you know where to find information and you know how to cite it in a manuscript, outline, or speech, let us turn to the specific kinds of materials that you can find in written resources or interviews.

Materials for Evidence, Proof, or Clarification

You already know that indices and card catalogs are supposed to lead you to new ideas and information about your topic, but what exactly are you supposed to be seeking when you find the magazine articles, journals, and books on the topic? You might find additional materials that help to clarify information or arguments that you can use to persuade. But the most useful material that you can find in written resources is the abundant supporting material, those materials that you can employ to support your ideas, to substantiate your arguments, and to clarify your position. The supporting materials that we will examine most closely are examples, surveys and studies, testimonial evidence, statistics, analogies, explanations, and definitions. Some of these supporting materials are used as evidence or proof; others are used mainly for clarification or amplification; but all are found in researching your topic.

Examples are one of the most common supporting materials found in speeches. Sometimes a single example will help to convince an audience; other times a relatively large number of examples may be necessary to achieve your purpose. For instance, if you are arguing in your speech that television commercials are sexist, you can support that claim with this example—men are never shown drinking tea on television commercials and women are never shown drinking beer, but we all know that both men and women drink tea and beer. Similarly in your informative speech on cell division, you can use as an example the cell division of an amoeba to demonstrate your point through a single example. When you find articles or when you interview an expert, you should keep your eyes and ears open for examples that might be appealing to your audience.

You should also be careful of examples or specific instances. Sometimes an example may be so unusual that an audience will not accept it as evidence or proof of anything. The student who referred to crime in his hometown as an example of the increasing crime problem was unconvincing because his hometown had considerably less crime than the audience was accustomed to. A good example must be plausible, typical, and related to the main point before it will be effective in a speech.

Surveys and studies are a second kind of supporting material commonly used in speeches. These studies and surveys are found most often in magazines or journals. They are usually seen as more credible than one person's experience or an example or two because they synthesize the experience of hundreds or thousands of people. Public opinion polls fall into this category. One person's experience with alcohol can have impact on an audience, but a survey indicating that one third of Americans are abstainers, one third are occasional drinkers, and one third are regular drinkers provides better support for an argument.

As with personal experience, there are some important questions you should ask about the evidence found in surveys and studies:

How reliable is the source that you used? A report in a professional journal of sociology, psychology, or speech is likely to be more thorough and more valid than one found in a local newspaper.

How broad was the sample used in the survey or study? Was it a survey of the entire nation, the region, the state, the city, the campus, or the class?

Who was included in the survey or study sample? Did everyone in the sample have an equally good chance of being selected or were volunteers asked to respond to the questions?

Playboy's readers may not be typical of the population in your state.

Who performed the survey or study? Was it a nationally recognized survey firm like Lou Harris or Gallup, or was it the local newspaper editor?

Was it performed by professionals like professors, researchers, or management consultants?

Why was the study done? Was it performed for any self-serving purpose—to attract more readers—or did the government make it to help establish policy or legislation?

      Testimonial evidence is the third kind of information that you can secure from interviews, television or radio, and printed sources. Testimonial evidence is the use of "testimony" or the words of others to support or clarify your points. The important part about using testimonial evidence is to either select persons or sources that the audience respects or choose quotations that state the ideas in a new, original, or better way. Testimonial evidence can be very convincing. Christian fundamentalists

often use testimonies of believers to help reinforce the beliefs of the group. Similarly, Alcoholics Anonymous members give testimonials about why they gave up drinking. Expert testimony is also a potent source of influence. We tend to believe an expert on cancer, politics, religion, drugs, or law. Nonetheless, there are some questions that should be asked about the sources of your testimonial evidence:

Is the person you quote an expert whose opinions or conclusions are worthier than most other people's opinions?

Is the quotation about a subject in the person's area of expertise?

Is the person's statement based on extensive personal experience, professional study or research, or another form of firsthand proof?

Will your classmates find the statement more believable because you got it from this outside source?

A fourth kind of evidence that makes useful supporting material for clarification or persuasion is **statistics.** Statistics is a kind of numerical shorthand that can summarize large quantities of data for easy consumption by an audience. This

data must be used with care, however, because it can be deceiving. To assist you in your use of statistics both as a speaker and as a critical listener, you should have a brief vocabulary relating to statistics and numbers, and you should know some of the questions that can be asked about them.

The terms below are only a partial list of words that are commonly used in describing statistics; along with each term is a brief explanation and some appropriate questions to ask about it.

Mean or Average   **Mean or average** refers to the total of a list of numbers divided by the number of items. For example, given these six scores—4,7,7,11,13, and 15—the mean would be 9.5, or the sum of the scores divided by the number of scores. Sometimes the average, or mean, is not a good indicator of central tendency. For example, if the scores were 1, 2, 2, 1, 14, 15, the average would be 5.8. But all the scores actually fell on the extremes and nobody received a score even close to the average. The average grade in a class could be C if everyone were given an equal number of *A*'s and *F*'s. Two good questions to ask about the mean, or average, are: Does the average tell us where most of the numbers or scores are clustered? and What was the range of the numbers?

Mode   The **mode** is the most frequently recurring number in a list of numbers or a distribution. If the mode on an examination were 7, it would mean that more people earned a 7 than any other score. However, the mode is not necessarily where most of the other numbers are clustered. The critical listener has to ask for several measures of central tendency: What was the mean? and Was the mode near the average?

Percentage   The term **percentage** literally means "by the hundred" because it refers to the ratio or fraction of one hundred. Percentage can be expressed as a decimal: .56 means 56 percent or 56/100. Among the questions that can be asked about percentages are: What is the basis for the whole? That is, what is 100 percent? A 500 percent increase in sales, for example, can mean that the person sold one car last year and five cars this year. One hundred percent, then, represented one car. Percentages can be difficult for an audience to comprehend unless you make them palatable. It is easier for an audience to understand percentages stated as percentages rather than as decimals, although they mean the same thing. It is also easier for an audience to comprehend percentages that are rounded off rather than percentages that are stated too specifically. A number like 49.67 percent is easier to understand if it is rounded off to 50 percent.

Range   The highest and lowest numbers in a distribution are the **range** of that distribution. For example, the examination scores ranged from 5 to 25 out of a possible 30 points. The range does not reveal where most of the numbers are clustered; it simply tells the two end points in a distribution of numbers. All the remaining numbers or scores must fall between these two points, but exactly where they cluster is unknown unless you ask the right questions. Two questions that will give you a better idea of where the numbers cluster are: Where was the mean, or average? Where was the mode?

Raw Numbers   **Raw numbers** are specific numbers that are often cited in population, production, and other measures of quantity. Say that the number of teenagers in the state increased by 325,465 this year. The raw number is often difficult to absorb because it is so specific. Raw numbers are easier for an audience to understand if they are rounded off (over 325,000) or stated as a percentage of increase (a 15 percent increase). Good questions to ask about a raw number are: What percentage of increase or decrease does that raw number represent? and What was the original number and what is the new total? Raw numbers are hard to interpret if you have no basis for comparison. If the speaker does not provide that basis, the critical listener must ask for additional information before the number can be understood. Listeners should not feel embarrassed about inquiring about statistics and numbers in speeches. They are often difficult to understand and interpret. As a speaker, you should strive to provide all the information necessary for interpreting numbers and statistics; as a listener you should ask for additional information when you need it.

Another kind of supporting material used in public speeches is the analogy. An **analogy** is a comparison of unlike things and of things in different classes. For instance, human beings and bees are fundamentally different, but one could draw a comparison of these two different classes by pointing out that in many ways human beings are like bees—we have the people who are like the queen bee who is pampered and cared for by others; we have the drones who do nothing and are cared for by others; and we have the workers who seem to do all of the labor without any pampering or any care from others. Similarly, analogies can be used to show that Roman society is analogous to American society, that a law applied in one state will work the same way in another, and that if animals get cancer from drinking too much diet soda so will human beings.

An analogy often provides clarification, but it is a risky means of arguing because somewhere along the line the comparison inevitably breaks down. So the speaker who argues that American society will fail just as Roman society did can carry that comparison only so far because the two societies exist in quite a different time frame, because the form of government and the institutions in the two societies are quite different, etc. Likewise, you can question the bee-human being analogy above by pointing out the vast differences between the two things being compared. Nonetheless, the analogy can be quite successful as a way to illustrate or clarify.

Explanations are another important means of clarification and persuasion that you can find in written sources and in interviews. How does the stock market work? What is a Dow Jones Industrial average? What does "buying on the margin" mean? What is a "bull market"? What is a "bear market"? All of these questions can be answered by explanations, by stating in ways that the audience can understand what these terms mean and how they work in the stock market. An explanation clarifies what something is or how it works to the audience.

A good explanation usually simplifies a concept or idea for an audience by explaining it from their point of view. William Safire, once a presidential speech writer and now a syndicated columnist, provided an explanation in one of his columns about how the spelling of a word gets changed. In his explanation, he pointed out that the experts who write the dictionaries observe how writers and editors use the language.

"When enough citations come in from cultivated writers, passed by trained copy editors," he quotes a lexicographer as saying, "the 'mistake' becomes the spelling."[16] You may find, too, that much of your informative speaking is explanation, explaining what an idea means or how something works.

Definitions are still another kind of clarifying information that you can garner from written sources or interviews. Often the jargon of your field of interest will be unfamiliar to your audience, and you will have to explain through definitions what the terms mean. Sometimes definitions are brief explanations—telling an audience that *hydroponics* is a system of growing plants in a chemical culture instead of in soil. Other times your best definition may be an operational definition, that is, a definition telling what operations need to be performed. An angel food cake can be defined by the recipe that must be followed to make it; a secretary can be defined by his or her job description; and a dash and a cross-country run can be differentiated by stating the distance and the speed that need to be employed in the two kinds of running.

Definitions, like explanations, simplify; they state what something is in terms that the audience can understand. If they try to clarify by using terms that the audience does not understand, then they fail as definitions. Some of the most complete definitions of words can be found in the *Oxford English Dictionary,* common words can be found in a college desk dictionary, and unusual words can be found in the specialized dictionaries and encyclopedias listed earlier in this chapter.

In your search through written works and in interviews you should seek the content or substance of your speech by finding good arguments and means of clarification. You should try to find supporting materials for your arguments and ideas in the form of examples, surveys and studies, testimonial evidence, statistics, analogies, explanations, and definitions.

Summary

As a public speaker, you should always remember that the choices you make in selecting a topic, in choosing an immediate purpose, in determining a long-range goal, in organizing your speech, in selecting supporting materials, and even in creating visual aids are all *strategic choices*. All these choices are made for the purpose of adapting the speaker and the subject to a particular audience. The larger your repertoire of supporting arguments, the better your chances are of having appropriate arguments. The larger your supply of supporting materials, the better your chances are of having evidence, illustrations, and visual aids that the audience will respond to. Your choices are strategic in that they are purposeful. The purpose is to choose, from among the available alternatives, the ones that will best achieve your objectives with the particular audience.

This chapter explores the concept of source credibility, by finding out what audiences look for in a speaker and how they evaluate the worthiness of a speaker. The four dimensions of source credibility are competency, trustworthiness, dynamism, and coorientation. Highly credible speakers have an initial advantage in changing audience opinion. To be an effective speaker you should employ common ground. As a speaker your credibility can be influenced by who introduces you and how you are introduced. A speaker's status and sincerity, and effective delivery can also influence credibility.

This chapter also discussed how to find credible or believable sources through interviews and library research. The names of indices were listed that can lead you to written resources. The card catalog can also lead you to books. How to write a notecard and footnotes and how to indicate sources through oral footnotes was discussed so you can cite credible sources. Finally, some supporting materials that could be used in your speech include examples, surveys and studies, testimonial evidence, statistics, analogies, explanations, and definitions.

Additional Readings

Hovland, Carl I.; Janis, Irving J.; and Kelly, Harold H. "Credibility of the Communicator." In *Dimensions in Communication: Readings,* edited by James H. Campbell and Hal W. Hepler. Belmont, Calif.: Wadsworth Publishing Co., 1970. Pages 146–69.
A discussion of the research on the effect of audience-rated source credibility on persuasiveness. A detailed exploration of the factors affecting the establishment of credibility to an audience and the manner in which credibility affects message acceptance.

Kruger, Arthur N. *Effective Speaking: A Complete Course.* New York: Van Nostrand Reinhold Company, 1970. Pages 243–77.
The use of statistics, evidence, and visual aids in the speech is explained. Some workable techniques are suggested for researching the topic and recording the information for easy reference as you develop the speech.

Robb, Stephen. "Fundamentals of Evidence and Argument." In *Modcom: Modules in Speech Communication.* Chicago: Science Research Associates, 1976.
Easily understood presentation of the issues underlying the use of evidence. Excellent section on the analysis of evidence and inference making. Shows the relationship between evidence and argument.

Swanson, Richard, and Marquardt, Charles. *On Communication: Listening, Reading, Speaking, and Writing.* Beverly Hills, Calif.: Glencoe Press, 1974. Chapter 8.
General strategies for changing attitudes. The credibility of the source as one method of proving an argument. A brief examination of credibility, but easy to understand and apply.

Thonssen, Lester, and Baird, A. Craig. "The Character of the Speaker." In *Readings in Speech,* edited by Haig A. Bosmajian. New York: Harper & Row, Publishers, 1971. Pages 118–28.
The authors discuss credibility as a source of proof, relate Aristotle's position on ethical proof to modern speeches, and list some ways in which speakers can enhance their credibility.

Notes

1. Aristotle, *Rhetoric*, in *The Basic Works of Aristotle,* trans. W. Rhys Roberts and ed. by Richard McKeon (New York: Random House, 1941), 1, 1356a, LL, 12–14.
2. Ralph L. Rosnow and Edward J. Robinson, eds., *Experiments in Persuasion* (New York: Academic Press, 1967), p. 18.
3. Derived from a study by Christopher J.S. Tuppen, "Dimensions of Communicator Credibility: An Oblique Solution," *Speech Monographs* 41 (1974), 253–60.
4. Rosnow and Robinson, p. 8. See also, Kenneth Andersen and Theodore Clevenger, Jr., "A Summary of Experimental Research in Ethos," *Speech Monographs* 30 (1963): 59–78.
5. Marvin Karlins and Herbert I. Abelson, *Persuasion* (New York: Springer Publishing Company, 1970), pp. 113–14.
6. Carl I. Hovland and Walter Weiss, "The Influence of Source Credibility on Communicator Effectiveness," in Rosnow and Robinson, p. 21.
7. Wayne N. Thompson, *Quantitative Research in Public Address and Communication* (New York: Random House, 1967), p. 54.
8. Andersen and Clevenger, pp. 59–78.
9. Harry Sharp, Jr., and Thomas McClung, "Effects of Organization on the Speaker's Ethos," *Speech Monographs* 33 (1966): 182–83.
10. L.S. Harms, "Listener Judgments of Status Cues in Speech," *Quarterly Journal of Speech* 47 (1961):168.
11. Thompson, p. 56.
12. Ibid.
13. Erwin P. Bettinghaus, *The Nature of Proof* (New York: Bobbs-Merrill Company, 1972), p. v.
14. *Ibid.*
15. *Ibid.*, p. 4.
16. William Safire, "When a Mistake Becomes Correct, and Vice Versa," *Des Moines Sunday Register,* 30 November 1980, p. 3C.

12

Sharing Your Message through Organization

Objectives

1. Explain five functions of an introduction
2. Compose an outline for your speech following the principles of outlining
3. Explain which patterns of organization are most appropriate for various topics
4. Provide examples of transitions
5. Explain the functions of a conclusion

Key Terms

introduction
body
conclusion
attention
interest
purpose
qualifications
forecast
immediate purpose
ultimate goal
abstract
outlining symbols
main points
subpoints
sub-subpoints
subordinate

parallel form
sentence outline
bibliography
key-word outline
organizational patterns
time sequence pattern
topical-sequence pattern
problem-and-solution pattern
spatial organization
cause-effect organization
climactic organization
anticlimactic organization
indirect sequencing
transitions
brakelight function
forewarning

I just can't get my act together. I don't know how to start a speech and I don't know how to end it.

I have ten pages of material to present to the class, but I have only five minutes to do it.

That's nothing. In my last speech on team sports, I forgot to tell the class that I'm a recreation major until the very end.

Each of these students is facing a problem in organizing a speech. The same problems are faced by every speaker inside and outside of the classroom. Anxiety about organizing the speech usually occurs after we have decided on a topic and after we have gathered some information that we wish to present. In this chapter, we will examine the three main parts of a speech: the **introduction,** the **body,** and the **conclusion.** The advice, the examples, and the explanations will help you avoid the problems faced by the students quoted above.

The Introduction: Gaining and Maintaining Attention

The five functions of the introduction to a speech are: to gain and maintain audience attention, to arouse the audience's interest in the subject matter, to indicate the purpose of the speech, to describe any qualifications that might improve your credibility, and to forecast the organization and development of your speech.

A number of techniques can be used to attract the audience's **attention.** One is to begin the speech with an eloquent quotation from one of your sources. A person giving a speech on new life-styles could begin her speech with a quotation such as this, from *Time* magazine:

From time immemorial—or at least since the first U.S. census was taken in 1790— the head of household has been identified for every house, hovel, plantation, apartment, co-op, condominium, igloo and wigwam to which an intrepid census taker could wend his way.[1]

The speaker could then point out that the new life-styles—unmarried men and women living together, women who earn more than men in the same family, and sometimes groups of people living together—have caused the Census Bureau to eliminate the designation "head of household" from the census forms. The quotation is appropriate, it introduces the topic in an imaginative way, and it will probably capture the audience's attention.

A second commonly used method of introducing a speech is to cite a striking statistic or fact. "People seem to be changing their eating habits to avoid heart attacks," the speaker might begin. "According to *U.S. News and World Report,* the

Figure 12.1 **Gaining attention.**

consumption of poultry has gone up 16 percent in the last ten years, fish is up 20 percent, eggs are down 14 percent, and animal fats are down 31 percent. But we still eat too much: total consumption of food has increased by nearly 6 percent."[2] Or the speaker might start by stating that "School vandalism costs taxpayers $600 million a year in repairs; there are 70,000 assaults each year against teachers; and assaults against both teachers and students rose 58 percent in just four years."[3] Striking facts and statistics can arouse the audience's interest.

A third way to introduce a speech is to begin with some action. One woman who was giving a speech on self-defense started her speech by inviting a cohort to attack her from behind, whereupon she flipped him neatly on his rear. A chemistry student began by showing the class a brief experiment. A motorcycle lover brought his chromed beauty right into the classroom. These active introductions were difficult to ignore.

These are just three out of dozens of possibilities. You can begin a speech with a vivid description, with two conflicting views that invite resolution, with a brief or extended story or narration, with a personal experience related to the topic, with emotional language of your own or from a source, with a statement of uncertainty that your speech will clarify, with a cause or effect that will be expanded in the speech, or with a statement that exploits an immediate concern or an unexpected development. There is no one way of starting a speech—every speaker should try to be creative and imaginative enough to invent ways of capturing and maintaining audience attention.

Some other suggestions can help you to plan your introduction. Remember that the time and effort that goes into composing an effective introduction is well worth the effort. We have already referred to research that indicates that audiences tend to make inferences about the speaker and the speech within the first 15 seconds. Your first exposure may have a disproportionate impact.

Your attention-getting introduction should also be related to your topic. Banging on the lectern or writing SEX on the board to capture an audience's attention, when these actions have nothing to do with the topic in hand, is self-defeating.

Avoid being overly dramatic. One of our colleagues had a harrowing experience in class. She was still writing down some comments about the previous speech when the next student rose to deliver his speech. She heard a horrifying groan and looked up to see the student on the floor with his whole leg laid open and bleeding. The students in the class leaped up and surrounded the injured student while she ran to the office to call emergency assistance. The student planned to give a speech on first aid. He had gotten a plastic leg wound in living color from the student health center. He had a bag of simulated blood on his stomach which he squeezed rhythmically so

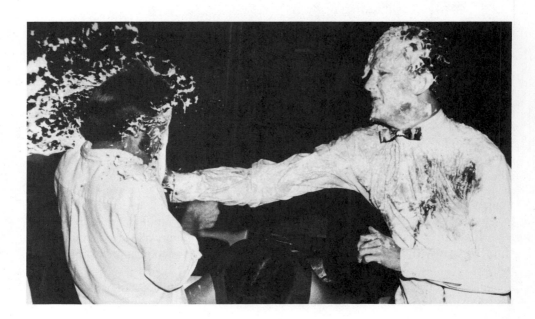

it would spurt like a severed artery. Unfortunately for the student, his attention-getting action introduction was too realistic. Instead of capturing the audience's attention, he managed to get so much adrenalin into their bloodstreams that they were in no mood to listen to any more speeches that day.

A second function of an introduction is to arouse audience **interest** in the subject matter. The best way to arouse audience interest is to show clearly how the topic is related to them. A highly skilled speaker can figure out how to adapt almost any topic to a particular audience by determining how it relates to them. Do you want to talk about collecting coins? Thousands of coins pass through each person's hands every year. Can you tell your audience how to spot a rare one? If you can arouse the audience's interest in currency, then you will find it easier to encourage them to listen to your speech about the rare coins that you have collected. Similarly, speeches about your life as mother of four, as bartender in a nightclub, as a camp counselor, or as the manager of a business can be linked to audience interests to fulfill the second function of an introduction.

A third function of the introduction is to state the **purpose** of the speech. Almost always, speakers should tell an audience what they want that audience to know, learn, or understand from the speech. Some exceptions to this general rule occur in persuasive speaking. When speakers face an audience with a proposition to which the audience is opposed, they are advised not to reveal their purpose at the outset. Ordinarily, though, the speaker will state the purpose of the speech very explicitly:

Today I will show you the basic construction of a simple electric motor.
There are three main causes of the inflation that reduces the value of your money.
I will provide you with a new way of looking at welfare.

In speaking, as in teaching, the members of an audience are more likely to learn and to understand if they know what is expected of them.

A fourth function of an introduction is to describe any special **qualifications** that you have. You can talk about your experience, your research, the experts that you interviewed, and your own education and training in the subject. You should be wary about self-praise, but you need not be reserved in stating why you can speak about the topic with authority. Chapter 11 will provide considerably more information about what behaviors audiences look for in a speaker along with some suggestions concerning what information should be included about the speaker.

A fifth function of an introduction is to **forecast** the organization and development of the speech. An audience will feel more comfortable if they know what to expect. You can help them by revealing your plan for the speech. Are you going to discuss a problem and its solution? Are you going to make three main arguments with supporting materials? Are you going to talk for five minutes or for twenty? Let your audience know what you plan to do early in your speech. A checklist may help you to consider some specific means of fulfilling the functions of an introduction.

Checklist for Your Introduction

Check the means you believe could be the most effective in developing the introduction to your speech.

1. Assisting the audience to attend to the speech
   a. An introductory quotation from a magazine, book, or interviewee _____
   b. A striking statistic or fact about the topic _____
   c. An action or demonstration related to the topic _____
   d. Other_____ _____
   _____ _____

2. An example or illustration that will arouse the audience's interest in the topic _____

3. An explicit statement that reveals the purpose of my speech and my expectations of the audience _____

4. A description of my qualifications to speak about this subject _____

5. A forecast of my organization and development _____

6. Other _____ _____
   _____ _____

Principles of Outlining

The most common way of organizing a speech or a written composition is to outline it. The following principles of outlining, the suggestions for composing an outline, and the samples of a full-content and a key-word outline should help you to organize the materials that you have gathered for your speech.

The first principle of outlining is that *all of the items of information in your outline should be directly related to your purpose.* In chapter 10 you learned that a speech can have an immediate purpose and a long-range goal. The **immediate purpose** is what you expect to achieve by the end of your speech. You might want the audience to be able to state your three main arguments; you might want the audience to respond to your speech by reading an article, signing a petition, or by trying some synthetic food; or you might want the audience to start changing their minds about the topic by discussing it with others. The **ultimate goal** is what you expect to achieve over a longer time period. Eventually you may want the audience to vote for your candidate, act more tolerantly toward persons of your race, sex, or religion, or join an activist group for a cause you represent. The first principle of outlining is that the content of your outline should reflect your immediate purpose and your long-range goal.

A second principle of outlining is that *the outline should be an* **abstract** *of the speech you will deliver;* that is, it should be less than every word you speak but should include all important points and supporting materials. Some instructors say that an outline should be about one third the length of the actual speech if it were in manuscript form. However, you should ask your instructor what he or she expects in an outline because some instructors like to see a very complete outline and others prefer a brief outline. Nonetheless, the outline is not a manuscript. Instead, it is an abstract of the speech you intend to deliver, a plan that includes the important arguments or information that you intend to present.

A third principle of outlining is that *the outline should consist of single units of information,* usually in the form of complete sentences that express a single idea. An item that looks like the following is incorrect because it expresses more than one idea in more than one sentence.

I. Gun control should be employed to reduce the number of deaths in the United States that result from the use of handguns. Half the deaths from handguns are because criminals murder other people with handguns.

The same idea can be outlined correctly by presenting ideas in sentences with a single idea in each sentence.

I. Government regulation of handguns should be implemented to reduce the number of murders in this country.
   A. Half of the murders in America are committed by criminals who are using handguns.
   B. Half of the murders in America are committed by relatives, friends, and acquaintances of the victim.
   C. Strict regulation of handguns could help to reduce the number of weapons available for murders of all kinds.

A fourth principle of outlining is that *the outline should indicate the importance of an item with an* **outlining symbol.** The **main points** or most important points in your speech are indicated with Roman numerals, such as I, II, III, IV, V, etc. The number of main points in a five-to-ten minute speech or even a longer one should be limited to the number you can reasonably cover, explain, or prove in the time permitted. Most five-minute speeches have from one to three main points. Even hour-long speeches must have a limited number of main points because audiences seem unable to remember more than seven main points.

Subpoints, those that are in support of the main point or those that are of less importance, should be indicated with capital letters, such as A, B, C, D, E, etc. Ordinarily two subpoints are regarded as the minimum if any subpoints are to be presented at all. As with the main points, the subpoints should be limited in number because the audience may otherwise lose sight of the main point you are trying to make. A good guideline is to present two or three of your best pieces of supporting material in support of your main point.

Sub-subpoints are even less important than the subpoints; they are introduced with Arabic numbers, such as 1, 2, 3, 4, 5, etc. Typically, the number of subpoints is limited like the number of subpoints. They usually do not exceed three in number. If you should have to present any additional ideas under a sub-subpoint, they are presented with lowercase alphabetical letters, such as a, b, c, d, e, etc.

A fifth principle of outlining is that *the outline should provide* **margins** *that indicate the relative importance of the items.* The larger the margin on the left, the less important is the item to your purpose. However, the margins are coordinated with the symbols explained above so that main points have the same left margin, the subpoints have a left margin with slightly more space on the left, the sub-subpoints have a left margin with slightly more space on the left, etc. A correct outline, then, would look like this with the appropriate symbols and margins:

I. The constitutional right to bear arms is being threatened by ineffective gun control.[4]

  A. Murders are being committed with handguns by psychopaths, criminals, and ordinary people.

    1. A psychopath killed John Lennon, a famous singer, with a .38-caliber handgun.[5]

    2. The same week an ex-convict killed a famous physician, Dr. Michael Halberstam, with a .32-caliber handgun.[6]

    3. Of the 20,000 persons killed by handguns each year, only 2,000 are murdered by criminals engaged in crime.[7]

  B. The number of handguns in circulation is immense.

    1. Nationally, 55 million handguns are in circulation.[8]

    2. Every year about 2.5 million handguns add to the total.[9]

    3. Handgun Control in Washington, D.C., estimates that we will have 100 million handguns in circulation by the end of the century.[10]

II. The solution may be federal gun control or harsher punishment for handgun offenders.

  A. *New York Times* columnist Tom Wicker recommends gun control.[11]

  B. Columnist James J. Kilpatrick recommends the death sentence for persons who murder with handguns.[12]

A sixth principle of outlining is that *the content of an item in an outline should be less than or* **subordinate** *to the content of items with higher order symbols or larger left-hand margins.* Notice in the outline illustrated above that the items with the highest order symbols (I, II) and the smallest margins are larger or more important ideas than the items that appear below them with lesser order symbols (A, B, C) and larger left-hand margins. Similarly, those items beneath the subpoints are less than or subordinate to the more important items that appear above them. The sub-subheadings merely amplify or provide additional evidence for the items that appear above them. Hence, items in an outline are ranked in importance by symbols, by margins, and by content.

A seventh principle of outlining is that *the items should appear in* **parallel form.** For example, a sentence outline should consist entirely of complete sentences and a key-word outline should consist entirely of important words or phrases. We will examine these two basic types of outlines and consider the advantages and disadvantages of each for the public speaker.

Composing a Sentence Outline

Before you begin composing your outline, you can save time and energy (1) by selecting a topic that is appropriate for you (see chap. 11), for your audience (see chap. 10), and for the situation; (2) by finding arguments, examples, illustrations, quotations, and other supporting materials from your experience, from interviews, and from library research; and (3) by narrowing your immediate purpose so you have to select the best materials from a much larger supply of available items than you could include in your outline and your speech.

Once you have gathered materials consistent with your purpose, you can begin by developing a rough draft of your outline. The most efficient way to develop an outline is to find the main points that are important for your purpose and your audience. The number of main points should be limited, especially in a five-to-ten-minute speech. In the outline from the previous section the speaker decided that the best approach to talking about gun control was to explore the problem (item I) first and then the two possible solutions (item II).

Next you should see what materials you have from your own experience, from interviews, and from your own reading to support these main ideas. In the outline from the previous section, the speaker determined that the number of murders and the number of handguns in circulation illustrated the lack of effective gun control. Similarly, you need to find out if you have any supporting materials that back up your subpoints. In the same outline, the speaker found two famous people murdered by handguns within a week and a statistic that illustrated the scope of the problem. In short, you assemble your main points, your subpoints, and your sub-subpoints for your speech always with your audience and purpose in mind. What arguments, illustrations, and supporting materials will be most likely to have impact on them? Sometimes a speaker gets so involved in a topic that he or she selects mainly those items that interest the speaker. In public speaking you should select the items that are likely to have maximum impact on the audience, not on the person giving the speech.

Composing a **sentence outline** for a speech is not easy. Even professional speech writers may have to make important changes on their first draft. Some of the questions that you need to consider as you revise your **rough draft** are the following.

1. Are my main points consistent with my purpose?
2. Are my subpoints and sub-subpoints subordinate to my main points?
3. Are the items in my outline the best possible ones for this particular audience, for this topic, for me, and for the occasion?
4. Does my outline follow the principles of outlining?

Even after you have rewritten your rough draft you would be wise to have another person, perhaps a classmate, examine your outline and provide an opinion about the contents.

When you have completed your outline, you may be asked to provide a **bibliography,** a list of the sources that you used in your speech. In chapter 11 we examined footnote form; in this chapter we must consider the correct form for the bibliography.

The most common source in student speeches is magazine articles, usually obtained by using the *Reader's Guide*. The correct form for a bibliography entry using a periodical or magazine article is as follows:

Allen, R. R., and Barbara Sundene Wood. "Beyond Reading and Writing to Communication Compentence," Communication Education 27(November 1978), 286–292.

"Teen-age Sex: The New Morality Hits Home," Newsweek 96 (September 1, 1980), 48–53.

Notice that in bibliography form the name of the first author appears in reverse order so that the list can be alphabetized. Notice also that if there is no author, then the bibliography entry begins with the next available information. In the case of the second entry the first information is the title of the article. Your teacher may or may not require volume numbers for magazine articles, but if a volume number is included, then you do not write "p." or "pp." in the entry. Thus a simpler way to write the second entry might be:

"Teen-age Sex: The New Morality Hits Home," Newsweek, September 1, 1980, pp. 48–53.

In this instance, because there is no volume number, you should include "p." for a single page or "pp." for more than one page. Finally, unlike the footnote form, the name of the author or authors is followed by a period.

Correct bibliographic form for a book in your list of sources is as follows:

Higgins, Jack. Solo. New York: Stein and Day, Publishers, 1980.

The author's name is in reverse order for accurate alphabetization. The name of the author and the name of the book are followed by a period. The place of publication is followed by a colon, the name of the publisher is followed by a comma, and the date of publication is followed by a period.

If you use an interview for your source, then the bibliography entry would look like this:

Perkins, Dann. Professor of telecommunicative arts. Interviewed on September 15, 1981.

Pamphlets, handbooks, and manuals may not have complete information about who wrote them, who published them, or when they were published. In that case you will be expected to provide as much information as possible so others can verify the source. The main idea behind a bibliography is to inform others what sources you used for your speech and to permit others to check those sources for themselves. If you run across sources that you do not know how to footnote or to place in bibliographic form, you can ask your bookstore or a librarian for *The MLA Style Sheet* or *A Manual of Style*. College composition texts also include the standard forms for footnote and bibliographic entries.

The Sentence Outline

One of the most useful forms of organization is the sentence outline. This kind of outline is a plan for your speech that will be useful in showing your order of presentation and in showing where and what kind of arguments, points, supporting materials, and evidence you are going to use in your speech. A look at your own outline might indicate, for example, that you have insufficient information to back one of your points or, perhaps, a surplus of information for another. It helps you to see if you really do have a limited number of main points for your speech and to see if the main points and subpoints are consistent with your stated purpose for the speech.

In addition to the outline itself, you may want to write in the functions that are being served by each part of your outline. For example, where are you trying to gain and maintain attention? Where are you trying to back up a major argument with supporting materials like statistics, testimony, or specific instances? The end result of a sentence outline along with sidenotes indicating functions is a blueprint, a plan for your speech that can strengthen your speech performance by aiding you in presenting materials that will make sense to your audience and with evidence or supporting materials that will help inform or persuade them.

The following outline is based on a student's speech.[13] Its immediate purpose was to challenge the belief that a materialistic society based on consumption is wrong by having the audience state at the conclusion of the speech some qualities of life besides wealth that they should strive for in a life-style designed for permanence.

As you read the outline, see if you think that the main points are consistent with the immediate purpose and the ultimate goal, which is to convince the audience to adopt a nonmaterialistic life-style after college. Notice also that the outline is called a sentence outline because every entry whether it is a main point, a subpoint, or a sub-subpoint, is a complete sentence. Finally, notice that the student finished the outline with a bibliography of sources indicating where she found the information for her speech.

Functions

Rhetorical questions to gain attention with topic-relevant means.

A Life-Style Designed for Permanence

Introduction

I. I want to ask all of you three general questions.

   A. Do you want to preserve the world's natural resources?

   B. Do you want our country to be independent of other nations for energy supplies?

   C. Do you want to insure a good future for your children?

Questions to relate the topic to the audience.	II. Next, I want to ask you three questions that pertain to us as college students.
	A. Do you want to become wealthy?
	B. Do you want to drive a big, prestigious Cadillac?
	C. Do you want to live in a big house?
Qualifications of speaker on this topic.	III. I have been listening to and reading about some very serious facts concerning the scarcity of natural resources in the world.
Forecast and statement of expectations.	IV. I am going to show you that if you answered "yes" to the first three questions, then you are going to have to answer "no" to the last three.

Body

Paraphrase an authority to demonstrate that speaker has read about the topic and to make the first main point in the speech.	I. E. F. Schumacher's book, *Small Is Beautiful*, says our most fateful error is in believing that the problems of production have been solved.
	A. We have come to believe that anything can be produced by technology and good old American ingenuity.
	B. Unfortunately, our technology depends on fossil fuels, which are being rapidly depleted.
Speaker gives the audience credit for what they have done before asking them to do more.	II. We are trying to conserve our resources by decreasing energy consumption.
	A. Statistics indicate that mass transit systems are being utilized more and more.
	B. The automobile industry has greatly increased the production of small cars.
Paraphrases an authority, presents second main point and demonstrates again the speaker's interest in the topic.	III. Kenneth Boulding, a world-renowned economist, gave a lecture last week on campus in which he promoted the idea of a new moral order within a new life-style.
	A. The new moral order is based on being, living, and working together.
	B. The new life-style is one in which we learn to get along with less and accept it.
Third main point with three subpoints to clarify the idea.	IV. Boulding's "mature world" has implications for our careers, for production, and for our attitudes.
	A. Instead of seeking jobs to give us wealth, we should strive for occupations that enable everyone to have a decent existence.

Advances the idea of smaller places of production.	B. Instead of large-scale, highly complex, and highly capital-intensive production, we should try smaller units of production.
Example of one change.	1. Instead of one big factory, we would have many smaller plants located closer to where resources are located.
Specific instances of a possible change.	a. Gasohol plants could be located near large corn supplies from which the alcohol is made.
	b. Food processing plants could be located closer to the supply of animals and grain.
Advances the idea of area instead of national companies.	2. Instead of encouraging bigger and bigger megacorporations, we could encourage a wider assortment of smaller, locally or regionally owned companies.
	C. We have to overcome our "bigger is better" notion that has been encouraged during most of this century.
Mentions an attitude that must be overcome.	Conclusion I. A life-style designed for permanence is possible!
	A. Do we want a world where quality means more than quantity?
Challenge to the audience: two alternatives.	B. Do we want a world that exhausts its resources on the way to self-destruction?

Bibliography

Boulding, Kenneth. "The Economic Implications of Living in a World of Limits," a lecture-seminar held at Iowa State University, November 3, 1980.

Satin, Mark. *New Age Politics*. New York: Delta Publishing Company, 1979.

Schumacher, E. F. *Small is Beautiful*. London: Perennial, 1973.

Wood, Donald F., and James C. Johnson. *Contemporary Transportation*. Tulsa, Okla.: Petroleum Publishing Company, 1980.

The Key-Word Outline

The public speaker can use a number of methods in delivering a speech. The speaker can use a manuscript of the entire speech, a complete sentence outline, or a **key-word outline.** The manuscript or outlines may be written on 8 ½-by-11-inch paper or on notecards. You should ask your teacher what he or she prefers because teachers often have strong feelings about which method works best. In this section we will look at the key-word outline and the use of **notecards** in case they are the preferred method.

Speakers sometimes become too dependent on a manuscript; it reduces their eye contact and minimizes their attention to audience responses. Nonetheless, some speakers become very proficient at reading from a manuscript on which they have highlighted the important words, phrases, and quotations. A complete sentence outline may be superior to a manuscript in that it forces the speaker to extemporize, to maintain eye contact, and to respond to audience feedback. Key words and phrases can be underlined or highlighted on a sentence outline. An alternative method is to simply use a key-word outline, which includes only those items that you would normally highlight on a complete sentence outline.

The key-word outline consists of important words and phrases that will serve as cues for the speaker to remind him or her of the topic or main idea being addressed. The key-word outline may contain statistics or quotations that are too long or complicated to memorize. The key-word outline abstracts the ideas in the speech considerably more than a sentence outline. The student who gave the speech based on the following key word outline[14] had as an immediate purpose the reduction of sugar in the audience's diet. Her long-range goal was to persuade the audience to alter their eating habits by becoming increasingly aware of how much sugar is in the food they eat and by recognizing that overconsumption of sugar can lead to unhealthy results.

Where Sugar Goes, Trouble Follows

Introduction

  I. Heavy consumption

 II. Sugar dependency

III. Myths

Body

  I. American consumption

     A. 125 pounds per year

     B. 60% hidden in foods

 II. Myths

     A. No physiological need

     B. No need for "quick energy"

     C. All carbohydrates not the same

        1. Sugar absorbed quickly

        2. Encourages tooth decay

           a. 98% of kids

           b. Loss of teeth in adults

III. Excessive weight

    A. 500 calories per day

        1. 10–20% of kids overweight

        2. 35–50% of middle-aged overweight

    B. Same calories in 2-oz. candy bar and 1 lb. of apples

IV. Diabetes

    A. 5–12 million American diabetics

    B. 1,000 new cases per day

    C. Diabetes linked to sugar

Conclusion

  I. Be intelligent consumer

  II. Be a healthier individual

III. Sugar is villain

Bibliography

Brody, J. E. "Sugar: Villain in Disguise," *Reader's Digest,* October 1977, pp. 163–165.

Mayer, Jean. "The Bitter Truth About Sugar," *New York Times Magazine,* June 20, 1976, pp. 26–34.

The key-word outline fits easily on three-by-five-inch or four-by-six-inch notecards or on 8½-by-11-inch paper. If you choose notecards on which you write or type a key-word outline, these suggestions may be helpful.

1. Write down instructions to yourself on your notecards. For instance, if you are supposed to write a title for your speech and your name on the board before your speech begins, then you can write that instruction on the top of your first card.
2. Write on one side of the card only. It is better to use more cards with your key-word outline on one side only than to write front and back because the latter method is more likely to result in confusion.
3. Number your notecards on the top so they will be unlikely to get out of order or, if dropped, can be quickly reassembled.
4. Write out items that might be difficult to remember. Extended quotations, difficult names, unfamiliar terms, and statistics are examples of items that you may want to include on your notecard to reduce the chances for error.
5. Practice delivering your speech at least two times using your notecards. Effective extemporaneous delivery may be difficult to achieve if you have to fumble with unfamiliar cards.

A sentence outline or key-word outline helps the speaker visualize many different patterns of organization that may be useful in speeches.

Organizational Patterns

The outline is a form into which many **organizational patterns** can be fitted. We will examine some of the most commonly used patterns of organization. Three organizational patterns will be examined in some detail—with a description, an application, and an example. Four others will be named and briefly described. However, these seven patterns of organization are just a few of the basic patterns from which a skilled speaker can construct many additional patterns. The three patterns of organization that will be examined in detail are the time-sequence pattern, the topical-sequence pattern, and the problem-and-solution pattern.

Time-Sequence Pattern

The first of these—**time-sequence pattern**—is also known as chronological order because it is used to indicate what happens to something over time. This pattern of organization is applied in speeches that consider the past, present, and future of some idea, issue, group, plan, or project. It is most useful on topics like the following:

How the Salvation Army Began
The Origins of the Electoral College
The Today Show: A Brief History
The Naming of a Stadium
The Future for Space Exploration
The Steps in Making a Cedar Chest
The Formula for Foolproof Gravy

Any topic that requires attention to events, incidents, or steps that take place in time is appropriate for this pattern of organization. In a brief outline such a speech would look like this:[15]

South Africa
  I. The "Bushmen" first came to South Africa seeking better land only to be pushed aside and enslaved by others.
     A. The San or "Bushmen" were nomadic hunters.
     B. The "Bushmen" later worked the African gold mines.
 II. Europeans (the Dutch) established an outpost at the Cape of Good Hope in 1652.
     A. The Dutch overcame the San and the Khoikhoi.
     B. The Dutch settlers and the black natives produced a repressed class of persons labeled "coloureds."
     C. The Dutch fought formidable black tribes like the Zulu and the Xhosa.
III. The 19th century brought armed conflict between the English settlers and the Dutch Boers.
     A. The British won a military victory in the Boer War (1899–1902).
     B. The Boers won a political victory by becoming Afrikaners with their own language, laws, and culture.

IV. In the 20th century the Afrikaners establish the concept of apartheid to control blacks, coloureds, and Asians.

Notice that the emphasis in this brief outline is on the history of South Africa, on the events that took place over the centuries and resulted in the society that is in such trouble today. A simpler example might be a recipe that depends on the combining of ingredients in the correct order.

Topical-Sequence Pattern

The second pattern of organization is the **topical-sequence pattern,** a pattern that addresses the advantages, disadvantages, qualities, and types of persons, places, or things. The topical-sequence pattern can be used to explain to an audience why you want them to adopt a certain point of view. It is appropriate when you have three to five points to make: three reasons why people should buy used cars, four of the main benefits of studying speech, five characteristics of a good football player. This pattern of organization is among the most versatile. In a student speech encouraging the audience to adopt a spider, a tarantula, for a pet of their own, the topical outline looked like this:[16]

I. The name *tarantula* has an interesting history.
   A. The word *tarantula* is derived from the name of a small town in Italy.
      1. Taranto was a town in Italy where the people experienced a large number of spider bites.
      2. The people of Taranto were bitten so frequently that they developed a dance to sweat the spider poison out of their blood.
   B. The name *tarantula* was applied originally to the European wolf spider, the one encountered in Taranto.
   C. The name was transfered to the tropical spider, which is now known as the tarantula.
II. The tarantula is characterized by five unusual characteristics.
   A. One unusual feature of the tarantula is its size.
      1. Tropical tarantulas are as large as three inches in body length and ten inches in leg span.
      2. Species in the United States range from one to three inches in body length and up to five inches in leg span.
   B. A second unusual feature of the tarantula is that it is nocturnal, that it hunts at night.
   C. A third interesting feature of the tarantula is that it can see only two inches and relies on leg hairs to sense the presence of other things.
   D. A fourth characteristic of the tarantula is that the species is cannibalistic.
   E. A fifth characteristic of the tarantula is that they moult.
      1. Moulting decreases with age.
      2. Moulting can be accompanied by regeneration of lost parts such as legs.

The outline continues to develop main points on why tarantulas make interesting and economical pets and on the myths about their poison. However, the portion shown here illustrates the main advantage of the topical outline—it can be used to organize diverse ideas in a common sense sequence that will appeal to an audience.

Problem-and-Solution Pattern

The third pattern of organization that we will consider in detail is the **problem-and-solution pattern.** As the name of this pattern suggests, the pattern describes a problem and proposes a solution. A speech based on this pattern is divisible into two distinct parts, with an optional third part in which the speaker meets any anticipated objections to the proposed solution. The problem-and-solution pattern can have other patterns within it. For example, you might discuss the problem in chronological or time-sequence order and you might discuss the solution using a topical-sequence pattern. The problem-and-solution pattern of organization requires close audience analysis because you have to decide how much time and effort to spend on each portion of the speech. Does the audience already know the problem? If so, you might be able to discuss it briefly with a few reminders of its seriousness or importance to the audience. On the other hand, the problem may be so complex that both the problem and the solution cannot be covered in a single speech. In that case you may have found a topic that requires a problem speech and a solution speech or speeches. In any case, your audience analysis should be an important first step in determining the ratio of time devoted to the problem and to the solution in this pattern.

The problem-and-solution speech in outline form might look like this:

Physical Fitness for College Students

I. Many college students are in poor physical condition.

   A. Fewer colleges are requiring physical education courses.

   B. Increasing numbers of college students are overweight.

   C. Increasing numbers of college students suffer from physical problems caused by poor physical conditioning.

II. Jogging is good for social, psychological, and physical reasons.

   A. People who jog together get to know each other very well.

   B. Joggers can take out some of their frustrations, anxieties, and aggressions on the track.

   C. Joggers can gain and maintain good physical conditioning through regular workouts.

III. The main objections to jogging are the time and the energy that it takes.

   A. We should take the time to keep our bodies in good condition just as we do our minds and spirits.

   B. The effort required in jogging is its main benefit—strengthening our cardiovascular system.

The problem-and-solution pattern has many applications in speeches on contemporary problems and issues. It can be used to discuss inflation, price-fixing, poverty, welfare, housing costs, quality of goods, quality of services, and problems of being a student.

Other Organizational Patterns

Spatial Organization   A speech can be organized spatially, with emphasis on where the parts of a whole exist in space. Examples of speeches that could be organized spatially are descriptions of a control panel from center to periphery, the electrical transmission from an energy source to the home, a dress design from top to bottom.

Cause-Effect Organization   In a cause-effect organization the speaker explains the cause or causes and the consequences, results, or effects similar to the problem-solution pattern. An example of a speech that could be organized in a cause-effect pattern is the causes of inflation and some possible solutions to the problem. Ratio of cause to effect is decided by audience analysis. If causes are well known to the audience, then more attention can be concentrated on the effect.

Climactic and Anticlimactic Organization   In a climactic organization, strongest or best information and arguments are stated last. In an anticlimactic organization, best or strongest arguments and evidence are presented early.

Indirect Sequencing   The speaker first states the grounds for an argument or conclusion, then the generalization or conclusion is based on that information. For example:

Grounds:
1. Our present waste-disposal system is outdated, ineffective, and expensive.
2. Our present waste-disposal system does not permit the recycling of metals, glass, and paper.
3. Our present waste-disposal system does not allow for the burning of combustible waste products.

Conclusion:
Our present waste-disposal system needs to be replaced.

The indirect sequencing pattern uses an inductive method of arriving at a reasonable conclusion.

Transitions

One aspect of speech organization that is not readily apparent in the overall organization of the speech are the linkages between sections of the speech known as *transitions.* The purpose of a transition is to help the audience move from one point to another in a speech as smoothly as possible. Audiences appreciate forewarning, and a transition is a verbal indication of a move. Rarely is it appropriate to indicate blatantly that the speaker is moving from one point to another. We do not state "This is my introduction" or "Now I am approaching my conclusion." Nonetheless, we do announce that we are going to present arguments favoring some proposition, and we do state, in transition, "My second point is," "To summarize my position on this subject," or "The best argument in favor of legalized gambling is." Transitions are a way of telling an audience where you are going, of mapping the organization of your speech, and of summarizing what you have already covered.

The most important transitions are between the introduction and the body, between the main points of the body, and between the body and the conclusion of the speech. Many others can appear in a speech: between the main heading and the main points, between the main points and the subpoints, between examples, and between visual aids and the point being illustrated. Transitions consist of forecasts, or previews, of coming attractions; of internal summaries that inform listeners how far the speech has progressed; and of statements of relationship telling how the parts of the whole are related in the speech's organization. Transitions are the mortar between the building blocks of the speech. Without them, cracks appear and the structure is less solid.

Much of the emphasis so far has been on how to start a speech and how to develop or organize the body. You also need to know how to end a speech which is the subject of the next section.

Figure 12.2

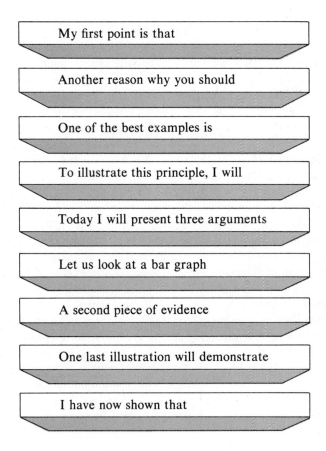

My first point is that

Another reason why you should

One of the best examples is

To illustrate this principle, I will

Today I will present three arguments

Let us look at a bar graph

A second piece of evidence

One last illustration will demonstrate

I have now shown that

The Conclusion

Like the introduction and the body of a speech, the conclusion has certain functions. Complex speeches frequently conclude with a summary of main points from the body of the speech. Persuasive speeches frequently end with an appeal to the audience to think or behave in some manner that is consistent with the persuader's purpose. The means of ending speeches are numerous. The speaker can terminate a speech with a rhetorical question— "Knowing what you now know, will you feel safe riding with a driver who drinks?" or with a quotation from some famous person—"As Patrick Henry said, 'Give me liberty or give me death.' " or with a literary passage— "We conclude with the words of Ralph Waldo Emerson, who said, 'It is one light which beams out of a thousand stars; it is one soul which animates all men.' " or perhaps with some action that demonstrates the point of the speech—the quickly assembled electric motor works for the class to see, the speaker twirls and does a split in one graceful motion, the experiment is completed and the mixture of soda and vinegar boils and smokes.

Introductions and conclusions—getting started and drawing to a close—are often difficult for beginning speakers. Because of this, these two parts of the speech should be rehearsed so they will be presented as planned. The speaker who fails to plan a conclusion may near the end with nothing more to say.

Audiences need to be warned by your words, your tone, or your actions that the speech is nearly completed. Otherwise, you might end your speech with the audience dangling in the wind as you head for your seat. Audiences appreciate a sense of closure, a sense of completeness, and a sense of finality in the conclusion of a speech. Speakers who ignore this expectation risk offending the very people that they seek to influence.

In conversations with friends we indicate that the conversation must stop by our words, facial expressions, gestures, and movements. Similarly in public speaking you signal that the end of your speech is near by signaling your audience with words and actions. Notice how this ending signals the impending conclusion of the speech— "Now that you have heard my three arguments concerning why we should encourage the student newspaper to cover assaults on campus, I want to leave you with these words from the editor of the student newspaper. . . ." You can also signal the conclusion of your speech with your movement—some speakers literally fade back and away from the audience as they draw to a conclusion because they want to show that they are almost done; others end their speech with a challenge in which they approach the audience for their final words. Either may be appropriate depending on whether a tranquil or a challenging ending is invited by the topic. Finally, you can simply tell your audience that you are finished by using the words that most often signal a conclusion— "Finally . . .," "To summarize . . .," "And my final words for you tonight are . . .," or "Wendell Johnson once summed up the main message that I have tried to convey to you this afternoon when he said. . . ."

There are certain functions that are fulfilled by a conclusion. Those functions are:

1. To forewarn the audience that you are about to stop, which is the brakelight function.
2. To remind the audience of your central idea or main points in your message.
3. To specify precisely what the audience should think or do in response to your speech.
4. To end the speech in an upbeat manner that will make the audience members want to think and do what you recommend.

Let's examine each of these functions of a conclusion in greater detail. The **brakelight function** warns the audience that you are about to stop. Can you tell when a song is about to end? Do you know when someone in a conversation is about to complete a story? Can you tell in a TV drama that the narrative is drawing to a close? The answer to these questions is usually "yes," because we get verbal and nonverbal signals that songs, stories, and dramas are about to end. But, how do you use the brakelight function in a speech?

One student signaled the end of her speech by saying "Five minutes is hardly time to consider all the complications of abortion. . . ." By stating that her time was up, she signaled her conclusion. Another said "Thus men have the potential for much greater role flexibility than our society encourages. . . ." The word "thus," like the word "therefore," is like the conclusion for a logical argument and indicates that the argument is drawing to a close.

A second function of a conclusion is to remind the audience of your central idea or the main points in the message. This can be done by restating the main points, by summarizing them briefly, or by selecting the most important one for special treatment. A woman who was delivering a pro-choice speech on abortion ended it by reminding her audience of the main point. Her method[17] was to use two contrasting quotations:

We need to protect ourselves from close-minded opinions like that of Senator Jesse Helms who proposed the following amendment:

The paramount right to life is vested in each human being from the moment of fertilization without regard to age, health, or condition of dependency.

Instead, let's consider the words of Rhonda Copelon, a staff lawyer with the Center for Constitutional Rights:

To use the Bill of Rights—which also and not incidently guarantees the separation of church and state—to establish laws as a religious belief on a matter of private moral conduct would be unprecedented. It would transform into a tool of oppression a document which guarantees rights by limiting the power of the state to invade people's lives.

All I ask you to do is to look at the woman's side for a moment. Consider all the implications upon her life. The unborn is not the only one with a right to life. The woman has one too.

Whether you agree with the position stated in the conclusion or not, it was an insightful way to restate the main message and to reiterate the conflicting viewpoints on the issue.

A third function of a conclusion is to specify exactly what you expect the audience to do as a result of your speech. Do you want them to simply remember a few of your important points? Then tell them one last time the points you think are worth remembering. Do you want the audience members to write down the argument they found most convincing, sign a petition, talk to their friends? If so, then you should specify what you would regard as an appropriate response to your speech. One student who gave her speech on unions ended her speech with the slogan— "Buy the union label." The ending statement specified exactly what the speaker expected of the audience.

A fourth function of a conclusion is to end the speech in an upbeat manner that will make the audience glad that they listened to you. Perhaps you taught the audience how to do something during the speech—how to help a choking victim, how to defend themselves, or how to find a better product. If you successfully teach the audience how to do something, they may already feel better because they know more than they did before they heard your speech.

In concluding, as in beginning, it is possible to be overly dramatic. At one big Midwestern college, the speech classes were taught in a block-long building that held several thousand students every class hour. On the third floor of this building, students were giving their final speeches. In one room, a student was delivering a speech about insanity. As the speech progressed, the class became increasingly aware that the young man delivering the speech had a few problems. At first, it was difficult to understand what he was saying: words were run together, parts of sentences were incoherent, pauses were too long. Near the end of the speech, the young man's eyes were rolling and his jaw had fallen slack. At the very end of the speech, he looked wildly at the audience, ran over to the open window, and jumped. The class was aghast. Teacher and students rushed to the window expecting to see his shattered remains. Far below, on the ground, were twenty fraternity brothers holding a large fireman's net with the speaker waving happily from the center.

A better idea is to conclude your speech with an inspirational statement, with words that make the audience glad they took the time and energy to listen to you. One student that I heard over ten years ago came up with a single line at the end of his speech on automobile accidents that summarized his speech and give his audience a line to remember— "It is not who is right in a traffic accident that really counts," he said, "it is who is left." That conclusion was clever, was a brief summary of the speech, and was an intelligent and safe way to end a speech.

Figure 12.3   The end.

Summary

Chapter 12 discussed the three basic parts of a speech—the introduction, the body, and the conclusion—and their functions.

An introduction fulfills five basic functions. 1. It gains and maintains the audience's attention. 2. It arouses the audience's interest in the topic. 3. It reveals the purpose of the speech. 4. It describes the speaker's qualifications. 5. It forecasts the organization and development of your speech.

This chapter also examined speech organization of the body. The seven principles of outlining included: 1. Relating all items in an outline to the immediate purpose and the ultimate goal. 2. Limiting the outline to an abstract of the speech itself. 3. Expressing ideas in single sentences. 4. Indicating the importance of items with rank-ordered symbols. 5. Indicating the importance of items with margins that increase with decreasing importance. 6. Coordinating less important content with less important symbols and larger margins. 7. Stating items in parallel form. There were illustrations of a sentence outline and a key-word outline. The correct bibliographic form was given so you can indicate your sources of information. Some of the typical patterns of organization commonly used in public speaking were discussed: the time-sequence pattern, the topical-sequence pattern, the problem-and-solution pattern, spatial organization, cause-effect organization, climax and anticlimax organization, and indirect sequencing.

After a brief look at transitions, we discussed the functions of a speech conclusion. 1. To forewarn the audience that the speech is about to end. 2. To remind the audience of the central idea or main points of the message. 3. To specify the desired audience response. 4. To end the speech in an upbeat manner that will encourage your audience to think and do as you recommend.

Additional Readings

Connolly, James E. *Public Speaking as Communication.* Minneapolis: Burgess Publishing Company, 1974. Pages 35–47.
Provides insights into patterns of organization: chronological, spatial, cause-effect, problem-solution, and so forth. Also contains a rationale for organizing messages so the audience can process the information more readily.

Ellingsworth, Huber W., and Clevenger, Theodore, Jr. *Speech and Social Action: A Strategy of Oral Communication.* Englewood Cliffs, N.J.: Prentice-Hall, 1967. Pages 56–103.
An inventive and insightful examination of organization. The authors show how context affects meaning and discuss the elements of organization as ways in which to provide the best context for the information to be presented. Interesting and worthwhile reading.

Kruger, Arthur N. *Effective Speaking: A Complete Course.* New York: Van Nostrand Reinhold Company, 1970. Pages 201–42.
Kruger suggests ways to analyze topics in order to discover their subpoints, presents organization as a means of thinking through a speech, and views organization as a process by which to develop the subject rather than as an end in itself.

Mills, Glen E. *Message Preparation: Analysis and Structure.* Indianapolis: Bobbs-Merrill Co., 1966, Pages 47–69.
Purposes and kinds of outlines are discussed. General principles of outlining are presented with examples of correct and incorrect outlines. Organizational patterns are related to the informative and the persuasive speech.

Oliver, Robert T.; Zelko, Harold P.; and Holtzman, Paul D. *Communicative Speaking and Listening.* 4th ed. New York: Holt, Rinehart & Winston, 1968. Pages 112–32.
The authors relate the principles and techniques of outlining to audience involvement. Organization makes the message clearer to the audience and helps the audience respond in a manner consistent with the speaker's purpose.

Thomas, Coramae, and Howard, C. Jeriel. *Contact: A Textbook in Applied Communication.* Englewood Cliffs, N.J.: Prentice-Hall, 1970. Pages 193–211.
A discussion of principles of outlining in an easy-to-understand format. Examples of subordination and division are given. Excellent help in understanding and improving your outlining skills.

Walter, Otis M. *Speaking to Inform and Persuade.* New York: Macmillan, 1966. Chapters 2, 3, and 4.
Walter develops the principles of introductions and conclusions. A straightforward style clearly identifies the basic elements of good organization for informative speaking. Walter also describes the use of internal summaries and transitions to carry the speech from one point to another.

Notes

1. "Headless," *Time,* July 18, 1977, p. 21.
2. "Tomorrow," *U.S. News and World Report,* July 18, 1977, p. 8.
3. "American Youth," *U.S. News and World Report,* July 18, 1977, p. 19.
4. James J. Kilpatrick, "Death Sentence as Gun Control?" *Des Moines Tribune,* December 12, 1980, p. 18.
5. "The Killing Goes On," *Des Moines Tribune,* December 11, 1980, p. 18.
6. "The Killing Goes On," p. 18.
7. Kilpatrick, p. 18.
8. Tom Wicker, "You, Me and Handguns," *Ames Daily Tribune,* December 18, 1980, p. A4.
9. Wicker, p. A4.
10. Wicker, p. A.4
11. Wicker, p. A.4
12. Kilpatrick, p. 18.
13. Based on a speech manuscript submitted by Jane Wolf in Speech 211H, Iowa State University, Fall 1980.
14. Based on a speech manuscript submitted by Melanie Comito in speech 211H, Iowa State University, Fall 1980.
15. For a fictional account based on historical facts read James A. Michener's two volume work entitled, *The Covenant* (New York: Random House, 1980).
16. Based on an outline submitted by Terry Hermiston in Speech 211, Iowa State University, Winter 1981.
17. From a speech delivered by Nancy Stuss in speech 211H, Iowa State University, Fall 1980.

13

Sharing Yourself through Delivery and Visual Aids

Objectives

1. Differentiate four modes of delivery
2. Define seven aspects of vocal delivery
3. Discuss the uses of gestures, eye contact, and movement
4. Use visual aids effectively
5. Demonstrate effective vocal and bodily delivery

Key Terms

delivery of a speech
modes of delivery
manuscript mode
extemporaneous mode
impromptu mode
memorized mode
pitch
rate
pause
volume
enunciation
fluency

vocal variety
listenability
comprehension
vocalized pauses
projection
pronunciation
articulation
gestures
eye contact
facial expression
movement
visual aids

Sharing Yourself through Delivery and Visual Aids

Reverend Heathweather was so good today. I just loved his sermon. He is such a fine speaker.

What was it that he said that impressed you so much?

Well, I don't know. He just has such a way with words.

The response to Reverend Heathweather's sermon is not uncommon among listeners who have heard a speaker who has impressive delivery. Sometimes the speech is so smooth that the audience misses the message and focuses instead on how it is said.

Delivery of a speech is an important part of public speaking. It includes the nonverbal messages we convey that were discussed in chapter 4 on nonverbal communication. The words of a speech are only part of the message; the remainder of the message may be carried by the speaker's vocal and bodily actions. For example, the speaker can deliver a speech with a tone of voice that expresses conviction, unhappiness, anger, or irony. Similarly, the speaker's smile, alert posture, and forceful gestures convey a message to the audience. In this chapter we will examine four modes of delivery, explore the vocal and bodily aspects of delivery, survey the use of visual aids, and conclude with some suggestions on how to effectively deliver your speeches.

Four Modes of Delivery

Four **modes of delivery** are possible choices for the public speaker: the reading of manuscripts, the delivery of memorized speeches, extemporaneous speeches, and impromptu speeches. We shall look at each and point out the appropriate circumstances for selecting them.

Manuscripts and Papers

Speakers who have to be very careful about what they say and how they say it choose to present manuscripts. In other words, the speaker has a script of the entire speech. The advantage of the **manuscript mode** of delivery is that the speaker is never at a loss for words—they are all right there. The disadvantage of a manuscript speech is that it is often a mere reading of the words, that it invites the speaker to watch the script instead of the audience, and that it discourages the speaker from responding to the listeners.

The best time to read a manuscript is when every word, phrase, and sentence must be exact. An error can be very serious, as when the president makes an important address. He may appear to be speaking without any notes at all, but he is actually reading his speech off a teleprompter that permits him to read every word while looking directly at the television camera or his audience. Many ministers write out their sermons so that their main points are correctly supported with Biblical verses. College teachers often lecture from a manuscript so that they give the same lesson to each section that they teach. Students may be asked to use a manuscript, but usually the emphasis for beginning speakers is on the next mode we will consider—the extemporaneous mode of delivery.

The Extemporaneous Speech

Extemporaneous speeches are the most common in the classroom where students are learning how to prepare and deliver speeches. The extemporaneous speech is carefully prepared and researched, but it appears to be conversational in its delivery. The **extemporaneous mode** of delivery does not have the disadvantages of the manuscript speech. While reading a manuscript invites reading of the script, reduces eye contact, and makes changes difficult, extemporaneous delivery invites freedom from the notes, encourages eye contact, and makes adaptation easier. The speaker who employs the extemporaneous mode delivers the speech from key words, an outline, or a list of main points. Because much of the speech is composed in the speaker's head as the speech is being delivered, it appears to be done "on the spur of the moment," the literal Latin meaning of the term *extemporaneous*.

The Impromptu Speech

The **impromptu mode** is delivery of a speech without notes and without plans or preparation. The term *impromptu* comes from Latin and French roots meaning "in readiness." You have already given impromptu speeches. When you answer a question in class, you are giving an impromptu answer. When someone asks you to explain something at a meeting, your explanation is usually impromptu. When you are asked to introduce yourself, to say a few words about yourself, or to reveal what you know about some subject, you are making an impromptu speech. You may be prepared for the speech in that you do have something to say, but you did not prepare to give a speech the way you would prepare for an extemporaneous speech. Some teachers give students an opportunity to practice impromptu speaking by having each student introduce himself or herself; others have students draw topics out of a hat for an impromptu speech. One of the advantages of this mode of delivery is that you learn how to think on your feet without benefit of notes. A disadvantage is that this mode of delivery does not encourage research, preparation, or practice.

The Memorized Speech

The **memorized mode** of delivery is simply one in which the speaker has committed the speech to memory. The speaker learns the speech either by rote memory or by delivering it so many times that it is not forgotten. This type of delivery is common in oratory contests, on the lecture circuit, and at banquets. Many politicians have a stock speech that they have committed to memory so it can be used wherever the politically faithful might gather. The main advantage of a memorized address is that it permits the speaker to concentrate on delivery. Eye contact can be continuous; searching for words is eliminated. The main disadvantage is that the memorized address permits little or no adaptation during the speech. The speaker risks having a speech that sounds memorized. However, in some formal situations there may be little need for adaptation—some speakers have delivered the same speech so many times that they even know when the audience is going to applaud, and for how long.

Different speakers prefer different modes of delivery. Whereas the impromptu mode teaches students very little about preparing a speech, both the reading of manuscripts and the delivery of memorized speeches require a great deal of time. The extemporaneous mode is favored in the public speaking classroom because it is useful, because it is efficient, because it allows for maximum adaptation to the audience before and during the speech, and because it helps students learn how to prepare a speech.

Nonetheless, the mode of delivery does not determine the effectiveness of a speech. In a study to determine whether the extemporaneous or the manuscript mode of delivery was more effective, two researchers concluded that the mode of delivery simply did not determine effectiveness. The ability of the speaker was more important—some speakers were more effective with extemporaneous speeches than with manuscripts, but others used both modes with equal effectiveness.[1]

Selecting a Mode of Delivery

Examine each of the topics, audiences, and situations below and indicate which mode of delivery would be best by placing the appropriate letter in the blank on the left.

A = Manuscript mode
B = Extemporaneous mode
C = Impromptu mode
D = Memorized mode

_____ 1. You have to answer questions from the class at the conclusion of your speech.

_____ 2. You have to tell the student government's new statement of policy on student rights to a group of high-level administrators.

_____ 3. You have to deliver the same speech about student life at your college three times per week to incoming freshmen.

_____ 4. You have to give parents a "walking tour" of the campus, including information about the buildings, the history of the college, and the background of significant places on campus.

_____ 5. You have to go door to door demonstrating and explaining a vacuum cleaner and its attachments that you are selling.

Vocal and Bodily Aspects of Delivery

Delivery, as we have already observed, is concerned with how the voice and body affect the meaning of your speech. They are important parts of the message you communicate to your audience. We turn now to those vocal and bodily aspects of public speaking.

Vocal Aspects of Delivery

Studying the vocal aspects of delivery is like studying the music that comes from the notes. Musical notes are like the words of the speech. The music results in the sounds that we hear when someone says the words. Just as different musicians can make the same notes sound quite different, public speakers can say words in different ways to get the audience to repond in various ways. We will examine this music of delivering a speech by defining the different vocal characteristics, by referring to relevant studies, and by offering some suggestions about your delivery. The seven vocal aspects of delivery are pitch, rate, pauses, volume, enunciation, fluency, and vocal variety.

Pitch is the highness or lowness of the speaker's voice, its upward and downward movement, the melody produced by the voice. Pitch is what makes the difference between the "ohhh" that you utter when you earn a poor grade in a class and the "ohhh" that you utter when you see something or someone really attractive. The "ohhh" looks the same in print, but when the notes turn to music the difference between the two expressions is vast. The pitch of your voice can make you sound lively or it can make you sound listless. As a speaker you learn to avoid the two extremes: you avoid the lack of change in pitch that results in a monotone, and you avoid repeated changes in pitch that result in a singsong delivery. The best public speakers employ the full range of their normal pitch.

Some studies indicate that control of pitch does more than make a speech sound pleasing. One study indicated that changes in pitch can actually help an audience remember information.[2] Another scholar found that voices perceived as "good" were characterized by a greater range of pitch, more upward inflections, more downward inflections, and more pitch shifts.[3] Certainly, one of the important features of pitch control is that it can be employed to alter the way an audience will respond to the words. Many subtle changes in meaning are accomplished by changes in pitch. The speaker's pitch tells an audience whether the words are a statement or a question, whether the words mean what they say, and whether the speaker is expressing doubt, determination, or surprise.

Pitch control, whether in baseball or speech, is learned only by regular practice. An actor who is learning to utter a line has to practice it many times and in many ways before he or she can be sure that most people in the audience will understand the words as intended. The public speaker practices a speech before friends to discover whether the words are being understood as intended. Sometimes we sound angry when we do not intend to; sometimes we sound opposed when we intend to sound doubtful; and sometimes we sound frightened when we are only surprised. We are not always the best judge of how we sound to others, so we have to place some trust in other people's evaluations. Practicing pitch is one way to control this important vocal aspect of delivery.

Rate, the second characteristic of vocal delivery, is the speed of delivery. The normal rate for American speakers is between 125 and 190 words per minute. But our minds can understand many more words per minute than that. That is why some medical schools are recording professors' lectures in a compressed form. Mechanically speeding up the lecture allows the student to hear a one-hour lecture in forty-five minutes. However, there is some question about what public speakers should conclude from this information. Perhaps information from studies on the subject of rate, listenability, and comprehension will help us to decide.

An early study of students who won collegiate oratory contests indicated that they spoke an average of 120 words per minute.[4] That rate is slightly below the average speaking rate for Americans. In oratorical contests, there may be some advantage to a slow delivery. There have also been studies of the relationship between rate and **listenability.** Can the audience understand the speaker when the rate varies? One scholar used recorded stories and found no differences in listenability when they were played back at 125, 150, 175, and 200 words per minute.[5] Notice that only the 200-word-per-minute rate exceeds the normal range of 125–190 words per minute and that it exceeds the normal rate only slightly. We may safely conclude from this study that, with recorded stories at least, a rate within the normal range does not adversely affect listenability.

How does rate relate to **comprehension** or understanding of the content of a speech? One study indicated that comprehension at 282 words per minute, well above the normal range, was only 10 percent less than it was at 141 words per minute, near the middle of normal range.[6] Given the rather large increase in rate, the loss in comprehension was relatively small. Another study related to rate and comprehension indicated that with just ten minutes of practice, students could learn to listen to double the amount without a loss of comprehension.[7]

These research findings seem to indicate that speakers can talk faster than normal without affecting listening and without affecting the audience's understanding. Indeed, one study showed that when students shortened their pauses and raised their speaking rate from 126 words to 172 words per minute, neither the audience's understanding nor their rating of the speaker's delivery was affected.[8] It appears, then, that the human mind can understand information delivered at a faster rate than we normally speak and that rapid delivery can increase the amount of material covered without negatively affecting the audience's rating of the speaker's delivery. Then why do winners of oratory contests speak even more slowly than most speakers? Perhaps because speech teachers tell their students more often to slow down than to speed up. Many speakers show their anxiety by speeding up, which is unpleasant to an audience. Then again, perhaps the studies are not conclusive. One of them demonstrated that increasing the speed of recorded stories did not reduce listenability, but all but one speed was well within the normal range. Stories are among the easiest verbal material to understand, anyway. In another study, the speed was increased from 126 to 172 words per minute without reducing comprehension or the audience's evaluation of delivery. But both speeds are within the normal range. One study that included a rate well beyond normal resulted in a 10 percent loss of comprehension. Instead of reading the studies as an indication that faster is better, it turns out that a speaker need only to stay within a normal range of rates.

The essential point, not revealed in the studies, is that speaking rate needs to be adapted to the audience and the situation. A grade-school teacher does not rip through a fairy tale—the audience is just learning how to understand words. The public speaker addressing a large audience without a microphone should speak slowly and distinctly to enhance the audience's understanding of the words. If audience and situation need to be taken into account in determining appropriate rate, so does content. Stories delivered at a relatively fast rate may be easy to understand, but a string of statistics may have to be delivered slowly and be repeated to be fully understood. The rate may depend on what effect you are seeking. Telling a scary story would be difficult to do at a high speed. Effective public speakers adjust their speed according to the audience, the situation, the content of the speech, and the effect they are trying to produce.

A third vocal characteristic is the **pause.** Speeches seem to be meant for a steady stream of words, without silences. Yet pauses and silence can be used for dramatic effect and to get an audience to consider content. The speaker may begin a speech with rhetorical questions: "Have you had a cigarette today? Have you had two or three? Ten or eleven? Do you know what your habit is costing you in a year? A decade? A lifetime?" After each rhetorical question a pause allows each member of the audience to answer the question in his or her own mind.

On the other hand, **vocalized pauses** are interruptions that negatively affect an audience's perception of the speaker's competence and dynamism. The "ahhhs," "nows," and "you knows" of the beginning speaker are disturbing to the public speaking teacher. Unfortunately, even some highly experienced speakers have the habit of filling silences with vocalized pauses. At least one group teaches public speaking to laypersons by having members of the audience drop a marble into a can every time a speaker uses a vocalized pause. The resulting punishment, the clanging of the cans, is supposed to break the habit. A more humane method might be to rehearse your speech before a friend who signals you every time you vocalize a pause, so you do it less often when you deliver your speech to an audience. One speech teacher hit on the idea of rigging a light to the lectern so that every time the student speaker used a vocalized pause, the light went on for a moment. Perhaps we should be less afraid of silence—many audiences would prefer a little silence to vocalized pauses.

One way to learn how to use pauses effectively in public speaking is to listen to how your classmates use them. You should also listen to professional speakers. Paul Harvey, the radio commentator, practically orchestrates his pauses. His delivery of the "Page Two" section of his news broadcast helps make him unique. Oral Roberts, Billy Graham, or any of a dozen radio and television evangelists also use pauses effectively.

A fourth vocal characteristic of delivery is **volume,** the relative loudness of your voice. We are accustomed to speaking to people at a close distance, about an arm's length in conversation. In order to speak effectively in front of a class, a meeting, or an auditorium full of people, we have to speak louder or project our voices so all may hear. Telling speech students to speak louder might sound like very elementary advice, but many beginning speakers see those people in the first few rows and speak only to them. We project our voices (**projection**) by making sure that the most distant people in the room can hear what we say. Even when practicing in an empty room, it is a good idea to project your voice so someone sitting at the rear could hear with ease.

Volume is more than just projection. Variations in volume can convey emotion, importance, suspense, and changes of meaning. We whisper a secret and we use a stage whisper in front of an audience. We may speak loudly and strongly on important points and let our voices carry our conviction. An orchestra never plays so quietly that the patrons cannot hear, but the musicians vary their volume. Similarly, a public speaker who considers the voice an instrument learns how to speak softly, loudly, and everywhere in between to convey meaning.

Enunciation, the fifth vocal aspect of delivery, is the pronunciation and articulation of words. Because our reading vocabulary is larger than our speaking vocabulary, we may use, in our speeches, words that we have rarely or never heard before. It is risky to deliver unfamiliar words. One student in a speech class gave a speech about the human reproductive system. During the speech he managed to mispronounce nearly half the words used to describe the female anatomy. The speaker sounded incompetent to his audience. Rehearsing in front of friends, roommates, or family is a safer way to try out your vocabulary and pronunciation on an audience.

The best way to avoid **pronunciation** problems is to find the words in a dictionary. Every dictionary has a pronunciation key. For instance, the entry for the word *belie* in the *Random House Dictionary of the English Language* looks like this:

be·lie (bi–lī′), v.t., -lied, -ly·ing. 1. to show to be false; contradict: His trembling hands belied his calm voice. . . .[9]

The entry indicates that the word *belie* has two syllables. The pronunciation key says that the *i* should be pronounced like the *i* in *if,* the *u* in *busy,* or the *ee* in *been.* The ī, according to the pronunciation key, should be pronounced like the *ye* in *lye,* the *i* in *ice,* or the *ais* in *aisle.* The accent mark (′) indicates which syllable should receive heavier emphasis. You should learn how to use the pronunciation key in a dictionary, but if you still have some misgivings about how to pronounce a word, you should ask your speech teacher for assistance.

Another way to improve your enunciation is to learn how to prolong syllables. This makes you easier to understand, especially if you are addressing a large audience, an audience assembled outside, or an audience in an auditorium without a microphone. The drawing out of syllables can be overdone, however. Some radio and TV newspersons hang onto the final syllable so long that the practice draws attention to itself. In general, a student speaker can improve pronunciation, articulation, and the audience's understanding by learning how to hold syllables.

Pronunciation and articulation are the important parts of enunciation. Poor **articulation,** poor production of sounds, is so common that there are popular jokes about it. One adult remembers hearing in Sunday school, a song about Willie the cross-eyed bear. The song was "Willing the Cross I Bear." Some children have heard the Lord's Prayer mumbled so many times that they think that one of the lines is "hollow be thy name."

The problem of articulation is less humorous when it happens in your own speech. It occurs in part because so many English words are spelled differently and sound alike and because people often fail to articulate carefully. Consequently, their words are conveyed inaccurately. A class experiment will illustrate this problem. One student whispered a phrase from a presidential address, and a line of students whispered the message from person to person. The phrase was, "We must seek fresh answers, unhindered by the stale prescriptions of the past." By the time the message left the third person, it was "When we seek stale answers to the prescription." The eighth person heard the message "When the snakes now answer the question." Similar problems can occur in a public speech if a speaker does not take care to articulate words properly.

Figure 13.1

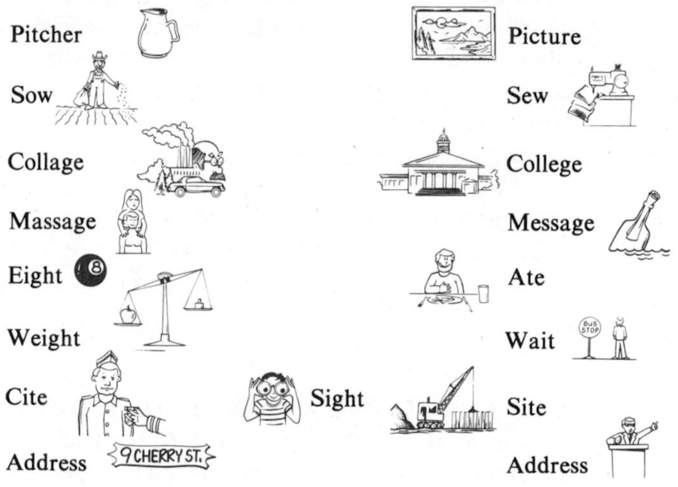

Pitcher

Sow

Collage

Massage

Eight

Weight

Cite

Address

Sight

Picture

Sew

College

Message

Ate

Wait

Site

Address

The sixth vocal characteristic of delivery is **fluency**—the smoothness of delivery, the flow of the words, and the absence of vocalized pauses. Fluency is difficult because it cannot be achieved by looking up words in a dictionary or by any other simple solution. Fluency is not even very noticeable. Listeners are more likely to notice errors than to notice the seemingly effortless flow of words in a well-delivered speech. It is possible to be too fluent. A speaker who seems too glib is sometimes considered "slick," "smooth as a used car salesman," or "so greasy that you could tap him for oil." The importance of fluency is emphasized in a study in which audiences tended to perceive a speaker's fluency, the smoothness of presentation, as a main ingredient of effectiveness.[10]

To achieve fluency, public speakers must be confident of the content of their speeches. If the speakers know what they are going to say and have said it over and over in practice, then disruptive repetition and vocalized pauses are reduced. If speakers master what they are going to say and focus on the overall rhythm of the speech, their fluency will improve. Speakers must pace, build, and time various parts of the speech so they all fit together in a coherent whole.

The seventh vocal aspect of delivery—one that summarizes many of the others—is **vocal variety.** This term refers to voice quality, intonation patterns, inflections of pitch, and syllabic duration. Vocal variety is encouraged in public speaking because studies indicate that it improves effectiveness. Charles Woolbert, in a very early study of public reading, found that audiences seem to retain more information when there are large variations in rate, force, pitch, and voice quality. More recently, George Glasgow studied an audience's comprehension of prose and poetry and found that it decreased 10 percent when the material was delivered in a monotone. A third study indicated that audiences understood more when listening to skilled speakers than when listening to unskilled speakers. They also recalled more information immediately after the speech and at a later date. The skilled speakers were more effective, whether or not the material was organized, disorganized, easy, or difficult. Good vocalization was also found to include fewer but longer pauses, greater ranges of pitch, and more upward and downward inflections.[11]

Testing Vocal Aspects of Your Delivery

Read the following poem to a classmate, roommate, relative, or friend with special attention to the pitch, rate, pauses, volume, enunciation, fluency, and vocal variety. See if you can let the way you say the words affect your audience. Allow your listener or listeners to tell you how to deliver the poem more effectively.

Ozymandias
I met a traveller from an antique land
Who said: Two vast and trunkless legs of stone
Stand in the desert. Near them, on the sand,
Half sunk, a shattered visage lies, whose frown,
And wrinkled lip, and sneer of cold command,
Tell that its sculptor well those passions read
Which yet survive, stamped on these lifeless things,
The hand that mocked them and the heart that fed:
And on the pedestal these words appear:
"My name is Ozymandias, king of kings:
Look on my works, ye Mighty, and despair!"
Nothing beside remains. Round the decay
Of that colossal wreck, boundless and bare
The lone and level sands stretch far away.
                                        Percy Bysshe Shelley

Bodily Aspects of Delivery

There are four *bodily aspects of delivery*—nonverbal indicators of meaning—that are important to the public speaker. In any communication, speakers indicate how they relate to the material and the audience by posture, facial expression, and bodily movements. When we observe two persons busily engaged in conversation, we can judge their interest in the conversation without hearing their words. Similarly, in public speaking, the nonverbal bodily aspects of delivery reinforce what the speaker is saying. Researchers have found that audience members who can see the speaker comprehend more of the speech than audience members who cannot see the speaker.[12]

Apparently, the speaker's actions convey enough meaning to improve the audience's understanding of what is being said. Among the important bodily aspects of delivery are gestures, eye contact, facial expression, and movement.

Gestures are movements of the head, arms, and hands that we use to describe what we are talking about, to emphasize certain points, and to signal a change to another part of the speech. We rarely worry about gestures in a conversation, but when we give a speech in front of an audience, arms and hands seem to be bothersome. Perhaps we feel unnatural because public speaking is an unfamiliar situation. Do you remember the first time you drove a car, the first time you tried to swim or dive, or the first time you tried to kiss your date? The first time that you give a speech you might not feel any more natural than you did then. Nonetheless, physically or artistically skilled people make their actions look easy. A skilled golfer, a talented painter, an excellent runner, and a graceful dancer all perform with seeming ease. The beginners are the ones who make a performance look difficult. Apparently human beings have to work hard to make physical or artistic feats look easy.

What can you do to help yourself gesture naturally when you deliver your speech? The answer lies in feelings and practice. Angry farmers and angry miners appear on television to protest low prices and poor working conditions. These speakers have not spent a lot of time practicing, but they deliver their speeches with gusto and a lot of strong gestures. They also look very natural. The main reason for their natural delivery may be their feelings about the issue they are discussing. They are upset, and they show it in their words and actions. They are mainly concerned with getting their message across. The student of public speaking can also deliver a speech more naturally if his or her attention is concentrated on getting the message across. Self-conscious attention to our own gestures is often self-defeating—the gestures look studied, rehearsed, or slightly out of rhythm with our message. Selecting a topic that you find involving can have the unexpected benefit of improving your delivery, especially if you concentrate on your audience and your message.

Another way of learning to make appropriate gestures is to practice a speech in front of friends who are willing to make positive suggestions. Indeed, constructive criticism is also one of the benefits you can receive from your speech teacher and your fellow students. Actors spend hours rehearsing lines and gestures so that they will look spontaneous and unrehearsed on stage. Public speakers appear before many audiences until they learn to speak and move naturally. In time and after many practice sessions, they learn which arm, head, and hand movements seem to help and which seem to hinder their message. You too can learn, through practice, to gesture naturally—in a way that reinforces your message instead of detracting from it.

Another physical aspect of delivery that is important to the public speaker is **eye contact.** This term refers to the way a speaker watches the audience. Studies and experience indicate that audiences prefer maintenance of good eye contact,[13] and that it improves source credibility.[14] Eye contact is one of the ways we indicate to others how we feel about them. We are wary of persons who, in conversation, will not look us in the eye. Similarly, in public speaking, eye contact conveys our relationship with our audience. The public speaker who rarely or never looks at the audience may appear uninterested in the audience, and the audience may resent it. The public speaker who looks over the heads of audience members or scans them so quickly that eye contact is not established may appear to be afraid of the audience. The proper relationship between audience and speaker is one of purposeful communication. We signal that sense of purpose by treating members of the audience as individuals with whom we wish to communicate. The appropriate way to treat people with whom we wish to communicate is to look at them for responses to our message.

How can you learn to maintain eye contact with your audience? One way is to know your speech so well that you have to make only occasional glances at your notes. The speaker who does not know the speech well is manuscript-bound. Delivering an extemporaneous speech from key words or an outline is a way of encouraging yourself to keep an eye on the audience. One of the purposes of extemporaneous delivery is to enable you to adapt to your audience. That adaptation is not possible unless you are continually observing the audience's behavior to see if the individuals understand your message. Other ways of learning to use eye contact include scanning or continually looking over your entire audience, addressing various sections of the audience as you progress through your speech, and concentrating on the head nodders. In almost every audience there are some individuals who overtly indicate whether your message is coming across. These individuals usually nod "yes" or "no" with their heads, thus the name, *nodders.* Some speakers find that it helps their delivery to find friendly faces and positive nodders who signal when the message is getting through.

A third physical aspect of delivery is **facial expression.** Your face is the most expressive part of your body. It consists of eyebrows that rise and fall; eyes that twinkle, glare, invite, and cry; lips that pout or smile; cheeks that can dimple or harden; and a chin that can jut out in anger or recede in yielding. Some people's faces are a regular barometer of their feelings; others seem to maintain the same appearance whether they are happy or in pain or sorrow. Because you do not ordinarily see your own face when you are in action, you may not be fully aware of how you appear when you give a speech. In general, speakers are trying to maintain a warm and positive relationship with the audience, and they signal that intent by smiling as they would in conversation with someone they like. However, the topic, the speaker's intent, the situation, and the audience all help to determine the appropriate facial expressions in a public speech. You can discover the appropriateness of your own facial expression by having friends, relatives, or classmates tell you how you look when practicing your speech.

A fourth physical aspect of delivery is **movement,** what the speaker does with the entire body during a speech presentation. Sometimes the situation limits movement. The presence of a fixed microphone, a lectern, a pulpit, or some other physical feature of the environment may limit your activity. The length of the speech can also make a difference. A short speech without movement is less difficult for both speaker and audience than a very long one. Good movement for the public speaker is appropriate and purposeful movement. The "caged lion" who paces back and forth to work off anxiety is moving inappropriately and purposelessly in relation to the content of the speech.

Because of the importance of eye contact, the speaker should always strive to face the audience, even when moving. Some other suggestions on movement relate to the use of visual aids. The speaker who writes on the blackboard during a speech has to turn his or her back on the audience. This can be avoided either by writing information on the board between classes or by using a poster instead. Some speakers move during transitions in the speech to give a visual indication of advancement in the speech; others move forward on the points that they regard as most important. The college classroom is a laboratory for the student who wants to learn movement. The college student can watch professors, lecturers, and fellow students when they deliver public speeches. You can learn through observation and practice what works for others and what works for you.

Effective delivery has many advantages. Research indicates that effective delivery, the appropriate use of voice and body in public speaking, contributes to the credibility of the speaker.[15] Indeed, student audiences characterize the poorest speakers by their voices and the physical aspects of delivery.[16] Poor speakers are judged to be fidgety, nervous, and monotonous. They also maintain little eye contact and show little animation or facial expression.[17] It has also been found that good delivery increases the audience's capacity for handling complex information.[18] Thus, public speakers' credibility, the audience's evaluation of them as good or poor speakers, and their ability to convey complex information may all be affected by the vocal and physical aspects of delivery.

Physical Aspects of Delivery

Observe a talented public speaker—a visiting lecturer, a political speaker, a sales manager—and study his or her gestures, facial expressions, eye contact, and movement. Then answer the following questions.

1. Do the speaker's gestures reinforce the important points in the speech?
2. Does the speaker's facial expression reflect the message and show concern for the audience and the topic?
3. Does the speaker maintain eye contact with the audience, respond to the audience's reactions, and keep himself or herself from becoming immersed in the manuscript, outline, or notes?
4. Does the speaker's movement reflect the organization of the speech and the important points in it?
5. Are the speaker's gestures, facial expressions, and movements consistent with the occasion, the personality of the speaker, and the message being communicated?

Using Visual Aids

Do you learn best when you read something? Or do you learn best when you see something? Or do you learn best when you do something? Certainly some skills are best learned by doing—reading about how to make a dress from a pattern or watching another person do it are no substitute for trying it yourself. However, many things that we know do not lend themselves to doing. You cannot do economics in the same way that you can make a dress, change a tire, or build a shed. Because so much public speaking deals with issues, with communicating information, and with other topics that cannot be performed, we must know what are the most effective methods of communicating that can be used in a public speech.

Researchers have tried to determine if people tended to remember best through telling alone, through showing alone, or through both showing and telling. Their results were measured three hours and three days after the communication attempt. The items below show the results.[19]

Method	Three hours later	Three days later
Telling alone	70%	10%
Showing alone	72%	20%
Showing and telling	85%	65%

Apparently, people tend to retain information longer when they receive it both in their eyes and in their ears. There is some evidence that visual aids are an important part of your message.

What are **visual aids?** They can be anything from the way you dress, to writing on the blackboard, to items brought in to show what you are talking about. The student who wears a white lab coat while talking about paramedical training, the student who lists her three main points on the board, and the student who brings in his pet malamute are all using visual aids.

Why use visual aids? One of the main reasons is cited above—people tend to learn more and retain it better when they both see and listen. Also some messages are more effectively communicated through one medium than through another. In other words, if you are trying to tell an audience about a particularly complex problem in calculus, then you might have considerable difficulty communicating that problem with voice only. Complex math problems are more effectively communicated through writing so the problem can be seen. Likewise, describing a ringneck pheasant is less effective than actually showing one. Can the audience compare ten items in their minds? No, but they can if you show the ten items on a bar graph. Can the audience visualize the Phillipines? Perhaps, but some travel posters or slides would result in a more accurate visualization. The first thing to remember in using visual aids is that some messages are more effectively communicated through sight, touch, smell, and taste, and the effective speaker knows when words will not be sufficient to carry the message.

When should you use visual aids? Visual aids are not appropriate for all speeches at all times. In fact, because they take preparation and planning, they may not be possible in many impromptu situations. Also, visual aids should not be used for their own sake—there is no virtue in having visual aids unless they aid the audience in understanding your message or contribute in some other way to your purpose. Use visual aids when the message is easier to understand visually than orally; use visual aids when they reduce complexity for easier understanding as when you are employing many or complex statistics or ideas; and use visual aids when they support your message in ways that cannot be accomplished with words such as when you hang a travel poster of a sandy beach during your speech on Hawaii. Using visual aids demands that you become sensitive to what an audience will be unable to understand only through your words. A number of different kinds of visual aids can be used to accomplish this purpose when it is appropriate.

Types of Visual Aids

What kind of visual aids can you choose from? They may be too numerous to catalogue here, but some of the main visual aids used by public speakers and some hints about their use are listed.

Chalkboards are the most readily available visual aid. You can write your name and the title of your speech on the chalkboard. You can use it to write down important or unusual words that you employ in your speech. Or you can use the board to list the items from your speech that you want your audience to remember. Any statistics, facts, or details that are difficult to convey orally should be written on the board. Some inquiries for using the chalkboard are:

1. When should the information go on the chalkboard? Some teachers prefer that you place the information on the chalkboard before class begins. They dislike the delay caused by

writing information on the board between the classroom speeches. Other teachers feel just as strongly that having information on the board before a speech is distracting. Few instructors object to having the speaker write his or her name and the title of the speech on the board. You and your classmates should make a point of asking your speech teacher his or her preference concerning information on the chalkboard.

2. How should you write on the chalkboard? You should print legibly and large enough so people in the last row can read it with ease. Also you can avoid that tooth shattering squeal by using chalk that has already been used and by angling the chalk so it makes no noise. As any teacher can tell you, you should practice writing on the board between classes or when no one else is using the room because writing on the board takes some skill. If you don't practice you might find that your words look as if they are misspelled, that your letters are too small, and that your lines tend to go up or down as you proceed through a sentence.

3. How should you deliver your speech when you are talking about items that you have written on the chalkboard? You should try to face your audience while you speak. A pointer, a yardstick, or even your hand can direct the audience's attention to statements or illustrations on the chalkboard.

A skillful speaker knows when to place the information on the chalkboard, how to write it on the chalkboard, and how to deliver the speech when using the chalkboard. The effective speaker also knows what kinds of information should be placed on the board and whether—telling or showing or doing both—will help the audience the most. Effective speakers use the chalkboard for "point clinchers,"[20] as a way to indicate to the audience the most important points in the speech.

Posters are another way to present your ideas visually. They are handier than using the chalkboard because they can be prepared ahead of time. This makes the speaker appear more efficient than the person who has to spend time writing while speaking. The general directions for creating an effective poster are similar to those listed for the chalkboard: the information on the poster should be information that is difficult to convey or to understand through listening; the information should be drawn or written in large scale so that people in the back of the room will be able to see every word or illustration; the speaker should face the audience while working with the information on the poster; and the visual message should highlight important points.

The message on a poster may be a written message showing the number of calories in hamburgers from fast-food joints, stating the three primary reasons why tuition should be raised, or listing the advantages to co-op bookstores. The message could also be an illustration such as a bar graph illustrating inflation rates, the increasing average age of the population, or the decrease in housing starts. A poster could be a pie chart showing the percentage of expenditures for defense, social welfare, education, and government; it could be a picture of a slum, a sandy beach, or a resort hotel in Hawaii. Often posters show numbers: percentages, averages, calories per hour, or miles per minute. When using numbers, you should remember to round off the numbers for easier understanding. Finally, do not hesitate to use the talents of your roommates, relatives, or yourself in making your posters more attractive. Colors, cartoon characters, and drawings can invite your audience's attention.

Figures 13.2–13.7 illustrate the uses of posters—to announce a topic, to illustrate a point, and to state a message. Here are some suggestions for using posters for visual aids:

1. Keep the message simple. A common problem with visual aids is too much clutter. The audience should be able to grasp your point quickly.

2. Use bar graphs rather than circle or pie charts whenever possible because people tend to underestimate the relative area of circles.[21]

3. Use color and artistic talents to make the poster attractive—to gain and maintain attention.

4. Be sure the poster is large enough for everyone to see.

5. Use ready-made posters or pictures such as travel posters or get hints for your own illustrations from those used on TV commercials. Television advertisers tend to use outdoor, daytime shots, with one person, but not crowds, present.[22]

6. Learn to use flip charts—a series of posters. Uncover each item as you come to it for special effects.

Whatever kind of poster you use, keep them in front of the audience as long as you are talking about the subject portrayed. In many cases it is appropriate to place the used poster on the chalk tray so you can refer to it again in the conclusion as you review the content of your speech.

Movies and *slides* are good visual supplements to your speech as long as they do not become the speech. Both have the disadvantage of placing the audience and the speaker in the dark where audience response is hidden. Even so, a one- or two-minute film showing violence on the basketball court or five or six slides showing alternative energy sources can add force to your speech. When you use slides and films you should check out equipment and rehearse. An upside-down slide or a jittery film can ruin your speech.

Figure 13.2   A poster with a written message.

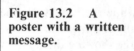

How much are you worth?

    Income _____
 + Savings _____
 _____
 − Food _____
 − Shelter _____
 − Transportation _____
 _____

Figure 13.3   A poster with a bar graph. "Average Private-College Tuition Hits $3,279, Up 10 Pct. in Year," *The Chronicle of Higher Education* **20 (July 21, 1980): 1. Used with permission.**

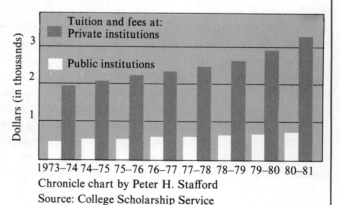

Chronicle chart by Peter H. Stafford
Source: College Scholarship Service

Figure 13.4   A poster with a pie chart.

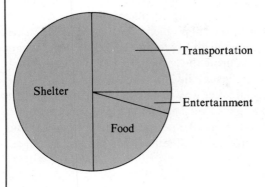

Figure 13.5   A poster with a picture. "Major Quake Rocks North California," *Des Moines Tribune*, November 8, 1980, p. 1. Used with permission.

Figure 13.6   A poster with a drawing.

Eat 3 ☐ meals
Sleep 8 hours
Work 8 hours
Exercise 3 times a week
Avoid
Avoid

Figure 13.7   A poster with rounded off numbers showing where business executives earned their undergraduate degrees. "12 Colleges Granted Nearly Half of Executives' Graduate Degrees," *The Chronicle of Higher Education* 21 (September 29, 1980): 1. Used with permission.

Ten Top Undergraduate
Schools for Business Executives

Yale University	1800
Harvard University	1500
City University of New York	1300
Princeton University	1300
New York University	1200
University of Pennsylvania	1200
University of Michigan	1100
University of Illinois	1100
University of Wisconsin	1000
Northwestern	900

Opaque and *overhead projectors* also demand special equipment and practice, but they, too, have special advantages in a speech. An opaque projector is a machine that can project a picture or print from a magazine or book. It can also be used for relatively small, flat objects. An overhead projector is a machine that can project transparencies or sheets of clear plastic on which the speaker can write with a special pencil. Transparencies are best prepared ahead of time, but short messages can be printed on them as the speaker talks. Both machines require dim lights and an empty wall or screen.

Living models and *physical objects* are visual aids. For a speech on body building, you might bring to class a 250-pound weight lifter to flex his muscles. In a speech on classical ballet, you can bring in a ballerina to demonstrate a few sophisticated turns. Physical objects might be the best visual aid if your speech is about something small enough or controllable enough to show. Students have brought in polished rocks, model cars, chemistry sets, musical instruments, rappelling equipment, weights, and volcanic lava. Live pets can pose special problems for the speaker. Snakes, dogs, cats, hamsters, and monkeys have a unique ability to make fools of their owners; they are often highly distracting before and during the speech. However, a particularly well-trained gorilla might be an appropriate visual aid for your speech.

Handouts are an especially effective way to communicate messages that are difficult to convey orally. One student gave every person in class a letter to open before his speech. It was a draft notice that stated the person's name and invited him or her down to the induction center for processing. The handout got the audience's attention for his speech on the draft. Another student distributed a handout with all of the names and call numbers of country western music stations because he knew that such information would be impossible to communicate orally. Still another student distributed the contract used when people will parts of their body to a medical center. Such handouts carry the impact of your speech beyond the classroom. They are usually kept, sometimes taken home where they are seen by others and serve as a reminder of the speech.

Finally, *you* might be the best visual aid for your speech. You can demonstrate karate, show some dance steps, or wear a lead apron. You can wear clothing that is appropriate for your speech: a suit when telling how to succeed in a job interview for a white collar job, a lab coat when demonstrating chemical reactions, or a uniform when telling why other students should join the ROTC program. One student wore an old flannel shirt, tattered jeans, and a rag tied around his head. He carried a large lantern. His speech was about "steam tunneling," a sport in which students explored the university's steam tunnels. He was faulted for encouraging his audience to participate in an activity that was strongly discouraged by the university administration, but he certainly was appropriately dressed for his speech.

Some Helpful Hints for Delivery

This chapter has discussed the vocal and bodily aspects of delivery and the use of visual aids. Perhaps how to deliver a speech effectively is obvious. However, the following hints should help you in delivering your speech and in using your visual aids.

1. Practice your speech so that you can deliver it with only occasional glances at your notes.
2. Keep your eyes on your audience so you can sense whether you are communicating your message.
3. Use your facial expressions, gestures, and movements to help communicate your message.

4. Use your voice like a musical instrument to keep the sounds interesting and to affect the audience's response.

5. Speak loudly enough for your audience to hear, slowly enough so they can listen with understanding, and smoothly enough so they do not focus on your faults.

6. Use visual aids to communicate material that does not lend itself easily to understanding through listening.

7. Make your writing on the chalkboard or on posters large enough for all to see and simple enough for all to understand.

8. Consider using live models, objects, slides, film, handouts, and audiovisual equipment to help communicate your message.

9. Sound conversational, look natural, and strive to get your message across to your listeners.

10. Watch how your classmates, your professors, and other speakers deliver their speeches so you can learn from them.

Evaluating Your Delivery

For your next speech, have a classmate, friend, or relative observe and evaluate your speech for delivery skills. Have your critic use this scale to fill in the blanks on the left.

1 = Excellent, 2 = Good,
3 = Average, 4 = Fair, 5 = Weak

Vocal Aspects of Delivery

_____ Pitch: highness and lowness of voice; upward and downward inflections.

_____ Rate: words per minute; appropriate variation of rate for the difficulty of content.

_____ Pause: intentional silence designed to aid understanding at appropriate places.

_____ Volume: loud enough to hear; variation with the content.

_____ Enunciation: correct pronunciation and articulation.

_____ Fluency: smoothness of delivery; lack of vocalized pauses; good pacing, rhythm, and cadence without being so smooth as to sound artificial, contrived, or overly glib.

_____ Vocal Variety: voice quality, intonation patterns, pitch inflections, and syllabic duration.

Bodily Aspects of Delivery

_____ Gestures: natural movement of the head, hands, arms, and torso consistent with the speaker, topic, and situation.

_____ Facial Expression: consistent with message; used to relate to the audience; appropriate for audience and situation.

_____ Eye Contact: natural, steady without staring, includes entire audience and is responsive to audience feedback.

_____ Movement: purposeful, used to indicate organization, natural, without anxiety.

Use of Visual Aids

_____ Speaker uses smooth transitions into and away from visuals.

_____ Visuals are easy to see with large print and/or pictures.

_____ Visuals highlight message.

_____ Any equipment is used without difficulty.

_____ Visual aids are appropriate for the speaker, the audience, the topic, and the situation.

Summary

After reading this chapter on delivery, you might have the impression that what you say is less important than how you say it. You might believe that delivery is so important that the person who is fluent, who pauses appropriately, who speaks at the best pitch and rate, and who gestures and moves well does not have to worry much about the substance of the speech. You should be wary about drawing this conclusion from the evidence presented here. Eye contact, gestures, and enunciation are important, but content may be even more important. The very same researcher who found that poor speakers are identified by their voices and by the physical aspects of their delivery also found that the best speakers were identified on the basis of the content of their speeches.[23] Two other researchers found that more of an audience's evaluation of a speaker is based on the content of the speech than on vocal characteristics such as intonation, pitch, and rate, and still another pair of researchers found that a well-composed speech can mask poor delivery.[24] Finally, one researcher reviewed all of the studies on informative speaking made prior to 1963 and reported that, while some research indicates that audiences that have listened to good speakers have significantly greater immediate recall, other findings show that the differences are slight. His conclusion: the influence of delivery on comprehension is overrated.[25]

What is the student of speech supposed to do in the face of these reports that good delivery influences audience comprehension positively but also that the influence of delivery on comprehension is overrated? What is the student of speech supposed to do when one study says that poor vocal characteristics result in evaluation as a poor speaker and another says that good content can mask poor delivery? Perhaps we all tend to oversimplify problems by not recognizing degrees of importance. If we recognize degrees of importance, then we may be able to resolve the apparent conflict—at least until more evidence comes in. The studies cited in this chapter emphasize the importance of delivery. The researchers who challenge those findings do not say that delivery is unimportant; instead, they say that in evaluating the relative importance of delivery and substance, or content, there is reason to believe that content may be more important than delivery. However, the jury is still out on this question. Additional studies may modify what we think and believe at this time. For the moment, the safest position for the speech student is to regard both delivery and content as important in public speaking. What you say and how you say it are both important.

Visual aids should be used in speeches when they are appropriate. They are appropriate when they contribute something to the message or help the audience understand the message or purpose of the speech. Visual aids are broadly defined to include the chalkboard, posters, movies, slides, opaque and overhead projectors, living models, physical objects, and handouts. Appropriately and skillfully employed in your speech, the visual aids can be a big asset; used inappropriately or unskillfully, they can detract from the message.

Additional Readings

*Black, John W., and Moore, Wilbur E. *Speech: Code, Meaning, and Communication.* New York: McGraw-Hill Book Company, 1955. Chapters 2, 3 and 4.
A rather technical explanation of the mechanics and uses of voice to produce intelligible speech. A good resource book for the student who may have problems developing good vocal delivery technique.

Bradley, Bert. *Speech Performance.* Dubuque, Iowa: Wm. C. Brown Company Publishers, 1967.
An exploration of various aspects of delivery, including modes of delivery, movement, poise, use of the microphone, appearance, and adaptation of delivery to the setting and the audience. Ways of reducing or controlling stage fright are suggested.

DeVito, Joseph A.; Giattino, Jill; and Schon, T.D. *Articulation and Voice: Effective Communication.* Indianapolis: Bobbs-Merrill Co., 1975.
The physiological bases of speech and hearing and the role of correct vocal techniques in effective communication are explained. Excellent exercises for improving articulation and vocal quality. Excellent resource for the nonclinical improvement of vocal delivery.

Kruger, Arthur N. *Effective Speaking: A Complete Course.* New York: Van Nostrand Reinhold Company, 1970. Pages 21–150, 355–76.
The vocal production of sounds is explained with advice and exercises to help improve vocal delivery. Poise, movement, and gestures are also discussed, with some suggestions about effective ways to practice the speech and reduce nervousness.

Weaver, Andrew T., and Ness, Ordean G. *An Introduction to Public Speaking.* New York: Odyssey Press, 1961.
Contains an excellent discussion of delivery techniques, including gestures, movement, and posture. Good delivery must be direct, animated, and have vitality.

Winans, James A. "Conversing With an Audience." In *Selected Readings in Public Speaking,* edited by Jane Blankenship and Robert Wilhoit. Belmont, Calif.: Dickenson Publishing Co., 1968. Pages 163–81.
Winans argues that public speaking does not differ significantly from conversational speech and suggests clear, workable guidelines for developing a direct, communicative delivery. Thinking about what you want to say, rather than how you are going to say it, is the key to effective delivery.

*Indicates more advanced readings.

Notes

1. Herbert W. Hildebrandt and Walter Stevens, "Manuscript and Extemporaneous Delivery in Communicating Information," *Speech Monographs* 30 (1963): 369–72.
2. Charles Woolbert, "The Effects of Various Modes of Public Reading," *Journal of Applied Psychology* 4 (1920): 162–85.
3. John W. Black, "A Study of Voice Merit," *Quarterly Journal of Speech* 28 (1942): 67–74.
4. William N. Brigance, "How Fast Do We Talk?" *Quarterly Journal of Speech* 12 (1926): 337–42.
5. Kenneth A. Harwood, "Listenability and Rate of Presentation," *Speech Monographs* 22 (1955): 57–59.
6. Grant Fairbanks, Newman Guttman, and Miron S. Murray, "Effects of Time Compression upon the Comprehension of Connected Speech," *Journal of Speech and Hearing Disorders* 22 (1957): 10–19.
7. John B. Voor and Joseph M. Miller, "The Effect of Practice upon the Comprehension of Time-compressed Speech," *Speech Monographs* 32 (1965): 452–54.
8. Charles F. Diehl, Richard C. White, and Kenneth W. Burk, "Rate and Communication," *Speech Monographs* 26 (1959): 229–32.
9. From *The Random House Dictionary of the English Language.* Copyright © Random House, Inc. Reprinted by permission of Random House, Inc.
10. Donald Hayworth, "A Search for Facts on the Teaching of Public Speaking," *Quarterly Journal of Speech* 28 (1942): 247–354.
11. Charles Woolbert, "The Effects of Various Modes of Public Reading," *Journal of Applied Psychology* 4 (1920): 162–85; George M. Glasgow, "A Semantic Index of Vocal Pitch," *Speech Monographs* 19 (1952): 64–68; Kenneth C. Beighley, "An Experimental Study of the Effect of Four Speech Variables on Listener Comprehension," *Speech Monographs* 19 (1952): 249–58 and 21 (1954): 248–53; Black, pp. 67–74.
12. Edward J.J. Kramer and Thomas R. Lewis, "Comparison of Visual and Nonvisual Listening," *Journal of Communication* 1 (1951): 16–20.
13. Martin Cobin, "Response to Eye-Contact," *Quarterly Journal of Speech* 48 (1962): 415–18.
14. Steven A. Beebe, "Eye Contact: A Nonverbal Determinant of Speaker Credibility," *Speech Teacher* 23 (1974): 21–25.
15. Erwin Bettinghaus, "The Operation of Congruity in an Oral Communication Situation," *Speech Monographs* 28 (1961): 131–42.
16. Ernest H. Henrikson, "An Analysis of the Characteristics of Some 'Good' and 'Poor' Speakers," *Speech Monographs* 11 (1944): 120–24.
17. Howard Gilkinson and Franklin H. Knower, "Individual Differences Among Students of Speech as Revealed by Psychological Tests—I," *Journal of Educational Psychology* 32 (1941): 161–75.
18. John L. Vohs, "An Empirical Approach to the Concept of Attention," *Speech Monographs* 31 (1964): 355–60.
19. Elena P. Zayas-Baya, "Instructional Media in the Total Language Picture," *International Journal of Instructional Media* 5(1977–78): 145–50.
20. Kenneth B. Haas and Harry Q. Packer, *Preparation and Use of Audiovisual Aids* (New York: Prentice-Hall, 1955), pp. 163–68.
21. Michael MacDonald-Ross, "How Numbers are Shown. A Review of Research on the Presentation of Quantitative Data in Texts," *AV Communication Review* 25 (Winter 1977): 359–409.
22. Isbrabim M. Hebyallah and W. Paul Maloney, "Content Analysis of T.V. Commercials," *International Journal of Instructional Media* 5 (1977–78): 9–16.
23. Henrikson, pp. 120–24.
24. Roland J. Hard and Bruce L. Brown, "Interpersonal Information Conveyed by the Content and Vocal Aspects of Speech," *Speech Monographs* 41 (1974): 371–80; D.F. Gundersen and Robert Hopper, "Relationships between Speech Delivery and Speech Effectiveness," *Speech Monographs* 43 (1976): 158–65.
25. Charles R. Petrie, Jr., "Informative Speaking: A Summary and Bibliography of Related Research," *Speech Monographs* 30 (1963): 81.

14

The Informative Speech

An Application of the Principles of Public Communication

Objectives

1. State the purposes of your informative speech behaviorally
2. Explain the concepts of information hunger and information relevance
3. Practice the skills of defining, describing, and explaining
4. Deliver an informative speech effectively

Key Terms

clarity
significance
informative-persuasive continuum
behavioral purposes
defining
describing
explaining
comparison
contrast
synonym
antonym
etymology
recognize
distinguish

compare
define
state
operational definition
abstract
concrete
evaluative
descriptive
information hunger
information relevance
information overload
extrinsic motivation
overt audience response
advance organizers

Speech is the mirror of the soul: as a man speaks, so is he.
Syrus

It is with narrow-souled people as with narrow-necked bottles; the less they have in them, the more noise they make in pouring out.
Alexander Pope

Nothing is so firmly believed as what we least know.
Michel de Montaigne

As a student, you have already spent the better part of thirteen or fourteen years hearing informative speeches from teachers of history, literature, grammar, music, art, math, physics, chemistry, social studies, typing, shop, home economics, health, and physical education. As an employee, you may have to tell others about products, sales goals, policies, and ways to sell, service, and salvage products. As a religious person, you might want to explain scripture, morals or ideals to others. As a citizen, you may have to speak to others about domestic politics, foreign affairs, or impending legislation. Teachers inform students, lawyers inform clients, priests inform parishioners, fire fighters inform groups about safety, police inform citizens about protecting person and property, managers inform employees and foremen inform workers. You, like all of these people, will likely find yourself informing others in verbal reports, instructions, and speeches. This chapter focuses on the primary vehicle for informing others—the informative speech.

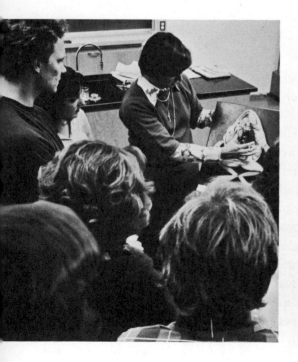 

Figure 14.1

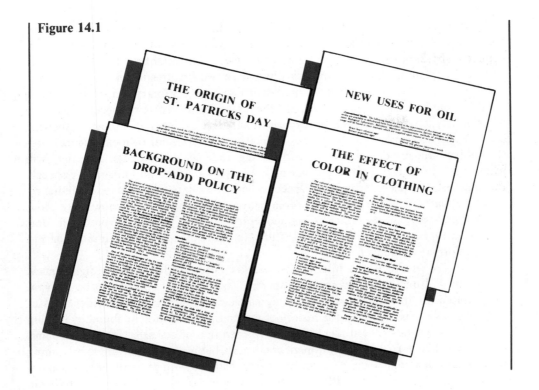

Preparing An Informative Speech

In order to prepare an informative speech, you should know first the intent and the goal of informative speaking; second, the kinds of topics that lend themselves best to informative speaking; and, third, the kinds of immediate behavioral purposes and how to determine if you have fulfilled them.

Understanding the goal or intent of informative speaking requires that you understand the "end product" that you seek and how to reach that end in ways that enlighten the audience and clarify the topic. The "end product" of informative speaking is *to increase an audience's knowledge or understanding of a topic.* You accomplish that goal by clarifying your topic in ways that retain the interest of your audience. The primary purpose of informational speaking is to clarify a topic for an audience. **Clarify** means "to make clear," coming as it does from Latin, Middle English, and Old French roots denoting "to make clear" or "to make bright." To clarify some concept for an audience assumes that the audience does not understand the topic clearly until the speaker has an opportunity to explain it. Typically, a majority of the audience members have insufficient knowledge or understanding to master or comprehend the informative speech topic. For example, you might know that a set of stereophonic speakers has a "woofer" and a "tweeter," but might need an informative speech to explain more clearly exactly what those two features mean.

Clarifying a topic for an audience may be a primary goal of informative speaking, but a second concern is to make the topic of an informative speech interesting and significant to the audience. We arouse an audience's interest in a topic by showing how the subject can be of importance, by relating stories of our own experiences with the subject, and by demonstrating gaps in the audience's knowledge that they will want to fill. In fact, if a bit of persuasion is likely to slip into an informative speech, the appropriate place is early in the speech where you relate the topic to the audience. It is here that you quite rightly may reveal why the audience should know more about Wagnerian opera, cross-country skiing, monetary inflation, or hamster breeding. How to make a topic palatable, literally digestible, to the audience is a continuing concern of the informative speaker.

Similarly, the informative speaker needs to demonstrate **significance.** Later you will find that relevance is important as well, but a topic can be relevant (i.e., related to) an audience without being particularly significant. Consider the student who gave a speech about the history of matches, information he found by looking in two encyclopedias. The student could have been faulted for selecting a topic about which he had no particular commitment or concern, but a more important shortcoming was the lack of significance. An informative speech on how to play tiddly winks is not as significant as a speech on CPR training; understanding other people's race, religion, and fields of study; or clarifying concepts on our economy, politics, philosophy, or technology. You, as an informative speaker, then, are expected to increase an audience's knowledge by clarifying concepts of significance.

The Topics for Informative Speaking

Selecting the topic for an informative speech and restricting its length is an early concern for the informative speaker. What topics are most appropriate for an informative speech? Chapter 10 provided some general information on topic selection: how to brainstorm for topics, how to assess your own reading habits to determine your own interests. But even with that information, you may not know exactly what kind of topics are most appropriate for informative speeches.

An informative speech is supposed to be predominantly informative; that is, most of the content of the speech should be stated for the purpose of increasing what the audience knows, clarifying concepts for greater understanding. Perhaps the notion of "predominantly informative" can be clarified by considering an **informative-**

persuasive continuum along which speeches could be placed. On one end of the continuum we might have "highly informative" discourse; on the other, "highly persuasive" discourse.

Highly	Partly Informative	Highly
Informative	Partly Persuasive	Persuasive

What kinds of discourse or speech would be placed at the two extremes?

Think first of the most highly persuasive speeches you are likely to hear. How about a senator who is addressing a group of undecided voters in a tight election campaign? How about a super salesperson hot on your trail in a auto dealer's display room? Or how about an evangelist on campus trying to save large numbers of sinners? These might qualify as speeches that would be placed correctly on the "highly persuasive" end of the continuum.

An example of discourse that would more appropriately appear at the other end of the continuum, the "highly informative" end, would be a math professor explaining the answer to a complex problem or your boss explaining the new accounting procedure to the employees or you telling a group of friends what you did during break.

Between the two extremes fall many other kinds of discourse. A sermon might fall in various places on the continuum, depending on your religion and your religious leader. A coach telling the team how to run a play might be partly informing and partly persuading the team that it will work. A teacher may have to persuade the class to do the assignment well, and the employer is not only telling you about the new accounting system, he also expects you to use it in your work. Your informative speech should be predominantly informative in its content so it will fall toward the "highly informative" end of the scale. Of course it may contain some elements of persuasion, especially where you are convincing your audience that the topic is relevant and significant to them.

Now that you know what "predominantly informative" means, you can discover what kind of topic is appropriate for an informative speech. Many informative speeches reveal how to do something, what something is or how something happens—namely, speeches of exposition, definition, and description. The following list contains the topics of student speeches that received the highest grades over the last two years in our classes. The topics are listed, not necessarily the titles of the speeches. Therefore, many of them look broader than they were when they were delivered as speeches. The speech topic, "The Intoxicated Driver," for example, was limited to information about intoxicated drivers in the town around the campus. Nonetheless, this list of topics may give you some ideas for your own informative speech. Once you have selected and narrowed the topic in a manner appropriate for you, your audience, and the situation, you will be ready to specify your behavioral purpose.

Sample Topics for Informative Speeches

The Intoxicated Driver
What Is Agribusiness?
Food Irradiation
Etiquette
Rappelling
Genetic Cloning
Aerobic Conditioning
First Aid
Obesity
What Coins Are Made Of
My Visit to Spain
Communicating with Dress
The Penalty for Possession
Underground Homes
College Alcoholics
Salt in Your Diet
Automobile Accidents
Divorce: The Facts
Chiropractors
The Basics of Interviewing
Anorexia Nervosa
The Autistic Child
Eye Surgery
The Irish Universities
Unidentified Flying Objects
Exam Anxiety
The Dormitory System
Door-to-Door Sales
Jogging
Personality Tests
Soft Drinks
What Is *Habeas Corpus*?
Who Are the Libertarians?
Substance Abuse Centers
Natural Childbirth
Grounds for Divorce
The Minimum Wage

The Social Security System
What is a Pacifist?
Pewter
Salt Water Aquariums
Popcorn Poppers Compared
Winterizing Your Car
Unique Wood Products
Clearcutting in Forestry
Ski Boots
What Is an Engineer?
Sleep and the College Student
Handling Handguns
Disc-Washers
The Concert Business
Inner-City Living
Adventures of a Bartender
My Tarantula
Generic Labeling
What Is Construction Management?
Writing Your Resume
How Computer Science Makes Your
  Job Easier
What Is Active Listening?
Food Preservatives
What Is a Finance Major?
Motorcycle Safety
Radiation and Plutonium
Evolution and the Bible
Cardiopulmonary Resuscitation
What Is Political Philosophy?
More about Iran
Solar Energy for Your Home
Police Codes
Volcanoes
Cricket
Simple Automobile Repairs
Hair Styling Made Easy

Behavioral Purposes for Informative Speaking

Important considerations for you as an informative speaker are what you want your audience to know or do as a result of your speech and how to know if you have succeeded. A teacher can teach more effectively if the students know exactly what they are expected to know; an audience learns more from an informative speech if the speaker states his or her expectations early in the speech. However, the effects of your informative speech will be unknown unless you make them behavioral; that is, your speech should result in behavioral change—change that is observable. A teacher discovers whether the class learned from a lesson by having them answer questions in class, answer examination questions, or even give speeches according to directions. Similarly, the informative speaker seeks to discover whether or not a message was effectively communicated by seeking overt feedback from the audience. The overt feedback that you seek is your immediate **behavioral purpose.**

The most common immediate behavioral purposes in an informative speech are to get the audience to do the following:

1. **Recognize** differences or similarities among objects, persons, and issues. After hearing a speech on the subject, the audience can recognize an English setter, a person suffering from Downs' syndrome, or the Libertarian position on welfare.
2. **Distinguish** among different things. After hearing a speech on the subject, the audience can distinguish between fool's gold and real gold, between a counterfeit dollar and a real one, or between a conservative position and a liberal one.
3. **Compare** items. After hearing a speech on the subject, the audience can compare prices on automobiles with the same features and options, can compare a poetic song and a sonnet, or can compare diamonds for cut, clarity, and carats.
4. **Define** words, objects, or concepts. After hearing a speech on the subject, the audience can tell what kerogen is, can describe an English Tudor house, and explain the concept of macroeconomics.
5. **State** what they have learned. After hearing a speech, the audience will be able to tell you or to write down your most important points or will be able to tell others what you said.

If the common purposes of an informative speech are to recognize, distinguish, compare, define, and state, then how does a speaker discover whether or not these behavioral purposes were accomplished?

One method of discovering whether an audience learned anything from your speech is to find out what they know both at the beginning and at the end of the speech. For example, you might ask early in your speech "How many of you know the significance of kerogen embedded in marl?" If all you get is blank looks, then you know that you are going to inform this audience about something that they do not know. After your speech explaining that kerogen is "shale oil," that it is embedded in marl or "limestone," and that this resource may be our most important supply of fuel in the future, you can ask a few of your classmates at the end of your speech to tell you the significance of kerogen embedded in marl to demonstrate that your message was received and understood.

Similarly, you may ask your classmates to write down something that indicates whether or not they understood your message. If you gave four reasons to buy food at a discount market, you might ask your classmates at the conclusion of your speech to restate two of those reasons to verify your message. Or if your purpose was to enable the audience to distinguish between edible mushrooms and toadstools, you might ask some people in your audience to point to the mushroom that will provide nutrition or to the toadstool that will make them sick. In each case, the purpose is stated in such a way that the speaker can determine whether or not the purpose was accomplished. Once you have decided on the specific purpose of addressing an audience, strategies for achieving that purpose must be selected. In other words, the speaker must decide how to adapt that purpose and the materials of the speech to a particular audience.

Presenting Information to an Audience

The informative speaker who wants to relate to an audience should first review the sections in chapter 10 dealing with selecting and narrowing the topic, as well as the material about audience analysis. Then he or she will be ready to determine how to adapt the topic and purpose to a particular audience. Audience analysis should help you determine how much the audience already knows and how much you will have to tell them to engender understanding. Then you will have to decide how to generate information hunger, achieve information relevance, employ extrinsic motivation, and select content for your speech.

Information Hunger

An informative speech will be more effective if you can generate **information hunger** in the audience; that is, the speaker can create a need for information in the audience. Information hunger is easiest to create when a speaker has analyzed the audience and has reason to believe that hunger for the information can be aroused. The audience does not have to possess prior interest in the topic, but indications of potential interest through audience analysis can help. Interest in the subject matter of a speech before listening to it is not significantly related to comprehension, but arousal of interest during the speech is related to how much the audience will comprehend.[1] Here, for example, are some rhetorical questions that could be used to introduce an informative speech and to arouse audience interest: Do you know how to protect yourself from skin cancer? Do you know how to save money on food? Can you repair your own stereo? Can you tell a good used car from a bad one? Depending on the audience, these rhetorical questions could be of interest to the audience.

Rhetorical questions are just one method of arousing information hunger. Another method is to arouse the audience's curiosity: "I have finally found a solution to our local problem of water purity," "The answer to the mysterious disappearance of our organizational funds has just been discovered in a most unlikely place," or "Every educated American should know the meaning of the word *cryogenics*." A brief quiz on your topic early in the speech is a method that arouses interest in finding the answers; unusual clothing is likely to raise interest in why you are so attired; and an object that you created will likely inspire the audience to wonder how you made it. These are just some ways that the public speaker can generate information hunger.

ANIMAL CRACKERS

Information Relevance

A second factor in relating an informative speech to an audience is **information relevance.** When selecting a topic for an informative speech, the speaker should carefully consider the relevance of the topic. Skin cancer might be a better topic in the summer when students are sunbathing than in the winter when they are not.

An audience might find a speech on tax laws dull; a speech on how the present tax laws cost you more than they cost the rich might be more relevant; and a speech on three ways to reduce your taxes might be the most salient. However, if your audience happens to be composed of eighteen to twenty-one year olds who have never paid taxes, none of the three topics might be relevant. Similarly, a speech on raising race horses, writing a textbook, or living on a pension would be informative but not relevant because of the financial status, occupation, or age of the listeners. The informative speaker, then, should exercise some care to select a topic that interests the audience.[2]

Research indicates that people expose themselves first to information that is supportive or that fits in with what they already believe or know. It also indicates that people reject less supportive information first. So an audience's predisposition toward a topic can determine whether a voluntary audience will show up to hear a speech and whether a captive audience will listen.[3]

Information Overload

The informative speaker needs to be wary about the amount of information included in a speech. The danger is **information overload.** Information overload comes in two forms. One is when the speaker tells us more than we ever wanted to know about a subject, even when we are interested in it. The speaker tries to cram as much information as possible into the time limits. Unfortunately this cramming of information makes it more difficult to be understood. A second form of information overload is when the speaker uses language or ideas that are beyond the capacity of the audience to understand. The engineer or mathematician who unloads her latest formulas on the audience or the philosopher who soars into the ethereal heights of high ideas may leave the audience feeling frustrated and less knowledgeable than before the speech. The solution to information overload is to select a limited number of main points with only the best supporting materials and to keep the message at a level the audience will understand.

Extrinsic Motivation

A third factor in relating an informative speech to an audience is **extrinsic motivation.** An audience is more likely to listen to and to comprehend a speech if there are reasons outside the speech itself for concentrating on its content.[4] A teacher who tells students to listen carefully today because they will be tested at the end of the hour is using extrinsic motivation. A student can use extrinsic motivation at the beginning of a speech by telling an audience: "Careful attention to this informative speech will help you improve your grades on objective tests," or "Listening to this speech today will save you money on gasoline," or as one student said, "I will give each of you one dollar for listening to my speech today, and I will tell you how to turn it into five dollars by the end of the week."

Informative Content

A fourth factor in relating an informative speech to an audience is the selection of **informative content.** In chapter 11, we discussed research and the selection of evidence and gave examples and illustrations to support our contentions. We will briefly examine some principles of learning and some research findings that can guide you in selecting your speech content.

The first finding is that audiences tend to remember and comprehend generalizations and main ideas better than details and specific facts.[5] The usual advice to speakers, that content should be limited to a relatively small number of main points and generalizations, seems to be well grounded. Specifically, public speakers are well advised to limit themselves to two to five main points or contentions in a speech. Even if the speech is very long, audiences are unlikely to remember a larger number of main points.

Figure 14.2

A second finding about content is that relatively simple words and concrete ideas are significantly easier to retain than more complex materials.[6] Long or abstruse words may dazzle an audience into thinking that you are intellectually gifted or verbally skilled, but it may also reduce understanding of the content. The best advice is to keep the ideas, and the words used to express them, at an appropriate level.

Humor can make a dull speech more interesting to an audience, but it does not seem to increase information retention. The use of humor also improves the audience's perception of the character of the speaker, and it can increase a speaker's authoritativeness when a speech is dull, although not when it is interesting.[7]

Early remarks about how the speech will meet the audience's needs can create anticipation and increase the chances that the audience will listen and understand.[8] Whatever topic you select, you should reveal to the members of an audience early in your speech how the topic is related to them. Unless you relate the topic to their needs, they may choose not to listen.

Figure 14.3

Another finding is that calling for **overt audience response** increases comprehension more than repetition. In a study of this subject, the overt responses that were invited were specific, "programmed" questions to which the appropriate overt responses were anticipated.[9] The results were consistent with other studies that show the virtue of active participation by an audience.

An informative speaker can ask for overt responses from the audience by having them perform the task being demonstrated (e.g., folding a paper airplane to demonstrate a principle of aerodynamics); by having them stand, raise hands, or move chairs to indicate affirmative understanding of the speaker's statements (e.g., stand up if you are over 25 years old); or by having them write answers that will indicate understanding of the informative speech (e.g., picture of four plants are drawn on the board and the audience members are instructed to identify the plant that they believe is marijuana). Having an audience go through some overt motion provides feedback to the speaker and can be rewarding and reinforcing for both speaker and listener.

Now that you have examined information hunger, information relevance, extrinsic motivation, and findings about content, you are ready to review some specific suggestions about organizing the informative speech.

Organizing Content

Chapter 12 contained detailed information about the overall organization of speeches. The following additional suggestions are based on studies that reveal specific ways that the informative speaker can help an audience to understand the content of the speech. In general, the research supports the old saying that you should tell an audience what you are going to tell them, tell them, and then tell them what you told them. Petrie, in his studies of informative speaking, found that the use of transitions can increase an audience's comprehension.[10] That finding underlines the importance of building, into the organization of your informative speech, transitions between your introduction and body and between your body and conclusion. Other places for transitions include the moves from one point to another in your speech and into and out of visual aids.

In organizing your informative speech you should determine which ideas, points, or supporting materials are of greatest importance. Apparently, an audience will understand the important points better if the speaker signals their importance by saying "now get this" or "this is very important." Some redundancy, or planned repetition, can also help to increase comprehension.[11] Some of that planned repetition can be included in the previews and reviews in your informative speech.[12] One researcher demonstrated that **advance organizers,** or previews in written work, aided retention by providing the reader with key points prior to their presentation in a meaningful, but unfamiliar, passage.[13] Perhaps it is true in speaking as well as writing that listeners can more easily grasp information when they are invited to anticipate and to review both the organization and the content of a speech.

When you have completed a sentence outline or some other form of outline that includes everything that you plan to say, you should check your speech for informational overload. Overload is a special problem in the informative speech because speakers have a tendency to inundate the listeners with information. Just as some writers believe that a longer paper is a better paper, some speakers think that the sheer quantity of information that they present in a speech makes it better. The most effective public speakers know that the quantity of material in a speech makes less difference than the quality of the material. They also know that listeners will pay more attention to carefully selected material that is well adapted to their needs. In a five-to-eight-minute informative speech, the speaker has only four to six minutes to actually present supporting materials; the remainder of the time is spent introducing the subject, making transitions, and making internal and final summaries. Your organizational plan should show you what material you intend to include in your speech. It can also be your final check on the quantity and quality of the information that you intend to present.

Special Skills for Informative Speaking

Public speakers who are highly effective at informative speaking demonstrate certain special skills that lead to their effectiveness. One of these skills is **defining.** Much of what an informative speaker does is revealing to an audience what certain terms, words, and concepts mean. Another skill is **describing,** for the informative speaker often finds himself or herself telling an audience how something appears, what it looks like, sounds like, feels like, and even smells like. A third skill is **explaining** or trying to say what something is in terms or words that the audience can understand.

Definitions

A student who was a model gave a speech in which she talked about "parts modeling"; a student who made his own butter gave an informative speech in which he talked about the "dasher" and the "clabber," "bilky" milk and butter that "gathers"; and an informative speech on aerobics included terms like "arteriosclerosis," "cardiovascular-pulmonary system," and "cardiorespiratory endurance." What were these students talking about? In each case they were using words that most persons in the audience did not understand. There is nothing particularly wrong with using terms that an audience does not understand as long as you explain the terms in language they *can* understand. You do that by *defining* your terms.

There are many ways to define your terms. You can define through **comparison.** The student who told about making butter explained that "The dasher consists of a stick similar to a broom handle. A cross made of two slats, four inches long and two inches wide, is nailed to the end of the handle. The dasher is inserted into the churn, and the churn's opening is covered by a tightly fitted wooden lid with a hole in the middle for the dasher." The student defined a *dasher* by comparing it to the better-known broomstick and by revealing how it was constructed.

Another method of definition is through **contrast,** which means by telling what it is not. An informative speaker who is attempting to distinguish among drunkenness, diabetic comas, and epileptic fits, may do so by contrasting the causes and characteristics of each. A speaker might define through a **synonym**—a word, term, or concept that is very close or similar in meaning. In an informative speech the speaker might say that depressive psychosis is characterized by loss of interest, dejection, stupor, and silence—a series of words that are similar to behaviors exhibited by the depressive psychotic patient. An **antonym** defines by stating the opposite of the term being defined—a hyperactive child is not quiet, immobile, silent, patient, or unexpressive.

Sometimes you may find it easier to explain a concept or term by revealing its **etymology** or history. A desk dictionary gives a very brief statement on the origin of a word. More complete origins can be located in specialized dictionaries like the *Oxford English Dictionary* or the *Etymological Dictionary of Modern English.* A speaker talking about sexual variations might use the term *lesbianism* and could define the term by explaining that the Greek poet Sappho wrote poetry about sexual love between women about 600 years before Christ. Because Sappho lived on the island of Lesbos, lesbians are "followers of Sappho" or female homosexuals. The story about the origins of the word provides a memorable way for the audience to relate to it.

Another means of defining is the **operational definition** or defining something by revealing how it is made or what it consists of. The earlier description of a "dasher" was an operational definition because it defined by revealing how a dasher is constructed. A student delivering an informative speech on rhinoplasty or "a nose job" did so through an operational definition:

Modern rhinoplasty is done for both cosmetic and health reasons. It consists of several mini-operations. First, if the septum separating the nostrils has become deviated as a result of an injury or some other means, it is straightened with surgical pliers. Then, if the nose is to be remodeled, small incisions are made within each nostril, and working entirely within the nose, the surgeon is able to remove, reshape, or redistribute the bone and cartilage lying underneath the skin. Finally, if the nose is crooked, a chisel is taken to the bones of the upper nose and they are broken so that they may be straightened and centered.[14]

An operational definition, then, defines by revealing the formula for the thing named: rhinoplasty is the surgery described above; a cake is its recipe; concrete is lime, cement, and water; a secretary is what a secretary does: typing, filing, answering phones, etc.

Remember that one important skill in informative speaking is skill in defining and that among the most useful methods of defining are the use of comparison, contrast, synonym, antonym, etymology, and operational definitions.

Descriptions

In informative speaking you should distinguish between words that are abstract and words that are concrete, between words that are general and words that are specific, and between words that are **evaluative** and words that are **descriptive.** One of the best ways to make your informative speech interesting is by using language forcefully and effectively. You can do that best if you recognize certain differences in words. For instance, some words refer generally to ideas, qualities, acts, or relationships: these are called **abstract.** Examples might be existentialism (an idea), beauty (a quality), violence (an act), and marriage (a relationship). Other words are more specific or concrete because they refer to definite persons, places, objects, and acts: Dr. Linda Busby, Carver Hall, my economics textbook, and those two men hitting each other in the face.

Abstract words are useful in theorizing, summarizing, and discussing and are more commonly used by educated persons discussing ideas. **Concrete** words are most useful in relating your personal experiences, direct observations, and feelings or attitudes. The important point about abstract and concrete or general and specific language is to use each where it is most appropriate. The most common error in informative speeches is the use of abstract terms where concrete words would be more forceful and clear. "I have really liked some courses of study here at Eastern College," says a student to his classmates as he adds, "but others I have disliked." That is an abstract, general statement that has minimal impact. Stated concretely and specifically the same student might say "I most enjoyed English, speech, and political science courses and I disliked Eastern College's courses in chemistry, mathematics, and physics."

Descriptions in informative speeches tend to be specific, accurate, and detailed rather than general and ambiguous. There may be a tendency, too, in informative speaking to use colorful language that appeals to the senses. A speaker describing a place might say that "the sun sets in an orange sky against the purple mountain," that a victim of shock "appears lifeless, pallid, and feels clammy," or that a manufactured meat "tastes like top-grade sirloin." A valuable exercise for the informative speaker is to review the rough draft of the speech by carefully discovering abstract, general, ambiguous words that can be replaced by concrete, specific details.

Explanations

A third special skill for the informative speaker is explaining an idea in terms that the audience can understand. An explanation is an alternative way of stating an idea or concept. Often an explanation will simplify or clarify an idea while at the same time making it interesting to the audience.

An important step in explaining something is dissecting, analyzing, or taking it apart so the audience can understand it. Unless you become skilled at dissembling the concept, your explanation may leave the audience more confused than they were before your speech. Thus you have to figure out what you can do to make the concept more palatable to the audience, what you can do to increase audience understanding. John Kenneth Galbraith, a retired professor of economics from Harvard University, wrote many books explaining economics to people who did not necessarily know very much about the subject. A close look at one of his explanations is instructive.

Galbraith is trying to make the point that politicians and the public often take the voices of a few influential persons as a shift-of-opinion by the majority.

On the need for tax relief, investment incentives or a curb on welfare costs, the views of one articulate and affluent banker, businessman, lawyer or acolyte economist are the equal of those of several thousand welfare mothers. In any recent year the pleas by Walter Wriston of Citibank or David Rockefeller of Chase Manhattan for relief from oppressive taxation, regulation or intrusive government have commanded at least as much attention as the expressions of discontent of all the deprived of the South Bronx.[15]

Galbraith is analyzing a situation: why do the persons of economic advantage have a bigger say in our economy than the millions who live with it? His language is specific and concrete. He is expanding on an idea with descriptive language, and he is doing so by dissecting the concept so we can understand its parts.

Explaining can require comparisons, analogies, anecdotes, and many other forms of support that have been discussed earlier. Your task as an informative speaker is to use the skills of defining, describing, and explaining to help your audience understand what they did not understand before they heard your speech.

An Example of an Informative Speech

So far in this chapter you have learned additional information on how to select a topic for your speech, how to determine behavioral purposes and goals for the speech, how to define, describe, and explain the concepts in your speech, and how to organize the informative speech. The following is an informative speech delivered by a student.[16] The idea behind this section is to look at another person's informative speech as an example or model of what you can do in your own.

Notice in this speech how the speaker gains and maintains the audience's attention, relates the topic to himself and to the audience, and forecasts the organization and development of the topic. Notice also how the speaker attempts to clarify the idea with examples that are high in audience interest, how ideas are translated into language that the audience can understand, and how the speaker employs definitions, descriptions, and explanations. The sidenotes will help to identify how the speaker is fulfilling the important functions of the introduction, the body, and the conclusion of an informative speech.

The Trouble with Codes

Speaker gains attention with a very brief tape recording of the opening for a TV police show.

I would like you to listen to a very important type of communication: (at this point the speaker plays a few seconds of tape-recorded sound, the introduction to the televised police show called "Adam-12")

Adam-12, Adam-12. 211 in progress at 1443 52nd. Handle Code 3.

Speaker identifies with the audience's lack of knowledge by raising rhetorical questions that most cannot answer.

What you just heard was the beginning of the T.V. show "Adam-12." The voice you heard was the radio dispatcher giving a call to a patrol car. The first time that I heard those words and numbers I could only wonder what in the world she was saying. Who's Adam-12? What's a 211 "in progress," and how do you handle something "code 3"?

Speaker relates topic to himself and describes his credibility on the topic.

Speaker announces the topic.

Speaker relates topic to the audience.

Speaker forecasts the development of the speech.

Well you could say that I found out the meaning of the message the hard way. After graduating at the top of my class from the state Law Enforcement Academy and after spending two years on our own city Police Department, I can tell you what the dispatcher just said. But there are some problems with coding systems like the one you just heard because coding systems are used these days by police, computer scientists, physicians, lawyers, and everyday people. So today I'd like to explain to you troubles that can arise from the use of a coding system by telling you of some of my personal experiences with them.

Speaker reminds audience of his credibility.

Speaker raises his first question about the code system.

At the Law Enforcement Academy the instructors who taught us the police communication system told us how easy and efficient the system is. At the Academy, the system sounded good, but the thought kept running through my mind: how will the system work when the officer is under pressure?

Speaker defines the police code system.

Speaker raises second issue concerning code.

The code system we use is based on numbers. The code contains 100 entries: 10-1 to 10-100. We learned the codes at the Academy, but like things we learn in college, if we don't practice we forget them.

Speaker relates personal experience to arouse audience interest and attention.

As I started my career in police work I found out at times the system worked very well. The times I'm talking about are the routine calls we'd receive every day. Things like prowler calls and accidents.

Speaker uses hypothetical example to make his point more specific and concrete.

For example, if a woman called in and said someone was trying to get into her house, the dispatcher would key the microphone and call the police car designated to be patroling in that area. It would sound something like this:

Speaker employs specific instance

Ames 124, 10-14, West Street, Code 2.

Translated, it would sound like this:

Speaker compares coded message with its translation.

Ames Radio to West Area patrol car number 124; 10-14: there is a prowler there now at 1004 West Street; Code 2: get there as soon as possible.

Or another routine call would sound like this:

Speaker employs second specific example.

Ames 124, 10-50 P. I. L-Way and State, Code 3.

Translated the message would sound like this:

Speaker compares coded message with its translation.

West area patrol car, there is an accident with personal injury involved at the intersection of Lincoln Way and State Avenue; because this is an emergency, use your red light and siren.

Speaker uses specific,
concrete language in his
description.

Speaker contrasts routine
code use with emergency
code use.

Speaker uses personal
experience to relate
stories illustrating the
problem with codes.

Speaker uses specific,
concrete example.

Speaker's story arouses
human interest in the
topic.

Speaker employs humor
to communicate his
message about codes.

Speaker uses descriptive
language to depict the
situation in his story.

From these examples you can see that the code system does cut down time and make the message easier to say. But what about the calls that aren't routine? What about situations in which the adrenalin is flowing?

I discovered how easy it is to forget these codes in a couple of scary ways. I received the following radio transmission from my dispatcher late one night toward the end of a hectic day:

Ames 124 & 126, 10–94, Happy Chef west, Code 2.

Well, this is what I'd been afraid of! What the heck is a 10–94? So I reached for my handy code sheet that I hadn't used for ages—but it wasn't there. I hoped that the backup officer in car 126 would have the answer I needed. As we pulled up to the restaurant we both got out of our cars and said at the same time to each other: "What the heck is a 10–94?"

We figured the only way to save our pride was to walk in and find out what was wrong. As we walked calmly in, we were met by a very frantic and excited waitress who said that a man had just called to say that he had planted a bomb in the building. Now we knew! A 10–94 was a bomb threat and we had just walked into the middle of it. So much for the code system.

Speaker uses a second
narrative to illustrate the
problem with the code in
actual use.

Speaker uses specific
example.

Another confusing situation happened one night at the scene of a very bad accident. I arrived at the scene of the accident to see a very bloody man running toward my car. Immediately, I picked up my mike and shouted into it:

124 Ames, 10–23, 10–50 P. I., 10–56 several injured.

It wasn't until I saw the dispatcher the next day that I realized my mistake. The message I had transmitted was:

West area car to Ames Radio: I have arrived at the scene of a personal injury accident; send a wrecker to pick up the several injured.

Speaker uses humor to
maintain audience
interest in the topic.

Speaker signals an
impending ending—
breaklight function.

Speaker uses an oral
footnote to indicate
interview.

In my excited state, instead of saying 10–57—send an ambulance—I said 10–56, send a wrecker. Fortunately, the dispatcher caught my error and corrected it herself.

You can see the problems that can result with the system. Not understanding messages sent out by dispatchers who use the codes everyday and have them posted by their radios, many police officers have to call back and ask them to repeat the message in English. Last week, I went in to talk with Ann Benson, the head dispatcher and a 12-year veteran of the Ames Police Department. I confronted her with these problems; this was her reply:

Speaker uses an outside authoritative source to summarize his information on the police code system.

> The code system is designed for speed and efficiency. One problem is that police calls are monitored by everybody from housewives to the press, and there are things that we do not want them to know. So until something better is figured out, we're stuck with it. It's the best we've got, and we'll have to learn to live with it.

Well, that didn't solve my problem, the problem of confusion from forgetfulness or nonuse. I also do not know a better way for an officer to communicate when he or she is under pressure.

Speaker is reviewing by repetition.

I learned the codes the hard way and I won't forget them, but under pressure I can still slip up. I don't know the answers to the problem of code communication, but I do know what the dispatcher said on the tape that introduced this speech:

Speaker uses circular organization to bring us back to his initial attention-getter.

> Adam-12 is a police patrol car; the 211 in progess is an armed robbery taking place; and code 3 is an emergency.

So now I thank you for your attention and say:

Speaker uses clever ending.

10–8, 12–24, 10–42.

The immediate purpose of this informative speech was to demonstrate to the audience some problems with a code system. The primary information that the audience should have been able to write down after the speech was two causes of code failure; namely, the inability to use a code when much of it is not routinely used and the chances for error in an emergency situation. The speaker taught the audience parts of the police code by translating specific examples; he demonstrated the problems with the code by citing personal experiences in which he as a police officer had made mistakes with the code; and he clarified the code by defining what certain code numbers meant and by explaining how police utilize the code system. The speaker included a bibliography that cited his term of instruction at the police academy, his interview with the dispatcher, and his use of the police code book.

Summary

In this chapter on the informative speech we have tried to synthesize previous chapters on topic selection, audience analysis, and organization by applying them to the informative speech. The following checklist for the informative speech can help you to prepare your speech and can serve as a summary of the chapter's contents.

As you prepare your informative speech, you may want to check off each item in the space on the left.

After you have checked off all of these important considerations for the informative speech, you should be ready to try the informative speech assignment at the end of this chapter.

Checklist for an Informative Speech

Topic

_____ 1. Have you selected a topic about which your content can be predominantly informative?

_____ 2. Have you selected a topic in which you are interested?

_____ 3. Have you selected a topic that the majority of your audience members do not know or understand?

_____ 4. Have you narrowed the topic to fit the time limit?

_____ 5. Have you considered the significance and relevance of your topic to your audience?

_____ 6. Have you reviewed chapter 10 on topic selection?

Purpose

_____ 1. Have you determined an immediate behavioral purpose?

_____ 2. Have you included methods of discovering whether or not your immediate purposes have been achieved?

Organization

_____ 1. Have you highlighted your main points by forecasting, by including transitions, by repeating them, and by summarizing them?

_____ 2. Have you limited your main points and illustrative materials to improve clarity and avoid information overkill?

_____ 3. Have you reviewed chapter 12 on organization to help you determine which patterns of organization are most appropriate for you, your topic, your situation, and your audience?

_____ 4. Have you explained by analyzing or dissecting the concept being explained in ways that invite audience understanding?

Content

_____ 1. Have you included ways to arouse information hunger, to arouse audience interest in the information you present?

_____ 2. Can you use extrinsic motivation to encourage your audience to listen carefully?

_____ 3. Have you selected information that will meet audience needs, reduce complexity, and increase understanding?

_____ 4. Have you used personal experience, stories, analogies, and comparisons to increase audience interest in your information?

_____ 5. Have you reviewed chapter 11 so you know how to find the most effective materials for your informative speech?

Language

_____ 1. Have you employed your skills in defining, describing, and explaining?

_____ 2. Have you tried defining through comparisons, contrasts, synonyms, antonyms, etymologies, or operational definitions?

_____ 3. Have you used specific, concrete detail and abstract language where it is appropriate?

_____ 4. Have you tried to be as descriptive as possible by using precise, accurate, and detailed descriptors?

Special Features

_____ 1. Have you reviewed chapter 10 on audience analysis so you know what the audience knows and needs to know?

_____ 2. Have you reviewed chapter 13 on visual aids so you can employ them where appropriate in your speech?

_____ 3. Have you reviewed chapter 11 so you know how to indicate your credibility on the topic you select?

_____ 4. Have you reviewed chapter 13 on delivery so you know how to effectively deliver your informative speech?

An Informative Speech Assignment

Deliver a 5–8 minute speech that is predominantly informative, that has immediate behavioral purposes that can be checked during or after the speech, that employs visual aids if and when appropriate, that is delivered extemporaneously, that includes oral footnotes, and that signals the important points in ways that will help the audience remember them. The speech should include an introduction that gains and maintains attention, that describes the origins of your credibility on the topic. that relates the topic to the audience, that reveals what you want the audience to learn from your speech, and that indicates the organization and development of your speech. Finally, the speech should include a conclusion that indicates the end is near, that summarizes the main point or points of the speech, and that makes the audience pleased that they listened to you.

A Written Assignment for the Informative Speech

Compose a paper with the title and your name on the top, a statement of your immediate purpose and how you will know if your behavioral purpose is fulfilled, a sentence outline of the content of your speech including the introduction and the conclusion, and a bibliography of the sources—both written sources and/or interviews—at the end in appropriate form.

Additional Readings

*Baird, John A. "The Effects of Speech Summaries Upon Audience Comprehension of Expository Speeches of Varying Quality and Complexity." *Central States Speech Journal* 25(1974): 119–27.
This article addresses itself specifically to the conclusion of an informative speech by comparing the effects of summaries in speeches that vary in quality and complexity as the title implies. The reading is not simple, but the article is informative.

Gruner, Charles R. "The Effect of Humor in Dull and Interesting Speeches." *Central States Speech Journal* 21 (1970): 160–66.
This article is one of the rare articles on the use of humor in public speaking. The reading level is not difficult.

Hart, Roderick P.; Friedrich, Gustav W.; and Brooks, William. *Public Communication*. New York: Harper & Row, Publishers, 1975. Pages 178–206.
Informative speeches are discussed in detail, and barriers to communication of ideas are examined. The book contains advice on clarifying, intensifying, sequencing, and timing the presentation of factual information.

*Petrie, Charles R., Jr. "Informative Speaking: A Summary and Bibliography of Related Research." *Speech Monographs* 30(1963): 79–91.
Although this article is not current, it is the most complete synthesis of information about informative speaking in the literature. Reading level is relatively difficult.

*Petrie, Charles R., Jr., and Carrell, Susan D. "The Relationship of Motivation, Listening Capability, Initial Information, and Verbal Organization Ability to Lecture Comprehension and Retention." *Speech Monographs* 43 (1976): 187–94.
This article is written at a relatively difficult level, but it does investigate many variables related to informative speaking.

*Indicates more advanced readings.

Notes

1. Charles R. Petrie, Jr., "Informative Speaking: A Summary and Bibliography of Related Research," *Speech Monographs* 30(1963):79–91.
2. See N.C. Cofer, *Verbal Learning and Verbal Behavior* (New York: McGraw-Hill Book Company, 1961).
3. Lawrence R. Wheeless, "The Effects of Attitude, Credibility, and Homophily on Selective Exposure to Information," *Speech Monographs* 41 (1974):329–38.
4. Charles R. Petrie, Jr. and Susan D. Carrel, "The Relationship of Motivation, Listening Capability, Initial Information, and Verbal Organization Ability to Lecture Comprehension and Retention," *Speech Monographs* 43 (1976): 187–94.
5. Petrie, p. 80.
6. Carole Ernest, "Listening Comprehension as a Function of Type of Material and Rate of Presentation," *Speech Monographs* 35 (1968): 154–58. See also, John A. Baird, "The Effects of Speech Summaries upon Audience Comprehension of Expository Speeches of Varying Quality and Complexity," *Central States Speech Journal* 25 (1974): 119–27.
7. Charles R. Gruner, "The Effect of Humor in Dull and Interesting Informative Speeches," *Central States Speech Journal* 21 (1970): 160–66.
8. Petrie, p. 84.

9. Charles O. Tucker, "An Application of Programmed Learning to Informative Speech," *Speech Monographs* 31 (1964): 142–52.
10. Petrie, p. 81.
11. See O.L. Pence, "Emotionally Loaded Argument: Its Effectiveness in Stimulating Recall," *Quarterly Journal of Speech* 40 (1954): 272–76.
12. Baird, pp. 119–27.
13. David Ausubel, "The Use of Advance Organizers in the Learning and Retention of Meaningful Material," *Journal of Educational Psychology* 51 (1960):267–72.
14. From a speech delivered by Mark Dupont in the Honors Section of Fundamentals of Public Speaking, Iowa State University. Used with permission.
15. John Kenneth Galbraith, "The 3 Attacks on Social and Economic Consensus," *Des Moines Sunday Register,* January 4, 1981. Reprinted from an article in the *New York Review of Books.* Reprinted with permission.
16. From a speech manuscript submitted by Steven D. Shupp in Speech 312, Business and Professional Speaking, Iowa State University. Used with permission.

15

The Persuasive Speech

An Application of the Principles of Public Communication

Objectives

1. State the behavioral goals of persuasive speaking
2. Recognize some methods of persuading an audience
3. Practice your skills in developing arguments, selecting evidence, and refuting arguments
4. Observe the rules of ethics in your persuasive speech
5. Deliver an effective persuasive speech

Key Terms

ultimate persuasive goal
adoption
discontinuance
deterrence
continuance
immediate persuasive purpose
boomerang effects
motivation
biological motives
primary needs
secondary needs
secondary drive
intra-psychic motives
social/behavioral motives
logical appeals
proposition
status quo
proof
evidence

emotional appeals
fear appeal
reassurance
arguments
counterarguments
novel arguments
ethics of persuasion
justification
inference
deductive arguments
valid
tests of evidence
believability
refutation
turning the tables
reducto ad absurdum
post hoc, ergo propter hoc
special pleading
red herring

You cannot convince a man against his will.
    Samuel Johnson

We are more easily persuaded, in general, by the reasons that we ourselves discover than by those which are given to us by others.
    Pascal

Information by itself almost never changes attitudes.
    Karlins and Abelson

Persuasive speaking is one of the most practical skills that you will learn in your speech communication class. You use persuasion every day in your interpersonal relations: you try to convince someone that he or she should (or should not) go out with you; you try to explain to your professor why you missed class or an examination; and you try to persuade someone to give you a job. But public persuasion is equally common. Coaches try to persuade a team that they can win; managers persuade employees to try a new approach; ministers persuade congregations to obey scripture; lawyers persuade juries; and people persuade legislators. Public persuasion pervades the mass media through advertising and public relations, and people learn to respond to, and to resist, their appeals.

This chapter will explore persuasive speaking by looking at preparing the persuasive speech, by examining some methods of persuasion, and by reviewing some special skills useful to the persuader. At the end of the chapter you will find an example of a persuasive speech.

Preparing a Persuasive Speech

To assist you in delivering an effective persuasive speech we will discuss what persuasion is, what the goals of persuasive speaking are, what kinds of topics are appropriate for a persuasive speech, and what kind of behavioral purposes are most appropriate in persuasive speaking.

Persuasion Defined

Persuasion is an on-going process in which verbal and nonverbal messages are employed to shape, reinforce, or change people's responses.[1] Persuasion is called an "on-going process" because our behavior is always undergoing modification based on alterations in our attitudes, beliefs, and values. Many people changed their attitude toward drinking coffee recently when a scientific report from Harvard University demonstrated a correlation between coffee drinking and cancer of the pancreas. Their change in attitude may or may not have resulted in a behavioral change—they may have stopped or reduced their coffee drinking.

People's attitudes, beliefs, and values and the resulting behavior are most often influenced by "verbal and nonverbal messages." Your friend's words or her frown may be sufficient to persuade you to stop moving her books. Our use of symbols in the form of language and the use of nonverbal signals are the medium that we use to convey our persuasive messages. Sometimes we use the message to "shape" responses; that is, after hearing a number of your friends talk about a particular movie your usually negative attitude toward horror movies is reduced just enough so that you decide to see just this one. Your friends were *shaping* your response with a number of messages over time. Sometimes we use the message to "reinforce" responses; that is, we need constant nourishment for our attitudes, beliefs, and values if we are to continue holding them. So you might keep going to church to reinforce your religious beliefs, keep going to meetings of the conservation club to reinforce your value toward natural resources, and keep going out on breaks with your fellow workers to maintain your positive attitude toward them.

Sometimes we use the message to "change" people's responses, to replace one attitude, belief, value, or the resulting behavior with another. The mother nags the children to pick up their clothing, to change their uncaring attitude toward their clothing, and to change their belief in orderliness. The persuader works on audience attitudes, beliefs, and values with persuasive messages so the audience will start, stop, continue, or discontinue behavior.

The Goals of Persuasive Speaking

The **ultimate persuasive goal** is always behavioral; that is, its effectiveness can be evaluated by audience behavior, some action on the part of the audience. On the way to that action on the part of the audience, the persuader tries to increase or change what the audience knows, change attitudes, beliefs, or values, or change the way the audience perceives something. But ultimately the goal of persuasion is some action by the audience.

A single example might illustrate the importance of behavior in evaluating persuasive effects. The evangelist can give sermon after sermon on the concept of human love in an effort to change the audience's attitudes toward loved ones, neighbors, and other human beings. All of this "attitude change" comes to naught, however, unless it is borne out in their behavior—unless they really do *behave* differently toward others. The "attitude change" is something that takes place inside people's heads; it is only measurable when the person acts in accord with the attitude. The evangelist should not be satisfied until the behavioral change occurs.

There are four action goals in persuasion: adoption, discontinuance, deterrence, and continuance.[2] **Adoption** means acceptance of a new idea, attitude, or belief as indicated by behavior. The advertiser wants you to try a new soap, deodorant, coffee maker, perfume, or whiskey. The advertiser is not content with a change in attitude toward the product unless it is evidenced in behavioral change—you buy the product. Similarly you might try for an adoption goal in your persuasive speech by trying to convince your classmates to car pool, ride a bicycle, or take the bus instead of filling the roads with gas-guzzling automobiles.

The second action goal of persuasion, **discontinuance,** means convincing an audience to stop doing something they do now—smoking, drinking, taking dope, using too much energy, or ignoring their studies. Your action goal is achieved when the members of the audience stop doing those things.

The third action goal of persuasion, **deterrence,** means getting the audience to avoid some activity—if you don't drink now, don't start; if you believe in special creation, don't listen to the evolutionists; or if you believe in hunting, don't vote for gun control.

The fourth action goal of persuasion, **continuance,** means convincing the audience that they should continue to behave as they do now—don't falter in your religious belief, keep studying, and keep buying Avon.

As you can see, the first two action goals, adoption and discontinuance, require the audience to change behaviors, while the last two, deterrence and continuance, ask the audience not to change behaviors. In general, it is easier to persuade people to continue their present behavior and to avoid new behavior than it is to persuade them to quit their present behavior and to start new ones. So attitude change may be taking place in the minds of persons who respond to these action goals, but the persuader ultimately seeks behavioral change.

Topics for Persuasive Speeches

Some topics are more appropriate for persuasive speeches than others. For instance, a topic that is current and controversial lends itself to persuasion better than topics that are outdated and accepted by nearly everyone. In chapter 14 you saw a continuum ranging from highly informative to highly persuasive. In the persuasive speech your speech content will be toward the "highly persuasive" end of that continuum. Some teachers believe that the best topics for persuasive speeches are those in which a majority of audience members disagree with the position advocated by the speaker. However, that position would disregard speeches with a continuance or deterrence goal.

Chapter 10 focused on some methods of selecting a topic through brainstorming and personal inventories. A review of that chapter will help you in finding appropriate topics. Another method is to survey topics that have been used in persuasive speeches. You may use that method by examining the following topics and titles. As you read over the list of topics for persuasive speeches, you should recognize that what is current and controversial in one college is bland as oatmeal at another, that many topics and titles are broader than their treatment in the speech, and that other excellent topics emerge every day. Nonetheless, this list may give you an idea for your own persuasive speech.

Topics for Persuasive Speeches

Register to Vote

Should News Be Entertaining?

Gay Liberation

In Favor of Nuclear Power

Against Gun Control

The Megavitamin Myth

Take Training for Parents

In Favor of Gun Control

The Trouble with Christianity

Child Abuse

Equal Rights for Women

Vegetarianism

Political Apathy

Selecting Wines

Advantages of a Home Computer

Youth Gangs

Affirmative Action

Ghetto Housing

Buying Used Cars

Cured Meats and Cancer

The Truth about Pesticides

Less Money for Defense

Improve Your Nutrition

Should You Be a Parent?

The Power of Nonviolence

Getting Involved in Government

Do We Need Trade Unions?

Sex Bias on the Job

Selling Automobiles

The Pro-Life Position

In Favor of Abortion

Against the Minimum Wage

Hauling Nuclear Waste

Killing Harp Seals

Strengthening Our Defense

Marijuana Is Dangerous

Advantages of ROTC

Why You Shouldn't Vote

Celibacy

Male Chauvinism

Against Football

The Food Service

Hiring the Handicapped

Legalizing Drugs

Buying Real Estate

Inexpensive Travel

Try Effective Listening

The Facts about Hunting

Watch Less TV

Student Drinking

Cohabitation

Stop Sexual Assaults

Appreciating Modern Art

X-Rays Are Dangerous

Legalize Gambling

Cocaine

TV Violence

Misbehavior at Games

Be Assertive

Volunteer Your Time

Generic Drugs

Child Discipline

Against Jogging

Motorcycle Safety

Behavioral Purposes for Persuasive Speeches

Your action goal for your persuasive speech whether it be adoption, discontinuance, deterrence, or continuance is an *ultimate goal*. It is something that you might achieve if you had word enough and time enough to work on the audience.

With your ultimate goal in mind you need to select more immediate behavioral purposes for your persuasive speech so you can estimate your effectiveness. You may wish to review the behavioral goals for an informative speech because many of them are applicable to the persuasive speech as well. On the way to your ultimate goal, you may want the audience to be able to recognize, distinguish, or state something just as you would in an informative speech. After all, part of persuasion is informing the audience, just as part of informing an audience is convincing them that they ought to listen to your information. Persuasion and information are interrelated.

In a persuasive speech you may include **immediate behavioral purposes** that are consistent with your ultimate goal but go beyond those you would expect in an informative speech. For example, persuasive speeches often call for the audience *to do* something: sign a petition, join a group, read a pamphlet, buy a product, write a letter, or eat a particular food. In selecting your immediate purposes for your persuasive speech you must exercise care to pick actions that are reasonable after a very short exercise in persuasion.

If you ask an audience to do too much as a result of your speech, you may find **boomerang effects;** that is, the audience will be even less likely to do what you ask than they were before they heard your appeal. Imagine, for instance, that a speaker asks you in a persuasive speech to change your religion, give up your major, quit school, or start taking hard drugs. Chances are that the speaker is asking too much of you and that you will respond by disliking the speaker and the topic even more than you did before.

On the other hand, you can move an audience toward an ultimate goal that they would not accept before by selecting immediate purposes that are more acceptable or reasonable. You try to convince the audience to do something that is consistent with an ultimate goal that they may be unprepared to accept at the moment. Your ultimate goal may be to have the audience vote for a candidate that is unknown to them. You are unlikely to enlist the group to work in campaign headquarters, but you might be able to get many of them to read a brief handout about the candidate or even to pass that handout to others who may be even more interested. You may not be able to get your classmates to join your religious group, but you probably can persuade them to write down three of the group's central beliefs.

You can improve your own chances of persuading an audience if you can write out your ultimate goal and your immediate purposes. For example, a student delivering a persuasive speech against jogging might state the following for an ultimate goal:

The ultimate goal of my persuasive speech is to convince people who jog that they should quit (discontinuance) and to convince people who do not jog that they should never start (deterrence).

The same speaker might state his or her immediate purposes like this:

One of my immediate purposes is to have the audience write down at the conclusion of my speech the three harmful effects of running on the body: shin splints, bone bruises, and knee problems. A second immediate purpose of my speech is to have the runners start reducing their workout times to avoid problems encouraged by fatigue.

The speaker does not have to reveal the ultimate purpose in the speech itself, but ordinarily it is wise to reveal the immediate purposes in the speech. The audience will more likely write down the names of the harmful effects if they are told early in the speech of that expectation. They may resist the persuader, however, if they know the ultimate goal of the speech.

Persuading an Audience

There are many ways to persuade an audience—using motivational appeals, employing source credibility, using reason or logical appeals, organizing your materials effectively, and observing ethical guidelines for persuasion.

Motive Appeals

The word *motivation* is based on a Latin term that means "to move," and in this section the word **motivation** is based on the idea of "moving" people to do something. The persuader through careful audience analysis discovers what will move an audience to fulfill immediate purposes and ultimate goals. Our motives can be classified into three categories, none of which completely explains why people do what they do but which together can provide probable explanations for human behavior. The three kinds of motivation are biological motives, intrapsychic motives, and social/behavioral motives.[3]

Biological motives are based on such bodily needs as food, water, air, and comfortable temperature. When these needs are not being met, the person is driven to satisfy them. The **primary needs** listed above are simply part of being a human being, but we learn **secondary needs** or ways to fulfill them. For example, as a human being you have a need for food, but the **secondary drive** to fulfill that need with steak, or a pizza, or a vegetarian diet is learned.

The persuader who is arguing for new regulation to clear the polluted air of Denver, Colorado, by imposing stronger automobile emission standards is appealing to the audience's need for clean air to breathe. That persuader is appealing to the primary need for air and is using the primary drive for air to breathe. The persuader who is trying to convince that same audience to get out of the city to enjoy the clean, clear mountain air of the surrounding region is appealing to a secondary or learned need, to satisfy a secondary drive for a particular kind of clean air. Similarly, the beer company appeals to our primary drive for drink, but to a secondary drive for drink made with "mountain water."

Our biological needs do not explain all that we do. In fact it is insufficient to simply satisfy biological needs. There are **intra-psychic motives** as well as biological ones. Some of our behavior is best explained not by drives but by emotions, feelings, and perceptions. Have you ever eaten popcorn, sometimes an entire bag or bowl, even though you were not particularly hungry? Perhaps you see the eating of popcorn or ice cream as a reward for yourself whether you are deprived of food or not. Our perception of popcorn as rewarding, as a pleasure, is intra-psychic; that is, it is psychological, not physiological like the biologically based needs.

Advertisers are persuaders who exploit our intra-psychic motives. Do we have a biologically based need for good grades? For perfume? For a particular political party? No; we do, however, find that good grades, cologne, and adherence to certain beliefs provide psychological pleasure. So the persuasive speaker has to determine the intra-psychic motives that are important to an audience because the psychological pleasures, the rewards, and the punishments will vary from person to person, from audience to audience.

A third kind of motivation, **social/behavioral** motives, is based on satisfying what others want us to do, how others want us to behave. Why do people join athletic teams, the Methodist church, or social groups like the Elks, Shriners, Rainbow Girls, Knights of Columbus? There is satisfaction in conforming to the beliefs and activities of a social group, and there are punishments for the person who does not belong. The persuader can use social/behavioral motivation in speeches on how to get along with others, how to join a support group, and how to win friends and keep a spouse.

Human behavior is very complicated. No explanation of why human beings behave the way they do is entirely satisfactory. Knowing the three kinds of motivation will not permit you to pull strings with an audience to elicit the behavior that you seek. Nonetheless, the most effective persuaders—advertisers, politicians, preachers, and lawyers—have learned how to analyze their audience—consumers, voters, parishioners, and juries—so that they are more often successful than unsuccessful in reaching their objectives.

Source Credibility

Who and what you are can make a powerful difference in persuasion. In chapter 11 you explored the concept of source credibility; a review of that chapter will help you to understand what audiences look for in a speaker: competence, trustworthiness, dynamism, and co-orientation. A high credibility speaker has more impact on an audience than a low credibility speaker. A persuader who is seen as similar to the audience is more likely to be effective than one who is seen as quite dissimilar. Sometimes a highly credible speaker can attain more attitude change when he or she asks for more.[4]

An example of how source credibility works occurred when Harvard University sent a recruiter to a large midwestern university in an effort to secure more first-rate students from that part of the country. The pre-law students gathered in a room to meet the recruiter who turned out to be a second-year law student from Harvard. The all-white audience of pre-law students seemed quite surprised when the recruiter turned out to be black. They showed their skepticism with their initial questions. "What was your grade-point average as an undergraduate?" asked one member of the audience. "3.9 on a 4.0 scale," answered the recruiter. "Well," inquired another student who may not have been suitably impressed with the grade-point average, "what did you earn on the LSAT?" "Seven hundred seventy," replied the recruiter. The pre-law students asked no more questions. The speaker may have been of a different race and from a different part of the country, but his grade-point average and his LSAT score (800 is top) were higher than anyone's in the room. The audience listened with respect to his speech on how to get into one of the best law schools in the land.

You can also signal the origins of your credibility to your audience by describing how you earned the right to speak on the topic. Perhaps your major will help: a nuclear engineer has the authority to speak on nuclear energy; a business major is a credible source on buying stocks and bonds; and a physical education major can speak with authority on exercise programs. Maybe your experience is the key to your credibility: your years in the military gave you some insights into military waste; your years as a mother and homemaker gave you some authority on time efficiency, raising children, or relating to a spouse; or your part-time job at a fast-food establishment permitted you some authority on management-labor relations.

Whatever the origins of your credibility, remember to reveal them early in the speech. Your authority may very well provide a reason for the audience to listen. If you reveal your credibility late in the speech, the audience may have paid little attention because they did not know you spoke with authority on the topic.

Logical Appeals

Motive appeals and source credibility are just two ways to persuade an audience; a third important method is the use of reasoning or logic to convince an audience. The main ingredients of **logical appeals** are propositions and proofs.

A **proposition** is a statement that asserts or proposes something: the United States should have uniform regulations for child support; the city should reduce the fines for traffic offenses; or the college should change its definition of "a student in good standing." Notice that a proposition always recommends a change in the **status quo,** the way things are right now. The primary method of persuading an audience that current policies should be changed and that another policy should be adopted is through the use of **proof** or **evidence.**

The persuader can use a wide array of evidence to demonstrate the wisdom of retaining present practice or of changing current policies: quotations from authoritative persons, conclusions from studies and reports, or experiences of individuals injured or helped by current policies. The underlying principle in logical appeals is that the audience should accept the side that presents the most convincing or the "best" evidence to support that side. In other words, our behavior should be based on the best evidence; it should be consistent with the persuader who provides the most effective "proof" that his or her position is the best position to adopt.

Logical appeals can also be refuted; that is, they can be attacked. Another persuader can analyze the situation suggested in the proposition and find the analysis faulty—the present policy will likely work better than the suggested alternative. The opposing persuader may find that the authorities who were quoted were biased, that the reports and studies were flawed, or that even better evidence would invite a different conclusion.

Finally, you should recognize that the world does not run by logic or evidence alone, that sometimes beliefs are irrational or not based on evidence. A persuader might come up with considerable evidence why you should eat beans and cheese instead of steak without changing your behavior or your beliefs on that subject. The persuader is always faced with the disconcerting fact that even the best evidence or proof in support of a persuasive proposition might not alter audience behavior.

Emotional Appeals

Although logical and **emotional appeals** are often seen as diametrically opposed concepts, most of our behavior is based on a mixture of emotional and rational "reasons." A speaker may persuade an audience to accept his or her immediate purposes for emotional rather than logical reasons. A story about one person's bad experience with the campus bookstore may inspire many persons in the audience to bring their business to another store. It matters little that the experience was a one-in-a-thousand situation, that it may have been as much the customer's fault as the manager's, or that it never happened before. Such is the power of our emotions that they can persuade us to defy the law, fight another nation, or ignore evidence. As one writer put it:

The creature man is best persuaded
When heart, not mind, is inundated;
Affect is what drives the will;
Rationality keeps it still.[5]

The emotional appeal that has been most studied is the **fear appeal.** Janis and Feshbach examined three levels of fear appeals in communication on dental hygiene and found that the least threat worked better than moderate threat, which worked better than strong threats.[6] Fredric Powell used strong and weak fear appeals in a civil-defense communication that threatened loved ones. He found more change of opinion when the fear appeal was strong.[7] In other words, the research findings on fear appeals are mixed and do not provide a formula for using them. One research result, however, is well established. If you use fear appeals to persuade your audience, you are advised to include in your speech some way that the audience can avoid or escape the fear. A fear appeal can make an audience aware of danger; the **reassurance** can tell them how to contend with the danger. Omitting such reassurance does not influence the audience's ability to recall the facts in a speech, but a speech with reassurance results in greater shifts of opinion than one without reassurance; the speaker who includes reassurance is regarded as a better speaker than one who does not.[8] Clearly, the best advice is when you use fear appeals, include reassurance.

Organizational Plans

Chapter 12 included considerable information on how to organize a speech. After reviewing that information, you should note that some organizational patterns lend themselves best to persuasive speaking. The problem-solution pattern, for example, is common in persuasive speaking. Sometimes an entire speech will be devoted to analyzing a problem that was unrecognized by the audience. At other times, the problem is recognized by all, so the focus falls heavily on solutions. Similarly, the cause-effect pattern is often utilized in persuasive speaking. These broad patterns of organization should be considered along with the more particular information that follows.

The introduction to your persuasive speech should fulfill the same functions as the introduction for an informative speech, with one exception. The introduction should relate the topic to the audience, relate the topic to the speaker (source credibility), gain and maintain audience attention, and forecast the organization and development of the speech as explained in chapter 12. The one aspect of the introduction that may differ in a persuasive speech is introducing the topic. In an informative speech where clarity is one of the most important considerations, you should reveal your expectations early in the speech. You tell the audience exactly what you expect them to know, understand, and do as a result of the speech. In persuasive speaking your expectations for the audience may have to be delayed until late in the speech because either the audience will be unprepared for your persuasive proposition or they may be hostile to the idea at first.

Persuasion is a kind of seduction in which you may have to convince an audience to accept your position. Most people do not begin a relationship with another by announcing "I want to marry you." The idea may be too early or too much. Similarly, an effective persuader knows how much to ask for. The effective persuader knows that some convincing may have to take place before the immediate purpose or ultimate goal is announced. So the persuasive speaker may not reveal in the introduction exactly what he or she wants from the audience unless they are in a state of readiness to accept the persuasive proposition.

Other considerations for the persuasive speaker include: Should my best arguments come first, in the middle, or last in my speech organization? Should I present one side of the issue or both or many? Should I refute counterarguments? And should I use familiar arguments or novel arguments to persuade my audience?

Should my best arguments come first, in the middle, or last in my persuasive speech? Arguments are information that supports your stated proposition. Arguments presented first or early in the body of the speech seem to have more impact in speeches on controversial issues, on topics with which the audience is uninvolved, on topics that the audience perceives as interesting, and on topics that are highly familiar to the audience. On the other hand, arguments and information seem to have more impact on an audience later in the persuasive speech when they are involved in the issue, when the topic is likely to be less interesting, and when the issue is moderately unfamiliar to the audience.[9] No research to date indicates that your most important materials should be presented in the middle of your speech. The middle is the place where attention is likely to wane so the effective speaker usually builds in human interest stories and interesting supporting materials to maintain audience attention.

Should I present one side of the issue or both or many? A persuasive speaker should present one side of an issue when the audience is friendly, when the speaker's position is the only one the audience is likely to hear, and when the speaker is seeking immediate but temporary change of opinion. The persuasive speaker should present both sides or a number of sides when the audience initially disagrees with the speaker or when it is likely that the audience will hear other sides from other people.[10] Presenting both sides or multiple sides to a hostile audience may make the speaker seem more open-minded or less rigid to the audience. Also, hearing the other sides of the issue, as you will see, reduces the impact of counterarguments.

Should I refute counterarguments? When you deliver your persuasive speech, you are likely to employ a number of arguments with supporting materials to encourage your audience to accept your persuasive proposition. The arguments against your stated position are called **counterarguments.** In a both- or multi-sided persuasive speech you are revealing other arguments including those that might be against your position. The best advice based on current research is to refute counterarguments before proceeding to your own position on the issue, especially when the audience is likely to already know the counterarguments.[11] If you favor freedom of choice on the abortion issue and your audience is familiar with the pro-life (anti-abortion) side of the issue, then you should refute those known counterarguments before you reveal your own position on the issue.

Should I use familiar or novel arguments in my persuasive speech? On most topics you will have to recognize familiar arguments even if it is for the purpose of refuting them. However, research indicates that **novel arguments** or new arguments that the audience has not heard before have more impact than familiar ones.[12] A student who delivered a persuasive speech in favor of gun control pointed out that a common counterargument from anti-control forces was that gun registration would provide national enemies with a ready-made list of gun owners. The student who favored gun control pointed out that the membership list of the National Rifle Association already provided an extensive list of gun owners that could be used by national enemies. The argument was novel and served to nullify the claim made by the anti-control side on the issue. You too should seek new, novel, or original arguments in support of your own case and against the positions of others. Old and familiar arguments may be useful in your persuasive speech, but the ones that the audience has not heard before will have greater impact.

Ethical Considerations

Ethics or standards of moral conduct are written and unwritten rules of conduct. Many of our standards for ethical behavior are codified into law: we may not slander in speech or in writing someone who is not a public figure; we may not start a panic that can endanger the lives of others; and we may not advocate the overthrow of our form of government. Many of our **ethics of persuasion** are not matters of law, but violations of those unwritten or uncodified rules do have consequences. There is no law against showing a picture of a fetus in the bottom of a wastebasket in your speech against abortion, pointing out acne sufferers in your speech on dermatology, or having your audience unknowingly eat cooked rat meat, but your audience may find your methods so distasteful that as a consequence they will reject you and your persuasive message.

The following are some of the unwritten rules that govern the preparation and delivery of persuasive speeches:

1. Accurate citation of sources. When you are preparing and delivering your speeches, you should be very careful to gather your information and to state it accurately. Specifically, you should reveal where or from whom you received information if it was not your own idea or information. Oral footnotes, written footnotes, and bibliographies should be a continuing reminder to speakers that who said something or where it was found is important. Making up quotations, attributing ideas to someone who never said it, omitting important qualifiers, quoting out of context, and distorting the information from others are all examples of ethical violations that spring from this rule.

2. Respect for sources of information. Have you ever gone to the library to do research for a paper or speech only to find that some inconsiderate individual has already cut out the information you seek? Removing or defacing information that is meant for everyone is a serious violation of ethics that is punishable in most colleges and universities. Unfortunately, few of the offenders are caught, but the idea of "doing unto others as you would have them do unto you" is in operation here. Unless students in the beginning speech course respect public sources of information, everyone will suffer. This rule extends to respect for persons whom you interview. They were willing to share information with you so it behooves you to treat them and their information with respect in your speech.

3. Respect for your audience. Persuasion is a process that works most effectively when there is mutual respect between speaker and audience. Attempts to trick the audience into believing something, lying to the audience, distorting the views of your opposition, or exaggerating claims for your own position are all ethically questionable acts. It helps if you already accept the idea that a speaker should speak truthfully and accurately, that the persuasive speaker is best if he or she can accurately portray the oppositions' arguments and still win with arguments and evidence. If you do not believe that the truth works better than the alternatives, then perhaps the fact that there are negative consequences for you as a person might sway you. Audiences can be very hostile to a person who has tricked them or who has lied, distorted, or exaggerated simply to meet an immediate purpose or an ultimate goal.

4. Respect for your opponent. Persuasive speeches invite rebuttal. Nearly always there is someone inside or outside your audience who thinks your ideas, positions, or issues are wrong. A good rule of thumb is to respect your opponent, not only because he or she may be right but because an effective persuader can take the best that the opposition has to offer and still convince the audience that he or she should be believed. The idea that you should respect your opponent means that you should not indulge in namecalling, in bringing up past behaviors that are irrelevant to the issue. It means that you should attack the other person's evidence, sources, or logic, not the person. A very practical reason for observing and practicing this rule of ethics is that few of the issues about which we persuade are settled yet, that you may find in time that your opponent's position is better in many respects than your own, and that you will have to live with many issues that are not resolved in the manner you most desire.

You may get the impression from these four ethical guidelines that every persuader must be part angel. Not quite. Our ethical rules for persuasive speaking allow for considerable verbal combat, for devastating the arguments of others with better or more persuasive evidence, for finding new supporting materials that your opposition has not found, and for majority acceptance of your ideas. Persuasive speaking is not for the faint of heart, but it is much cleaner verbal combat if you obey the ethical guidelines that call for accurate citation of sources, respect for written and human sources of information, respect for your audience, and respect for your opponent's ideas.

Special Skills for Persuasive Speaking

Just as the informative speaker must learn special skills in defining, describing, and explaining, the persuasive speaker must learn special skills in arguing, providing evidence, and rebutting the arguments of others. In this section you will discover what an argument is, what the tests of evidence are, and how to counter the arguments of others.

Argumentation

An argument[13] consists of a proposition and its justification. In persuasive speaking the proposition embodies what you want the audience to believe or do: communication classes should be required, physicians fees should be competitive, or federal money for human services should be returned to the state for distribution. Because persuasive propositions suggest change from present practice, they are usually controversial and state that something "should" or "ought to" be changed. The **justification** is all of the evidence that can be gathered in support of the proposition: facts, statistics, quotations, reports, studies, stories, pictures, objects, illustrations, and demonstrations.

The proposition is a conclusion that can be inferred from the justification or evidence. The pattern in a persuasive speech often looks like this:

Proposition		Evidence
Evidence		Evidence
Evidence	or	Evidence
Evidence		Proposition

It might begin with the proposition followed by the evidence or it might start with evidence that leads to a conclusion. In either case, the argument hinges on an **inference;** that is, a conclusion that is consistent with, but beyond or larger than, the evidence used to support it. A lawyer might argue: he was at the scene of the murder, he held a smoking gun, the bullets in the weapon matched the slugs in the body, and the suspect had just publicly threatened the victim. Therefore, this person is the murderer. He could have just as well argued that the person was a murderer and then cited the evidence. In either case the conclusion—this person is the murderer—follows from, but is beyond, the evidence itself. Notice that even given the evidence of the case, it is possible that the suspect was framed, that someone else did the shooting and stuck the smoking gun in the hapless suspect's hand just before the police arrived.

Another kind of argument reaches a conclusion deductively. **Deductive arguments** are based on premises rather than on evidence and the conclusion drawn from the premises includes them:

Major premise: All rats are undesirable pests.
Minor premise: This animal is a rat.
Conclusion: Therefore, this animal is an undesirable pest.

The conclusion is not an inference that goes beyond evidence, but a deduction that includes two of the three terms (rats, undesirable pests, animal) already included in the two premises. Deductive arguments follow certain rules. If they follow the rules, they are called **valid** even if the three terms (rats, undesirable pests, and animal) are arranged in premises that are false. For instance, the deductive argument stated above is valid, but one could question the major premise—are all rats undesirable pests? Are laboratory rats undesirable? Or in the minor premise, are you sure the animal is actually a rat and not a hamster? The effective persuader makes sure that evidence is consistent with and leads to the conclusion. The effective persuader makes sure that the premises in the deductive argument are valid (correctly arranged) and true. The most common kind of argument to emerge in persuasive speaking is deductive argument. You will find next some ways to evaluate evidence.

Evidence

Evidence is data or information intended to get the audience to accept the persuasive proposition it purportedly supports.[14] The best evidence has to meet two criteria: does it meet the **tests of evidence** and does the audience believe it? Evidence usually consists of statements from authorities or from examples. A speaker supporting the idea that the college should supply childcare service for students with children might use as evidence a statement from an authority: "Dr. Rodney Higgins, Director of the Counseling Bureau, says that colleges should provide childcare facilities and personnel for students." Perhaps the speaker could use himself or herself as an example of why the service is needed.

Evidence must meet certain tests. Let us say that one of your classmates argues that the students should establish their own cooperative bookstore (proposition) because other schools have done so successfully (evidence), because students could get better value for used books (evidence), and because the vice-president for student affairs favors the idea (evidence). Let us assume also that the speaker expanded on the evidence to provide specific examples of schools that have successfully provided student co-op bookstores, has demonstrated that used books bring a better price at student co-ops, and that he or she has a quotation from the vice-president for student affairs.

How would you evaluate this evidence? What questions would you ask about it? What are the tests of evidence that are applicable in this case? Here are some of the questions that test this evidence:

1. Is the evidence consistent with other known facts? Did the speaker look at a relatively large number of student co-ops to show that other schools have done so successfully? Have any student co-op stores failed?
2. Would another observer draw the same conclusions? Has anyone other than the speaker determined that other student co-ops are successful? What does the speaker mean by "success."
3. Does the evidence come from unbiased sources? Does the vice-president for student affairs have anything to gain by favoring student co-op bookstores? Who made the claim that students will get better value for their used books? Who said that other schools have established successful student co-ops?
4. Is the source of the information qualified by education and/or experience to make a statement about the issue? The vice-president may be well educated, but what does he or she know about co-op bookstores? What about the qualifications of the sources for the information on used books or successful co-ops?
5. If the evidence is based on personal experience, how typical was that personal experience? Unless the personal experience was typical, generalizable, realistic, and relevant, it is questionable as evidence.
6. If statistics were used as evidence, then they must be from a reliable source, comparable with other known information, current, applicable, and interpreted so that the audience could understand them.
7. If studies and surveys were employed, then they must be authoritative, valid, reliable, objective, and generalizable. A study done by persons who favor student co-op bookstores, for instance, may be questionable because the source of the study had a bias favoring them.
8. Were the speaker's inferences appropriate to the data presented? Did the speaker go too far beyond the evidence in reaching the conclusion that students should establish their own cooperative bookstore?
9. Was important counter-evidence overlooked? Often in our haste to make a positive case, counter-evidence is ignored or omitted. What evidence against student co-ops was left out?
10. What is the speaker's credibility on the topic? Did the speaker "earn the right to speak" on the topic through research, interviews, and a thorough examination of the issue? Has the speaker had experience related to the issue?

The answers to these ten questions are important. Evidence that meets these tests has met the first requirement of good evidence.

The second requirement of good evidence is that the audience believe in it, trust it, and accept it—**believability.** Finding evidence that meets the tests of evidence is difficult enough, but at least the speaker has some guidelines. Why an audience will not accept evidence is more mysterious. The effective public speaker knows all of the major arguments for and against the persuasive proposition. The evidence that is selected is chosen from a multitude of arguments both because it meets the tests of evidence and because the speaker's audience analysis indicates that this evidence is most likely to be believed. A speaker addressing a group of fundamentalist Christians may know that supporting material from scripture will fall on friendly ears; that same evidence may not be believed by groups that do not accept the authority of the Bible. The effective public speaker chooses evidence both because it meets the tests of evidence and because it meets audience requirements for believability.

Refutation

Refutation is the art of opposing the arguments presented by someone else. You can oppose the arguments of another speaker by showing how the evidence does not meet the tests of evidence and by demonstrating that for this particular audience the evidence is not the most believable. By carefully reviewing the tests of evidence you will see that they can be employed to attack the persuasive proposition, the inferences, and the evidence presented by another speaker. Other methods of refutation are more subtle.

Turning the tables is one refutational strategy in which the same evidence that one speaker used in support of a proposition is used by the opposition to attack it. The speaker mentioned earlier who argued that the membership list of the National Rifle Association already provides a national enemy with a ready-made list of ardent gun owners was using that strategy. Another speaker arguing against gun control said that North Dakota, South Dakota, Wyoming, and Montana did not have gun control, yet their murder rate was very low. An opposing speaker turned the tables by arguing that all of the states mentioned were devoid of large metropolitan areas, a reason for few murders, not the lack of gun control laws.

Another refutational strategy is **reducto ad absurdum** or reducing the issue to absurdity. One speaker argued that there should be no laws against gun possession because "people, not guns, kill other people." An opposing speaker reduced the argument to absurdity by pointing out that such reasoning would justify the ownership of submachine guns, flame throwers, and hand grenades. Listen carefully to the arguments presented by others. Are there any ways that the principle they advocate can be applied in ways undesirable to the audience?

A common fault in public speeches is the fallacy called **post hoc, ergo propter hoc;**[15] that is, the assumption that just because one thing occurred after another is no reason to believe that one thing caused the other. The Latin statement means "after this; therefore, because of this." Most superstitions are based on this fallacy— I saw a black cat on the way into the office and I slipped and broke my wrist going into the building. Make sure in listening to the speeches of others that events are really causally linked and not simply two events that happened to occur close together in time.

Special pleading is still another kind of arguing that is susceptible to refutation.[16] Special pleading means that the speaker blissfully ignores contrary evidence. Often an otherwise strong case can be critically weakened when one audience member or an opposing speaker brings up a convincing piece of evidence to the contrary. A student argued that hearty eaters need not despair; the National Academy of Sciences had declared no specific link existed between eating habits and heart disease. The argument was shot down in rebuttal by an opposing speaker who produced a current study of 1900 men over a nineteen-year period. The study demonstrated that men who ate more fat and cholesterol had more heart attacks than those who restricted their diets. The latter student found the study in the high prestige *New England Journal of Medicine*. The first speaker had been special pleading; the second produced a single piece of good evidence that destroyed the case.

Still another characteristic for the refutational speaker to watch for is the **red herring**,[17] an irrelevancy that is introduced to draw attention away from the main issue. In a recent court case a lawyer argued that his clients, a respected couple in the community, had been faithful church members who enhanced community life by sponsoring garage sales and by giving the money to the church. This glowing report was presented in an attempt to get the jury to overlook the fact that the goods sold at the garage sale had been stolen from the firm where the couple worked. Another type of red herring is found in cases where the persuader presents a mountain of largely irrelevent evidence in an attempt to make quantity look like quality. Both types of red herring are readily attackable by the public speaker who can distinguish between relevent and irrelevant evidence.

There are other kinds of refutation, but beginning with turning the tables, reducto ad absurdum, post hoc, ergo propter hoc, special pleading, and the red herring will give the beginning public speaker a sufficient arsenal with which to attack the evidence in a persuasive speech.

An Example of a Persuasive Speech

The following speech was delivered by a student to meet the persuasive speaking assignment. It is provided here, not because it is a perfect speech, but because it will show you specifically how one person chose to compose a persuasive message. The sidenotes show what is occurring in the message.

Where Sugar Goes, Trouble Follows[18]

Speaker gains audience attention.

Appeal to biological motive, a secondary drive—the learned preference for sugar.

Are you closing your eyes to a situation you do not wish to acknowledge? Are you aware of the dangers in your diet? Yes, my friends, you are in trouble, and that trouble is sugar. You may think that you consume reasonable amounts of sugar, but today I am going to demonstrate that you may be consuming considerably more than you think.

Speaker states immediate purpose, a discontinuance goal: Stop eating so much sugar.

Source credibility: Did research and reduced consumption (experience).

Forecast.

Specific statement of purpose and expectations.

Evidence that Americans consume large quantities of sugar.

Statistical evidence.

Visual aid: List of foods containing hidden sugar as a main ingredient.

Immediate behavioral purpose: Check the label before buying.

Organization: Reviews first myth and moves to second.

Argument: Bodily needs can be met with nutritious foods.

Organization: signals third point in speech.

Counterarguments: Each myth is an argument the speaker refutes thus reviewing the arguments that could be leveled against her case.

A main point with three subpoints: Tooth problems, diabetes, and weight problems.

This habitual consumption of large amounts of sugar is truly undesirable so all of us should cut down immediately. We are all sugar addicts. After reviewing the evidence, I tried to consciously reduce my sugar consumption. That made me more fully aware of how much sugar I really do consume and how dependent I am on it. As a result of my speech in which I will dispel a few myths and talk of the adverse effects of sugar, you too may make a conscious effort to reduce your sugar consumption.

The average American consumes about 125 pounds of sugar annually. Even with the increasing price of sugar, the figure remains relatively constant. Of this sugar consumption, 70% is hidden, is contained in foods and beverages prepared outside the home.[1] Here is a list of the common foods that contain a lot of hidden sugar. (Speaker refers to visual aid). Go to a supermarket, glance at the labels, and if sugar is listed among the first ingredients, then it is a major component.

A second myth, besides the one that we don't think that we consume much sugar, is that the body needs sugar for energy. The body has no physiological need for sugar that cannot be satisfied by other, more nutritious foods. Your body can convert starches to sugar or use the sugar in fruits and vegetables for energy. The alleged need for sugar as "quick energy" is a myth—except in such rare situations as insulin shock.

A third myth is that all carbohydrates are the same, that it is the number of calories that really matters. On the contrary, sugar is essentially a pure chemical species that is broken down in one step and quickly absorbed in the bloodstream. Other carbohydrates are complex and are digested relatively slowly. Eventually these complex carbohydrates become blood sugar, the primary fuel for your body. This metabolic difference may have different effects on your health.

One adverse effect that sugar can have on your health is tooth decay. Bacteria in the mouth digest the sugar on tooth surfaces. This bacterial action produces an acid that etches the protective tooth enamel and fosters gum disease. Interestingly, it is the amount of time that sugar remains on the teeth—not the quantity eaten—that makes the difference. In the United States today, it has been estimated in a recent *New York Times Magazine* article that 98% of American children have some tooth decay; by age 55 approximately half the population have no teeth.[2]

A second metabolic difference that sugar can make besides tooth decay is excessive weight. According to Jean Mayer in an article entitled "The Bitter Truth about Sugar," 10% to 20% of all U.S. children and 35% to 50% of all middle-aged Americans are overweight.[3] Each person on the average consumes 500 calories worth of sugar per day. This is the energy equivalent of more than 50 pounds of fat per year for each one of us.[4] The basic cause of obesity is not sugar; it is excess calories. But since calories can be highly concentrated in sugar-sweetened foods, you may eat more calories than you need of such foods before you feel full or even realize how much you have consumed. Compare the satiety value of a pound of apples with that of a two-ounce candy bar: both have the same caloric content. I'm not trying to say that everyone should cut down on calories, but instead of having one-fourth of your daily calories being supplied by sugar, which is essentially devoid of nutrients, replace it with foods that make a significant contribution to your nutrition.

A third metabolic problem related to sugar—besides tooth decay and obesity—is diabetes in adults who have a genetic predispositon for the disease. Diabetes is a major cause of death in the U.S. and between five and twelve million Americans are classified as diabetics. About 1000 new cases are reported every day.[5] There is a strong suspicion that a large sugar consumption may be causally related to diabetes both indirectly by promoting obesity and directly as a source of repeated stress on the insulin-producing mechanism of the body.

I have suggested today that we Americans consume more sugar than we think we do, that we do not really need refined sugar to gain energy for our bodies, and that all carbohydrates are not the same. To demonstrate that all carbohydrates are not the same, I showed that refined sugar is related to tooth decay, that sugar encourages excess weight, and that sugar is bad for adults who are predisposed to diabetes. With these arguments and evidence in mind, I urge you to join me in reducing the sugar in your diet. Be an intelligent consumer who reads the labels, who eats healthy, nutritious foods instead of sugar-laden food and drink. Remember, sugar is a villain in disguise: where sugar goes, trouble follows.

Organization: First subpoint.

Explanation.

Statistical evidence.

Oral footnote.

Organization: Second subpoint.

Oral footnote.

Statistical evidence.

Relates statistics to audience with alternative explanation.

Argument from comparison.

Immediate behavioral purpose.

Organization: Third subpoint and repetition of first two subpoints.

Statistical evidence.

Suggested causal link.

Conclusion:

Breaklight function.

Summary of main arguments and subpoints.

Relates arguments, evidence with speaker and audience.

Immediate behavioral purpose repeated.

Upbeat ending.

Endnotes or Footnotes   1. J.E. Brody, "Sugar: Villain in Disguise," *Reader's Digest,* October 1977, p. 164.
2. Jean Mayer, "The Bitter *Truth* About Sugar," *New York Times Magazine,* June 20, 1976, p. 31.
3. Mayer, p. 31.
4. Mayer, p. 31.
5. Mayer, p. 31.

Bibliography   Brody, J.E. "Sugar: Villain in Disguise." *Reader's Digest.* October 1977, pp. 163–165.
Mayer, Jean. "The Bitter *Truth* About Sugar." *New York Times Magazine,* June 20, 1976, pp. 26–34.

The ultimate goal of this persuasive speech on sugar in the diet was discontinuence, to persuade the audience to reduce consumption of refined sugar. The speech also had an explicit ultimate goal of adoption, to get the audience to start eating more nutritious foods instead of sugar-laden foods and drink. The immediate goals were stated intermittently through the speech: check labels to determine the amount of hidden sugar in food and drink products, and eat natural sugars in fruits and vegetables instead of refined sugars in candy and other junk foods. The main motivational appeal was biological: alter your secondary drive, the learned preference for sugar, and avoid tooth decay, obesity, and diabetes. Much of the evidence was in the form of statistics from authoritative sources.

Perhaps this specific example of a persuasive speech by a student will give you a more concrete idea of how the advice and the information in this chapter can be applied in an actual instance of persuasion.

Persuasive Speech Performance

Deliver an 8 to 10 minute persuasive speech in which you try to achieve immediate behavioral goals consistent with an ultimate action goal like adoption or discontinuance. The speech should include an introduction that fulfills the functions of an introduction (see chap. 12) with special emphasis on establishing your credibility (see chap. 11) and a conclusion that fulfills the functions of a conclusion (see chap. 12).

The body of the speech should consist of at least three major arguments with supporting materials (evidence) that has been selected because of its appropriateness for your audience. The speech should include oral footnotes and, if appropriate, visual aids (see chap. 13). The speech should be delivered extemporaneously with as much eye contact and as little attention to notes as possible.

Persuasive Speech Document

Write a paper with your name and the title of your persuasive speech on top. Start by stating your ultimate behavioral goal and your immediate behavioral purposes. Then include a manuscript of your persuasive speech with sidenotes to indicate what functions you are fulfilling in the introduction and conclusion, what your main and subpoints are, and what kinds of evidence you are using. The paper should conclude with endnotes or footnotes and a bibliography in proper form.

Summary

This chapter on persuasive speaking began with advice on how to prepare a persuasive speech: how to classify ultimate purposes in behavioral terms as speeches of adoption, discontinuence, deterrence, or continuance; how to find an appropriate topic; and how to write an ultimate goal and immediate behavioral purposes for persuasion. The second section of the chapter examined how an audience may be persuaded through motive appeals (biological, intra-psychic, and social/behavioral motives), source credibility, logical appeals, and emotional appeals. The organization of a persuasive speech dealt with taking into account the placement of arguments and evidence, the number of sides presented to different kinds of audiences, the use of refutation, and the use of familiar and novel arguments. Ethical considerations that should be observed in persuasive speaking included accurate citation of sources, respect for sources of information, respect for the audience, and respect for your opponent.

The third section of this chapter reviewed some special skills for persuasive speaking including argumentation with its propositions, justifications, tests of evidence, and believability; methods of refutation including turning the tables, reducto ad absurdum, post hoc, ergo propter hoc, special pleading, and the red herring. The chapter ended with a specific example of a persuasive speech.

Additional Readings

*Bem, Daryl J. *Beliefs, Attitudes, & Human Affairs.* Belmont, Calif.: Brooks/Cole Publishing Company, 1970.
A thorough discussion of the psychological, social, cognitive, and behavioral bases of attitude formation and maintenance. Information about attitudes is theoretical, but a good foundation is laid for making decisions about designing persuasive strategies and predicting audience response to persuasive messages.

Bettinghaus, Erwin P. *Persuasive Communication.* 3rd ed. New York: Holt, Rinehart and Winston, 1980.
A behaviorally based textbook on persuasion that covers some of the

*Indicates more advanced readings.

current theories of persuasion and many experimental studies in persuasion. Intended for students who have an interest in persuasion beyond the introduction to the subject provided in *Understanding and Sharing.*

————. *The Nature of Proof.* New York: Bobbs-Merrill, 1972.
A good book for students who want to know more about proof, belief, evidence, inference, and strategies. Reading level is slightly more difficult than *Understanding and Sharing.*

Cronkhite, Gary. *Persuasion: Speech and Behavioral Change.* New York: Bobbs-Merrill Co., 1969.
A thorough exploration of persuasive theories, techniques, and effects. Includes discussions of audience analysis, credibility, organization, and language as they relate to persuasive speaking. The classical theories of persuasion are examined.

Ehninger, Douglas. *Influence, Belief, and Argument.* Glenview, Ill.: Scott, Foresman and Company, 1974.
Contains clear and precise definitions of types and uses of evidence as support for persuasive arguments, as well as fallacies of reasoning to avoid. Includes exercises designed to help you apply the concepts to your own speech assignments.

Karlins, Marvin, and Abelson, Herbert I. *Persuasion: How Opinions and Attitudes Are Changed.* New York: Springer Publishing Co., 1970.
A summary of the research on persuasion, with emphasis on the effects of persuasion, the "sleeper

effect," one-sided vs. two-sided messages, and the relation of information to persuasion. Each chapter contains questions that stimulate thinking about the decisions the speaker must make to prepare a successful persuasive message.

Larson, Charles U. *Persuasion: Reception and Responsibility.* Belmont, Calif.: Wadsworth Publishing Co., 1974.
Larson places persuasion into the context of our social structure and cultural environment and finds the psychological roots of persuasion in human needs. He also discusses ways in which a speaker can ethically adapt materials and arguments to meet those needs.

Miller, Gerald R., and Burgoon, Michael. *New Techniques of Persuasion.* New York: Harper & Row, 1973.
A small book heavy with research findings and current thought on persuasion. Covers many ideas untouched in most persuasion textbooks. Written at an advanced level.

Roloff, Michael E., and Miller, Gerald. *Persuasion: New Directions in Theory and Research.* Beverly Hills: Sage Publications, 1980.
This book is an edited work consisting of eleven chapters by various authors many of whom apply persuasion theory and research to persuasion in bargaining, negotiating, and marketing; and in trials, in the family, and in mass communication. This book is not intended for the casual reader.

Notes

1. Based on Gerald R. Miller, "On Being Persuaded: Some Basic Distinctions," in *Persuasion: New Directions in Theory and Research,* edited by Michael E. Roloff and Gerald R. Miller (Beverly Hills: Sage Publications, 1980).

2. Adapted from Wallace Fotheringham, *Perspectives on Persuasion* (Boston: Allyn & Bacon, 1966), p. 33.
3. Based on James V. McConnell, *Understanding Human Behavior: An Introduction to Psychology* (New York:

Holt, Rinehart and Winston, 1977), pp. 243–51.

4. C. Hovland and H. Pritzker, "Extent of Opinion Change as a Function of Amount of Change Advocated," *Journal of Abnormal and Social Psychology* 54(1957): 257–61.

5. Reprinted from Marvin Karlins and Herbert I. Abelson, *Persuasion: How Opinions and Attitudes Are Changed,* 2d ed., p. 35. Copyright 1970 by Springer Publishing Company, New York. Used by permission.

6. I.S. Janis and S. Feshbach, "Effects of Fear-Arousing Communications," *Journal of Abnormal and Social Psychology* 48 (1953): 78–92.

7. Fredric A. Powell, "The Effects of Anxiety-Arousing Messages when Related to Personal, Familial, and Impersonal Referents," *Speech Monographs* 32(1965): 102–6.

8. Frances Cope and Don Richardson, "The Effects of Measuring Recommendations in a Fear-Arousing Speech," *Speech Monographs* 39(1972): 148–50.

9. R. L. Rosnow and E. Robinson, *Experiments in Persuasion* (New York: Academic Press, 1967), pp. 99–104.

10. Karlins and Abelson, pp. 22–26.

11. Karlins and Abelson, pp. 22–26.

12. D. Sears and J. Freedman, "Effects of Expected Familiarity with Arguments upon Opinion Change and Selective Exposure," *Journal of Personality and Social Psychology* 2(1965): 420–26.

13. For additional information on the uses and limits of argument, see Douglas Ehninger, "Argument as Method: Its Nature, Its Limitations, and Its Uses," *Speech Monographs* 37(1970): 101–10.

14. Gerald R. Miller, "Evidence and Argument," in *Perspectives on Argument,* edited by Gerald R. Miller and Thomas R. Nilsen (Chicago: Scott, Foresman, 1966), p. 25. See also, Robert P. Newman and Dale R. Newman, *Evidence* (Boston: Houghton Mifflin Company, 1969).

15. Erwin P. Bettinghaus, *The Nature of Proof,* 2d ed. (New York: Bobbs-Merrill, 1972), p. 135.

16. Bettinghaus, pp. 137–138.

17. Bettinghaus, p. 138.

18. From a persuasive speech delivered by Melanie Comito in the Honors Section of Fundamentals of Public Speaking, Iowa State University. Used with permission.

Topics for Activities

1 The Nature of Communication

Case of Sharon Black	15
Communication Breakdown	20

2 Perception: The Process of Understanding Interpretation

Differences in Perception	42

3 Verbal Codes: A Tool of Sharing

Clichés and Euphemisms	52
Definitions	56
Definitional Differences	58
Helter Skelter	62–64
Paraphrasing	66–67
Concreteness	70

4 Nonverbal Codes: A Tool of Sharing

Nonverbal Meeting	77
Clothes Communicate!	88

5 Understanding Yourself

Kampf Um Dein Leben	103
"Children Learn What They Live"	106
Here I Am Again	114

6 Sharing Yourself

The Risk of Self-Disclosure	130
Applying the Principles	135

7 Understanding Another

Who's Right	147–48
Sources of Interference with Listening	154
Paraphrasing	157

8 The Interview

Types of Questions	168
Guidelines for Answers	170
In-Class Informational	

Interview   173

Persuasive Interview Role-Play   174–75

Employment Interview Preparation   180

9 The Small Group Discussion

Social, Task, or No Small Group at All?   192

Identify the Category of Each of These Questions for Discussion   194

10 Understanding through Topic Selection and Audience Analysis

Brainstorming Exercise   211

Newspaper Inventory   212

Newsmagazine Inventory   212

Captive vs. Voluntary Audiences   218

Speech Topics   222

Ranking Values   225

Attitudinal Scale   229

11 Sharing Yourself: Source Credibility and Credible Sources

Four aspects of source credibility   245

Strategies for Improvement   249

Library Scavenger Hunt   254

12 Sharing Your Message Through Organization

Checklist for Your Introduction   274

13 Sharing Yourself through Delivery and Visual Aids

Selecting a Mode of Delivery   301

Testing Vocal Aspects of Your Delivery   309

Physical Aspects of Delivery   313

Evaluating Your Delivery   319

14 The Informative Speech

Checklist for an Informative Speech   346–47

An Informative Speech Assignment   347

15 The Persuasive Speech

Persuasive Speech Performance   371

abstract
When used as a noun, words or phrases that are not rooted in physical reality. When used as a verb, less than a complete manuscript but includes all important points and supporting materials, e.g., an outline.

action view of communication
The view that communication occurs when one person sends a message to another.

active listening
Involved listening with a purpose.

active participation
Asking the audience to write, reply, or act in a certain way during the speech in order to demonstrate ideas, ascertain audience attitudes, or involve the audience in the topic.

active perception
The view that people select the stimuli they receive.

ad hominem attacks
Irrelevant attacks on a person who supports views different from the speaker's; a tabooed strategy.

adoption
Aimed at inducing an audience to accept a new idea, attitude, belief, or product and to demonstrate that acceptance by behavioral change; an action goal of the persuasive speech.

advance organizers
Previews of the forthcoming content.

affective domain
The way the audience feels about what it knows; the audience's emotions and attitudes about a topic.

analogy
A comparison of unlike things and like things in different classes.

anticlimactic organization
A method of organization in which the speaker presents the best or strongest arguments and evidence early in the speech.

antonym
A word that means the opposite of another.

Glossary

appointed leadership
Leaders who are selected by someone outside the group, elected by the group members, or selected in some formal way.

appropriate self-disclosure
Self-disclosure that is appropriate to oneself, the other person, the topic, and the length and intimacy of the relationship.

arguments
Propositions and proof or evidence used to persuade.

arousal
Initiating and maintaining audience interest, focusing attention on the speaker, stating the specific purpose of the speech, and describing the speaker's qualifications; a function of the introduction.

articulation
The production of sounds; a component of enunciation.

assertiveness
The ability to communicate your feelings, attitudes, and beliefs honestly and directly; a communication skill associated with positive self-concept.

attention
Causing the audience to focus on the speaker and the message.

attitude
A predisposition to respond favorably or unfavorably to some person, object, idea, or event.

audience adaptation
Adjusting the verbal and nonverbal elements of the speech on the basis of data derived from audience analysis.

audience analysis
The collection and interpretation of data on the demographics, attitudes, values, and beliefs of the audience obtained by observation, questionnaires, or interviews.

audience interest
The relevance and importance of the topic to an audience; sometimes related to the uniqueness of the topic.

audience knowledge
The amount of information the audience already has about the topic.

autocratic leadership
Leaders who exert complete control.

Barnlund's "six persons"
Each person involved in a two-person communication has three points of view: a view of herself or himself; a view of the other person; and a view of the other's perception of him or her.

behavioral purposes
Actions a speaker seeks in an audience.

belief
A conviction.

believability
The extent to which an audience accepts evidence.

bibliography
A list of written sources used in a speech.

biological motives
Moving people based on bodily needs such as food, water, air, and temperature.

blind area
The quadrant of the Johari Window that illustrates the proportion of information about oneself that is known to others but not to oneself.

body
Part of the speech that contains the arguments, evidence, and main content of a speech.

boomerang effect
Occurs when the audience's attitudes toward the speaker's position on a topic become more negative during the speech.

brainstorming
Listing or naming as many ideas as a group can in a limited period of time.

brakelight function
A function of a conclusion fulfilled by warning that the end of the speech is near.

captive audience
An audience that did not choose to hear a particular speaker or speech.

cause-effect organization
A method of organization in which the speaker first explains the causes of an event, problem, or issue, and then discusses its consequences.

clarity
To make a message clearly understood by an audience.

classification
The process of ordering stimuli into meaningful groups or classes using language to identify similarities and ignore differences; abstraction.

clichés
Words or phrases that have lost their meaning and effectiveness through overuse.

climactic organization
A method of organization in which the speaker presents the strongest or best arguments and evidence last.

closed question
A question framed so that the possible answers are specified or restricted; an interview question.

closure
The organization of stimuli so that information missing in the original is filled in by the perceiver in order to provide the appearance of a complete unit or whole.

code
Any systematic arrangement or comprehensive collection of symbols, letters, or words that have been given arbitrary meanings and are used for communication.

cognitive change
A change in what an audience knows or understands about the speaker's topic; a purpose of the informative speech.

cohesiveness
The sense of belonging or groupness.

commitment
Individual dedication to a group because of interpersonal attraction, commonality, fulfillment, or reinforcement.

common ground
The experience, ideas, or behavior that the speaker shares with the audience.

communication
Making common; understanding and sharing.

communication apprehension
The generalized fear of communication regardless of context.

communication network
The pattern of communication among members in a small group.

communication situation
The environment and context of a communication, usually defined in terms of the number of people involved and the function of the communication.

comparison
A behavioral goal of the informative speech in which the audience weighs the relative values and characteristics of the speech or its uses of objects, events, or issues.

competence
The degree to which the speaker is perceived as skilled, experienced, qualified, authoritative, and informed; an aspect of credibility.

comprehension
The understanding of the meaning of a message; sometimes tested by retention.

conciliatory remarks
Compliments or commendations that a speaker gives to an audience.

conclusion
The last part of the speech; a summary of the major ideas designed to induce some mental or behavioral change in an audience.

concreteness
Specificity of expression; using words that are not ambiguous or abstract.

connotative meaning
Individualized or personalized meaning; the emotional content of words.

consensus
General agreement among members and their support of the decisions that are made by the group.

content
The evidence, illustrations, proof, arguments, and examples that are used to develop a speech topic.

continuance
Persuading the audience to continue present behavior.

contrast
The comparison of unlike things.

co-orientation
The degree to which the speaker's values, beliefs, attitudes, and interests are shared with the audience.

counterarguments
Rebuttals to an argument.

creative perception
The view that meaning is imparted to stimuli by the perceiver rather than being an inherent property of the thing perceived.

credibility
The audience's perception of a speaker's competence, dynamism, trustworthiness, and co-orientation.

credibility is earned
The view that credibility is not inherent in the speaker, but is perceived by the audience, based on the speaker's life, experiences, and accomplishments.

criteria-application pattern
A method of presenting arguments for a persuasive message in which the speaker establishes criteria that the audience will accept and then shows how the proposition meets the criteria; the pattern asks that the audience be consistent.

critical listeners
Listening in which the receiver attempts to discriminate among the information and ideas that are presented and attempts to make analytical judgments about the validity and usefulness of the message.

cultural differences
The influence on perception of stimuli by the environments and situations imposed by the culture.

cultural role
The pattern of behavior imposed upon a person by the culture of which the person is part.

culture and subculture
Groups or classes of people defined in terms of their heritage, traditions, social structure, and value systems. The meaning assigned to words differs among cultures and subcultures.

dating
A component skill of concreteness; identification and statement when an inference or observation was made.

decode
To assign meaning to a verbal code that we receive.

deductive arguments
Arguments based on major premise, minor premise, and conclusion rather than on evidence.

defensiveness
The act of protecting and supporting our ideas and attitudes against attack by others; induced by the feeling that the self and the validity of self-expression are threatened.

definition
A behavioral goal of the informative speech in which the audience is expected to be able to define a concept of the speech upon its completion.

delayed revelation
The postponement of the statement of purpose until late in the persuasive speech; used especially when the audience is initially opposed to the speaker's purpose.

delivery of a speech
Use of voice and body to communicate a message.

democratic leadership
Leaders who exert a balance of control and freedom.

demographic analysis
Collection and interpretation of data about the characteristics of people, excluding their attitudes and beliefs.

denotative meaning
An agreed-upon meaning of a word or phrase; a formal meaning determined by agreement within a society or culture.

description
A technique for improving or establishing credibility; the speaker objectively describes his or her accomplishments or credentials.

descriptive feedback
Describing to another person his or her nonverbal and verbal behavior; telling the other person your objective understanding of messages that you are receiving.

descriptiveness
The describing of observed behavior or phenomena instead of offering personal reactions or judgments.

deterrence
Persuading the audience to avoid some activity.

Dewey's method of reflective thinking
A sequence of steps for organizing, defining, researching, and solving problems in groups.

discontinuance
Inducing an audience to stop doing something; a behavioral goal of the persuasive speech.

distinguish
The ability of an audience to differentiate the characteristics of events or objects; a behavioral goal of the informative speech.

double bind
The conflict caused by a difference between verbal and nonverbal messages.

dyadic communication
Communication between two persons.

dynamism
The degree to which the speaker is perceived as bold, active, energetic, strong, empathic, and assertive; an aspect of credibility.

egocentrism
The tendency to view oneself as the center of any exchange or activity; an overconcern with the presentation of oneself to others.

emergent leadership
A leader who is not officially elected or chosen, but whom the group identifies as a leader.

emotional appeals
Persuading an audience to change based on some narrative basis.

empathic listening
Listening in which we attempt to perceive the other person's view of the world.

empathy
The ability to perceive another person's view of the world as though the view were your own.

employment interview
An interview for the purpose of screening job applicants or hiring a person.

encode
To put a message or thought into a code.

enunciation
The pronunciation and articulation of sounds and words; a vocal aspect of delivery.

ethics and persuasion
Unwritten or uncodified rules concerning how people persuade.

etymology
The historical origins of a word.

euphemisms
Words or phrases that are considered inoffensive as compared to those that have vulgar or unacceptable connotations, e.g., *washroom* as a substitute for *toilet*.

evaluation
A kind of self-description that does not usually enhance credibility; speakers evaluate their own accomplishments, usually in a complimentary fashion.

evaluative
To be judgmental or unobjective.

evidence
Anything that constitutes proof of a proposition.

example
To illustrate by using a specific instance.

experiential superiority
The attitude that our experiences are more important and valid than the experiences of others.

explanation
To clarify by simplifying or amplifying.

extemporaneous mode
A delivery style; the speech is carefully prepared and researched, but it appears to be spontaneous in its delivery.

extrinsic motivation
A method of making information relevant by providing the audience with reasons outside the speech itself for attending to its content.

eye contact
The way a speaker watches the audience; an aspect of bodily delivery.

facial expression
Use of face to reinforce a message.

fact question
A discussion question that deals with truth and falsity; concerns the occurrence, existence, or particular properties of something.

factual distractions
The tendency to listen to facts rather than main ideas; a barrier to listening.

fear appeals
A strategy of the rhetoric of emotions that attempts to create anxiety in the audience and then offers reassurance that the speaker's ideas will reduce the anxiety.

feedback
The verbal and nonverbal responses to messages that are received and understood by the speaker.

figure and ground
The organization of perception so that some stimuli are brought into focus and the rest become the background.

finale
The last statement made by the speaker; ideally, a clever, insightful, or memorable statement that concludes an informative speech or a visionary, rewarding, or motivating statement that concludes a persuasive speech.

fluency
The smoothness of delivery, the flow of words, and the absence of vocalized pauses; an aspect of vocal delivery.

forecast
An overview of the speech's organization; occurs in the introduction or early in the body of the speech.

forewarning, or preview
A transition that serves to advise the audience of the next main idea.

functions of communication
Survival of self and survival of society.

gestures
The movements of head, arms, and hands to illustrate, emphasize, or signal ideas in the speech; an aspect of bodily delivery.

group
A small number of persons who share common interests or goals, who regularly engage in communication with each other, and who all contribute to the functioning of the group.

hearing
The physiological process by which sound is received by the ear.

hidden agenda
When the underlying goal of the communication is different than the stated goal; the underlying goal is the hidden agenda.

hidden area
The quadrant of the Johari Window that illustrates the proportion of information about oneself that is known to oneself but not to others.

immediate goal
The short-range change the persuasive speaker hopes the audience will adopt.

immediate purpose
The short-range immediate goal that the speaker wishes to achieve.

impromptu mode
A delivery style; the speech is delivered without notes and without preparation.

indexing
A component of concreteness; identifying the uniqueness of objects, events, and people and stating that one's observations and inferences are specific rather than generalizable.

indirect sequencing
A method of organization in which the speaker first states the grounds for an argument or conclusion and then states the generalization or conclusion based on that information.

inferences
Conclusions drawn from observation.

inferential method
A method of audience analysis in which inferences or tentative conclusions are drawn about an audience on the basis of partial or incomplete information.

inflection
The patterns of alteration, or lack of alteration, in the pitch of a person's voice.

informational interview
An interview for the purpose of collecting information, opinions, or data about a specific topic.

informational overload
Occurs when the quantity of information presented is greater than the audience can assimilate within the given time.

information hunger
The audience's need for the information contained in the speech.

information relevance
The importance, novelty, and usefulness of the topic and the information; a factor in adapting an informative speech to an audience.

informative persuasion continuum
The degree to which a message is informative or persuasive.

informative speaking
A speech whose purpose is to get an audience to understand, learn, or change its behavior.

inherent meaning
The view that meaning is inherent in stimuli; hence, that perception is passive.

interactional view of communication
The view that communication occurs when communicators take turns encoding and decoding messages.

interest
A function of an introduction that enhances the audience's concentration on the subject matter.

interpersonal communication
The process of sharing and understanding between oneself and at least one other person.

interpretation
The assignment of meaning to stimuli.

interviewing
Communication, usually between two persons, involving the asking and answering of questions for a predetermined purpose.

intimate distance
Extends from touch to eighteen inches, the distance used with persons to whom we are emotionally close.

intimate self-disclosure
Disclosure of information that is highly personal and risky.

intrapersonal communication
The process of sharing and understanding within oneself.

intrapsychic motives
Behavior that is best explained by emotion, feelings, and perceptions rather than drives such as people who eat when they are not hungry.

introduction
The first part of the speech; its function is to arouse the audience and lead into the main ideas presented in the body.

involvement
The importance of the topic to the speaker; determined by the strength of the feelings the speaker has about the topic and the time and energy the speaker devotes to that subject area or topic.

Johari Window
A model of self-disclosure that indicates the proportion of information about oneself that is known and unknown to oneself, others, and both.

journal
A daily or periodic record of personal experience and impressions.

justification
All of the evidence that can be gathered in support of a proposition.

key-word outline
An outline consisting of important words or phrases to remind the speaker of the speech's content.

kinesics
The study of bodily movements, including posture, gestures, and facial expressions.

laissez-faire leadership
Leaders who exert minimal control on a group.

language distortion
The use of ambiguous or misleading language for the purpose of confusing others.

leader
Anyone who acts as a leader or is selected or designated the leader of a particular group.

leadership
Any behavior that helps to clarify or achieve a group's goals; influence.

leading question
A question that suggests the answer; a question worded so that there is only one acceptable answer.

limiting the topic
The process of reducing a general topic to a less abstract and more concrete topic.

listenability
The degree to which sounds and meaning can be easily ascertained by listeners; closely related to comprehension.

listening
The selective process of receiving and interpreting sounds.

logical appeals
Use of propositions and proofs to persuade an audience.

main points, subpoints, sub-subpoints
Statements listed in decreasing order of importance.

manipulation
A controlled, planned communication for the purpose of influencing or controlling the behavior of others.

manuscript mode
A delivery style; the speech is written and is read verbatim.

Maslow's hierarchy of needs
A ranking order of physical, safety, social, self-esteem, and self-actualization needs. Maslow states that lower-order needs must be satisfied before higher-order needs.

mean, or average
The arithmetic sum of a series of numbers divided by the total number of items in the series.

meaning
What we share and understand in the process of communication; that which is felt to be the significance of something. A more accurate and useful descriptor of the object of communication than *message* or *thought*.

memorized mode
A delivery style; the speech is committed to memory either by rote or repeated delivery.

mental distraction
Communicating with ourselves while we are engaged in communication with others; a barrier to listening.

message
A unit containing verbal and nonverbal symbols, but in which meaning is not inherent.

mode
The most frequently recurring number in a series of numbers.

modes of delivery
Four styles of delivery that vary in the amount of preparation required and their degree of spontaneity.

motivation
The inclination to do something.

movement
The speaker's use of the entire body; an aspect of physical delivery.

negative self-disclosure
Disclosure of information about oneself that tends to decrease our esteem in the eyes of others.

neutrality
Indifference to another person.

neutral question
A question that does not suggest any particular or preferred response or direction.

noise
Any interference in the encoding and decoding processes that lessens the fidelity of the message.

nonfluency
Delivery characteristics, usually vocal, that break the smooth and fluid delivery of the speech and are judged negatively by the audience.

nonverbal code
A code that consists of any symbols that are not words, including nonword vocalizations.

norms
Unwritten rules of acceptable and unacceptable behavior in a group.

novel arguments
New and original evidence or reasoning that the audience has seldom or never heard; often has more impact than the repetition of familiar arguments.

objectics
The study of the human use of artifacts as cues; object language.

objective perception
The view that the perceiver is a non-evaluative recorder of stimuli.

observation
Active observation of the behavior and characteristics of an audience.

obstacles
The characteristics of the speaker, audience, topic, situation, or content of a speech that are likely to hamper the effectiveness of the presentation.

one-sided message
Presentation of the arguments and evidence that support only the speaker's position on a persuasive topic; used when the audience is generally friendly, when the audience will hear only the speaker's position, or when the speaker is seeking immediate but temporary opinion change.

open area
The quadrant of the Johari Window that illustrates the proportion of information about oneself that is known to oneself and others.

open question
A question that is broad in nature, generally unstructured in form, and that requires a rather lengthy response.

operational definition
An explanation of the meaning of words by describing the behavior, actions, or property that words signify.

organization
The structuring of stimuli into meaningful units or wholes. As a form, the outline, structure, or design of a speech. As a function, the functions of the parts of the speech; how organization governs content.

organizational patterns
Methods of arranging the contents of the speech, e.g., problem-solution pattern.

outlining symbols
Roman numerals, Arabic capital letters and numerals to indicate subordination.

overt audience response
The involvement of an audience with a topic through signalling or actual performance of a task.

paralanguage
The vocal or physical aspects of delivery that accompany the language used.

parallel form
The consistent use of complete sentences, clauses, phrases, or words in an outline.

paraphrasing
Restating the other person's message by rephrasing the content or intent of the message.

passive participation
The nonbehavioral involvement of the audience in a persuasive speech; cognitive change.

passive perception
The view that perceivers are mere recorders of stimuli.

pause
The absence of vocal sound used for dramatic effect, transition, or emphasis of ideas; an aspect of vocal delivery.

percentage
The ratio or fraction of 100 represented by a specific number; obtained by dividing the number by 100.

perception
What a person sees, hears, smells, feels, or tastes; the process by which one comes to understand.

perceptual constancy
The invariable nature of the perception of a stimulus once it has been selected, organized, and interpreted by the perceiver.

permissive leadership
Leaders who exert slight control.

personal distance
Extends from eighteen inches to four feet; the distance used most often in ordinary conversation.

personal inventory
A speaker's survey of his or her reading habits and behavior to discover what topics and subjects are of interest.

personal language
The language of the individual, which varies slightly from the agreed-upon meanings because of past experience and present condition. The meaning of words is personal and changeable.

personal space
The space between one person and another; the space a person controls and that moves with the person.

persuasive interview
An interview for the purpose of selling a particular idea, product, or service.

persuasive speaking
A form of communication in which the speaker attempts to modify the audience's behavior by changing its perceptions, attitudes, beliefs, or values.

persuasive strategies
Means for achieving the goals of a persuasive speech.

physical distraction
Environmental stimuli that interfere with our focus on another person's message; a barrier to listening.

pitch
The highness or lowness of a speaker's voice; technically, the frequency of sound made by the vocal cords.

policy question
A type of discussion question that concerns future action.

positive self-disclosure
The expression of information about oneself that tends to increase our esteem in the eyes of others.

post hoc, ergo propter hoc
Confusing causation with correlation.

primary needs
Physiological needs for food, water, air, and temperature.

primary question
A question asked in an interview to introduce a new topic or a new area of a topic under discussion.

primary research
Firsthand research; the acquisition of information from personal experience, interviews, surveys, questionnaires, or experiment.

principle of division
In outlining, the content must be divisible into at least two parallel parts.

principle of parallel construction
In outlining, the verbal forms of the main heads, subheads, main points, and subpoints should be consistent and similar.

principle of subordination
In outlining, the main headings, subheadings, main points, and subpoints should be distinguished from each other so the speaker can convey to the audience which items are of greater or lesser importance.

problem-and-solution pattern
A method of organization in which the speaker describes a problem and proposes a solution to that problem.

problem-solving discussion
A discussion in which the nature and solution of a problem are determined.

process
Action, change, exchange, and movement.

projection
The body's support of the voice that ensures that the most distant people in the room can hear what is said.

pronunciation
The conformance of the speaker's production of words with agreed-upon rules about the sounds of vowels and consonants, and for syllabic emphasis.

proof
Evidence offered in support of a proposition.

proposition
A statement that asserts or proposes something.

proxemics
The study of the human use of space and distance.

proximity
The organization of stimuli into meaningful units or wholes according to their perceived physical or psychological distance from each other.

public communication
The process of sharing and understanding between oneself and a large number of other people.

public distance
Exceeds twelve feet; the distance used in public speaking situations.

purpose
Stating what the speaker expects the audience to learn or do as a result of the speech.

qualifications
The speaker's experience, education, or expertise on the topic.

quality
The pleasant or unpleasant characteristics of a person's voice, including nasality, raspiness, and whininess; the timbre of the sounds produced by the vocal cords.

questionnaire
A method of obtaining information about an audience by asking written questions about its members' demographic characteristics or attitudes.

range
The highest and lowest numbers in a distribution.

rate
The speed of delivery, normally between 125 and 190 words per minute.

raw numbers
Exact numbers cited in measures of population, production, and other measures of quantity.

reassurance
Permitting an audience a means of avoiding the consequences of a fear appeal.

recognition
The ability of an audience to identify the presence or absence of characteristics, properties, or elements of objects and events; a behavioral goal of the informative speech.

red herring
An irrelevancy introduced to distract from the main issue.

reducto ad absurdum
Reducing an argument to a ridiculous extreme.

redundancy
Planned repetition of words, phrases, or ideas.

refutation
The art of opposing the arguments presented by another.

reliability
The credibility of the source of specific information or evidence.

repetition
A restatement of the persuasive appeal after its initial presentation.

review and inspiration
The indication that the speech is near its conclusion by language, tone, nonverbal behavior, and summary and motivational statements.

review of exposition
A review of the main points of the speech that helps the audience focus on the overall purpose and content of the speech.

rhetorical questions
Questions asked by the speaker to stimulate an audience's thinking, but to which no overt response is expected.

rhetoric of emotion
A speaker's appeals to the feelings and emotions of the audience in order to gain support for his ideas; a persuasive strategy.

rhetoric of reason
A speaker's attempts to prove by reasoning, logic, and consistency that a proposition is acceptable to the audience; a persuasive strategy.

rhetoric of refutation
A speaker's attempts to gain support for a proposition or idea by attacking or discrediting another person's evidence, logic, or credibility; a persuasive strategy.

role
Behavior expected by others because of the social category in which a person is placed.

sample
The people who received a questionnaire or were interviewed; a large sample is usually more useful, generalizable, and valid than a small sample.

Sapir-Whorf hypothesis
The theory that our perception of reality is determined by our thought processes and that our thoughts are limited by our language; language shapes our perception of reality.

secondary drives
Fulfilling learned or acculturated needs such as fulfilling the need for food by eating steak.

secondary needs
Learned or acculturated needs such as the need for money, love, and power.

secondary question
A question asked in an interview to follow up or develop a primary question.

secondary research
Second-hand research; the acquisition of information from published sources.

selection
Neglecting some stimuli to focus on other stimuli.

selective attention
A focus on particular stimuli so that other stimuli are ignored.

selective exposure
The perception of stimuli that we want to perceive and the ignoring of stimuli we do not want to perceive.

selective retention
The recollection of information after selection, organization, and interpretation have occurred; the mental categorization, storage, and retrieval of selected information.

self-awareness
The ability to consciously distinguish between one's self-image and one's self-esteem.

self-concept
A person's consciousness of his or her total, essential, and particular being; self-image and self-esteem.

self-consciousness
An excessive concern about self-esteem.

self-control
Our manipulative, strategic, and analytical responses to the demands and expectations of others and situations; unspontaneous self-expression.

self-disclosure
Intentional statements about oneself that impart information that the other person is unlikely to have.

self-esteem
Our attitudes and feelings toward our self-image; how well we like ourselves.

self-expression
Our open, genuine, and spontaneous response to people and situations.

self-focus
Developing a view of oneself from one's own perspective rather than through the eyes of others.

self-fulfilling prophecy
The self-image and self-esteem expected of one by others; the tendency to become what others expect us to become.

self-image
The sort of person we think we are; our own description of who we are and what we do.

self-improvement
The strengthening of the awareness of self; the development of clear goals for oneself; the development of self-esteem and self-expression.

self-praise
An evaluative, self-serving method of conveying the credentials of the speaker to an audience.

semantic distraction
Bits or units of information in the message that interfere with understanding the main ideas or total meaning of the entire message; a barrier to listening.

sentence outline
An outline consisting entirely of complete sentences.

sharing
Interaction between oneself and others, with the purpose of exchanging meaning.

significance
The relative importance of a topic or message.

similarity
A basis for organizing stimuli into meaningful units by perceiving the similarities among them.

sleeper effect
An increase in changes of opinion created by a speaker with little credibility; caused by the later separation of the content of the message from its source.

small
The number of persons in a group discussion; generally between three and twenty, more often between four and seven.

small group discussion
A discussion in a group of approximately three to twenty persons who share common interests or goals, who regularly engage in communication with each other, and who all contribute to the functioning of the group.

social-behavioral motives
Satisfying what others want us to do or behaving how others want us to behave.

social distance
Extends from four feet to twelve feet; the distance used by people conducting business.

social function
The function of a small group that meets the needs of the members to belong to something, to share pleasant companionship, and to satisfy interpersonal needs.

source credibility
The degree to which an audience perceives a speaker as credible; based on perceived competence, trustworthiness, dynamism, and co-orientation.

spatial organization
A method of organization in which the speaker explains where the parts of a problem exist in space.

special pleading
Blissfully ignoring contrary evidence.

speech delivery
The behavior of the speaker; the manner in which the verbal content of a message is enhanced or diminished by nonverbal vocal and physical behavior.

spontaneity
A voluntary, genuine reaction to feelings and ideas; nonmanipulative self-expression.

statement
The ability of an audience to verbally list the major ideas, reasons, or propositions of the speech; a behavioral goal of the informative speech.

statement of purpose
A statement in which the speaker tells the audience what he or she wants the audience to do, learn, or understand.

statistics
Numbers that summarize numerical information or compare quantities.

status
The relative social position, reputation, or importance of another person.

status quo
The way things currently are.

stereotypes
Categories into which we place other people.

stereotyping
The process of placing people and things into categories or of basing judgments about them on the categories into which they fit rather than on their individual characteristics.

strength of belief
The stability and importance of a belief held by the audience; can be inferred from the responses of its members to an attitudinal scale.

subcultural differences
The influence on perception and behavior of membership in a subgroup of a culture.

subjective perception
The view that perception is based on the physiological and psychological characteristics of the perceiver.

subordinate
A point that is less important than another point in an outline.

supervisory leadership
Leaders who exert considerable control with minimal freedom.

surveys and studies
Evidence consisting of questionnaires, experimental findings, and interviews.

symbol
Something that stands for, or represents, something else by association, resemblance, or convention.

sympathy
A response to a situation that is the same as another person's.

synonym
A word that means approximately the same as another.

tactile communication
Communicating by touch.

task function
A function of a small group that exists to share information or solve important and difficult problems.

territoriality
The need to establish and maintain certain space as one's own; the control of space that is typically unmovable and separate from the person.

testimonial evidence
Written or oral statements of the experience of people other than the speaker.

tests of evidence
The methods for evaluating information based on the qualifications of the source,

the recency of the information, the completeness and accuracy of the information, and the generalizability of the evidence.

thought
The cognitive process by which meaning is assigned to our perceptions.

time-sequence pattern
A method of organization in which the speaker explains a sequence of events.

topical-sequence pattern
A method of organization in which the speaker emphasizes the major reasons why an audience should accept a certain point of view.

transactional view of communication
The view that communication is the simultaneous encoding and decoding of messages by more than one person.

transitions
Linkages between sections of the speech that help the speaker move smoothly from one idea to another. Principal transitions are forecasts, internal summaries, and statements of relationship.

trustworthiness
The degree to which the speaker is perceived as honest, fair, sincere, honorable, friendly, and kind; an aspect of credibility.

turning the tables
The same evidence used in support of a proposition is used by the opposition to attack it.

ultimate goal
The long-range effect that the speaker hopes to have on the audience.

understanding
The perception and comprehension of the meaning of incoming stimuli, usually the verbal and nonverbal behavior of others.

unevaluative
To be objective or descriptive.

unknown area
The quadrant of the Johari Window that illustrates the proportion of information about oneself that is unknown to oneself and others.

valid
Deductive argument that follows the rules for arranging the terms.

value question
A type of discussion question that requires a judgment of good and bad.

values
Deeply rooted beliefs that govern our attitudes; goals rather than the means of reaching them.

verbal
Anything associated with or pertaining to words.

verbal codes
A code that consists of words.

visual aids
Any item that can be seen by an audience, for the purpose of reinforcing a message.

vocal cues
All the oral aspects of sound, excluding the words that we speak; part of paralanguage.

vocalized pauses
Breaks in fluency; the use of meaningless words or sounds to fill in silences.

vocal variety
Vocal quality, intonation patterns, inflections of pitch, and syllabic duration; a lack of sameness or repetitious patterns in vocal delivery; an aspect of vocal delivery.

volume
The loudness or softness of a person's voice.

voluntary audience
A collection of people who choose to listen to a particular speaker or speech.

words
Verbal symbols by which we codify and share our perceptions of reality.

Bibliography

Addis, B. R. "The Relationship of Physical Interpersonal Distance to Sex, Race, and Age." Master's thesis, University of Oklahoma, 1966.

Adler, Ronald B. *Confidence in Communication: A Guide to Assertive and Social Skills.* New York: Holt, Rinehart & Winston, 1977.

Adler, Ronald, and Towne, Neil. *Looking Out/Looking In.* San Francisco: Rinehart Press, 1975.

Aiken, L. R. "The Relationship of Dress to Selected Measures of Personality in Undergraduate Women." *Journal of Social Psychology,* S9 (1963):119–28.

Allport, Gordon W. *The Nature of Prejudice.* Garden City, N.Y.: Doubleday & Co., 1958.

Andersen, Kenneth, and Clevenger, Theodore, Jr. "A Summary of Experimental Research in Ethos." *Speech Monographs* 30 (1963):59–78.

Anderson, Jane. "Discover Yourself: Go Hiking Alone." Fort Wayne *Journal-Gazette,* March 21, 1976.

Argyle, Michael. *Social Interaction.* New York: Atherton Press, 1969.

Argyle, Michael, and Dean, Janet. "Eye-Contact, Distance, and Affiliation." *Sociometry* 28 (1965):289–304.

Aristotle. *Rhetoric.* Translated by W. Rhys Roberts. In *The Basic Works of Aristotle,* edited by Richard McKeon. New York: Random House, 1941.

Ausubel, David. "The Use of Advance Organizers in the Learning and Retention of Meaningful Material." *Journal of Educational Psychology* 51 (1960):267–72.

Baird, John A. "The Effects of Speech Summaries upon Audience Comprehension of Expository Speeches of Varying Quality and Complexity." *Central States Speech Journal* 25 (1974):119–27.

Banker, Larry L. *Listening Behavior.* Englewood Cliffs, N.J.: Prentice-Hall, 1971.

Barbara, D. "On Listening—The Role of the Ear in Psychic Life." *Today's Speech* 5(1957):12.

Barbour, John. "Edwin Newman Talks to Himself, but for a Good Reason." *Des Moines Sunday Register,* June 5, 1977.

Barnlund, Dean C. "Toward a Meaning Centered Philosophy of Communication." *Journal of Communication* 12(1962):198–202.

———. *"A Transactional Model of Communication."* In *Foundations of Communication Theory,* edited by Kenneth K. Sereno and C. David Mortensen. New York: Harper & Row, Publishers, 1970, pp. 98–101.

Bateson, Gregory; Jackson, D. D.: Haley, J.; and Weakland, J. H. "Toward a Theory of Schizophrenia." *Behavioral Science* 1 (1956):251–64.

Beach, Dale S. *Personnel: The Management of People at Work.* 3d ed. New York: Macmillan Publishing Co., 1975.

Becker, Samuel L. "New Approaches to Audience Analysis." In *Perspectives on Communication,* edited by Carl E. Larson and Frank E. X. Dance. Shorewood, Wis.: Helix Press, 1970.

Beebe, Steven A. "Eye Contact: A Nonverbal Determinant of Speaker Credibility." *Speech Teacher* 23 (1974):21–25.

Beighley, Kenneth C. "An Experimental Study of the Effect of Three Speech Variables on Listener Comprehension." *Speech Monographs* 21 (1954):248–53.

———. "An Experimental Study of the Effect of Four Speech Variables on Listener Comprehension." *Speech Monographs* 19 (1952):249–58.

Bem, Daryl J. *Beliefs, Attitudes and Human Affairs.* Belmont, Calif.: Brooks/Cole Publishing Co., 1970.

Berlo, David K. *The Process of Communication.* New York: Holt, Rinehart & Winston, 1960.

Bettinghaus, Erwin P. *The Nature of Proof.* New York: Bobbs-Merrill Co., 1972.

———. "The Operation of Congruity in an Oral Communication Situation." *Speech Monographs* 28(1961):131–42.

———. *Persuasive Communication.* 3d ed. New York: Holt, Rinehart & Winston, 1980.

Bird, D. "Teaching Listening Comprehension." *Journal of Communication* 3(1953):127–30.

———. "Have You Tried Listening?" *Journal of the American Dietetic Association* 30(1954):225–30.

Birdwhistell, Ray L. *Kinesics and Contexts.* Philadelphia: University of Pennsylvania Press, 1970.

Black, John W. "A Study of Voice Merit." *Quarterly Journal of Speech* 28(1942):67–74.

Black, John W., and Moore, Wilbur E. *Speech: Code, Meaning, and Communication.* New York: McGraw-Hill Book Company, 1955.

Blau, P. M. *Exchange and Power in Social Life.* New York: John Wiley & Sons, 1964.

Bochner, Arthur P., and Kelley, Clifford W. "Interpersonal Competence: Rationale, Philosophy, and Implementation of a Conceptual Framework." *Speech Teacher* 23(1974):279–301.

Bormann, Ernest G., and Bormann, Nancy C. *Effective Small Group Communication.* 2d ed. Minneapolis: Burgess Publishing Company, 1976.

Bowlby, John. *Maternal Care and Mental Health.* Geneva: World Health Organization, 1951.

Bradley, Bert. *Speech Performance.* Dubuque, Iowa: Wm. C. Brown Company Publishers, 1967.

Brigance, William N. "How Fast Do We Talk?" *Quarterly Journal of Speech* 12(1926):337–42.

Brilhart, John K. *Effective Group Discussion.* 3d ed. Dubuque, Iowa: Wm. C. Brown Company Publishers, 1978.

Brooks, Wm. D., and Emmert, Philip. *Interpersonal Communication.* 2d ed. Dubuque, Iowa: Wm. C. Brown Company Publishers, 1980.

Brown, Charles T., and Van Piper, Charles. *Speech and Man.* Englewood Cliffs, N.J.: Prentice-Hall, 1966.

Brown, James I. "The Objective Measurement of Listening Ability." *Journal of Communication* 1 (May 1951):44–48.

Bruskin Report. "What Are Americans Afraid Of?" Vol. 53. 1973.

Buchalo, Jack. "The Balanced Approach to Successful Screening Interviews." *Personnel Journal* 57 (August 1978):420–28.

Burgoon, Judee K., and Saine, Thomas. *The Unspoken Dialogue: An Introduction to Nonverbal Communication.* Boston: Houghton Mifflin Company, 1978.

Burke, Kenneth. *Permanence and Change.* Los Altos, Calif.: Hermes Publications, 1954.

Carney, Clarke G., and McMahon, Sarah L. *Exploring Contemporary Male/Female Roles.* La Jolla, Calif.: University Associates, 1977.

Carroll, Lewis. *Alice's Adventures in Wonderland.* New York: Random House, 1965.

————. *Through the Looking Glass.* New York: Random House, 1965.

Cathcart, Robert S., and Samovar, Larry A. *Small Group Communication: A Reader.* 3d ed. Dubuque, Iowa: Wm. C. Brown Company Publishers, 1978.

Chaikin, A. L., and Derlega, V. J. "Variables Affecting the Appropriateness of Self-Disclosure." *Journal of Consulting and Clinical Psychology* 42(1974):588–93.

Chelune, G. J. "Nature and Assessment of Self-Disclosing Behavior." In *Advances in Psychological Assessment,* edited by P. W. McReynolds. San Francisco: Jossey Bass, 1978.

Clay, V. S. "The Effect of Culture on Mother-Child Tactile Communication." *Family Coordinator* 17(1968):204–10.

Clevenger, Theodore, Jr. *Audience Analysis.* Indianapolis: Bobbs-Merrill Co., 1966.

Cobin, Martin. "Response to Eye-Contact." *Quarterly Journal of Speech* 48 (1962):415–18.

Cofer, N. C. *Verbal Learning and Verbal Behavior.* New York: McGraw-Hill Book Company, 1961.

Coffina, Richard M. "Management Recruitment Is a Two-Way Street." *Personnel Journal* 58(February 1979):86.

Cope, Frances, and Richardson, Don. "The Effects of Measuring Recommendations in a Fear-Arousing Speech." *Speech Monographs* 39 (1972):148–50.

Coramae, Thomas, and Howard, C. Jeriel. *Contact: A Textbook in Applied Communications.* Englewood Cliffs, N.J.: Prentice-Hall, 1970.

Cozby, P. C. "Self-Disclosure, Reciprocity, and Liking." *Sociometry* 35 (1972):151–60.

————. "Self-Disclosure: A Literature Review." *Psychological Bulletin* 79 (1973):73–91.

Cronkhite, Gary. *Persuasion: Speech and Behavioral Change.* Indianapolis: Bobbs-Merrill Co., 1969.

Culbert, S. A. "Trainer Self-Disclosure and Member Growth in Two T-Groups." *Journal of Applied Behavioral Science* 4(1968):47–73.

Dance, Frank E. X., and Larson, Carl E. *The Functions of Human Communication: A Theoretical Approach.* New York: Holt, Rinehart & Winston, 1976.

Danner, Jack. *People-Empathy: Key to Painless Supervision.* New York: Parker Publishing Company, 1976.

Davis, James H. *Group Performance.* Reading, Mass.: Addison-Wesley Publishing Co., 1969.

Desper, J. L. "Emotional Aspects of Speech and Language Development." *International Journal of Psychiatry and Neurology* 105(1941):193–222.

De Vito, Joseph A.; Giattino, Jill; and Schon, T. D. *Articulation and Voice: Effective Communication.* Indianapolis: Bobbs-Merrill Co., 1975.

Diehl, Charles F.; White, Richard C.; and Burk, Kenneth W. "Rate and Communication." *Speech Monographs* 26(1959):229–32.

Dohrenwend, Barbara Shell; Klein, David; and Richardson, Stephen A. *Interviewing: Its Forms and Functions.* New York: Basic Books, 1965.

Donty, H. I. "Influence of Clothing on Perception of Persons." *Journal of Home Economics* 55(1963):197–202.

Duker, S. *Listening Bibliography.* New York: Scarecrow Press, 1964.

————. *Listening Bibliography.* New York: Scarecrow Press, 1966.

Eakins, Barbara Westbrook, and Eakins, R. Gene. *Sex Differences in Human Communication.* Boston: Houghton Mifflin Company, 1978.

Edwards, David C. *General Psychology.* 3d ed. New York: Macmillan, 1980.

Edwards, Myles T.; Hollander, Edwin P.; and Fallon, Barry J. "Some Aspects of Influence and Acceptability for Appointed and Elected Group Leaders." *Journal of Psychology* 19(1977):289–96.

Egan, Gerard. *Interpersonal Living: A Skills/Contract Approach to Human Relations Training in Groups.* Belmont, Calif.: Wadsworth Publishing Co., 1976.

Ehninger, Douglas. "Argument as Method: Its Nature, Its Limitations, and Its Uses." *Speech Monographs* 37(1970):101–10.

————. *Influence, Belief, and Argument.* Glenview, Ill.: Scott, Foresman & Company, 1974.

Eirlich, H , and Graeven, D. "Reciprocal Self-Disclosure in a Dyad." *Journal of Experimental Social Psychology* 7(1971):389–400.

Ekman, Paul, and Friesen, Wallace V. "Head and Body Cues in the Judgment of Emotion: A Reformulation." *Perceptual and Motor Skills* 24(1967):711–24.

————. "The Repertoire of Nonverbal Behavior: Categories, Origins, Usages, and Coding." *Semiotica* 1(1969):49–98.

————. *Unmasking the Face: A Guide to Recognizing Emotions from Facial Cues.* Englewood Cliffs, N.J.: Prentice-Hall, 1975.

Ernest, Carole. "Listening Comprehension as a Function of Type of Material and Rate of Presentation." *Speech Monographs* 35 (1968):154–58.

Fairbanks, Grant; Guttman, Newman; and Murray, Miron S. "Effects of Time Compression upon the Comprehension of Connected Speech." *Journal of Speech and Hearing Disorders* 22(1957):10–19.

Fear, Richard A. *The Evaluation Interview.* New York: McGraw-Hill Book Company, 1978.

Fisher, B. Aubrey. *Small Group Decision Making: Communication and the Group Process.* 2d ed. New York: McGraw-Hill Book Company, 1980.

Fothergill, Robert A. *Private Chronicles: A Study of English Dianes.* London: Oxford University Press, 1974.

Fotheringham, Wallace. *Perspectives on Persuasion.* Boston: Allyn & Bacon, 1966.

Fraser, Alistair B. "Fata Morgana— The Grand Illusion." *Psychology Today* 9(January 1976):22.

Fromm, Eric. *The Art of Loving.* New York: Harper & Row, Publishers, 1956.

Galassi, John P., and Galassi, Merna D. "Preparing Individuals for Job Interviews." *Personnel and Guidance Journal* 57(December 1958):188–91.

Gatewood, Robert D., and Ledvinka, James. "Selection Interviewing and the EEOC: Mandate for Objectivity." *Personnel Administrator* 24(December 1979):51–54.

Gergen, Kenneth J. *The Concept of Self.* New York: Holt, Rinehart & Winston, 1971.

Gilbert, Shirley J., and Whiteneck, Gale G. "Toward A Multidimensional Approach to the Study of Self-Disclosure." *Human Communication Research* 4(1976):347–55.

Gilkinson, Howard, and Knower, Franklin H. "Individual Differences Among Students of Speech as Revealed by Psychological Tests—I." *Journal of Educational Psychology* 32(1941):161–75.

Glasgow, George M. "A Semantic Index of Vocal Pitch." *Speech Monographs* 19(1952):64–68.

Goffman, Erving. *The Presentation of Self in Everyday Life.* Garden City, N.Y.: Doubleday & Co., 1959.

Goldberg, S., and Lewis M. "Play Behavior in the Year Old Infant: Early Sex Differences." *Child Development* 40(1969):21–31.

Gordon, Chad, and Gergen, Kenneth J. *The Self in Social Interaction.* New York: John Wiley & Sons, 1968.

Gordon, Raymond L. *Interviewing Strategy, Techniques, Tactics.* Homewood, Ill.: The Dorsey Press, 1969.

Gruner, Charles R. "The Effect of Humor in Dull and Interesting Informative Speeches." *Central States Speech Journal* 21(1970):160–66.

Guardo, Carol J. "Personal Space in Children." *Child Development* 40(1969):143–51.

Gundersen, D. F., and Hopper, Robert. "Relationships between Speech Delivery and Speech Effectiveness." *Speech Monographs* 43(1976):158–65.

Haas, Kenneth B., and Parker, Harry L. *Preparation and Use of Audiovisual Aids.* New York: Prentice-Hall, 1955.

Hall, Edward T. *The Hidden Dimension.* New York: Doubleday, 1966.

————. *The Silent Language.* Greenwich, Conn.: Fawcett Publications, 1959.

————. "Proxemics—The Study of Man's Spatial Relations and Boundaries." *Man's Image in Medicine and Anthropology.* New York: International Universities Press, 1963.

Hamid, P. N. "Some Effects of Dress Cues on Observations, Accuracy, Perceptual Estimate, and Impression Formation." *Journal of Social Psychology* 86(1972):279–89.

Haney, William V. *Communication and Organizational Behavior.* Homewood, Ill.: Richard D. Irwin, 1967.

Hard, Roland J., and Brown, Bruce L. "Interpersonal Information Conveyed by the Content and Vocal Aspects of Speech." *Speech Monographs* 41(1974):371–80.

Harms, L. S. "Listener Judgments of Status Cues in Speech." *Quarterly Journal of Speech* 47(1961):164–69.

Hart, Roderick P.; Friedrich, Gustav W.; and Brooks, William. *Public Communication.* New York: Harper & Row, Publishers, 1975.

Harwood, Kenneth A. "Listenability and Rate of Presentation." *Speech Monographs* 22(1955):57–59.

Hastorf, Albert H.; Schneider, David J.; and Polefka, Judith. *Person Perception.* Reading, Mass.: Addison-Wesley Publishing Co., 1970.

Hayakawa, S. I. *Language in Thought and Action.* 3d ed. New York: Harcourt Brace Jovanovich, 1972.

Hayworth, Donald. "A Search for Facts on the Teaching of Public Speaking." *Quarterly Journal of Speech* 28(1942):247–354.

Heath, Robert L. "Variability in Value System Priorities as Decision-Making Adaptation to Situational Differences." *Communication Monographs* 43(1976):325–33.

Hebyallah, Isbrabim M., and Maloney, W. Paul. "Content Analysis of T.V. Commercials," *International Journal of Instructional Media* 5(1977–1978):9–16.

Hellman, Connie S. "An Investigation of the Communication Behavior of Emergent and Appointed Leaders in Small Group Discussion." Ph.D. dissertation, Indiana University, 1974.

Henley, Nancy M. *Body Politics: Power, Sex, and Nonverbal Communication.* Englewood Cliffs, N.J.: Prentice-Hall, 1977.

―――. "Power, Sex, and Nonverbal Communication." *Berkeley Journal of Sociology* 18(1973):10–11.

Henricks, S. H.; Kelley, E. A.; and Eicher, J. B. "Senior Girls' Appearance and Social Acceptance." *Journal of Home Economics* 60(1968):167–72.

Henrikson, Ernest H. "An Analysis of the Characteristics of Some 'Good' and 'Poor' Speakers." *Speech Monographs* 11(1944):120–24.

Hertzler, Joyce O. *A Sociology of Language.* New York: Random House, 1965.

Hildebrandt, Herbert W., and Stevens, Walter. "Manuscript and Extemporaneous Delivery in Communicating Information." *Speech Monographs* 30 (1963):369–72.

Holmes, Oliver Wendell. *The Autocrat of the Breakfast Table.* Boston: Phillips, Simpson & Co., 1858.

Holtzman, Paul D. *The Psychology of Speaker's Audiences.* Glenview, Ill.: Scott, Foresman & Company, 1970.

Horrocks, John E., and Jackson, Dorothy W. *Self and Role: A Theory of Self-Process and Role Behavior.* Boston: Houghton Mifflin Company, 1972.

Hopkins, John T. "The Top Twelve Questions for Employment Agency Interviews." *Personnel Journal* 59(May 1980):209–13.

Hovland, Carl I.; Janis, Irving J.; and Kelly, Harold H. "Credibility of the Communicator." In *Dimensions in Communication: Readings,* edited by James H. Campbell and Hal W. Hepler. Belmont, Calif.: Wadsworth Publishing Co., 1970.

Hovland, Carl I., and Pritzker, H. "Extent of Opinion Change as a Function cf Amount of Change Advocated." *Journal of Abnormal and Social Psychology* 54(1957):257–61.

Hovland, Carl I., and Weiss, Walter. "The Influence of Source Credibility on Communicator Effectiveness." In *Experiments in Persuasion,* edited by Ralph Rosnow and Edward J. Robinson. New York: Academic Press, 1967.

Janis, I. S., and Feshbach, S. "Effects of Fear-Arousing Communications." *Journal of Abnormal and Social Psychology* 48(1953):78–92.

Johnson, Wendell. *People in Quandaries.* New York: Harper & Row, Publishers, 1946.

Jourard, Sidney. "An Exploratory Study of Body Accessibility." *British Journal of Social and Clinical Psychology* 5(1966):221–31.

―――. "Self-Disclosure and Other Cathexis." *Journal of Abnormal and Social Psychology* 59(1959):428–31.

―――. "Healthy Personality and Self-Disclosure." In *The Self in Social Interaction,* edited by Chad Gordon and Kenneth J. Gergen. New York: John Wiley & Sons, 1968.

―――. *The Transparent Self.* 2d ed. New York: Van Nostrand Reinhold Co., 1971.

Jourard, Sidney, and Jaffe, P. "Influence of an Interviewer's Disclosure on the Self-Disclosing Behavior of Interviewees." *Journal of Counseling Psychology* 17(1970):252–97.

Jourard, Sidney, and Landsman, M. J. "Cognition, Cathexis, and the 'Dyadic Effect' in Men's Self-Disclosing Behavior." *Merrill-Palmer Quarterly of Behavior and Development* 9(1960):141–48.

Jourard, Sidney, and Lasakow, Paul. "Some Factors in Self-Disclosure." *Journal of Abnormal and Social Psychology* 51(1958):91–98.

Jourard, Sidney, and Resnick, J. L. "Some Effects on Self-Disclosure Among College Women." *Journal of Humanistic Psychology* 10(1970):84–93.

Jourard, Sidney, and Robin, J. E. "Self-Disclosure and Touching: A Study of Two Modes of Interpersonal Encounter and Their Inter-Relation." *Journal of Humanistic Psychology* 8(1968):39–48.

Kafka, Franz. "Give It Up!" In *The Complete Stories,* edited by Nathum N. Glatzer. New York: Schocken Books, 1972.

Kahn, Robert L., and Cannell, Charles, F. *The Dynamics of Interviewing.* New York: John Wiley & Sons, 1957.

Karlins, Marvin, and Abelson, Herbert I. *Persuasion: How Opinions and Attitudes Are Changed.* New York: Springer Publishing Co., 1970.

Karmar, Edward J. J., and Lewis, Thomas R. "Comparison of Visual and Nonvisual Listening." *Journal of Communication* 1(1951):16–20.

Katz, Elihu. "On Reopening the Question of Selectivity in Exposure to Mass Communication." In *Speech Communication Behavior: Perspectives & Principles,* edited by Larry Baker and Robert Kibler. Englewood Cliffs, N.J.: Prentice-Hall, 1971.

Keller, Paul W. "Major Findings in Listening in the Past Ten Years." *Journal of Communication* 10(March 1960):29–38.

Kiesler, C. A.; Kiesler, S.; and Pallack, M. "The Effects of Commitment on Future Interaction on Reactions to Norm Violations." *Journal of Personality* 35(1967):585–99.

Knapp, Mark L. *Nonverbal Communication in Human Interaction.* New York: Holt, Rinehart & Winston, 1972.

Korten, Frances F. "The Influence of Culture on the Perception of Persons." *International Journal of Psychology* 9(1974):31–44.

Kramer, Cheris. "Folk-Linguistics: Wishy-Washy Mommy Talk." *Psychology Today,* June 1974, p. 82–85.

Kramer, Ernest. "The Judgment of Personal Characteristics and Emotions from Nonverbal Properties of Speech." *Psychological Bulletin* 60(1963):408–20.

Kraut, Robert E. "Verbal and Nonverbal Cues in the Perception of Lying." *Journal of Personality and Social Psychology* 36(1978):380–91.

Kruger, Arthur N. *Effective Speaking: A Complete Course.* New York: Van Nostrand Reinhold Co., 1970.

Laing, R. D. *Knots.* New York: Pantheon Books, 1971.

Lair, Jess. *I Ain't Much Baby, but I'm All I've Got.* New York: Doubleday & Co., 1972.

Larson, Charles U. *Persuasion: Reception and Responsibility.* Belmont, Calif.: Wadsworth Publishing Co., 1974.

Lee, Irving J. *How to Talk With People.* New York: Harper & Row, Publishers, 1952.

Lee, Melvin; Zimbardo, Philip G.; and Bertholf, Minerva. "Shy Murderers." *Psychology Today* 11(November 1977):148.

Levin, F. M., and Gergen, K. "Revealingness, Ingratiation, and the Disclosure of Self." *Proceedings of the 77th Annual Convention,* American Psychological Association, 1969.

Levinger, G., and Senn, D. "Disclosure of Feelings in Marriage." *Merrill-Palmer Quarterly of Behavior and Development* 13(1967):237–49.

Lopez, Felix M. *Personnel Interviewing.* New York: McGraw-Hill Book Company, 1975.

McConnell, James V. *Understanding Human Behavior: An Introduction to Psychology.* New York: Holt, Rinehart & Winston, 1977.

McCroskey, James C. "Measures of Communication-Bound Anxiety." *Speech Monograph* 37(1970):269–70.

McCroskey, James C.; Doly, John A.; Richmond, Virginia P.; and Falcione, Raymond L. "Studies of the Relationship Between Communication Apprehension and Self-Esteem." *Human Communication Research* 3(1977):269–77.

McCroskey, James C.; Larson, Carl E.; and Knapp, Mark L. *An Introduction to Interpersonal Communication.* Englewood Cliffs, N.J.: Prentice-Hall, 1971.

MacDonald-Ross, Michael. "How Numbers Are Shown: A Review of Research on the Presentation of Quantitative Data in Texts." *AV Communication Review* 25(Winter 1977):359–409.

Markgraf, B. "An Observational Study Determining the Amount of Time that Students in the Tenth and Twelfth Grades Are Expected to Listen in the Classroom." Master's thesis, University of Wisconsin, 1957.

Maslow, Abraham H. "Hierarchy of Needs." In *Motivation and Personality.* 2d ed. New York: Harper & Row, Publishers, 1970, pp. 35–72.

Mehrabian, Albert. "Communication Without Words." *Psychology Today,* September 1968, pp. 53–55.

———. *Silent Messages.* Belmont, Calif.: Wadsworth Publishing Co., 1971.

Mehrabian, Albert, and Kerris, Susan R. "Inference of Attitude from Nonverbal Communication in Two Channels." *Journal of Consulting Psychology* 31(1967):248–52.

Miller, Gerald R. "Evidence and Arguments." In *Perspectives on Argument,* edited by Gerald R. Miller and Thomas R. Nilsen. Chicago: Scott, Foresman & Company, 1966.

Miller, Gerald R., and Burgoon, Michael. *New Techniques of Persuasion.* New York: Harper & Row, Pubishers, 1973.

Montagu, Ashley. *Touching: The Human Significance of the Skin.* New York: Harper & Row, Publishers, 1971.

Morris, Jud. *The Art of Listening.* Boston: Farnsworth Publishing Co., 1968.

Mortensen, C. David. "Communication Postulates." In *Messages,* edited by Jean Civikly. 2d ed. New York: Random House, 1977.

Newman, Edwin. *A Civil Tongue.* Indianapolis: Bobbs-Merrill Co., 1976.

Newman, Robert P., and Newman, Dale R. *Evidence.* Boston: Houghton Mifflin Company, 1969.

Nichols, Ralph, and Stevens, Leonard A. *Are You Listening.* New York: McGraw-Hill Book Company, 1957.

Nichols, Ralph, and Stevens, Leonard A. "Listening to People." *Harvard Business Review* 35(1957):no.5.

Nolte, Dorothy Law. "Children Learn What They Live," 1954.

Osborn, Alex F. *Applied Imagination: Principles and Procedures of Creative Thinking.* New York: Charles Scribner's Sons, 1953.

Parlee, Mary Brown. "Conversational Politics." *Psychology Today,* May 1979, pp. 48–56.

Partridge, Eric. *Slang: Today and Yesterday.* New York: Barnes & Noble Books, 1970.

Pei, Mario. *The Story of Language.* New York: New American Library of World Literature, 1949.

Pell, Arthur R. *Be a Better Employment Interviewer.* New York: Personnel Publications 1978.

Pence, O. L. "Emotionally Loaded Argument: Its Effectiveness in Stimulating Recall." *Quarterly Journal of Speech* 40(1954):272–76.

Petrie, Charles R. "Informative Speaking: A Summary and Bibliography of Related Research." *Speech Monographs* 30(1963):79–91.

Petrie, Charles R., Jr., and Carrel, Susan D. "The Relationship of Motivation, Listening Capability, Initial Information, and Verbal Organization Ability to Lecture Comprehension and Retention." *Speech Monographs* 43(1976):187–94.

Phillips, Gerald M.; Pedersen, Douglas J.; and Wood, Julia T. *Group Discussion: A Practical Guide to Participation and Leadership.* Boston: Houghton Mifflin Company, 1979.

"Playboy Interview: Abbie Hoffman." *Playboy,* May 1976, p. 64.

Powell, Fredric A. "The Effects of Anxiety-Arousing Messages when Related to Personal, Familial, and Impersonal Referents." *Speech Monographs* 32(1965):102–6.

Powell, John. *The Secret of Staying in Love.* Niles, Ill.: Argus Communications, 1974.

————. *Why Am I Afraid to Tell You Who I Am?* Niles, Ill.: Argus Communications, 1974.

————. *Fully Human, Fully Alive.* Niles, Ill.: Argus Communications, 1976.

Prather, Hugh. *Notes to Myself.* Moab, Utah: Real People Press, 1970.

Quinn, P. T. "Self-Disclosure as a Function of Degree of Acquaintance and Potential Power." Master's thesis, Ohio State University, 1965.

Rankin, Paul T. "Measurement of the Ability to Understand the Spoken Language." Ph.D. dissertation, University of Michigan, 1926, cited in *Dissertation Abstracts* 12(1926):847.

————. "Listening Ability: Its Importance, Measurement, and Development." *Chicago Schools Journal* 12(1930):177.

Richmond, V. P., and Robertson, D. "Communication Apprehension as a Function of Being Raised in an Urban or Rural Environment." Monograph, West Virginia Northern Community College, 1976.

Robb, Stephen. "Fundamentals of Evidence and Argument." In *Modcom: Modules in Speech Communication.* Chicago: Science Research Associations, 1976.

Rogers, Carl R. *Client-Centered Therapy.* Boston: Houghton Mifflin Company, 1951.

————. *On Becoming a Person.* Boston: Houghton Mifflin Company, 1961.

————. *Freedom to Learn.* Columbus, Ohio: Charles E. Merrill Publishing Company, 1969.

Rogers, Carl R., and Farson, Richard E. "Active Listening." In *Readings in Interpersonal and Organizational Communication,* edited by Richard C. Huseman, Cal M. Logue, and Dwight L. Freshly. Boston: Holbrook Press, 1969.

Rokeach, Milton. *Beliefs, Attitudes, and Values.* San Francisco: Jossey-Bass Publishers, 1968.

Roloff, Michael E., and Miller, Gerald R. *Persuasion: New Directions in Theory and Research.* Beverly Hills: Sage Publications, 1980.

Rosenthal, Robert, and Jacobson, Lenore. *Pygmalion in the Classroom: Teacher Expectation and Pupils' Intellectual Development.* New York: Holt, Rinehart & Winston, 1968.

Rosnow, Ralph L., and Robinson, Edward J. *Experiments in Persuasion.* New York: Academic Press, 1967.

Rubin, Zick. "The Rise and Fall of First Impressions." In *Interpersonal Communication in Action,* edited by Bobby R. Patton and Kim Griffin, 2d ed. New York: Harper & Row, Publishers, 1977.

Scheidel, Thomas M., and Crowell, Laura. *Discussing and Deciding: A Desk Book for Group Leaders and Members.* New York: Macmillan Publishing Co., 1979.

Schramm, Wilbur. "How Communication Works." In *The Processes and Effects of Mass Communication,* edited by Wilbur Schramm. Urbana, Ill.: University of Illinois Press, 1971.

Schutz, William. *Here Comes Everybody.* New York: Harper & Row, Publishers, 1971.

Sears, D., and Freedman, J. "Effects of Expected Familiarity with Arguments upon Opinion Change and Selective Exposure." *Journal of Personality and Social Psychology* 2(1965):420–26.

Shapiro, Jeffrey G.; Krauss, Herbert H.; and Truax, Charles B. "Therapeutic Conditions of Disclosure beyond the Therapeutic Encounter." *Journal of Counseling Psychology* 16(1969):290–94.

Sharp, Harry, Jr., and McClung, Thomas. "Effects of Organization on the Speaker's Ethos." *Speech Monographs* 33(1966):182–83.

Shaw, Marvin E. "Communication Networks." In *Advances in Experimental Social Psychology* edited by Leonard Benkowitz, vol. 1. New York: Academic Press, 1964, pp. 111–47.

———. *Group Dynamics: The Psychology of Small Group Behavior.* New York: McGraw-Hill Book Company, 1971.

Shostrum, Everett L. *Man, the Manipulator.* New York: Abingdon Press, 1967.

Simon, Wm. A., Jr. "A Practical Approach to the Uniform Selection Guidelines." *Personnel Administrator* 24(November 1969):75–79.

Smith, Raymond G. *Speech Communication: Theory and Models.* New York: Harper & Row, Publishers, 1970.

Sommer, Robert. "The Distance for Comfortable Conversation: A Further Study." *Sociometry* 25(1962):111–16.

Stewart, Charles J., and Cash, William B. *Interviewing: Principles and Practices.* 2d ed. Dubuque, Iowa: Wm. C. Brown Company Publishers, 1978.

Stewart, John. "An Interpersonal Approach to the Basic Course." *The Speech Teacher* 21(1972):7–14.

Swanson, Richard, and Marquardt, Charles. *On Communication: Listening, Reading, Speaking, and Writing.* Beverly Hills, Calif.: Glencoe Press, 1974.

Taylor, D. A. "Some Aspects of the Development of Interpersonal Relationships: Social Penetration Process." *Technical Report No. 1.* Center for Research on Social Behavior. University of Delaware, 1965.

Taylor, D. A., and Altman, I. "Intimacy Scaled Stimuli to Use in Studies of Interpersonal Relations." *Psychological Reports* 19(1966):729–30.

Taylor, L. C., and Compton, N.H. "Personality Correlates of Dress Conformity." *Journal of Home Economics* 60(1968):653–56.

Terkel, Studs. *Working.* New York: Avon Books, 1974.

Thompson, Wayne N. *Quantitative Research in Public Address and Communication.* New York: Random House, 1967.

Thonssen, Lester, and Baird, A. Craig. "The Character of the Speaker." In *Readings in Speech,* edited by Haig A. Bosmajian. New York: Harper & Row, Publishers, 1971.

Thorne, Barrie, and Henley, Nancy eds. *Language and Sex: Difference and Dominance.* Rowley, Mass.: Newbury House Publishers, 1975.

Triandis, Harry C. "Cultural Influences upon Perception." In *Intercultural Communication: A Reader,* edited by Larry A. Samovar and Richard E. Porter. 2d ed. Belmont, Calif.: Wadsworth Publishing Co., 1976.

Tucker, Charles O. "An Application of Programmed Learning to Informative Speech." *Speech Monographs* 31(1964):142–52.

Tuppen, Christopher J. S. "Dimensions of Communicator Credibility: An Oblique Solution." *Speech Monographs* 41(1974):253–60.

Verderber, Rudolph F. *The Challenge of Effective Speaking.* 4th ed. Belmont, Calif.: Wadsworth Publishing Co., 1979.

Vohs, John L. "An Empirical Approach to the Concept of Attention." *Speech Monographs* 31(1964):355–60.

Voor, John B., and Miller, Joseph M. "The Effect of Practice upon the Comprehension of Time-Compressed Speech." *Speech Monographs* 32(1965):452–54.

Voss, F. "The Relationships of Disclosure to Marital Satisfaction: An Exploratory Study." Master's thesis, University of Wisconsin, 1969.

Watzlawick, Paul; Beavin, Janet; and Jackson, Don. *Pragmatics of Human Communication.* New York: W. W. Norton & Co., 1967.

Weaver, Andrew T., and Ness, Ordean G. *An Introduction to Public Speaking.* New York: Odyssey Press, 1961.

Weinrauch, Donald J., and Swanda, John R., Jr. "Examining the Significance of Listening: An Exploratory Study of Contemporary Management." *Journal of Business Communication* 13(Fall 1975):25–32.

Wenburg, John R., and Wilmot, William. *The Personal Communication Process.* New York: John Wiley & Sons, 1973.

West, Morris L. *The Shoes of the Fisherman.* New York: William Morrow & Co., 1963.

Wheeless, Lawrence R. "The Effects of Attitude, Credibility, and Homophily on Selective Exposure to Information." *Speech Monographs* 41(1974):329–38.

White, R., and Lippit, R. "Leader Behavior and Member Reaction in Three 'Social Climates.' " In *Group Dynamics: Research and Theory,* edited by Dorwin Cartwright and Alvin Zander. 2d ed. New York: Harper & Row, Publishers, 1960, pp. 527–53.

Whorf, Benjamin Lee. "Science and Linguistics." In *Language, Thought and Reality,* edited by John B. Carroll. Cambridge, Mass.: M.I.T. Press, 1956.

Williams, M. C., and Eicher, J. B. "Teenagers' Appearance and Social Acceptance." *Journal of Home Economics* 58(1966):457–61.

Wilt, Miriam E. "A Study of Teacher Awareness of Listening as a Factor in Elementary Education." *Journal of Educational Research* 43(1950):626.

Winans, James A. "Conversing With an Audience." In *Selected Readings in Public Speaking,* edited by Jane Blankenship and Robert Wilhoit. Belmont, Calif.: Dickinson Publishing Co., 1968.

Woolbert, Charles. "The Effects of Various Modes of Public Reading." *Journal of Applied Psychology* 4(1920):162–85.

Worthy, W.; Gary, A.; and Kahn, G. M. "Self-Disclosure as an Exchange Process." *Journal of Personality and Social Psychology* 13(1969):59–63.

Zayas-Baya, Elena P. "Instructional Media in the Total Language Picture." *International Journal of Instructional Media* 5(1977–1978):145–50.

Zelko, Harold P., and Dance, Frank E. X. *Business and Professional Speech Communication*. New York: Holt, Rinehart & Winston, 1965.

Zimbardo, Philip G. *Shyness: What It Is and What To Do About It*. Reading, Mass.: Addison Wesley Publishing Co., 1977.

Name Index

Abelson, Herbert I., 254, 266, 373, 374
Addis, B. R., 92
Adler, Ronald, 92, 119
Aiken, L. R., 93
Allport, Gordon W., 43
Altman, I., 134, 138
Andersen, Kenneth, 266
Anderson, Jane, 120
Argyle, Michael, 92, 120
Aristotle, 238, 266
Ausubel, David, 349

Baird, A. Craig, 265
Baird, John A., 348
Barbara, D., 160
Barbour, John, 72
Barker, Larry L., 159, 160, 233
Barnlund, Dean C., 9, 10, 22, 24, 32
Bateson, Gregory, 93
Beach, Dale S., 182
Beavin, Janet, 23
Becker, Samuel, 233
Beebe, Steven A., 322
Beighley, Kenneth C., 322
Bem, Daryl J., 234, 372
Berkowitz, Leonard, 205
Berlo, David K., 7, 23, 24
Bertholf, Minerva, 128, 137
Bettinghaus, Erwin P., 266, 322, 372, 373, 374
Bird, D., 143, 160
Birdwhistell, Ray L., 91, 92
Black, John W., 321, 322
Blankenship, Jane, 321
Blau, P. M., 133, 138
Bochner, Arthur P., 145, 160
Borman, Ernest G., 204
Borman, Nancy C., 204
Bosmajian, Haig A., 265
Boswell, James, 117
Bowlby, John, 92
Bradley, Bert, 321
Brigance, William N., 322
Brilhart, John K., 201, 204, 205
Brooks, William D., 159, 348
Brown, Bruce L., 322
Brown, Charles T., 24
Brown, James I., 160
Bucalo, Jack, 184
Buckley, William F., 243
Bugliosi, Vincent, 63
Burgoon, Judee K., 91
Burgoon, Michael, 373

Burke, Kenneth W., 17, 24, 322

Caine, Lynn, 117
Campbell, James H., 265
Cannell, Charles F., 183
Carney, Clarke G., 43
Carrel, Susan D., 348
Carroll, John B., 72
Carroll, Lewis, 72
Carter, Jimmy, 51
Cartwright, Dorwin, 205
Cash, William B., 183, 184
Cathcart, Robert S., 204
Chaiken, A. L., 138
Chelune, G. J., 136
Clay, V. S., 92
Clevenger, Theodore, Jr., 233, 266, 293
Cobin, Martin, 322
Cofer, N. C., 348
Coffina, Richard M., 184
Colson, Charles W., 111
Compton, N. H., 93
Connolly, James E., 293
Cope, Frances, 374
Cozby, P. C., 137, 138
Cronkhite, Gary, 373
Crowell, Laura, 204
Culbert, S. A., 138

Daly, John A., 120
Dance, Frank E. X., 23, 24, 184, 233
Danner, Jack, 159
Davis, James H., 204
Dean, Janet, 92
Deihl, Charles F., 322
Derlega, V. J., 138
Desper, J. L., 92
De Vito, Joseph A., 321
Dohrenwend, Barbara, 182
Douty, H. I., 93
Doyle, Warren, 102
Duker, Sam, 160
Dylan, Bob, 7

Eakins, Barbara Westbrook, 93
Eakins, R. Gene, 93
Edwards, David C., 43, 205
Egan, Gerard, 136, 159
Ehninger, Douglas, 373, 374
Eicher, J. B., 93
Ekman, Paul, 78–80, 91, 92

Ellingsworth, Huber W., 293
Emerson, Ralph Waldo, 289
Emmert, Philip L., 159
Erlich, H., 137
Ernest, Carole, 348

Fairbanks, Grant, 322
Falcione, Raymond L., 120
Fallon, Barry J., 205
Farson, Richard E., 160
Fear, Richard A., 183
Feshbach, S., 360, 374
Fisher, B. Aubrey, 204
Fothergill, Robert A., 117, 120
Fotheringham, Wallace, 373
Fraser, Alistair B., 44
Freedman, J., 374
Friedrich, Gustav W., 348
Friesen, Wallace V., 78–80, 91, 92
Fromm, Eric, 159

Galassi, John P., 177, 184
Galassi, Merna D., 177, 184
Galbraith, John Kenneth, 341–42, 349
Gary, A., 132, 137, 138
Gatewood, Robert D., 184
Gentry, Curt, 63
Gergen, Kenneth J., 119, 136, 137
Giattino, Jill, 321
Gibbs, Jack R., 120
Giffin, Kim, 43
Gilbert, Shirley J., 133, 134, 135, 138
Gilkinson, Howard, 322
Glasgow, George M., 308, 322
Glatzer, Nathum N., 137
Goffman, Erving, 119, 136
Goldberg, S., 92
Gordon, Chad, 136
Gordon, Raymond L., 183
Graeven, D., 137
Grier, Rosey, 101
Gruner, Charles R., 348
Guardo, Carol J., 92
Gundersen, D. F., 322
Gunther, Bernard, 156
Guttman, Newman, 322

Haas, Kenneth B., 322
Haley, J., 93
Hall, Carol, 120
Hall, Edward T., 81, 91, 92
Hamid, P. N., 93
Haney, William V., 43
Hard, Roland J., 322
Harms, L. S., 266
Hart, Roderick P., 348
Harwood, Kenneth A., 322
Hastorf, Albert H., 43
Hayakawa, S. I., 71
Hayworth, Donald, 322
Hearst, Patricia, 110
Heath, Robert L., 234
Hebyallah, Isbrabim, 322
Hellman, Connie S., 205
Hendricks, S. H., 93
Henley, Nancy M., 72, 85, 91, 93
Henrikson, Ernest H., 322
Henry, Patrick, 289
Hepler, Hal W., 265
Hertzler, Joyce O., 71
Hildebrandt, Herbert, 322
Hoffman, Abbie, 111, 120
Hollander, Edwin P., 205
Holmes, Oliver Wendell, 14, 24
Holtzman, Paul D., 233, 294
Hooper, Robert, 322
Hopkins, John T., 184
Horrocks, John E., 119
Hovland, Carl I., 265, 266, 374
Howard, C. Jeriel, 183, 294

Ingham, Harrington, 125–26

Jackson, D. D., 93
Jackson, Don, 23
Jackson, Dorothy W., 119
Jacobson, Lenore, 106, 120
Jaffe, P., 137
Janis, Irving J., 265, 360, 374
Johnson, Wendell, 71
Johoda, Marie, 100
Jong, Erica, 115
Jourard, Sidney, 93, 100, 119, 134, 137, 138

Kafka, Franz, 130, 137
Kahn, G. M., 137, 138
Kahn, Robert L., 132, 183

Karlins, Marvin, 254, 266, 373, 374
Karmer, Edward J. J., 160
Katz, Elihu, 233
Keller, Paul W., 160
Kelley, E. A., 93
Kelly, Clifford W., 145, 160
Kelly, Harold H., 265
Kerris, Susan R., 92
Kibler, Robert, 233–34
Kiesler, C. A., 138
Kiesler, S., 138
Kilpatrick, James J., 294
King, Carole, 92
Klein, David, 182
Knapp, Mark L., 92, 93
Knower, Franklin, 322
Korten, Frances F., 43
Kramer, Cheris, 71
Kramer, Edward J. J., 92, 322
Kramer, Ernest, 93
Krauss, Herbert H., 138
Kraut, Robert E., 184
Kruger, Arthur N., 265, 294, 321

Laing, R. D., 42, 44
Lair, Jess, 119
Landman, Theodore, 100
Landsman, M. J., 137
Larson, Carl E., 23, 93
Larson, Charles U., 373
Lasakow, Paul, 134, 138
Ledvinka, James, 184
Lee, Irving J., 71
Lee, Melvin, 128, 137
Levin, F. M., 137
Levinger, G., 137, 138
Lewis, M., 92
Lewis, Thomas R., 92, 160, 322
Lippit, R., 205
Lopez, Felix M., 184
Luft, Joseph, 125–26

McClung, Thomas, 266
McConnell, James V., 373
McCroskey, James C., 93, 120
MacDonald-Ross, Michael, 322
McKeon, Richard, 266
McMahon, Sarah L., 43
MacMillan, Donald, 35
McReynolds, P. W., 136
Maloney, W. Paul, 322
Manson, Charles, 60

Markgraff, B., 160
Marquardt, Charles, 265
Maslow, Abraham H., 99, 120
Mehrabian, Albert, 76, 77, 79, 92
Merrill, Bob, 137
Messina, Jimmy, 24
Michener, James A., 294
Miller, Gerald R., 373, 374
Miller, Joseph M., 322
Mills, Glen E., 294
Montagu, Ashley, 92
Moore, Wilbur E., 321
Morris, Charles, 100
Morris, Jud, 159
Mortensen, C. David, 23, 24
Murray, Miron S., 322

Ness, Ordean G., 321
Newman, Dale R., 374
Newman, Edwin, 60, 71
Newman, Robert P., 374
Nichols, Ralph, 142, 159, 160
Nilsen, Thomas R., 374
Nixon, Richard M., 111
Nolte, Dorothy Law, 106, 120

Oliver, Robert T., 294
Osborn, Alex F., 205

Packer, Harry Q., 322
Pallack, M., 138
Parlee, Mary Brown, 71
Partridge, Eric, 71
Patton, Bobby R., 43
Peary, Robert, 35
Pedersen, Douglas J., 204
Pei, Mario, 72
Pell, Arthur R., 183
Pence, O. L., 349
Petrie, Charles R., Jr., 322, 348
Phillips, Gerald M., 204
Polefka, Judith, 43
Powell, Frederic A., 360, 374
Powell, John, 116, 119, 120, 130, 137
Prather, Hugh, 119, 137
Pritzker, H., 374

Quinn, P. T., 137

Rankin, Paul T., 24, 142, 160
Renuk, James M., 33, 44
Resnick, J. L., 137
Richardson, Don, 374
Richardson, Stephen A., 182
Richmond, V. P., 44, 120
Robb, Stephen, 265
Roberts, W. Rhys, 266
Robertson, D., 44
Robinson, Edward J., 266, 374
Rogers, Carl R., 7, 9, 24, 100, 137, 146, 160
Rokeach, Milton, 234
Roloff, Michael E., 373
Rosenthal, Robert, 106, 120
Rosnow, Ralph L., 266, 374
Rubin, J. E., 93
Rubin, Zick, 43

Safire, William, 263, 266
Saine, Thomas, 91
Samovar, Larry A., 204
Sapir, Edward, 59
Sappho, 344
Scheidel, Thomas, 204
Schneider, David J., 43
Schon, T. D., 321
Schramm, Wilbur, 23
Schutz, Will, 92, 100, 120
Sears, D., 374
Senn, D., 137, 138
Sereno, Kenneth K., 24
Shapiro, Jeffrey G., 138
Sharp, Harry, Jr., 266
Shaw, Marvin E., 204, 205
Simon, William A., Jr., 184
Smith, Raymond G., 23
Sommer, Robert, 81, 92
Stern, Toni, 91
Stevens, Leonard A., 159, 160
Stevens, Walter, 322
Stewart, Charles J., 183, 184
Stewart, John, 14, 24
Styne, Jule, 137
Swanda, John R., Jr., 24
Swanson, Richard, 265

Taylor, D. A., 134, 137, 138
Taylor, L. C., 93
Terkel, Studs, 17, 24
Thomas, Coramae, 183, 294
Thompson, Wayne N., 266
Thonssen, Lester, 265
Thorne, Barrie, 72
Towne, Neil, 92
Triandis, Harry C., 43
Truax, Charles B., 138
Tucker, Charles O., 349
Tuppen, Christopher J S., 266

Van Riper, Charles, 24
Verderber, Rudolph F., 234
Vohs, John L., 322
Voor, John B., 322
Voss, F., 138

Walter, Otis M., 294
Watzlawick, Paul, 23
Weakland, J. H., 93
Weaver, Andrew T., 321
Weinrauch, J. Donald, 24
Weiss, Walter, 266
Wenberg, John R., 23
West, Morris L., 130, 137
Wheeless, Lawrence R., 348
White, Richard C., 205, 322
Whiteneck, Gale G., 133, 134, 135, 138
Whorf, Benjamin Lee, 59, 72
Wicker, Tom, 294
Wilhoit, Robert, 321
Williams, M. C., 93
Williams, Mason, 114, 120
Wilmont, William, 23
Wilt, Miriam E., 160
Winans, James A., 321
Wood, Julia T., 204
Woolbert, Charles, 308, 322
Worthy, W., 132, 137, 138

Zander, Alvin, 205
Zayas-Baya, Elena P., 322
Zelko, Harold P., 24, 184, 294
Zimbardo, Philip G., 119–20, 128, 137

Action, 13
Adaptors, 80
Advance organizers, 338
Affect displays, 80
Analogy, 263
Answers and Answering,
      168–70
Antonym, 340
Articulation, 85
Assertiveness, 109–10
Attention, 270
      gaining and
            maintaining,
            270–74
Audience adaptation,
      229–32
      adapting supporting
            materials for, 232
      adapting your purpose
            for, 231–32
      adapting yourself for,
            230
      adapting your topic for,
            230–31
      adapting your verbal
            and nonverbal
            codes for, 230
Audience analysis, 216–32
      audience attitude,
            beliefs, values in,
            222–25
      audience interest in
            topic in, 220–22
      audience knowledge of
            topic in, 220–22
      captive and voluntary
            audiences in,
            216–18
      demographic analysis in,
            219–20
      levels of, 216–25
      methods of, 225–29
            inference in, 226–27
            observation in,
                  225–26
            questionnaires in,
                  227–29

Barnlund's "six people," 9
Bodily movement, 78–80
Boomerang effect, 356
Brainstorming, 193

Classification, 59
Clichés, 52–53
Closure, 38
Clothing, 87–88

...de, 12, 49
...nverbal, 12, 74–9i
Co...bal, 12, 47–70
Co...ness, 190
Co...ent, 190
Comm...und, 247
      app...
      defin...
      functio... 107, 110
      soci...9
      task, ...8
      networks,
      problems in,
      and self, 9–1...
Comparison, 339
Conclusions, 289–9...
      functions of, 290
            brakelight func...
            290
Concreteness, 68–70
Connotative meaning,
      56–57
Consensus, 190
Contexts, 10–12
Contrast, 340
Counterarguments, 362
Credibility defined, 238–39
Cultures, 54–56

Dating, 69
Decode, 13, 49
Defensiveness, 107–9
Definitions, 264, 339–40
Delivery, 296–313
      bodily aspects of,
            309–13
      comprehension, 304
      enunciation in, 307
      evaluating your, 319
      eye contact in, 311
      facial expression,
            311–12
      fluency in, 308
      four modes, 299–301
            extemporaneous, 299
            impromptu, 300
            manuscript, 299
            memorized, 300–301
      gestures in, 310
      helpful hints for,
            318–19
      listenability, 303
      movement in, 312
      pause in, 304
      pitch in, 302–3
      projection in, 306
      pronunciation in, 307
      rate of, 303

Subject Index

vocal aspects of, 302–9
vocalized pauses in, 305
vocal variety in, 308–9
volume in, 306
Denotative meaning, 56–57
Descriptions, 340–41
abstract, 341
concrete, 341
descriptive, 340
evaluative, 340
Descriptive feedback, 90
Descriptiveness, 61
Dewey's method of
reflective thinking,
197
Distance, 81–83
intimate, 82
personal, 82
public, 82
social, 82
Double bind, 89
Dyadic communication, 165

Emblems, 80
Emotional appeals, 360
fear appeals, 360
reassurance, 360
Empathy, 145
improving our ability in,
155–57
interference with,
148–54
defensiveness and,
150–51
egocentrism and,
153
experiential
superiority and,
151–52
factual distractions
and, 148–49
mental distractions
and, 149
physical distractions
and, 149–50
self-focus and, 150
semantic distractions
and, 149
status and, 153
stereotypes and, 153
Encode, 13, 49
Enunciation, 85
Etymology, 340
Euphemisms, 52–53
Evidence, 259–64
types of, 260–63
statistics, 261–63
surveys and studies,
259–60
testimonial, 260–61

Examples, 259
Explanations, 263–64,
341–42

Facial expression, 78–80
Feedback, 14–15
Figure and ground, 38
Footnote form, 256–58

Hearing, 143
Hidden agenda, 21

Illustrators, 80
Immediate purpose,
231–32, 274
Indexing, 69
Inferences, 65–66
Inflection, 85
Informative-Persuasive
Continuum,
328–29
Informative speech, 324–47
behavioral purposes of,
331
checklist for an, 346–47
example of an, 342–45
extrinsic motivation and
the, 335
information hunger and
the, 333
information overload
and the, 335
information relevance
and the, 334
informative content and
the, 335–36
organizing the, 338–39
overt audience response,
337
preparation of, 327–38
special skills for, 339–42
topics for, 328–30
Intentional confusion
avoidance of, 60–61
Interaction, 13
Interpersonal
communication,
11–12, 95
Interviewing, 162–82
definition of, 164–65
employment, 175–82
informational, 170–73
persuasive, 174–75
purposes of interviews,
170–82
Intrapersonal
communication,
11, 95

Introduction of a speech,
270–74
functions of, 270–73
attention, 270–73
forecast, 273
interest, 273
purpose, 273
qualifications, 273

Johari Window, 125–27
blind area in the, 126
hidden area in the, 126
open area in the, 126
unknown area in the,
126
Journal writing, 115–18

Key-word outline, 281–83
Kinesics, 78–80

Language, 46–72
used to distort meaning,
51–53
Leader, 200
Leadership, 200–203
appointed, 200
autocratic, 201
defined, 200
democratic, 201
emergent, 200
functions of, 201–2
Laissez-faire, 201
permissive, 201
styles of, 201
supervisory, 201
traits of, 200
Listening, 140–60
active, 144
behavioral components
of, 157–58
critical, 144
definition of, 142–43
empathic, 145
improving our ability in,
155–57
interference with,
148–54
defensiveness and,
150–51
egocentrism and,
153
experiential
superiority and,
151–52
factual distractions
and, 148–49

mental distractions
and, 149
physical distractions
and, 149
self-focus and, 150
semantic distractions
and, 149
misconceptions about,
142–43
status and, 153
stereotypes and, 153
three kinds of, 144–48
Logical appeals, 359–60
evidence in, 359
proposition in, 359
Long-range goals, 231–32,
353

Maslow's hierarchy of
needs, 99–100
Mean or average, 263
Meaning, 8
Message, 8
Mode, 262

Neutrality, 145
Noise, 15
Nonverbal codes, 74–91, 78
definition and
identification of,
78–87
importance of, 76–77
interpretation of, 88–90
problems of
interpreting, 88–89
solving problems of
interpreting, 90
Norms, 191
Novel arguments, 362

Objectives or object
language, 87–88
Observations, 65
Operational definitions, 61,
340
Organizational patterns,
284–88
cause-effect, 287
climactic and anti-
climactic, 287
indirect sequencing, 288
problem-and-solution,
286
spatial, 287
time-sequence, 284–85
topical sequence,
285–86

Outlining, 274–83
as an abstract, 275
key-word outline,
composing a,
281–83
main points, 275
margins in, 276
notecards, 282
principles of, 275–76
rough draft, 277
sentence outline,
composing a,
277–81
bibliography, 277
example of, 279–80
subordination, principle
of, 276
subpoints, 275
sub-subpoints, 276
symbols for, 275–76

Paralanguage, 85–86
Paraphrasing, 66–67
Percentage, 262
Perception, 28–42
active, 31
activities involved in,
36–42
creative, 31
cultural differences
influencing, 34
cultural roles
influencing, 34
inherent meaning, 30
interpretation in, 41–42
in understanding others,
29–30
involved with
communication, 29
objective, 30
organization in, 37–40
passive, 30
past experience
influencing, 33–34
physiological factors in,
32–33
present feelings and
circumstances
influencing, 35
reasons for differences
in, 32
selection in, 36–37
subcultural differences
influencing, 34–35
subjective, 31
what occurs in, 36–42
Perceptual constancy, 40
Personal language, 49–50
Personal space, 82

Persuasive speech, 350–72
an example of a, 368–71
argumentation, 364
deductive arguments,
365
inference, 364–65
justification, 364
validity in, 365
behavioral change as a
goal of the, 355–57
defined, 352–53
ethics of, 362–63
evidence, 365–67
believability, 366–67
tests of, 365
goals of, 353, 354
adoption, 353
continuance, 354
deterrence, 354
discontinuance, 354
immediate purpose in
the, 356
mode of appeals,
357–58
biological motives,
357
intra-psychic
motives, 357–58
motivation, defined,
357
primary needs, 357
secondary drives,
357
secondary needs, 357
social/behavioral
motives, 358
one-sided and two-sided
presentations in the,
361–62
order of arguments in
the, 361
organizational plan in,
360–62
preparing a, 352–57
refutation in the,
367–68
post hoc ergo propter
hoc, 367
red herring, 368
reducto ad
absurdum, 367
special pleading,
367–68
turning the tables,
367
topics for, 354–55
Pitch, 85
Primary research, 195–96
Problem-solving discussion,
197
Process, 7

Proxemics, 81–83
Proximity, 39
Public communication, 12

Questions and questioning,
  165–68
  closed questions in, 165
  leading questions in,
    166–67
  neutral questions in, 166
  open questions in, 165
  primary questions in,
    166
  secondary questions in,
    166
Questions of fact, 193
Questions of policy, 194
Questions of value, 194

Rate, 85
Raw numbers, 263
Regulators, 80
Roles, 191

Sapir-Whorf hypothesis,
  59–60
Secondary research, 195–96
Selective attention, 36
Selective exposure, 37
Selective retention, 36–37
Self-actualization, 100
Self-awareness, 98–103
  increasing, 116–17
Self-concept, 103–14, 118
  affects communication,
    107–10
  improving, 110–14,
    117–18
  in process, 104–7
Self-consciousness, 104
Self-control, 102
Self-disclosure, 123, 124–36
  appropriateness and,
    132
  definition of, 124
  guidelines for, 131–35
  importance of, 125–29
  in establishing
    meaningful
    relationships, 127
  in establishing positive
    attitudes toward
    self and others,
    128–29
  in self-improvement,
    127
  interference with,
    129–30

negative, 128
person disclosing,
  dependent upon,
  134–35
positive, 128
reciprocal nature of,
  131–32
related to duration of
  relationship, 133
related to topic under
  discussion, 134
Self-esteem, 104
Self-expression, 102
Self-fulfilling prophecy,
  106–7
Self-image, 103–4
Self-improvement, 117–18
Sentence outline, 277–81
Sharing, 7
Similarity, 40
Sleeper effect, 246
Small group discussion,
  186–203
  defined, 189–90
  evaluating primary
    research for,
    195–96
  evaluating secondary
    research for, 196
  function of, 191–92
  organization and
    presentation of,
    197
  preparation and
    presentation,
    192–97
  researching the topic
    for, 195
  selecting the topic for,
    193
  social function of,
    191–92
  task function of, 192
  unique features of,
    190–91
  wording the question
    for, 193
Source credibility, 238–50
  citing sources and,
    256–58
  competence and, 239–41
  coorientation and,
    243–44
  dynamism and, 241–43
  finding credible sources,
    250–64
  proof or
    classification,
    259–64
  increasing, 244–50

introduction by another
  and, 248
opinion change and,
  245–46
organization and, 248
persuasion and, 358–59
sincerity and, 248
status and, 248
strategies for improving,
  249–50
time and, 245–46
trustworthiness and, 241
Space, 81–83
Stereotyping, 37
Strategic choices, 232
Subcultures, 54–56
Surveys and studies,
  259–60
Symbol, 48–49
Sympathy, 145
Synonym, 340

Tactile communication,
  83–85
Territoriality, 81
Thought, 8
Topic
  narrowing the, 215–16
  selecting and limiting
    the, 210–16
Topic selection, 210–16
  brainstorming and,
    210–11
  involvement in, 213–14
  knowledge of, 214–15
  newsmagazine inventory
    and, 212
  newspaper inventory
    and, 212
  personal inventory and,
    212–13
Touching, 83–85
Transaction, 13–15
Transitions, 288

Ultimate goal, 274–353
Understanding, 7

Verbal, 48
Verbal skills, improvement
  of, 60–70
Visual aids, 313–18
  types of, 314–18
  using, 313–18
Vocal cues, 85–86
Vocal quality, 85
Volume, 85

Words, 48
    as an obstacle to
        communication,
        49–60
    do not have inherent,
        universal meaning,
        53–60
    vary in meaning among
        cultures, 53–54
        individuals, 56–57
        subcultures, 54–56
    vary in meaning
        depending on
        situation and
        context, 57–58

Chapter 1

page

8   Photograph by Rick Smolan

11   Photograph by Chuck Isaacs

17   FAO photo by Peyton Johnson

18   © King Features Syndicate Inc., 1976

19   © King Features Syndicate Inc., 1976

20   Photograph by Chuck Isaacs

Chapter 2

page

29   Photograph by David S. Strickler, Strix Pix

30   Photograph by Peter Karas

31   Photograph by Rick Smolan

32   *Funky Winkerbean* by Tom Batiuk. © Enterprises, Inc., 1978. Courtesy of Field Newspaper Syndicate

35   *Crock* by Bill Rechin and Brant Parker. © Field Enterprises, Inc., 1978. Courtesy of Field Newspaper Syndicate

36   Photograph by DocuAmerica

Chapter 3

page

48   Photograph by Rick Smolan

49   Photograph by Leonard Lee Rue III, Bruce Coleman Inc.

51   *The Wizard of Id* by permission of Johnny Hart and Field Enterprises, Inc.

52   (top) *The Wizard of Id* by permission of Johnny Hart and Field Enterprises, Inc.
(bottom) Reprinted by permission of the Chicago Tribune-New York News Syndicate, Inc.

54   Photograph by Chuck Isaacs

57   © 1976 King Features Syndicate, Inc.

61   Charles M. Schulz, *What Next, Charlie Brown?* Greenwich, Connecticut: Fawcett Publications, Inc., 1956

Illustrations

Chapter 4

page

76   © 1976 King Features Syndicate, Inc.

77   Photograph by Rick Smolan

78   (left) Photograph by Jean-Claude
      Lejeune
      (right) Photograph by Rick Smolan

81   Photograph by Richard L. Good

84   Photograph by Jean-Claude Lejeune

89   © 1956 United Feature Syndicate, Inc.

Chapter 5

page

98   Photograph by Peter Karas

99   Photograph by Jean-Claude Lejeune

101   Photograph courtesy of Wide World
      Photos

105   *The Wizard of Id* by permission of
      Johnny Hart and Field Enterprises,
      Inc.

107   Photograph by Rick Smolan

111   Reprinted by permission of the
      Chicago Tribune-New York News
      Syndicate, Inc.

115   Photograph by David S. Strickler,
      Strix Pix

Chapter 6

page

124   *Conchy* by James Childress, © Field
      Enterprises, Inc., 1975. Courtesy of
      Field Newspaper Syndicate

125   Photograph by Jean-Claude Lejeune

127   © 1979 King Features Syndicate, Inc.

131   © 1979 King Features Syndicate, Inc.

132   Photograph by David S. Strickler,
      Strix Pix

Chapter 7

page

145   © 1975 United Feature Syndicate,
      Inc.

146   (left) Photograph by Nell Campbell,
      UFW Photo
      (right) Photograph by Rick Smolan

149   Photograph by James L. Shaffer

153   © King Features Syndicate, Inc., 1976

155   Photograph by Laimute Druskis,
      © 1980

Chapter 8

page

164   *The Wizard of Id* by permission of
      Johnny Hart and Field Enterprises,
      Inc.

166   Photograph by John R. Maher

167   Photograph by Alan Ruid

Chapter 9

page

188   (top) Reprinted by permission of the
      Chicago Tribune-New York News
      Syndicate, Inc.
      (middle) © 1976 United Feature
      Syndicate, Inc.
      (bottom) Reprinted by permission of
      the Chicago Tribune-New York News
      Syndicate, Inc.

189   Photograph by James L. Shaffer

193   Photograph by Rick Smolan

195   Photograph by David S. Strickler,
      Strix Pix

203   Reprinted by permission of the
      Chicago Tribune-New York News
      Syndicate, Inc.

Chapter 10

page

211   Photograph by James L. Shaffer

213   Photograph by Kryn Peter Westhoven

220   Photograph by Robert V. Eckert, Jr.

222   (left) Photograph by Major Morris
      (right) Photograph by William Helsel
      © 1977

223   Photograph by David S. Strickler,
      Strix Pix

226   *B.C.* by permission of Johnny Hart
      and Field Enterprises, Inc.

228   Photograph by Jean-Claude Lejeune

231   © 1976, G. B. Trudeau/Distributed
      by Universal Press Syndicate

Chapter 11

page

239 © 1975 United Feature Syndicate, Inc.

240 Photograph by Bob Eckert

242 Photograph by Rick Smolan

243 Photograph by Paul V. Sherburne

246 Photograph by Paul V. Sherburne

247 *Dunagin's People* by Ralph Dunagin, 1975 Sentinel Star. Courtesy of Field Newspaper Syndicate

250 Photograph by Daniel S. Brody

251 Reprinted by permission of the Chicago Tribune-New York News Syndicate, Inc.

253 Photograph by David S. Strickler, Strix Pix

258 (left) Photograph by Rohn Engh (right) Photograph by David S. Strickler, Strix Pix

260 Photograph by David S. Strickler, Strix Pix

261 Photograph by David S. Strickler, Strix Pix

Chapter 12

page

272 Photograph by Chris Grajczyk

287 Copyright, 1972, Universal Press Syndicate

Chapter 13

page

298 Photograph by James L. Ballard

300 Photograph by James L. Shaffer

302 Photograph courtesy of Atlantic Records

305 Photograph by Brent Jones

306 Photograph by James L. Shaffer

310 Photograph by James L. Ballard

Chapter 14

page

326 (left) Photograph by John R. Maher (right) Photograph by Howard Simmons

332 Photograph by Robert Eckert

333 Reprinted by permission of the Chicago Tribune-New York News Syndicate, Inc.

334 Photograph by David S. Strickler, Strix Pix

338 *Crock* by Bill Rechin and Brant Parker. © 1978, Field Enterprises, Inc. Courtesy of Field Newspaper Syndicate